Goals of Economic Life

Goals of Economic Life

EDITED BY A. DUDLEY WARD

JOHN MAURICE CLARK   FRANK H. KNIGHT
KENNETH E. BOULDING   WALTON HAMILTON
CLARENCE H. DANHOF   ALFRED E. EMERSON
EDUARD HEIMANN   RALPH LINTON
WILLIAM VICKREY   DONALD SNYGG
ROBERT M. MACIVER   THEODORE M. GREENE
CLARK C. BLOOM   JOHN C. BENNETT
REINHOLD NIEBUHR

HARPER & BROTHERS · PUBLISHERS · NEW YORK

This volume has been prepared by a study group authorized by the Federal Council of the Churches in 1949. The National Council of the Churches, into which the Federal Council has been merged, states that the volume is not a statement or pronouncement of the National Council. Each of the fifteen chapters in the book is written by a different author, and each author is solely responsible for what appears under his name.

Contents

Foreword

by CHARLES P. TAFT

*Chairman of the Department of the Church and Economic
Life and of Its Study Committee*

This volume forms part of a larger study of *Christian Ethics and
Economic Life* which was begun by the Department of the Church
and Economic Life of the Federal Council of the Churches of
Christ in America in 1949. At the beginning of 1951 the Federal
Council was merged with other interdenominational agencies to
form the National Council of the Churches of Christ in the United
States of America, made up of twenty-nine Protestant and Orthodox
church bodies within the United States.

In recent years, religious leaders have recognized that the ethical
problems of economic life are becoming increasingly urgent. The
ethics of everyday decisions and practices in economic life, private
and public, as we earn our livings, are matters also of wide public
concern. We need to go behind the observed individual acts and
group pressures for a deeper understanding of the motives underlying what people do in order to eat, of how the system fits together,
and of how close our preconceived ideas are to reality.

Change is a dominant characteristic of our national life and perhaps nowhere so much as in its economic aspects. During the past
half-century our ways of life and work have undergone a vast alteration. This change has been accomplished without violence and
without great apparent upset, but the tempo of its pace is truly
revolutionary. Certainly if people whose span of life was in the
nineteenth century could see what we see in everyday life they
would hardly accept any word but revolution for the process that
has brought it about.

This accelerated change, for all thoughtful people, demands an
understanding of the effects of this revolution upon ethics and human values. How shall we deal with the dynamism in our economic

life as it affects every segment of national existence, in order to preserve and extend freedom and justice, concern for the dignity of the individual and respect for the rights of minorities, sensitivity to the public welfare, and free discussion and peaceful persuasion? We cannot rely upon business statistics to measure these intangibles. Judgments of even the best-qualified individuals about actual or impending changes, affected as they are by individual temperament, vested interests, or political partisanship, are equally inadequate if considered separately. The fullest use of all our resources for information and discussion is required for sound progress toward solution of our complex problems.

There is no vital threat to our inherited and cherished values either in the *status quo* or in change as such. We cannot take ethics into the stratosphere and separate it from practical economic concerns. What is needed is a better understanding both of economic facts and also of those ethical values which have special significance in the meaning and direction which they give to economic activity.

Our world finds many who adopt a fanatic cynicism or a false philosophy in opposition to the very foundations upon which Western society is based. What earlier generations took for granted, such as the value and integrity of the individual, the character of government as a tool only for service of the people, the capacity of human life for essential decency and justice—these are now challenged with emotional zeal in the name of other conflicting assumptions claimed also to be moral. Here lies the real crisis of the second half of the present century. We must meet this challenge of evil, insofar as it is evil, and clarify in relation to our own institutions the basic ethical affirmations which we support.

The Federal Council of Churches conducted for many years an educational program on the ethical issues involved in economic life. Many denominational bodies have likewise been active in this field. It has become clear, however, that we need a more careful and realistic investigation of economic life and its relation to spiritual and moral values. We need to make use of the capacities of social scientists and theologians, with their feet kept on the ground by association with lay persons drawn from many occupations.

Accordingly, as a beginning of such an investigation, a three-year research study was commenced in 1949 under a grant from the Rockefeller Foundation. The Foundation has not exercised any supervisory control over the studies and does not assume responsibility for any of the findings. The results of the study are to be presented in six volumes: *Goals of Economic Life; American Attitudes on Economic Problems; Social Responsibilities of the Businessman; The Organizational Revolution; American Income and Its Use; Ethics and Economic Life.*

In the preparation of the present volume, grateful acknowledgment is made to the authors and to many others whose contributions have been of special importance. The Reverend Cameron P. Hall, Executive Director of the Department of the Church and Economic Life, has given the project his unfailing and effective administrative support. Professor Howard R. Bowen, Economic Consultant to the Study, made an invaluable contribution in the formulation of the project and aided also in criticism of the manuscripts. The Reverend A. Dudley Ward, Director of the Study, has carried out his responsibilities as organizer and coordinator, and in the process of evaluation, with imagination and efficiency. A Study Committee of the Department, including both lay and clerical members and representing a variety of occupations, has reviewed the program of the study at various stages.

Special appreciation is due to the fifteen distinguished authors whose contributions make up this volume. All of them are deeply interested in the venture and gave generously of their time and talent in producing this series of essays related to the main theme of the study. Among them, special mention should be made of the Editorial Committee, consisting of Professors J. M. Clark, Theodore M. Greene, Reinhold Niebuhr, and William Vickrey. In addition, Mr. Charles H. Seaver, Secretary of the Department and a member of the Study Committee, has carefully edited all of the papers and has consistently been available for counsel. Each manuscript was reviewed by others of the group in one draft or another, and opinions were freely exchanged in several discussions. As in the other volumes, however, each author has been free to write as he wished and to accept or reject suggestions or criticisms. In the final analysis each chapter is the responsibility of the writer under whose name it appears.

The National Council of Churches has taken no official position and assumed no responsibility regarding the content of any of the volumes. In no sense, therefore, can or should any statement in this series be regarded as an official declaration of the National Council of Churches or of any of its units.

Introduction

Introduction

by Theodore M. Greene

Professor of Philosophy and Master of Silliman College,
Yale University

The present volume is the product of an inconclusive but illuminating cooperative study of the values and goals of our American economic life. The several contributors have enjoyed great latitude of approach, emphasis, and interpretation. All their essays, however, fall within a framework laid down at the outset.

This framework called for an analysis of our complex economy, with special regard to the values which it promotes and fails to promote; for a study of this economy in the context of wider secular and ethical perspectives; and, finally, for a critique of our economic society from the religious perspective of the Christian faith. The project is thus a factual *and* normative study of our Western democratic society—a study focused primarily upon our economy, but pursued within a wider interpretative framework and given (it is hoped without dogmatic religious bias) a final Christian orientation.

The fifteen participants whose essays constitute this volume were selected with an eye to the requirements of the project as thus envisaged. The central emphasis on our economic system dictated the choice of several economists who would be able to explore its intricacies with professional competence and who would undertake this task, each in his own way, with appropriate attention to problems of evaluation. We realized, moreover, that our economy can really be understood only in its relation to government and law, to man's psychological nature and motivations, to our culture as one among other cultures, and, finally, in the light of man's similarities to, and differences from, various subhuman living species. Hence, a political scientist and a student of law, a psychologist, an anthropologist, and a biologist were asked to contribute the perspectives of their several disciplines. A philosopher was asked to survey the volume as a whole in an Introduction, and to discuss the crucial problems of evaluation and religious commitment in a separate

3

essay. Finally, the specifically Christian orientation of the entire project was entrusted to two liberal Protestant theologians.

This cooperative venture has been conducted in a manner appropriate to scholarly inquiry in a free society. The fifteen participants gave their approval at the outset to the initial formulation and orientation of the project. Tentative outlines of most of the essays were discussed and criticized at an early meeting in New York. The fifteen essays were then written independently and circulated among the entire group and several consultants, eliciting extensive written comment. A second and final meeting was devoted to a discussion of all the essays, revised in the light of previous criticism. The several contributions were then sent to press with such further revisions as the authors felt inclined to make.

The ordering and grouping of the fifteen essays calls for a word of explanation. The five essays in Part I are all by economists and are all focused primarily upon economic theory and practice. The methodological problems of the presuppositions, nature, and limits of economic theory are raised more than once—first by Professor Clark, in historical and cultural perspective by Professor Danhof, and with major emphasis on the limits of pure economic theory by Professor Vickrey. Professor Boulding's chief interest is economic progress—its nature, criteria, and possibility. Professor Heimann studies our economic system as a whole by comparing it with alternative systems. These essays also deal with the more factual problems of the market and its fluctuations and cycles, of the effect of monopoly on competition, of the causes and effects of inflation and unemployment, of the problem of an ever-increasing population, etc. These and other issues are studied always with an eye to the central problem of the entire project, namely, the values which our complex economy tends to sustain, threaten, or ignore, and the ways in which it might be made to contribute more richly and surely to our own corporate welfare and that of other contemporary societies.

The authors of the four essays in Part II consider our economy in its wide democratic context—Professor MacIver, in its dependence upon government; Professor Hamilton, in its relation to law and court procedure; Professor Bloom, with special regard to the economic policies of government; and Professor Knight, with particular concern for the practical problem of how to reconcile the conflicting demands of justice and freedom.

These nine essays will be found to reflect interesting differences of emphasis and conviction on matters bearing on economic policy. Professors Knight, Bloom, and Hamilton, for example, stress the values of freedom, the tendency of competition to check antisocial self-interest, and the dangers of governmental regulation. Professor Heimann, in contrast, emphasizes rather the dangers of a relatively autonomous economy and the importance of having it controlled by the moral and spiritual forces of the community, not through totalitarian regimentation but in a manner consonant with democratic freedom and a Christian respect for the individual. Other participants, cognizant of the value of both freedom and social control, address themselves to more specific problems—Professor Clark, for example, to the values neglected by the market, and Professor Vickrey to the economist's need for basic moral standards.

The essays in Part III and the Conclusion study our society from various converging perspectives—biological, anthropological, psychological, philosophical, and theological. What analogies, asks Professor Emerson, can profitably be drawn between subhuman species and *homo sapiens?* What, inquires Professor Linton, are some of the most illuminating differences and similarities in basic economy and motivation between primitive and more advanced human societies? What light, asks Professor Snygg, can modern psychology throw upon human motivation and evaluation? What, I ask in my essay, is the status of values, what are the criteria of responsible evaluation, and how is reflective religious commitment possible? And what, ask Professors Bennett and Niebuhr, are the major implications of a liberal Christian faith for the individual, for our democratic way of life, and for our economic institutions, practices, and attitudes?

This must suffice to indicate the general nature of the project, its common focus and its multiple approach. All the essays contribute to a synoptic understanding of our complex and evolving society. They offer no simple panacea, no magic formula for human welfare. They are concerned, rather, to emphasize the difficulty of the problems which confront us, the multiplicity of relevant factors, the variety of tensions and conflicts, the everlasting need for compromise and social adjustment. They all reflect, however, our deep conviction that greater understanding can and will contribute to more enlightened social policy, and that knowledge can and should guide decision and action, both individual and corporate.

The volume as a whole may give some readers a first impression of baffling complexity. If the several essays are read with care in their relation to one another, however, various overlapping patterns of factual analysis and appraisal will be seen to emerge. The reader's task will perhaps be facilitated by a listing of some of the more notable areas of agreement and disagreement among us and some of the controversial questions which have arisen.

1. Man Can Be Understood Only in the Context of His Environment

All the participants recognize that the concept of "economic man" is an abstraction, useful on occasion but dangerous if used uncritically. They agree that a human being can be understood only in the context of his total environment. This includes his family, the various local groups to which he may belong, his nation in a world of other nations, and his total culture in its relation to other cultures. The human race as a whole, meanwhile, has admittedly evolved from more primitive forms of life, which, in turn, have come into being and maintained themselves in an orderly world of nature, organic and inorganic. One of our major premises, in short, is that man must be studied in the realistic setting of his society and its major institutions, of his biological antecedents, and of the entire spatio-temporal world of nature.

There is less agreement as to whether all natural phenomena, inanimate and animate, subhuman and human, should be conceived of within a still more embracing framework of "spiritual laws," and as the creation of a Deity who transcends the whole of nature and sustains it as its ultimate Ground. That this is the case is, of course, a basic affirmation of the Christian faith. The last three essays in this volume explore the validity and content of this affirmation, as well as its social implications. Some of the other essays reflect, more or less clearly, an acceptance of Christian theism; others express, directly or indirectly, an attitude of agnosticism or skepticism; some are silent on this issue.

But we all seem to agree that man can be understood only in his manifold relations to his *total* environment, in whatever terms the ultimate reaches of this environment can best be described. We are also at one in rejecting a purely "positivistic" or dogmatically anti-metaphysical approach. We all believe that the universe in which we find ourselves is, in some meaningful sense, a whole whose parts, aspects, and dimensions are related to one another in many ways, and that man's persistent attempts to discern the basic structure and character of this "whole" are themselves meaningful and significant. All of us are certainly impressed by the mystery of ultimate reality—a mystery which, at the least, dictates humility rather than dogmatism.

2. Man Is a Complex and Distinctive Being

There is also complete agreement among us that the components which, in sum, constitute human character are all significantly related to one another. There is, accordingly, no disposition on the part of any of the participants to claim self-sufficiency for that facet of man's nature and behavior which is the special area of his professional interest. It is assumed that man is *simultaneously* a physiological, psychological, and social being with a capacity for aesthetic, moral, and religious responses and decisions, and that all these aspects of his nature are somehow "organically" interrelated. These relationships, it is further recognized, reflect themselves in his private motives and individual actions as well as in his interlocking social institutions and in his various cooperative ventures.

It follows that, at least in principle, valid propositions regarding human nature and conduct which emanate from any one of the specialized disciplines will not contradict equally valid propositions emanating from other disciplines, but will rather complement them. Thus the psychologist does not expect to find himself in radical conflict with the biologist or the physicist, on the one hand, or with the economist, political scientist, or moralist on the other, provided that he and they are all able to escape the errors of ignorance and the provincialism of a too narrow specialization. Indeed, the common cry throughout the volume is for more collaboration: first, among scholarly specialists in the several disciplines; and, second, in society itself, since "progress" is felt to be possible only if government, business, the family, the school, and (some would add) the church join forces in working for desirable social objectives.

The emphasis on these "organic" relationships has not precluded, in these essays, full recognition of significant differences between species, societies, cultures, institutions, and disciplines. Nor has it led to a neglect of individual differences and uniquenesses. Thus, our biologist has scrupulously avoided the "reductionism" that would be involved in conceiving of man as *merely* animal. He has explored provocative similarities between man and various sub-human species, but he has also carefully emphasized the crucial ways in which men differ radically from insects and the higher animals. Similarly, there has been no disposition on the part of our psychologist to *reduce* man's moral conduct to psychological processes or to deny whatever is distinctive in responsible human volition; our anthropologist has not equated what he finds to be relatively universal in human societies with the humanly "good" or the "best"; power has not been identified with justice, or "legal" law with "moral" law, or economic efficiency with moral growth, or historical "trend" with "progress." All the participants, in turn, have consistently recognized and valued the individuality of men as persons, and all have sought to do full justice to the uniqueness of the "individual field," the concrete environment, and the specific potentialities and responsibilities of each man as an individual. The assumptions underlying the study, in short, have emphasized similarities *and* differences, social groups *and* individuals, distinguishable traits in men and institutions *and* their relationships to one another.

3. Nature and Society Are Dynamic

No less unanimous is the recognition that the world of nature is still in process of evolution, and that every society and all its inter-

meshed institutions, corporate beliefs, and patterns of social conduct
are forever changing and therefore part of an ongoing, dynamic
historical process. This process of transformation is seen by several
contributors to necessitate the balancing factor of some type of continuity or permanence; the repeated pleas for social and individual
flexibility and growth as the necessary condition of progress are frequently coupled with a reminder of man's need, both individual
and social, for some measure of stability. This dual emphasis on
change and continuity, experimentation and consolidation, dictates
a rejection both of violent revolution and of static orthodox conservatism in social policy. It underlines the perennial need for compromise and balance in all social planning and social action. How, in
concrete situations, to hit upon the most beneficial compromise and
to discover the balance most conducive to human welfare and progress is a recurrent query.

4. Evaluations Are Inescapable, Meaningful, and Important

A further presupposition of each writer is that man inevitably
evaluates, that his evaluations reflect the socially accepted values of
his society and culture, and that the distinction between the actual
and the ideal, between what is and what ought to be, is of major
importance. Much attention is given to what in fact is valued in
various societies, and particularly in our own, and several essays
summarize the chief stages in the evolution of our Western values
and list the successive normative attitudes of Western economists
since the Middle Ages. Attention is given also to the factors which
have contributed to diverse social and individual evaluations, and to
the conditions under which further changes might now be initiated, retarded, or accelerated. Underlying all these inquiries is the
common assumption that what is is not necessarily inevitable; there
will be found no defense of a mechanistic determinism in human
affairs. Rather is it assumed throughout that men can, by taking
thought, appraise themselves and their society in terms of normative
standards, envisage desirable goals, and, with appropriate ingenuity
and effort, make at least some progress toward their realization.

Far more controversial are the emergent problems relating to (a) the objectivity of values, i.e., whether or not values have an objective status; (b) the relation of values, if they are objective, to the God of religious worship; and (c) the methods and criteria of responsible or valid evaluation. Several of the participants refrain from discussing these problems, either as not falling within the area of their professional competence or else as not being immediately relevant to the specific concern of their essays. Some seem to reflect, at least indirectly, a skepticism regarding the ultimate objectivity of values and the possibility of discovering criteria of objective appraisal. Others assert, or imply, a belief in objective values, their significance for religion, and the possibility of responsible evaluation. I discuss these problems in my own essay and try to indicate the lines along which an affirmative philosophical theory of values and evaluation might be developed.

5. Major Types of Social Organization Can and Should Be Compared and Assessed

There is evident throughout this volume a notable agreement that our free democratic society differs in important ways from the "rugged individualism" of nineteenth-century "liberalism" on the one hand, and from communistic and fascistic totalitarianism, on the other; that it is superior to both, judged in terms of total human welfare; but that, at its present stage, it is far from ideal, and that it is possible to specify ways in which it could notably be improved. There is no disposition, in short, to espouse a nihilistic relativism which denies the possibility, *in principle*, of an intersocietal and transcultural appraisal that is rationally defensible. Bertrand Russell's insistence, for example, that a preference for our social philosophy over that of communism is ultimately irrational and indefensible finds no echo between these covers. This remarkable consensus on this controversial issue underlines the need for an intelligible philosophical account of objective values and responsible evaluation.

6. WHAT ARE THE BASIC CONDITIONS OF A LIBERAL COMMUNITY?

There is also clearly apparent in each of the following essays the recognition that a truly democratic society, conceived of as a free community of responsible persons who honor the intrinsic value of each of its members as a human being, can be approximated only in proportion as certain basic conditions are satisfied. Chief among these, as several writers insist, is freedom. There is some disposition to prefer the negative approach to freedom, defining it as freedom *from* obnoxious or harmful restraints and coercions. Many of man's most cherished liberties can, indeed, be stated in these negative terms, as is evident in our American Bill of Rights. It is clear, however, that freedom from tyrannical coercion means little apart from positive human desires and the power necessary to realize them. These factors of desire and power greatly complicate the problem of human liberty.

As regards desire, it becomes imperative to distinguish between actual need and conscious desire or want; between primary needs conditioning survival and secondary needs conditioning security, comfort, cultural development, and spiritual well-being; between the needs and desires which can be satisfied only at the expense of other people and the needs and desires whose satisfaction entails no such sacrifice. There is also the vexed question, discussed repeatedly in these essays, whether men's conscious desires, wise or unwise, fugitive or lasting, can be determined with any degree of accuracy; and underlying this issue is the more difficult problem, less often considered in this volume, of how man's actual needs, reflecting his cultural, moral, and spiritual potentialities, can best be determined. Professor Linton's distinction between "thematic" values, which are universal and basic, and "instrumental" values, which differ from culture to culture, will be found helpful in this connection.

Power, in turn, is seen to exist in many different forms and to be productive of both good and evil. To be beneficial, it must be wisely directed and its many possible misuses must somehow be controlled. How it can best be employed in our society is discussed in various contexts.

These considerations, explored in several of the following essays, lead to the conclusion that freedom without order is license and that power exercised without wisdom and effective restraint is tyranny. The ideal community which all the participants, with minor differences of emphasis, regard as normative is one in which freedom is implemented and safeguarded by various legal and extra-legal devices, and in which desire is informed and disciplined by education. It is a community whose members, institutions, and prevailing ethos are all characterized by a profound respect for personality, a mature sense of responsibility, and great technical and cultural enlightenment. In such a community, greater justice will prevail, cooperation and mutual sympathy will be more widely operative, and significant progress will be hastened.

These fine phrases are easily uttered and often too easily accepted as solutions of our most pressing human problems. Perhaps the chief merit of the present volume is the stubborn refusal of its contributors to accept these general truths as adequate diagnoses or practical solutions of the tortuous problems which in fact no sages and no human societies have ever satisfactorily understood or solved. Each contributor, in his own way, raises and explores the awkward questions of more detailed definition and practical implementation which lie hidden beneath the surface of these large and easy generalizations.

Thus, Professor Knight struggles with the meaning and implications of freedom and stresses convincingly the precariousness and the price of liberty. Professor Boulding explores the ambiguity of the concept of "progress" and demonstrates the difficulty of finding a satisfactory standard or criterion. Professor Hamilton exhibits the ambivalence of law, simultaneously the product of an evolving ethos and an important controlling and guiding factor in an evolving society. Various participants study the nature, value, and dangers of competition in the effort to determine how essential it is to human endeavor, how it can best be curbed when it becomes harmful to the individual and to society at large, and how it might be encouraged and redirected into more socially beneficial channels.

In short, what sort of noncompetitive life net can be placed under the institution of competition to safeguard its demonstrable values and to minimize its no less demonstrable dangers? The concept of equality is similarly scrutinized and the awkward questions of its true meaning, its proper scope, its relation to justice, etc., are analyzed with disconcerting and enlightening candor.

7. Can Self-Interest and Altruism Be Reconciled?

This question arose so frequently in our discussions and seemed so important that some mention should be made of it here. There was no disposition among the participants to oversimplify human motivation. Our economists were never guilty of reducing all motivation to acquisitiveness; our theologians never assumed that man is capable of simon-pure altruism. It was recognized by all of us that men in fact desire the greatest variety of things, including not only physical security and comfort, social prestige and power, but also aesthetic pleasure, the joys of friendship and love, and the satisfactions of ultimate religious dedication. The problem which we debated and never resolved was whether self-interest, defined inclusively to embrace all types of human satisfaction, is or is not in conflict with an altruism defined to include all types of concern for the welfare of others.

It can be argued, on the one hand, that since the welfare of the individual depends so essentially upon the welfare of others, a really enlightened egoism will, in fact, function altruistically. Such enlightenment would seem to dictate, moreover, a major emphasis upon those values (freedom, security, truth, etc.) which are by their very nature sharable, in preference to those widely desired objectives (property, prestige, etc.) which are not similarly sharable. On this view, there is no ultimate conflict between an *enlightened* egoism and an *enlightened* altruism. What is to my greatest advantage is of equal benefit to all my fellow men; I love myself most intelligently by loving my neighbor as myself; my own greatest felicity can best be secured by loving God with all my heart, soul, and mind; and such love, truly comprehended, *means* loving "my neighbor as myself."

In at least apparent opposition to this view is the view that man is, in fact, incorrigibly egoistic, preferring his own welfare to that of others whenever the two seem to be in conflict; and that, furthermore, these conflicts between our own welfare and the welfare of others do continually arise in any actual human culture, whatever may be the mutuality of benefit in some ideal utopian society. This diagnosis of human motivation and of the actualities of any human society, in turn, seems to dictate, at the high moral and spiritual level, a condemnation of such egoism and a challenge to contrition and redemption; and, at the practical level, the formulation of social policy which will recognize the fact of egoistic selfishness and the importance of so controlling and using it as to promote the greatest social good.

This plea for the recognition of ineradicable egoism in man is reinforced by the fact that all men have, in addition to their natural concern for their own private welfare, responsibilities to the several social groups to which they belong—groups whose welfare seems frequently to be in conflict with the welfare of other groups. Thus, it may indeed be my duty to sacrifice myself, even my life, for others; but have I a similar duty to sacrifice my family, or my nation? Do not my proper and inescapable loyalties to my group dictate a concern for it, at the expense of other groups, and is not such a concern an extended egoism which cannot be censured in the way in which purely private egoism can and should be censured? Professor Niebuhr has expounded this universal human predicament with great power in his Conclusion as well as in his other writings.

The problem is further complicated at the practical level in two ways. We must acknowledge, first, the real conflict which frequently arises between the long-range social good of all men and the short-run interest of particular groups and individuals. For example, the members of a well-organized union may really benefit from a series of strikes, even though these strikes precipitate other strikes which, in turn, have the eventual result of devaluating the currency and increasing the cost of living. Such groups may believe quite correctly that they have the power to keep ahead of the game for an indefinite period and that a net loss to the community means a net gain for themselves for the foreseeable future. The temptation to achieve this type of benefit is, of course, very great.

This temptation, in turn, is intensified by the ready availability of ideological defenses for individual or group selfishness. It is fatally easy to justify such acts by exhibiting genuine in-group need, by appealing to group loyalty, and by relying upon the approbation of the like-minded people by whom we are most immediately surrounded. Witness many of the arguments which are so often heard today in defense of management, or of high-pressure advertising, or of American imperialism—arguments which ignore the impact of predatory egoism upon other individuals and groups and which betray an insensitivity to, and an ultimate unconcern for, their welfare. Man's conscience finds many and varied cushions; it is all too easy to "justify" our own individual and group advantage.

These practical considerations will suffice to indicate that the problem of egoistic selfishness is poignantly actual for every individual and every social group, however indistinguishable may be completely enlightened egoism and altruism. The most ardent faith in an orderly and beneficent cosmos in which my *real* good, by definition, will coincide with the *real* good of all my fellow men must, in realistic honesty, be accompanied by the recognition that no human beings can ever discern this real common good of all with complete clarity, and that there is also in each of us an apparently ineradicable tendency to prefer my immediate good to yours, our good to theirs, our partial short-run advantage to a more inclusive universal human welfare.

Our practical task, therefore, starting with human nature as we find it, would seem to be to promote, to the best of our ability, (a) greater unselfishness, that is, greater concern for others for their own sake, even at the cost of personal sacrifice; and *also* (b) more intelligent selfishness, that is, a realization that some policies which are socially beneficial may also be more beneficial to myself and my group than are other policies which neglect or injure others. Ultimately, your good and mine may indeed be identical; the advent of this universal common good may indeed have to await the universal reign of perfect selfless love; and it may also be true that prudential motivation, however enlightened, is morally (and even psychologically) inconsistent with selfless dedication—that we cannot serve both God and Mammon. Yet man seems to be, in actuality, partly selfish and partly unselfish, his motivations mixed and his vision limited. Hence the apparent necessity for a dual practical objective, in part spiritual and selfless, in part practical and prudential. Only thus, it would seem, can we hope to improve our human lot here and now and promote a closer approximation to the Kingdom of God on earth.

8. How Significant Are Our Agreements and Disagreements?

These are only some of the baffling problems dealt with in this volume and only some of the areas of agreement and disagreement among us. We have discussed both the extent and the significance of these agreements and disagreements, and have asked ourselves several provocative questions regarding them which the reader may wish to bear in mind as he reads the following essays.

A.   To what extent are our agreements and disagreements more verbal than real? Are the enlightened naturalist and the enlightened Christian as far apart as their labels and common report would indicate? Here we face the ever-present problem of semantics and man's perennial difficulty in communicating his most cherished convictions to his fellows.

B.   How important are ultimate beliefs? What practical differences might be expected to issue from real differences in ultimate conviction? Professor Boulding believes that they would be noteworthy:[1]

I think it is pretty clear that the real division in the group comes between those for whom religious experience is something vital and central and those for whom religious experience is either meaningless or peripheral. . . . This suggests that study of the impact of religious experience on economic life would be of unusual interest as a follow-up.

Professor Clark also queries the ultimacy of what I have called "ultimate beliefs," as well as their practical effect:

[1] The following quotations are all taken from written memoranda to the author.

In the case of Greene, which is more nearly ultimate, his belief in objective values, or the fact that he is a humane man who can be trusted not to convert concepts of objective values into engines of inhuman devastation? I might also suggest, as a provisional hypothesis, that the beliefs you have classed as ultimate may make little difference to the best people, and to the worst, in their actions toward things of this world; but that in between there are various types to whom such intellectual beliefs may make a real difference, sometimes for better and sometimes for worse, according to the enlightenment of the individuals in question.

Mr. Dudley Ward, Director of the Project, believes, in contrast, that:

. . . there is apparent agreement among the participants on the ends being sought (philosophy of life) even though the basic presuppositions out of which their philosophies have developed are different.

C. What is the probable source of our agreements? Have we arrived at similar or identical conclusions regarding desirable goals by interpreting different sets of data with equal objectivity? If our diverse and independent inquiries have in fact reinforced each other, our resultant agreements take on added significance. But it is also possible that our agreements reflect our common membership in the same society and our common indebtedness to a common ethos. Professor Snygg has stated this possibility clearly:

I am much interested to find a close agreement between Dr. Niebuhr's view of human nature and my own. But I wonder how independent our points of view really are. To what extent is my interpretation due to the data and to what extent is it due to my Protestant American background? To what extent is his due to Christian theology, as such, and to what extent is it due to the fact that many theologians, including Niebuhr, have been very good observers of human nature?

If it is hard to determine the operative role of a prevailing ethos in the life of an individual, it is equally hard to assess the influence of a historical religion upon an entire culture. Historians have found it difficult to disentangle Christian from other influences upon a semi-Christian culture like ours. It is as natural, moreover, for professing Christians to overemphasize the Christian factor as it is for the secularist to minimize its importance. Professor Bennett's query is certainly germane:

Would the authors of these essays have accepted and emphasized so unanimously what can be described as Christian ideals and values had we been Moslems or Hindus, reflecting a Moslem or Hindu culture rather than our own? And to what extent can the ideas associated with a Christian ethic be divorced from the Christian faith?

D. How far is our agreement really no more than an absence of disagreement? For example, to what extent have our theologians and scientists avoided disagreement because they have operated at different levels of inquiry? As Professor Snygg has put it:

My feeling is that I have been employed as a psychologist and that it is my responsibility to stay, as well as I can, within my field of competence. Neither psychology nor any other science has any techniques for testing the existence of the supernatural. The result is that, as a psychologist, I have nothing to say on that question. I am not equipped to deal with it.

This statement may suggest to some a disjunction between factual inquiry and religious pronouncement. Is such a disjunction possible, or necessary, or valid? Can religious insights transcend, without contradicting, scientific knowledge? And can they assimilate such knowledge without transforming it? For example, does the Christian perspective merely add a new dimension to the scientific account of man's nature and behavior, stated in terms of heredity and natural environment, or does it substitute a distinctively Christian account of human freedom and responsibility? And, reversely, will not religious insights be modified by relevant scientific inquiry?

The same issue can be restated in secular terms. To what extent can factual inquiry safely be divorced from moral insight? In what sense can the latter transcend the former, and how, if at all, can moral insight be confirmed, corrected, or enriched by relevant factual inquiry? And, reversely, in what ways can scientific search be supplemented, and perhaps guided, by moral insight in a manner productive of greater understanding and wisdom?

9. How Can Vital Beliefs Be Generated and Strengthened?

One remaining problem must be mentioned, since it is one of the most urgent problems facing us today. How can vital beliefs be generated and strengthened in a free society? The totalitarian states have learned a great deal about how blind and uncritical beliefs can be "conditioned" into people, particularly in childhood and youth, by reiterative and emotional propaganda, by censorship, and by a system of social rewards and drastic punishments. Organized religions have too often used similar methods of indoctrination with conspicuous success, and even in a democracy like ours the temptation is great, with the advent of mass media of communication, to arouse patriotic and partisan loyalties in these ways. Yet all these devices, however successful in achieving their ends, are inconsistent with the spirit of liberalism as exemplified in scholarship, scientific inquiry, democracy, and enlightened religion at their best.

Our task, desperately urgent in a period of crisis such as the present, is to find and use educative devices as effective in the establishment and strengthening of critical beliefs in a free society as propaganda and other "conditioning" devices seem to be effective in instilling uncritical, fanatical beliefs in a rigid, monolithic society. How can formal liberal education be made more efficient than it is at present in the achievement of this objective? How can a democratic government not only safeguard the basic rights of free men but also impress upon them the value of these rights and arouse in them a lively sense of responsibility for their preservation? How can the family instill a sense of responsibility in early youth and generate loyalties that extend themselves gradually beyond the family circle to the local and national community and the whole world? How can business, particularly big business, combine the control requisite for efficiency with that free cooperation of all workers required for human dignity and a democratic morale? How can the churches be persuaded to abandon their dogmatisms and authoritarianisms and to foster the enlightened faith which "high" religion demands? How, in short, can we better cultivate the liberal attitude, at once idealistic and realistic, convinced and critical, dedicated and tolerant, in the historical situation in which we find ourselves?

This volume does not specifically address itself to this issue, but the inquiry with which it is concerned will remain sterile unless it eventually leads to intensive study of this crucial problem and, through such study, to vigorous constructive action.

PART I

The Role of Values in Our Economy

I

Aims of Economic Life as Seen by Economists

by John Maurice Clark
John Bates Clark Professor of Political Economy, Columbia University

1. Introduction

1. *Preview of the Problem*

Ask an economist what the goal or aim of the economic system is, in a free society such as ours, and he will probably reply that the system, as a system, has no specific aims; the service it renders is to give its members a maximum of means and opportunity to pursue their several aims, whatever they may be. The system is conceived as neutral, ready to serve any and all kinds of wants; the responsibility of directing it to good wants, rather than bad, lies with those to whom the service is rendered. For the economist, people's wants are facts; those expressed in markets are economic facts; and his task as a scientist is to study facts, not to approve or disapprove them.

If that were all, this paper might end here, having defined the attitude of economists toward the aims of economic life. But that is not all; the system is not as neutral as this definition suggests. No doubt its proper place is at the service of whatever ends the society may have. But the market naturally gives a preferred position to wants for marketable products. And it is taking generations of struggle to make slow progress in recognizing and making provision for other wants, some of which are far more important than an individualistic age has permitted itself to understand. To make

23

goods cheaper and more plentiful, technical improvement has driven forward, from Adam Smith's pin factory to modern mass production; and only after we are committed to this irreversible movement do we get the disturbing realization that something not fully understood has happened to conditions of work, to human relations on the job, and to the impact of work on the personality of the worker. Are we developing the kinds of personalities the modern society needs, if it is to hold together and keep working, while maintaining freedom? If we fail in eternal vigilance in such matters, economic techniques could become our masters, precisely through our failure to realize that they are anything but docile servants.[1]

Up to a point, economists realize that the market is not neutral, and express this realization in their policies, if not in their theories. But as to the more far-reaching human and social imponderables, even those who realize their importance are hardly equipped to deal with them. Economics is a quantitative discipline, and does not know how to handle such qualitative material. Its most unqualified criteria of economic progress are more goods to consume and, on the side of conditions of production itself, a shorter work week and more leisure.

If you catch an economist in an expansive mood, he may define the goal as "the good things of life for the many, as widely distributed as practicable, in an ever-increasing flow." This adds several elements, and raises more questions than it settles. "How wide a distribution is 'practicable'? And who is to be the judge of what things are good?" If the many are free to choose, they are free to choose wrong as well as right—that is what freedom means. We recognize this by practicing a limited censorship in the interest of health, safety, and, to a dwindling extent, morals. But outside of these limits, economists traditionally think that the things people want for themselves and their families are likely to be less harmful

[1] The writer has developed this theme in "The Empire of Machines," *Yale Review*, October 1922, reprinted in *Essays in Contemporary Civilization*, C. W. Thomas, ed., New York, Macmillan Co., 1931, pp. 146-157. Karl Polanyi's thesis, mentioned by Dr. Heimann, of the absorption of the society by the economy, seems to be a different way of putting essentially the same idea.

than the goals that self-appointed mentors or rulers set for them. This question of the wisdom of wants economists prevailingly regard as somebody else's business, and they have satisfied themselves that quantitative economic gains are good as far as they go.

Our system stressed the self-interested (or family-interested) side of human nature as a prime mover in the business of producing and distributing goods and services, and undertakes to harness it to the economic requirements of the community by the most nearly voluntary methods, involving the least interference with its natural expression. Traditionally, the harness has been viewed as a rather simple matter of legal rights of person and property, plus competition as a game in which, to serve oneself, one must serve others. Ethical motives were thought of mainly as entering into the spending of incomes; they were good but not necessary to the working of the system, and pretensions to moral motivations in business were actually suspect.

In fact, the traditional harness depends on a general underlying sense of right. And as group power is less precisely limited by competitive checks, the sense of right becomes an increasingly active feature of economic life, and social responsibility in the use of group power has become an absolute necessity, if the industrial system is to go on working on a basis containing enough freedom to be fairly characterized as voluntary. The tradition of utilizing self-interest has made us slow to realize this necessity, and thus the tradition is a source of weakness as well as of strength. Furthermore, whatever responsibility for social ends there may be in our system needs to become explicit and conscious. It is not enough that the system be serviceable; serviceability must appear to flow naturally from its inherent character. Otherwise, it concedes a dangerous propaganda advantage to rival systems. Our system must be animated by awareness of its obligation to be directed to serviceable ends, not merely tricked by an "unseen hand" into pursuing such ends in spite of the fact that the main preoccupation of its members is with self-interested motives.

In addition to self-interest, human nature has another and sharply contrasting side: the impulse to identify oneself with something bigger than oneself or one's family, to merge oneself in it, and to find there support, an inner sense of security and of sharing in a larger realization than an unattached individual could attain, supplying a sense of meaning that smaller objectives fail to convey. This self-identifying, self-merging, or self-dedicating impulse appears in many guises—in fraternal orders, in trade unions, in political parties, in any service that has a strong *esprit de corps,* and most profoundly in religions and in totalitarian systems. The last two have this in common, despite being poles apart in their objects of loyalty; and this is presumably the most deeply rooted reason for the attraction the Soviet system has had for many Western Christians, who set a high value on self-dedication and are repelled by the degree to which our economic system neglects this side of man's nature. While Soviet strength rests also on fear and ruthless coercion, it is a dangerous error to suppose that they are its sole source.

This system now threatens our own, in what amounts to an anti-religious holy war; and the requirements of defense against this threat will probably be the greatest single force determining the character of the changes our system will experience in the foreseeable future. Liberals are already warning us that we might win the contest and lose the thing we are fighting for. So we need not only to arm for defense, but to rediscover and redefine the qualities of our system which make it worth defending, the weaknesses of which it needs to be pruned, and the points at which the pruning may or may not involve risks to the essentials. Every generation needs such a rediscovery. Ours faces the need in the heat and confusion of conflict. It will make its decisions, with or without a clear eye to the values they affect and the valuations they imply.

2. *Some Basic Concepts*

If the term "goal" implies a final terminus, it had better be translated "aspirations"; since we look to endless change, and can hardly hope to resolve all the conflicts between different aspirations and organize them into a single unified goal. For economists, "goals" will remain plural, made up of wants of different sorts. In general, economists are most keenly alive to personal wants for personal use. They are tolerant of altruistic wants, so long as these do not assume too much power to interfere in others' affairs, for they continue to hold that people are on the whole better judges of their own needs than of others'. Wants as to the kind of community one wishes to live in they tend to relegate to the realms of the noneconomic. They accept the necessity of group decisions on collective matters, such as national defense, though alive to the defects of such decisions. And as to wants purporting to emanate from some superindividual entity, such as abstract "right"—which generally turns out to be customary—or the glory or prestige of the state as such, they are profoundly distrustful, suspecting a camouflaged sacrifice of the interests or welfare of the actual members of the society to some idea or interest that would not stand scrutiny in terms of democratic tests of welfare.

Problems of policy are always conflicts of values; and in making recommendations on them, economists reveal their working standards more dependably, if less explicitly, than in their theories. For such judgments between rival values, no ready-made yardsticks are available. Methods used in ethics and in law are suggestive, but not transferable just as they stand, if economists are to make the contribution which their background peculiarly qualifies them to make. They do not arrange generic values in an order of priority (e.g., health is, or is not, more important than freedom) and they would consider such a scale misleading. Their problems are always more specific. Should disease carriers be denied freedom to handle food in public restaurants? Should physiologically harmful use of tobacco be prohibited by law? Nearly everyone would decide the first question in favor of protecting the health value, and the second against the proposed method of protection. Such policy decisions deal with marginal increments; and, at some point, every generic class of values has to be limited in the interest of others.

Among value criteria, several grades may be distinguished. First comes the currently effective standard, expressed in the conditions society maintains or permits. This includes things approved as desirable, but it includes also many recognized abuses which society has merely not found effective ways of removing. The existing verdict of the market on the worth of different economic activities is a standard of this sort. It has the inertia of custom behind it, and this is entitled to some weight, but to limited weight only. Some economists regard their job, *qua* economists, as ending with this standard.

Second comes the known and expressed community judgment of what is desirable—where such a judgment exists. It implies a consensus prevalent enough to be regarded as representative—complete unanimity would be an unreasonable requirement. By this standard, many existing practices and conditions may be judged unsatisfactory, as evidenced by efforts to improve them. The persistence of the unsatisfactory condition means merely that these efforts have not been able to succeed completely, within the limits of means we are prepared to use and disturbance we are prepared to incur. This is presumably the kind of standard to which Justice Holmes appealed as the settled judgment of the people, which a judge should follow, even against his personal predilections. The present writer contends that economists can and should appeal from the first standard to the second, this being required in order to fulfill the ideal of neutrality between actual ends. In the process, they may modify existing standards, by developing their unrealized implications; or as Booth and Rowntree did, a half century and more ago, by reporting the facts of British urban poverty.

Third, there is the search for more ultimate ethical standards by which the prevailing community judgment might be held right or wrong. This is outside the economist's special field. But his training prepares him, when he encounters claims of right, to look into their consequences, and to scrutinize the standards themselves to see if they contain rationalizations of group interests or traditional and inherited preconceptions that should be freshly scrutinized, or both. In this area he can contribute a healthy skepticism which is the beginning of wisdom.

II. Historical Evolution of Economists' Attitudes

1. The Medieval Period

Current attitudes of economists are explainable partly in terms of their roots in the past development of their tradition. In sketching some high points of this development, we may take medieval thought as a point of departure. Here social and ethical goals were frankly set for economic activity, under the leadership of the church, which had sufficient authority and power to give its standards a considerable degree of effect. It accepted the customary class structure of society, and sanctioned the income suitable to one's station in life, as against unlimited arbitrary exploitation or unlimited business acquisition. Wealth was a trust, charity a duty, usury forbidden, and exchange subject to the (elastic) doctrine of the "just price."

In the large, this thinking was suited to a nearly static handicraft system, set in a strong frame of custom and obedience to authority, temporal and ecclesiastical. Its defects and abuses were many. Its strongest point was its insistence that men were members of one body, with mutual duties. This doctrine, largely submerged by early modern individualism, is having to be slowly and painfully recreated in different forms and in a less hospitable environment.

2. Mercantilist-Nationalist Attitudes

With the end of the fifteenth century, a dynamic, nationalistic commercialism broke the bonds of medieval customary authority and ecclesiastical control. The goals of the new nationalistic states were dynastic and militaristic, with growing influence exercised by the mercantile class, who were making the first large modern accumulations of capital. A large population was a national asset. Colonial empires were sought, and managed, with a view to allowing the mother country to do the manufacturing, which would support a dense population while the colonies sent home raw materials and took manufactured products in exchange.

One prominent aim was a favorable balance of trade, sometimes fortified by disapproval of imported luxuries. But liberal expenditure by the rich was generally approved, as giving employment to the poor, while for the mass of workers low wages were generally sought, in order that they might be under pressure to work hard for the benefit of the more fortunate classes.[2] And a working class was

[2] This aspect is well brought out in F. S. Furniss, *The Position of the Laborer in a System of Nationalism,* Boston, Houghton Mifflin Co., 1920, especially Chap. VI.

coming into existence, free of both the trammels and the protections of medieval status, and dependent on employment in what seems to have been a buyers' oftener than a sellers' market.

The mercantilists understood one thing which later economists ignored: namely, the importance of spending as conditioning the level of economic activity. They represent the earliest and crudest phase of the kind of economic thinking that seeks methods of increasing the "wealth of nations" (as they conceived it) by utilizing and channeling the "free" activities of private traders.

3. *The Physiocrats*

The physiocrats (whose name signifies "the rule of nature") made a rather remarkable attempt, under the circumstances, to rescue the sick economy of France from the abuses of the decaying Bourbon monarchy. Quesnay, court physician to king and economy alike, urged that taxes should be paid by the landed aristocracy, instead of falling with hampering or crushing weight on peasant cultivators and on trade and industry. The great landowners should also plow back capital into the land, to restore and maintain the productiveness of agriculture. This idea of direct taxation was a permanent contribution to economic thinking, though nowadays we do not confine it to land taxes. It is linked to the idea of the "natural order" of laissez faire, since direct taxes do not distort and hamper economic activity as indirect taxes do.

The physiocrats were probably sincere in believing that the resulting increase in productiveness would more than repay the landed nobility and enrich the king. One need not take too seriously any implication that in the physiocrats' minds this was the purpose of it all. Nobles and king were the powers who had to be persuaded, and Quesnay exhibited the wisdom of the serpent in devising ways of lubricating the insertion of his ideas into the mind of Louis XV. Moreover, the limits of free speech were narrow: the Abbé Galiani defined eloquence as the art of saying everything without going to the Bastille. Ideas of burden-sharing by the aristocracy could not safely have been presented in a less sugar-coated capsule.

4. *Adam Smith*

Adam Smith was a pioneer of the conception that the proper goal of economic policy was primarily the increase of goods for consumption by the common man, sold at the lowest prices the producers could afford and still have adequate incentive for vigorous production. His consumer standpoint was an antithesis to the sponsorship of producer interests by the mercantilists, who were his main object of attack. But for a quantitative concept, he was forced to fall back on the total exchange value of the nation's products, though he had already concluded that the exchange values of goods are not in proportion to their use values. Another criterion was a selection of occupations under which a given capital would set a maximum amount of productive labor in motion—but natural liberty would bring this about.

Smith evidenced solicitude for those with low incomes. Increased wealth does not bring proportional increase in happiness. People who gain substantial wealth, hoping to gain happiness thereby, are disappointed; but in the process they improve productive methods, and this brings a modest gain in real income to the masses, which does count in the scale of happiness. It tends to be eaten away by a consequent increase of population; but with continuing progress wages can be kept above a bare subsistence, and this is desirable. It is well that those who feed and clothe the rest of society should be themselves tolerably well fed and clothed. Hardly startling, but a notable advance over the mercantilist attitude.

A position of personal independence is a desideratum. Laws in favor of workers are always just, since they must run the gauntlet of a Parliament that represents the other classes. At one point Smith excoriated the deadening effect on workers' minds and characters of the monotonous jobs that the subdivision of labor was creating. His suggested countermeasure was education. He approved of the effect of small religious sects because, among other things, they gave more people a chance to count for something in the life of a group.

On the ground that "defense is more important than opulence," he justified some deviations from "natural liberty"; but, in the conditions of the time, a few minor exceptions were sufficient. Perhaps his greatest departure was his approval of the navigation acts, which had ruined the carrying trade of Britain's rival, Holland. His many-sided thinking included some mercantilist elements. He did not question the "natural right" of landowner and capitalist-employer to their shares of the product at their "natural levels," which in the case of capitalist-employers meant the necessary supply price of capital and enterprise. But his arguments for individualism were not applied to joint-stock companies.

As the physiocrats spoke for a sick economy in which agriculture was basic, and the mercantilists spoke for trade and protected manufactures, Smith spoke, in the infancy of the Industrial Revolution, for a freely balanced economy in which manufacturing was the most dynamic element, needing no leading strings. The problems and tasks of a more developed industrialism came later.

5. Bentham

Bentham rejected intuitive concepts of natural right as a standard of appraisal, and insisted that institutions should justify themselves by a rational scrutiny of their results. These were to be measured by maximum happiness, conceived as an algebraic sum on a scale of pleasure and pain, which in turn are the things people actually seek or avoid. The task of the legal framework of economic life is, by rules of general application, to prevent people from pursuing their interests to the injury of others, leaving them free to pursue them in any other way. Since each is supposed to pursue his own interest more faithfully than others can be trusted to do it for him, this system leads to the maximum result. Thus Bentham laid the basis for a more rationalistic and doctrinaire system of laissez faire than Smith. But it was built of elements that could lead, equally rationally, to quite different results; partly because law could not perform, or closely approximate, the miracle which the Benthamite system required.

In the Benthamite social sum of happiness, every person counted as one; and Bentham assumed that the pleasures of different persons could be compared and added. He felt that this, while not strictly accurate, came nearer to the truth than any other practicable assumption; furthermore, without it his whole social mechanics of happiness became impossible. It afforded a strong case for distribution according to need; but he rejected this on the ground that it was more important to promote a progressive increase in the total income, through the stimulus afforded by the assurance that the person investing capital and assuming risk would reap the rewards that might come from ownership of the results. Nowadays, of course, we practice many methods of striking an intermediate balance.

Bentham laid the basis for economics as a science of subjective feelings. And his optimistic confidence in the possibility of devising institutions as mechanisms to produce calculated results has been irresistibly attractive, despite difficulties and disappointments. This view of institutions has refused to stop with laissez faire, but has moved on to new deals and collectivist utopias. The Benthamite idea of the negative function of law —the "policeman state" (not to be confused with the totalitarian "police state")—has been buried under the growth of more positive state activities.

6. Malthus

Malthus' *Essay on Population* gave currency to the idea that limiting population was a prerequisite to any large and lasting raising of the standard of living of the masses, together with considerable skepticism as to the feasibility of such large improvements. With this went a hardening of poor-law policy. In a more general way, he may be said to have established, as a characteristic of the economic profession, the principle of hard-headed exclusion from economic goals of anything seen not to be feasible. (But some of the things that economists proved impracticable have subsequently come to pass.)

After Napoleon's blockade, Malthus wanted England to be less dependent on imported food, and to that end favored moderate agricultural protection. He also had the hardihood to suggest the need for a due balance between saving and consumption, and the possibility that saving might go too far. It is ironic that his heresy on this point has increased his stature in the eyes of the present generation, while his law of population, acclaimed in his day as basic orthodoxy, has been inoperative in the industrially developed part of the world. But for a majority of the world's population it is still to be reckoned with.

7. *Ricardo*

From our present standpoint, perhaps, Ricardo's chief impact was to reinforce the classical tendency to hold that ambitions for social betterment are narrowly limited by economic laws, which are independent of human institutions and which society transgresses at its peril. He emphasized national net income—surplus above subsistence—as an objective measuring a country's power to pay taxes and to support a war. Cheap food would increase this margin, resulting in lower money wages without reducing real wages; and on this ground he opposed agricultural protection. But his recommendations on policy are frequently bare of explanation of the criteria that underlie them.

8. *John Stuart Mill*

John Stuart Mill represented a transition from Benthamite-Ricardian orthodoxy to broader conceptions of human values, of institutions, of what is feasible, and of what government can and should undertake to do. Raising of real wages by trade-union action would be desirable if possible, but it is impossible (wages being limited by the ratio between the working population and the wages fund). In other ways, however, working with and not against economic law, gains may be made; and some of these may be substantial enough to become embodied in the standards of living which people will protect by restricting their birthrate, and may thus be perpetuated, in the face of the Malthusian law of population.

Mill sought to escape from the fatalism of economic laws independent of human institution, searching for an area of laws that were matters of human institution and therefore modifiable. His charter of justified functions of government accepts private activity as the general rule. But Bentham, in the act of defining the logical basis of laissez faire, had also provided Mill with opportunity and grounds for a list of exceptions, which we can now see to be pregnant with possibilities of almost indefinite expansion under changed conditions or changed attitudes.[3] His specific suggestions were modest, and his chief restriction was that only highly important values justify the compulsory variety of governmental interference. But with Mill, as with Smith, the presumption in favor of laissez faire did not apply to joint-stock companies.

Mill discusses collectivism tolerantly, and suggests that the decisive consideration might be which system affords the greater freedom, indicating that this did not automatically settle the issue in favor of private enterprise. Another criterion is a healthy balance between the public and private spheres, in terms of the levels of ability they are able to enlist, and the scope for its exercise. In addition to the gratification of wants, Mill appeared to be deeply concerned that individuals should exercise and develop their capacities in caring by their own efforts for the things that are important to them.

9. Other Ideas of the Classical Period

The thought of the early nineteenth century included forerunners of the historical school, institutionalists, aesthetic critics of early industrialism, early socialists, and other reformers. Sismondi noted that the Middle Ages afforded the security of belonging to a place in the community, a security which participants in the modern struggle lacked. The Middle Ages built enduringly, as modern builders did not. He was ahead of his time in viewing depressions as an inherent illness of the system. Fourier revolted against the waste and chicanery he saw in business. Robert Owen, successful industrialist, pioneered in welfare work and dissipated his fortune in collectivist experiments. Historical students envisioned social evolution, not bound by Benthamite specifications. Carlyle called economics the "dismal science" and blamed it for accepting poverty

[3] See his *Principles of Political Economy*, Book V, Chaps. I, X, XI.

too calmly. But he had no sympathy for plodding utilitarianism or for "democratic" rule by the drab values of industrialized masses. He would not make them kings. Ruskin, as against economists' abstractions, insisted that "there is no wealth but life."

The dissents influenced somewhat the attitudes of regular economists, without radically diverting their current of thought. To Marx, the actual goal of the existing system was exploitation of the workers; and the Marxian goal was the workers' seizure of the economy, without detailed attention to the ends to which they would subsequently put it.

10. Early Marginal Theory, 1871-1900

With the aid of Ricardo's great tool, the marginal method, an answer was found to the difficulty that had baffled the classicists—the apparent lack of correspondence between use value and exchange value. The solution hinged on the use value (or utility) dependent on the presence or absence of a little more or less of a commodity—a "marginal unit." Bentham's pleasure-pain mechanics could now be fulfilled in an economics of subjective values or utilities. Individuals' comparisons of utilities were accepted as meaningful, though the relative utilities of things to different individuals remained a problem, the more cautious theorists insisting that nothing can be known, scientifically, about it. (But when it comes to policy, most economists believe—scientifically or not—in reducing the inequalities of wealth and income which an unmitigated laissez-faire system would create.)

In the matter of incomes, the marginal-productivity theory—companion of marginal utility—rounded out a system in which, under competition, factors of production were allocated where they would be most productive, and their owners, including laborers, received the worth of their marginal contribution to the joint product. And this is not without an ethical element, though few would claim that it settles all ethical problems. It is the ethics of the parable of the talents, not that of the workers in the vineyard.

Under this theory, the bulk of the gain from improvements was seen as filtering rather quickly through to the workers (manual and directive) while business kept as profits no more than the minimum needed to attract capital and afford enterprise the necessary incentive to take the risks of pioneering. The Industrial Revolution in the Western world had progressed to the point of emancipating this area from the pressure of population as an insuperable barrier to prospects of progressive raising of the level of living of the masses. This and many related values were lifted out of the limbo of the unattainable, and became accepted goals of endeavor. Thus the tone of the period was optimistic.

The individual worker had the responsibility, as well as the opportunity, of finding employment and keeping it by satisfactory performance in a competitive struggle with others. It was assumed that he could always find some job, at some rate of pay. It was only later that this view was progressively altered by the impact of cycles of mass unemployment, arising from causes largely inherent in the business system and beyond the power of individual workers to remove.

The marginal economists were, however, moving in the direction of a moderate interventionism. They prevailingly viewed the system of private enterprise as basically sound, though with particular defects. These should be remediable by piecemeal methods, which would not alter the fundamental character of the system. Like John Stuart Mill, they found exceptions to the laissez-faire theory, or necessary conditions unfulfilled; and the exceptions multiplied. Nevertheless, a good deal—though not all—of the public intervention which was approved could be characterized as trying to make the actual system work more nearly like the ideal model of free and fluid competition. With limitations, this was accepted as the most pertinent economic objective for a society made up mostly of everyday human beings, neither saints, geniuses, nor criminals; ready to give value for value received but not to make a charity of business; people with many and important generous impulses, but people to whom the most dependable stimuli to daily toil were stimuli of self-interest.

So much for the antecedents of current ideas as to the goals of economic life. The story reflects the liberation of great productive forces by an individualism, not wholly undisciplined, but often ignorantly disruptive of the values of the society it replaced. Then came belated recognition that something more was needed, and attempts to rectify defects and abuses. As we go on into the twentieth century this movement gathers momentum, until ways of thinking are surprisingly transformed.

III. THE CURRENT CENTURY: MOVING TOWARD A NEW BALANCE BETWEEN INDIVIDUAL, GROUP, AND COMMUNITY

1. *Institutional Theory*

While piecemeal exceptions to laissez faire multiplied in the realm of policy, so also did divergent heterodoxies in the realm of theory. The term "institutionalism" has been applied to a number of such theories, some of them having little in common except departure from "marginalist" orthodoxy.

Charles H. Cooley performed the great service of showing that the mechanism of the market, which dominates the values that purport to be economic, is not a mere mechanism for neutral recording of people's preferences, but is a social institution with biases of its own, different from the biases of the institutions that purport to record, for example, aesthetic or ethical valuations. Policy-wise, his theories looked largely in the direction of making the market responsive to a more representative selection of the values actually prevalent in the society.

By way of contrast, Thorstein Veblen combined a merciless deflation of the pretensions of the business system with an Olympian detachment from questions of what to do about it. His critique had much more of Marxian thought in it than Veblen himself would have willingly recognized, and centered largely on failures in serviceability to the "material" interests of the common man. He appears to have taken democratic values as seriously as he took anything; but his final suggestion of a "soviet of technicians"—the germ of "technocracy"—was hardly a democratic proposal. His whole bent was against making purposive recommendations.

John R. Commons was at the opposite pole from the detachment of Veblen. A practical crusader, his thought was frankly purposive, and he defined institutions as "collective action in control of individual action." His dominant purpose was to make the business system serviceable enough to deserve to survive; though he was not certain this effort would succeed. His main emphasis was on labor conditions, including the maintenance of employment. In the field of theory, he wanted "to give to collective action, in all its varieties, its due place throughout economic theory"—a place which would be something more than a list of specific abuses or exceptions to laissez faire.[4] With this in view he broadened the concept of a "transaction" to include social action, and added the conceptions of a "going concern" and its "working rules"—similarly broadened to include both private and social forms.

What these very different thinkers had in common was a refusal to accept the market as an adequate vehicle for expressing the importance of things to society. They looked beyond it in varying ways, according to their differing personalities.

2. *Welfare Economics*

The reason for a separate subdiscipline labeled "welfare economics" arises as economics becomes growingly self-conscious in its attempt to separate its analysis of what is desirable from judgments of what is desirable. A. C. Pigou, in his *Wealth and Welfare*, published in 1912, proceeded on the basis of an "unverified probability" that welfare would be increased by an increase in the size of the national dividend, by a more equal distribution (unless it resulted in too great a reduction in the total), and by greater steadiness. But the use the poor make of relief funds should be supervised, or else the funds will be largely wasted. He justified, in principle, policies that would increase and regularize employment, but had only cautious and limited suggestions to offer.

One sector of his analysis was a form of social accounting, aiming to identify cases in which a given added use of resources would add either more or less to the national dividend than to the income of the person making the outlay. He also justified some forms of nega-

[4] *Institutional Economics*, New York, Macmillan Co., 1934, p. 5.

tive eugenics, and raised the question whether some economic policies aiming at welfare might not have their effects canceled by a resulting deterioration of the biological stock of the population.

Two years later, John A. Hobson brought out a welfare study of a very different kind, stemming from Ruskin's theme, "There is no wealth but life."[5] Hobson did not try, as Pigou did, to isolate *economic* welfare, but asked simply, "What is welfare, and how is it affected by existing methods of producing and circulating wealth?" His answer held that welfare is an organic whole, not an arithmetic sum of marginal units of gratification; and his particular contribution lay in giving primary emphasis to the effect of the character of work on the worker. Much earlier, he had ventured an underconsumption theory of depressions. Thus he put his finger on the two biggest blind spots in conventional economics. But economists were not impressed, regarding his treatment as nonscientific.

If Hobson's welfare economics left the scientific economics out, the form of theory which now bears the name can without real unfairness be described as welfare economics with the welfare left out, in a remarkably resolute attempt to meet the real or supposed requirements of economic science. Rejecting "interpersonal comparisons," this body of theory seems to end in rather complete agnosticism, aside from policies that increase the national dividend without making anyone worse off. But the existence of a single disadvantaged person acts as a veto on scientific approval of any policy—one cannot be scientifically certain that his loss does not outweigh the gains of many. Such a theory cannot recommend that we install tax-supported poor relief or a progressive income tax; but equally it could not recommend that they be not established. It seems clear that this theory has not reached satisfactory final form.

Meanwhile, no one has disproved the hypothesis that society cannot afford to let its less fortunate members starve, or that many highly important effects of industrialism are nonmarketable by-products, so that it appears almost a matter of chance whether they are beneficial or the opposite. Almost, but not quite, since men, even in economic life, have not wholly lost their moral sense, and

[5] J. A. Hobson, *Work and Wealth*, New York, Macmillan Co., 1914, pp. 10-12.

are not completely indifferent to the diffused good or harm they do. State action is no automatic panacea. Extensions of state power have unintended by-products also. And unmoral politics, like unmoral business, can fail to be directed to socially valid ends. Further, no one has disproved that if the moral fibre of the people deteriorates, and if the ethics of voluntary cooperation is submerged in self-seeking struggles, the material national dividend will suffer.

3. *Current Theories of Limited Competition*

Competitive theory is probably in a transitional state, tending to set objectives too precise for realization, and therefore to underrate the effectiveness of actual ("imperfect") competition, while policy does not follow theory with any consistency. Briefly, theory has stressed the effect of competition in bringing prices and costs into equilibrium at levels that minimize profits and promote an economical scale of operation in a given state of techniques. This is a static problem for which price theory can produce precise answers. At least equally important is dynamic improvement of methods and products, but formal theory cannot reduce this to precision, especially in the diagrammatic forms of which it is so fond.

As one result, current theory tends to regard quality differentiation as a defect of competition, rather than a means of progress in quality and an essential additional service which can be thoroughly competitive, although, like all services, it may take defective forms. Scarcely less important, perhaps, is the fact that these dynamic forms of competition do not require such large numbers of competitors as "perfect" competition does, and they allow some producers to make profits while others are making losses. And actual competition takes many important forms besides those "obvious and simple" enough to be embodied in formal theory.

4. *Attitudes toward Competition in General*

"Competition," as commonly used, refers to competition of business units in the production and sale of their products. In this sense, American economists support competition more consistently than prevailing policy does. For example, they generally oppose resale-price maintenance under the "fair-trade" laws. But it would be a rare economist who would hold that everything—employment, wages, agricultural production, and farm prices—should be settled by an unrestricted competitive struggle. Economists have accepted the idea that neither workers nor farmers should be exposed to the full rigors of competition in the sale of their labor or their products.

This country's legal enactment that "labor is not a commodity" took its meaning from Karl Marx's assertion that under capitalism labor *is* a commodity, "constantly exposed to all the vicissitudes of competition, to all the fluctuations of the market."[6] This particular statute freed unions from the antitrust laws; but as an expression of general policy the phrase had wider implications. Economists approved unions at first as an offset to the superior bargaining power of employers. The nearest practicable approach to equality of bargaining position, and one which economists of a generation ago typically set as an ideal, would be a situation in which, while bargaining is collective, neither side can control the supply of the thing it has to sell, or maintain its price regardless of an excess supply. This leaves unanswered such questions as that of industry-wide versus companywide bargaining, and the conditions under which an employer should be protected in filling the places of striking workers. Equity seems to lie somewhere between an absolute right of the striker to hold his job vacant and the older practice of hiring strikebreakers.

Collective bargaining has not stopped with any such vague balance, and by degrees economists have found themselves tolerating bargaining methods which would unquestionably be classed as monopolistic if employed by business in the sale of its products. This became ominous with the increasing number of vital services which can be cut off by a strike, giving numerous minorities coercive power over the public. So far, in this perplexing dilemma, economists have prevailingly approved of efforts to get settlements by mediation and arbitration without power; and have acquiesced in moderate injury to the public interest from stoppages of service pending settlement, chiefly because these are questions on which

[6] *Communist Manifesto*, 1847, authorized English translation, p. 15.

only a settlement voluntarily reached, or at least acquiesced in without outright compulsion, can provide a basis for healthy employment relations afterward.

A genuine attempt to break unions is unthinkable. Economists today probably discount union power to raise the general level of real wages as overrated, and judge that their greatest value lies in protecting workers' human rights on the job.

As to agriculture, there is general agreement that it is naturally subject to undue competitive pressure as compared to industry, and that this disparity needs to be remedied somehow; disagreements are mostly as to method. Other problem areas include bituminous coal, crude oil, rail-truck competition, and noncompetitive practices in the field of small trade.

To sum up, while current theory implies that competition can be too weak, but never too strong, attitudes on policy imply that it can be too severe, as well as not severe enough, even in business and still more in other fields. Economists are perhaps readier than others to recognize that it may not be strong enough unless it is sufficiently severe to be called "destructive" or "cutthroat" by some of those exposed to it. This is largely because one of its important services is to weed out inefficient enterprises more rigorously than a human judge or jury would have the hardihood to do. The assumption is that individuals bankrupted out of a business are merely forced to fall back on some second-choice livelihood. The chief exception occurs in the small trades, which unemployed workers may enter in order to have some kind of job, even though it pays less than standard wages.

5. Theory of Business Fluctuations and Unemployment

Statistics of business cycles have gone far to dispel the once-prevalent idea that "everyone can get a job" if he tries hard enough. The great depression of the thirties found government committed to assuming responsibility. This period also produced suggestions of effective remedies in the Keynesian theory. For the younger generation of economists, such remedies became the primary frontier objective of economic policy. New force has also been lent to older objectives, especially to widely diffused income as a necessity for the prosperity of a mass-production economy which sells most of its product at home, as ours does. When employment is short of a satisfactory level, increased consumption is less important as an ultimate end than as a means to more jobs—always provided its effect is not canceled by reduction of capital outlays.

However, American economists have not generally adopted the theory, espoused by various economists speaking for organized labor, that a general wage increase regularly stimulates employment and can help avert a threatened depression (as was urged in 1945-1946). Neither have American economists adopted the theory of recovery via wage reduction. A representative view would probably be that wages can be too low for maximum employment, but are not likely to be, the strength of organized labor being what it is; and that if wages are too high, the result may be either inflation or unemployment, according as employers are or are not able to pass on added costs in higher prices and still market an ample output.

6. *War, Overemployment, and Inflation*

War reverses the problem of depression and upsets many of the ratings in our ordinary scheme of values. Increased consumer gratification is temporarily subordinated, so far as practicable. As to the basic personal liberties, against our present adversary, the paramount fact is that if we lose, these values have no future, and temporary and limited restriction is better than permanent blackout. But since they are what we are fighting to defend, we must do our utmost to minimize any encroachments upon them. Their postwar restoration is safer in proportion as a large measure of them have been preserved during the struggle.

In major war, economic controls become indispensable; but they have to make terms with the fact that the country's war objective does not automatically wipe out habits of self-interested action. Since controls require a measure of voluntary compliance, compromise with ordinary incentives is necessary. But an uncompromising determination on the part of powerful groups that "whoever has to endure a shrunken real income, it won't be us"—this can be disastrous. It spells inflation, the most inequitable way of sharing shortages.

7. Price Stability and Price Flexibility

Over the long future, the question has been raised whether, if we succeed in maintaining employment at a satisfactorily high level, the result will be a progressive inflationary trend of prices, due not to shortages but to ample buying power, sustaining and inviting a bidding up of money costs of production. Economists would agree that, beyond some very moderate limit—the present writer suggests a long-run trend averaging 2 per cent per year— inflation is a serious evil. So also is any policy that results in such a harmful degree of inflation.

While approximate stability of the general level of prices has long been one of the objectives of economists, they have laid even greater stress on the need for sufficient flexibility of particular prices to keep them in a healthy relation to changing costs. As to whether they should fluctuate still more actively, responding to every shift of demand, or of supply of productive factors, opinions are divided. The majority probably holds that general price movements in response to changes in over-all demand can do little or nothing to restore stability of operation and employment that could not be done in other ways with less disturbing consequences.

8. The Social Minimum

Social insurance is now accepted, exclusive reliance on individualistic and voluntary methods in these matters having been gradually eroded away by time, statistics, and the impact of depressions. While unemployment benefits are in part a substitute for steady employment, they have some stabilizing effect on jobs, by mitigating the fluctuations of purchasing power through which depressions spread and cumulate. And the Beveridge Report of 1942 linked the two objectives with the proposition that really adequate "cradle-to-grave" social security was financially feasible only if unemployment was kept within rather modest limits.

cially what substitutes may be found for nonreproducible resources that are now essential.

12. *Maintaining Essential Freedoms*

Economists have obviously departed far from the attitude, prevalent a generation ago, which condemned any encroachment on the customary range of things that individuals were supposed to do for themselves, as contrary to the principles of our system. C. H. Cooley long ago disposed of the idea that the way to develop effective capacity for decision-making is to impose on everyone complete responsibility for all the decisions that affect his interests. It is no service to the principle of freedom and individual responsibility to overload the individual with more decisions than he can give proper attention to, or decisions of a character with which he cannot hope to cope successfully. The pertinent question, from this standpoint, is whether he has a sufficient range of such responsibilities, of sorts that he has a reasonable chance to deal with. To this end, since decision is an effort unpleasant to many, and retreat from freedom an attractive refuge, we probably need to be confronted with more and heavier "challenges" than most of us would voluntarily invite. Hence limits need to be set on the tendency to give the individual all the securities he is likely to seek.

There are some freedoms everyone needs to exercise, and others that are enormously important for their results to society, though only a few individuals have the rare combination of capacity and luck required to exercise them successfully. Such are the freedoms of leadership, including freedom to carve out new occupations or to introduce new products or new ideas. Business freedom is in this class, in differing degrees. The small self-employed enterprise is sometimes, though rarely, a source of pioneering improvements, and more often a refuge from unemployment. Corporate enterprise, on the other hand, makes possible mass production, using applied science, on a private basis; and this most economists continue to support. They do so only partly on grounds of efficiency, and in spite of a bad past record of unstable employment. Economists, who are against concentrated power in general, find private enterprise still subject to considerable (if imperfect) competitive checks; but beyond that, it affords multiple centers of decision which—after due deduction for intercorporate relations—are genuinely independent of one another. Freedom of criticism and dissent, which economists prize above the general run of "economic values," would be subject to obvious dangers in an economy with one supreme employing authority. And the meaning of freedom of the press under such conditions would be problematical, to say the least.

This kind of consideration appears to be gaining in importance in the typical economist's appraisal of the case for private enterprise, as problems of near-monopoly and unstable employment make the customary economic arguments relatively weaker. Danger to political and personal freedoms does not prevent some economists from espousing democratic collectivism, but it probably does deter others. They may admit the reality of the danger, even while they discount dogmatic statements that freedom is one and indivisible and that political and intellectual freedoms stand or fall with business freedom and the "profit system." If pressed, a representative group might hold that the methods which a democratic and decentralized socialism could use to deal with economic problems, including unemployment, are probably sufficiently available to the mixed system we now have; and that the chance that this is true is good enough to be worth a trial. Nearly all would give the benefit of the doubt to gradual and evolutionary change, as against either abrupt and complete transformation, or a futile attempt to preserve unchanged a past in which the forces of change were an inseparable part.

IV. CONCLUSION AND APPRAISAL

The changes here summarized have transformed the American economy, and our way of thinking about it, into something which is not recognizable as the "capitalism" or "individualism" of the mid-nineteenth century. The society is taking responsibility for basic elements in the welfare of its members. This raises the problem of the effect on the individual of doing so much for him without commensurate obligations laid upon him in return. The chal-

II

Economic Progress as a Goal of Economic Life

by KENNETH E. BOULDING
Professor of Economics, University of Michigan

I

The concept of economic progress, difficult and wide as its ramifications may be, is at bottom simple. It may be defined as an increase in efficiency. All the difficulties in the concept center around the definition and measurement of "efficiency," and it is to this problem that we shall first turn.

All concepts of efficiency define it as the ratio:

$$\frac{\text{Quantity of Output}}{\text{Quantity of Input}}$$

Efficiency, that is to say, is a quantity descriptive of some process of production or transformation, by means of which a quantity of something is transformed into a quantity of something else. The difficulties in the various concepts of efficiency all revolve around the definition and measurement of the output and input concerned.

At the simplest level are concepts of "engineering efficiency"— amounts of physical output per unit of physical input. The ratio of available kinetic energy to fuel-energy consumption in an engine is a good example. Engineering efficiency, however, is not necessarily economically significant. One engine may, for instance, have a higher ratio of output to input in terms of energy than another, but it may use a costlier fuel or be more expensive to run.

Accounting as a Measure

Evidently a more "significant" concept is that of accounting efficiency. Here we take into account not merely the energy transformation, but all the other inputs and outputs which are subject
to valuation in terms of money. The transformation process here is
regarded as a process of transformation of asset values, of "costs"
into "revenues." In any process of production, looked at from the
point of the balance sheet of the firm, certain assets are diminished.
Money is paid out in wages, raw materials are used up, fuels and
lubricants are consumed, plant and equipment depreciate, and so
on. As a result of all this consumption of assets, however, certain
other assets are created—the products of the process. Clearly another interesting measure of efficiency is the ratio:

$$\frac{\text{Assets produced (revenues)}}{\text{Assets destroyed in production (costs)}}$$

Even at this level, however, a second main problem presents itself
—that of *valuation*. Both input and output are not now usually
homogeneous quantities; they are aggregates of a number of different, incommensurable quantities. If 100 bushels of wheat and 5
tons of straw are produced at a "cost" of 5 acre-years of land, one
tenth of a man-year of labor, one hundredth of a tractor and a combine, and one ton of fertilizer, what is the "efficiency" of such a proc
ess? This question cannot be answered at all unless we have some
way of reducing these heterogeneous quantities to a common denominator; i.e., to a single dimension. This is done by valuation—
i.e., by multiplying each quantity by a valuation ratio expressing the
number of units of the "measure of value" which are equivalent to
one unit of the quantity concerned. Usually, of course, the common
denominator is money and the valuation ratio is a money price.

Thus, if in the above example wheat were $2 a bushel, straw
were $3 a ton, land use was $10 an acre-year, labor use was $1,000
per man-year, the tractor and combine were worth $2,000, and fer-
tilizer was $20 per ton, the value of both input and output could
be calculated and the efficiency ratio derived. The value of the

input is $(50+100+20+20)$ or \$190; the value of output is $(200+15)$ or \$215, and the efficiency is $\frac{215}{190}$ or 1.13. With different *relative* values of the different inputs and outputs a different result will be obtained for the efficiency ratio, even with the identical physical quantities of inputs and outputs. Thus, even if all other values remain the same and the valuation ratio of wheat falls to \$1 a bushel, the value of output will now be \$115, and the efficiency is $\frac{115}{190}$, or .61.

Without the valuation ratios we cannot even tell whether the process has an efficiency greater or less than one—i.e., whether it results in an increase or in a decrease in the total stock of assets. Mere physical transformation alone, therefore, can never serve as a measure of efficiency. The necessity for valuation raises acutely the question of *what* valuation ratios should be used. The most obvious ratios to use are, of course, the market prices of the various assets. The concept of a valuation ratio, as well as the process of valuation, is, however, independent of the concept of market price. There are many assets which do not have a market; specialized plant and machinery, for instance, has no regular market and no regular market price. There are other assets for which the market price is an inadequate guide to relative significance—where, for instance, markets are narrow or otherwise imperfect, or where the market price is highly fluctuating. Nevertheless it is to market price, whether actual, average, corrected, or in some sense ideal, that we turn to find an objective system of relative valuation ratios; indeed, there is no other source of an *objective* system.

It is perhaps the greatest contribution of the institution of the market to the conduct of human affairs that over a wide area of life it provides us with some sort of standard of relative values which is objective at least to the degree that it results from a consensus of a multitude of individual valuations. There is an analogy here with political opinion; the market does for commodities what the process of argument does for public opinion—it forms a general judgment out of a multitude of individual opinions.

The most significant concept of accounting efficiency is that of the *rate* of profit; that is, the rate of growth of the value of assets in the course of their transformations. Even this concept, however, is inadequate as a measure of economic progress. The accounting-efficiency concept breaks down for two reasons. One reason is that at the level of the individual account there are a good many costs and revenues which are clearly significant from the point of view of well-being but which slip through the broad net of the accounting system. There are, for instance, social costs which for one reason or another do not get into the accountant's ledger because the assets (or liabilities) concerned cannot be appropriated. A famous example is the nuisance created by smoke, which the owner of the offending chimney (or pipe!) does not have to pay for. Another significant example is the unseen labor costs due to health hazards, etc. There are also social revenues which do not get into the accounts; a man who beautifies his garden thereby enhances the value of his neighbor's property as well as his own. One of the major objects of economic legislation should be to catch these hidden costs and revenues, so that accounting results may bear a closer relation to social costs and benefits. Much rather ill-founded criticism of the private-property economy is based also on the failure to distinguish between this defect in the definition of property and the concept of property itself.

The second reason why the concepts of accounting efficiency are not applicable to social efficiency is more fundamental. Even if the accounting net were made fine enough to catch every cost and every benefit, the accounting concepts would still not yield us a measure of social efficiency, for the costs and benefits cannot be *aggregated*. Accounting, no matter how socially refined, is a device for measuring the *relative* efficiency of different enterprises or of different uses of resources. It is not suited to the measurement of the total efficiency of a society. Suppose, for instance, that we tried to define the efficiency of a whole society by the ratio of its total revenues to its total costs. If we include "profits" in costs, defining costs to include all disbursements out of total revenue, costs and revenues are by definition equal, and their ratio is unity. If we exclude profits from costs the "efficiency ratio" becomes total income divided by total income less profits, and becomes simply a measure of the way in which income is distributed, and is not a measure of efficiency at all.

OTHER MEASURES

In order to get a measure of social efficiency, therefore, we must ask ourselves what are the outputs and inputs which are significant in assessing the total efficiency of a society. Clearly the ultimate input is human time and energy. The ultimate output is human living, human satisfaction, call it what you will. Do we get "more" out of life than our ancestors? This is the crucial problem of progress. And it cannot be answered satisfactorily unless we can ask, more of *what*? What do we get out of life? And what do we put in? Now perhaps we have jumped too far; right outside the realm of the economist, in fact into that of the philosopher and the theologian. Perhaps before asking the ultimate question it would be better to ask some penultimate questions which have more hope of being answered.

Suppose, then, we limit the input concept to human time and the output concept to the value of economic product—i.e., a money value of that product which can be so valued. What we have now is "income per man-hour." We can call this concept without too much strain the "economic efficiency" of a society. There are some points, however, at which we must be careful. If two societies, or two periods in the same society, are to be compared in this respect the same schedule of valuation coefficients must be used in both cases. Otherwise a mere inflation of the monetary unit will result in an apparent rise in economic efficiency. But the use of the same schedule of relative valuation coefficients introduces an inescapable indeterminacy into the measurement, because the set of relative values which is appropriate to the one society or period is not necessarily appropriate to the other, and there are no clear objective criteria for selecting a set of valuation coefficients which are equally significant for both periods. Where the societies or periods compared are not widely different, this indeterminacy does not have a wide enough range to invalidate the use of the concept. Where, however, the societies compared are widely different, the comparison becomes almost meaningless. How, for instance, can we compare the nightingales' tongues and chariots of ancient Rome with the caviar and automobiles of today?

Fortunately the problem of comparison is not quite so hopeless as the above example would suggest, because there are certain products, or categories of products—"necessities"—which are common to all societies. All societies, for instance, produce food and warmth. It is not beyond the bounds of imagination to compare even two very different societies in this respect, in regard to the amount of man-time which is necessary for the provision of the caloric requirements of living. Any actual statistical definition of "necessities," of course, will have to be somewhat arbitrary; the arbitrariness need not be so great, however, as to impair the meaning of the comparisons.

A useful rough index of economic progress is the proportion of the economic resources of a society (say, its labor force) which is not employed in agriculture; for agriculture, by and large, produces the basic necessities.[1] A society in which only 20 per cent of the people are employed in agriculture, leaving 80 per cent to be employed in producing the "conveniences and luxuries of life," is clearly richer than one in which 90 per cent of the people have to be employed in agriculture, leaving only 10 per cent to produce the other things.

As long as the output of necessities is a large part of the total, the measure is likely to be fairly significant. Improvements in techniques in industry, however, may raise general standards of life without affecting the proportion of resources in agriculture, so that especially for more advanced countries the measure is not conclusive. If the demand for necessities is completely inelastic—i.e., if the society will wish to consume only a certain amount of them no matter how rich it is—an improvement in the methods of producing necessities will not result in an increase in the production of necessities (population being held constant) but will result in a

---

[1] The export industries of a food-importing country should, of course, be included in its "agriculture," and vice versa for a food-exporting country. Thus England grows wheat in her cotton mills, for the final process of the cotton industry can be thought of as the exchange of cotton goods for wheat.

transfer of resources from the "necessities" industries. The end result of the improvement is that the same quantity of necessities as before is produced with fewer resources, and the resources so released are available to produce conveniences and luxuries.

The figure below (related to "Agricultural Power and Machinery" in *Encyclopaedia Britannica*, 1947, Vol. I. p. 381) shows this force operating graphically in the case of American agriculture. The improvements in agriculture in the past hundred years have released something like 30 million workers—about half the present labor force—for employment in producing telephones, automobiles, refrigerators—and, it must be added, guns and bombs.

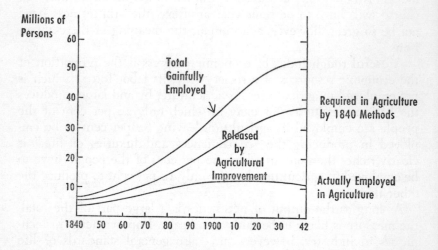

THE FACT, MEASURED OR UNMEASURED

We may well leave the question of the *measure* of economic progress at this point, even though the question must be left partially unanswered. As with all questions involving complex aggregates, there is no single measure or simple answer. We cannot always measure even the direction of economic development. Nevertheless we have a strong feeling that we have made enormous economic progress in the Western world in the past two hundred years, and that no matter how it is measured the figure that measures it must be so large that there can be no doubt of its significance or direction. The crudity of our measures is amply justified by the magnitude of the change.

We are so accustomed to a rapid rate of economic progress in the Western world that we are apt to regard it as a natural law that average real income shall increase at the rate of 3 per cent per annum! In fact, of course, periods of rapid economic progress have been relatively rare even in the history of civilization, and are almost unheard of in precivilized societies. Furthermore, there has never been anything like the last two or three hundred years in human history before. It is no exaggeration to say that all previous civilizations have existed on an economic shoestring, and that the typical abode even of civilized man has been on the edge of starvation. It is doubtful whether any previous civilization was ever able to spare more than 20 per cent of its labor force for all its nonsubsistence occupations. There may have been short-lived exceptions, but two almost universal forces have conspired to make any age of plenty brief. One is the Malthusian principle—that in the absence of deliberate checks on the growth of population, an improvement in the food supply will simply enable the population to grow to the point where numbers are once more checked by malnutrition. The other is the pride of the powerful, which leads to the expenditure of resources on luxury, buildings, and war beyond what the agricultural base can support, with consequent capital consumption and decline.

Over the long pull our own age may be no exception to these dismal "laws." But it differs from all previous ages in the sheer quantity of its economic power. The United States at present produces all the food that it needs, and more, with less than 20 per cent of its population: less than two hundred years ago it required something like 95 per cent of the population to produce its food supply. Nor are we at the end of this process. Even if there is no further improvement in the knowledge of agricultural techniques —even if present techniques were merely applied more extensively —it would be possible to produce our food with 10 per cent of the population or even less. People are not generally aware of the significance of this change. It was shown during World War II that the United States could devote half its national product to war, and still maintain a comfortable level of consumption, without anything (in the mass) that could be called real privation. This hundred billion dollars' worth of extra product could take other forms. In less than ten years, for instance, we could replace *all* our capital equipment—all our cities, roads, railroads, all our stores and houses and everything which they contain. Economic power on this scale has never existed in history before.

SOCIOLOGICAL FACTORS IN A DYNAMIC ECONOMY

How, then, did this remarkable development come about? Unfortunately we do not really know more than fragmentary answers to this question. The study of economic progress has been strangely neglected by most reputable economists, historians, and philosophers alike, in spite of its being the dominant characteristic of our age. Economic theory has been too much concerned with equilibrium, not enough with change. Economic history has been written largely by literary romanticists, who have not even been aware of what insights economic theory has to offer on this question. Finally, the moral philosophers have argued too much as if we were already in a stationary state, and as if the problem of economic justice were mainly one of distributing a fixed product, rather than encouraging an increasing product.

Any theory of economic progress therefore must be tentative. Nevertheless we can claim to know something. It is evident, for instance, that change, although not synonymous with progress, is at least a prerequisite. Not all change is progress, but without change no progress is possible. A society, therefore, which is resistant to change must also be resistant to progress; one which is open to change has the possibility of progress, though it has also possibilities of retrogression. We need to know much more, therefore, about what determines the willingness to change. This is more in the domain of the social psychologist, where the economist does not feel particularly competent.

One principle may nevertheless be suggested. If change itself, in any connection, is valued highly in itself in any aspect of the culture it is more likely to be valued highly in other aspects, and so will reduce the society's resistance to economic change. In this connection, therefore, the nature of religious attitudes to change is extremely important. One may venture a hypothesis that those societies in which conversion or convincement has been an important part of the religious experience of individuals will be much more open to change than those societies in which the prevailing pattern is to grow up without any conversion experience into a secure and established pattern of life. This may be one of the main reasons for the clear historical connection between "newness" and reforming zeal in religion and progressiveness in economic life. The immense influence of the Protestant Reformation and the Catholic Counter Reformation on economic development is a commonplace among historians. Less well recognized, but perhaps even more important, has been the influence of the perfectionist and evangelical sects, especially the Quakers and Methodists. An astonishing number of the basic developments of the so-called Industrial Revolution were the work of the Quakers and other nonconformists. Looking outside the boundaries of Christendom we find a similar connection between reforming religion and economic development in the early days of Mohammedanism.

The converse side of the medal is, of course, that when a religion gets "old," when it relies for its propagation and maintenance on the coercive power of the family or of the state, when it loses its "prophetic" quality and becomes "priestly," it correspondingly acts as a damper on change of any kind and on economic progress in particular. The greatest enemy of change is the spirit of orthodoxy —the feeling that the fundamental problems of life have been solved and embodied in writing or in organization, and that the main task of each generation is to transmit this solution to the next. Christianity has passed through several such "orthodox" phases; Mohammedanism provides one of the best examples of the ossifying effects of orthodoxy. It now looks as if Russian communism is repeating the same pattern—the vigor of revolutionary days being replaced by the sterile orthodoxy of Marx-Lenin-Stalin worship.

Although the religious element in a culture is of great importance in explaining its attitudes to change, other elements also are at work. We must not underestimate the importance of the high value which the development of science has given to disinterested curiosity. Science can exist only in a world that tolerates change; by its successes it reinforces that tolerance. Nor, in explaining the willingness to change, can we leave out of account the physical factors of climate, nutrition, and disease. Any change involves an expenditure of human energy; the easiest thing to do today is usually what we did yesterday, and the inertia of primitive societies may be closely related to their low human-energy levels. The relation between high productivity and cool, temperate climates is obvious to anyone with even a slight knowledge of human geography. One does not need to go so far as Markham and identify the 70° isotherm as the prime source of civilization;[2] but the northward drift of civilization with the invention of window glass and adequate heating of houses is beyond doubt, and it will be surprising if the invention of air conditioning does not produce a corresponding expansion toward the equator. Malnutrition and diseases such as malaria or hookworm are also important in explaining the failure of the tropics and warm-temperate zones to produce high-productivity cultures. Favorable physical conditions, however, while they may be necessary for the development of high productivity, are by no means sufficient. An almost classic example is the old German-Polish frontier, which divided two economic regions virtually identical in the physical factors of soil and climate, but differing widely in their economic productivity—a difference which could be explained only in terms of the whole culture pattern of the two peoples.

The most difficult question of all is that of the effect of social institutions, organizations, laws, and customs on economic progress. It is clear from human history that there is nothing automatic about economic progress; it is all too easy, in fact, to devise a set of social institutions which will prevent it. We need to know much more about the impact of various institutions and habits in these respects, and in the criticism of institutions their impact on economic progress should receive much more attention.

[2] S. F. Markham, *Climate and the Energy of Nations* (Oxford, Oxford University Press, 1944).

Economic progress cannot take place unless there is some provision in society for processes which are judged in some way "superior" to displace those which are judged by similar criteria to be "inferior." As a dynamic process economic progress means the development of better ways of doing things; this implies as a corollary that worse ways must be abandoned. The opportunity for the better to displace the worse is one of the meanings that may be given to that much-abused word "competition."[3] It is in this sense that competition can be said to be a prerequisite of progress.

Its opposite is "protection"—the setting up of institutions to protect the "vested interests," or the established ways of doing things, and to prevent their abandonment. If enough people and institutions are so "protected" from the necessity of substituting better for worse ways of doing things, progress may be made impossible. There are, of course, ethical problems involved in the "rights" of vested interests. There are also practical problems involved in overcoming the resistances to desirable changes, and modern welfare economics has developed quite an elaborate discussion of the "compensation" of vested interests. All we are concerned to do now, however, is to point out that there must be some arrangements for displacement of the obsolete methods, skills, equipments, and commodities.

There are a number of possible institutional systems under which competition of this sort can take place. One of the main justifications for the free market as an institution is that it permits rapid displacement of one process by another—though there may be real question as to the tests of inferiority or superiority. The free market is not, of course, the only conceivable institutional framework within which competition of this kind is possible; even within a highly organized and planned society it is possible for superior processes to knock out the inferior. The test of superiority, how-

[3] One of the most deplorable failures of modern social ethics has been its inability to develop a proper ethical taxonomy or classification of competition, and hence its tendency to regard all "competition" as bad. The truth is that some kinds of competition are bad and some are very good. The lumping of all kinds of competition together results mainly in a quite false imputation of badness to the good kinds, and imputations of goodness to all kinds of substitutes for competition, both good and bad.

ever, in this case is ability of the successful process to displace the unsuccessful one in the opinions of the planners rather than in the opinions of those who would benefit directly.

Another institutional factor on which economic progress depends is the ability of innovators to acquire control over the resources which are necessary to make the innovations. The capacity for genuine innovation, whether for invention itself or for the practical application of new methods, is rare in society. It would be remarkable indeed if the individuals whose heredity and upbringing had granted them unusual capacities for innovation were at the same time individuals whose position in society automatically gave them control over the resources needed to make innovations. If a society is to progress, therefore, some apparatus is necessary which will enable—or compel—the established controllers of resources to relinquish some of that control to the innovators.

In a capitalist society this is one of the main tasks of the financial system. The ultimate control of resources is invested in the owners of the physical capital and the money stocks of the system. These owners, however, are not necessarily, or even usually, the people best adapted to control these resources, whether as innovators or even as routine operators. Some means need to be devised, therefore, whereby the owners can relinquish the administration of resources to specialists in this task. This "divorce of ownership from control" is the main achievement of finance—i.e., of the system of debt and securities. The banking system is an important part of this process; through its power of creating bank deposits it has enabled borrowers to withdraw resources from unemployment or from the less active members of society by the process of inflation.

In the Western world, therefore, the innovator has obtained the necessary resources by persuading those who have the equity in the capital of society to relinquish to him some of their "purchasing power." Indeed, he does not even have to do the persuasion. The growth of the financial system has bred a class of financial experts whose job it is to persuade capitalists to relinquish their capital to enterprisers, and then discover enterprisers who can be entrusted with capital. It is impossible to assess how much of the rapid growth of the Western economy is due to its specialized system of finance, but there may be a strong connection, and the matter needs careful investigation.

A socialist society, of course, faces the same problem, and has generally found it much more difficult of solution. The virtue of capitalism has been its decentralization. Because ownership has been scattered among many individuals and groups, the man with an idea who is repulsed by one group of potential backers may, and frequently does, find another. Studies of innovations are revealing the importance of *informal* methods of finance in this connection. As society moves toward the formalization of its economic life, the capitalist "angel" willing to take a flyer on a crazy new idea is replaced by the bureaucratic bank and the even more bureaucratic government lending agency, whose operations are conducted in the limelight of politics and which is therefore prejudiced in favor of a cautious respectability. It would be rash to say that a socialist society cannot solve this problem. It is hardly too much to say, however, that the ultimate success of a socialist or of any highly integrated, monolithic society depends largely on its ability to devise administrative substitutes for capitalist casualness and flexibility.

In order to have economic progress there must not only be innovators—there must be imitators. The institutions and customs in a society which encourage the imitation of successful new methods deserve careful study. We have already noticed the significance of the free market in this regard. Innovation often results in a cheapening of the product, which will reduce the rewards of those who are still using the obsolete methods, thus forcing them either to change their occupation altogether or to increase their rewards by adopting the improved methods. There are, however, other factors in society which encourage imitation. To get very far into this problem would involve us in the sociology of fashion—most of which is yet to be written—but it is clear that the greater the positive desire to emulate the successful innovator, the more rapidly will the change take place, and in all probability the less will be the social cost. It is when the practitioners of the old methods are highly resistant to change that the process of competitive displacement results in so much human suffering.

There are also other elements in the fabric of society which may be of great importance in determining the rate of economic progress, and which should at least be mentioned, even if they cannot be treated very adequately.

There is first the whole problem of "incentives." The problem here is how to ensure that the rewards of those who pioneer are adequate to insure a sufficient supply of pioneering, or of productive activity in general. This is a problem which it is extremely difficult for any large collectivized system of distribution to solve. It is interesting to note that the Pilgrim Fathers at New Plymouth started with an "experiment of communal living," but got along much better when this was abandoned and each man was allowed to plant corn for his own household! If in fact productive activity of any kind has a "supply price"—i.e., if there is some level of reward below which the activity will not be undertaken—any system of distribution which results in a return to the productive activity of less than its supply price will simply result in the disappearance of the product. In other words, it is only the surplus of product over and above what is necessary to pay out to producers to keep them producing that is "available" to society, either for pomp, for war, or for redistribution.

There is, however, a difficult problem of fact here. A good deal of economic activity, and even a good deal of innovation, is done for its own sake and has a zero or even negative supply price—i.e., it will be done whether it is rewarded or not, or even if it is penalized. This spontaneous activity, however, has rarely been sufficient for the needs of society. Consequently in virtually all societies it has been necessary to reward the producer somewhat in proportion to his product. By our patent and copyright laws also we seek to reward the innovator. It is a moot question whether the granting of a monopoly, even a temporary one, is the best method of rewarding the innovator. It seems clear, however, that unless the institutions of society permit a reward of some sort there will not be a rapid rate of economic progress. It is desirable, of course, that the "supply prices" should be as low as possible; and insofar as honor, for instance, can substitute for more tangible rewards, that is all to the good. The more unselfish people there are in society, the better it is for the selfish, and, no doubt, for the unselfish as well.

Another factor which is difficult to define but which is unquestionably real is the stimulus of necessity, which is reputed to be the mother of invention, or that challenge, in the language of Toynbee, which is just adequate to provoke the proper response. The importance, in this connection, of a *disequilibrium* in the price system is something which most economists have overlooked. Often it is not the prospect of reward as much as the prospect of disaster which spurs us to effort, and failure is often the goad which has spurred a man on to success. A system in equilibrium in which everybody was doing moderately well might afford much less of a stimulus to progress than a system in disequilibrium in which there was a wide dispersion of profits and losses. There may be a case here for price fluctuations, which perpetually stir up the economic elites and make them circulate; also for interferences with the pricing system, such as the minimum wage, which has sometimes been a spur to innovation. Depressions and even wars have played their part in stimulating innovations. The quantitative importance of this factor, however, is difficult to assess, and I merely warn against overlooking it.

SPECIFIC ECONOMIC FACTORS

The factors we have mentioned above might well be called "sociological"; in fact their discussion carries us far beyond the conventional bounds of economics. There are also some more narrowly "economic" factors, most of which have been recognized at least as far back as the classical economists.

There are, for instance, the influence of specialization (i.e., the division of labor) on human productivity and the influence of the "extent of the market" on the development of specialization. Adam Smith's eloquent exposition of these theorems (*Wealth of Nations*, Book 1, Chapters 1-3) has never been bettered. The contribution of specialization to economic progress can be visualized dramatically. Suppose that the present population of the world were placed with each family on its own five acres of land and forbidden to trade with any other, so that each family had to raise its own food, weave its own cloth, build its own houses, paint its own pictures, and write its own books—in short, suppose we had a world of Swiss Family Robinsons. The material and cultural poverty of such a world compared with our own would be beyond measure. It must be emphasized also that specialization and trade are inseparable partners; without trade specialization would be absurd, and without specialization trade would be useless.

There are, however, certain qualifications which must be noticed. Like everything else, specialization can be carried to excess, and in any one state of the arts there is clearly an optimum degree of specialization. Most men employ barbers to cut their hair, but shave themselves. There are also certain human costs of extreme specialization (for instance, loss of significance of daily work) which do not get into the accounting system and which therefore need the attention of social policymakers. There are also certain technical qualifications of the doctrine that an increase in the extent of the market is always desirable, such as the "infant industry" argument for protection or the case for patents and copyright. These qualifications, however, serve but to underline the basic significance of the central doctrine.

Another theorem regarding economic progress which also dates back to Adam Smith is that economic progress almost invariably requires the "accumulation of stock." If we extend the concept of accumulation to include the accumulation of knowledge and skills in the minds and muscles of men, the proposition is incontrovertible. The "better ways of doing things" which economic progress implies nearly always involve the use of more elaborate and costly implements; and so, especially in poor societies, the difficulty of accumulation may be the most significant factor limiting the rate of progress. Accumulation is the excess of production over consumption. If production is small the sheer physical necessities of consumption press so hard upon the heels of the meager productive capacity that it requires the utmost parsimony and "abstinence" to refrain enough from consuming to allow much accumulation. In such circumstances "foreign investment"—i.e., an arrangement which enables the poor region to import without exporting—may be of great help in permitting the poor region to accumulate enough to start it on the path of progress.

In this respect, as in so many others, "to him that hath shall be given." There is some critical point of poverty below which consumption presses so hard on production that no accumulation is possible, and the people tread round and round in an endless squirrel cage—low production meeting only their barest necessities and allowing no surplus for improvement, either of human or of physical capital. Once above this critical point, however, a benevolent spiral is set up, with accumulation leading to higher productivity, and higher productivity leading to easier accumulation, which in turn leads to still higher productivity. One of the great problems facing the world today is how to get the poverty-stricken three quarters of the world over this initial "hump."

In this whole problem of accumulation the vital importance of human capital (i.e., improvement in the abilities of men) must be stressed. Education, training, and health services may easily be by far the most profitable kinds of investment. The rise in the average length of life which is an almost universal characteristic of a progressive society is itself a substantial contribution to economic progress, for it means a reduction in the "consumption" of skills and abilities by death. In a society in which the average age at death is thirty—as it is, for instance, in most of the overcrowded nations of the Far East—a large proportion of the resources of the society must be spent in replacing the population, and little can be devoted to improving it. Where the average age at death rises toward sixty and seventy, as it is doing in the Western world, a much smaller proportion of the resources of the society need be devoted to replacing the population, children and young people will form a much smaller percentage of the society, and much higher standards of education can be attained.

At this point, however, it is necessary to introduce again the "dismal theorem" of Malthus—a theorem which, incidentally, also goes back to Adam Smith. The "dismal theorem" can be stated very simply. It is that if nothing checks the growth of population except misery and starvation, then the population will grow until it is miserable and starves. It is necessary at this point to make a sharp distinction between *technical* and *economic* progress. Technical progress consists in the discovery and application of better ways of doing things. Such technical progress, however, does not necessarily result in economic progress—i.e., in a rise in income per head. This is because income per head depends not merely on the techniques available but also on the proportion of the human to the nonhuman resources.

We have here the famous law of diminishing returns in one of its forms. For our purposes it may be stated as follows: With *given* techniques there is some proportion of human to nonhuman resources at which income per head is a maximum; with given nonhuman resources, therefore, there is some population at which income per head is a maximum. This is usually called the "optimum population." As the population rises beyond this point, with given techniques and nonhuman resources, income per head must fall. And if the only check on the growth of population is poverty and the high death rate which poverty brings in its train, then, no matter how advanced the techniques of the society, the population will grow until poverty checks its growth.

This is a dismal theorem indeed. It implies that the end result of technical progress under strictly Malthusian conditions is an actual *increase* in the sum of human misery—if indeed misery can be summed—for it means that a larger population is enabled to live in precisely the same state of misery as its forefathers.

Fortunately, however, the dismal theorem is a strictly conditional one. Its dismal conclusion rests on an alterable premise, and it can be readily restated in a cheerful form: if there are checks other than misery which prevent the unlimited growth of population, then there can be a stable condition both of population and of plenty. Fortunately, also, rising standards of life themselves seem to bring these preventive checks in their train. Or perhaps the matter should be stated more generally: the same cultural changes which are favorable to technical change also seem to be associated with voluntary limitation of the population.

We are here dealing with a field where more is surmised than is known. The Malthusian specter does seem to have been laid in the Western world—though even there the apparent slowing down of population growth may have been merely a depression phenomenon, and a permanent state of full employment and increasing levels of income may produce results at present unsuspected and may raise the specter once more. Nevertheless the dismal theorem operates in full gloom over the greater part of mankind. If technical change comes too slowly to the underdeveloped parts of the world, its benefits will be swallowed up in population increase before the rising level of living has a chance to operate sufficiently as a check to the birth rate. It may well be that in these areas the change must be rapid and dramatic or it will be worse than useless and will merely set off a disastrous population explosion. Technical change, whether in agriculture, manufactures, transportation, education, or health, must be viewed in the light of the population situation and the whole cultural pattern of the society.

The growth of population is not the only way in which the fruits of technical progress can be dissipated. In some societies these fruits have been dissipated in the pomp and display of the ruling classes —in the building of pyramids, of palaces, even of temples. A much more frequent source of dissipation is war. In a world of warring states there is no true equilibrium of national power, and the normal condition of international relations is that of the arms race. Each nation attempts to establish its security by being stronger than its neighbors. It is only under rare circumstances that this situation can be stable for anything more than brief periods, and the competition for relative strength results in the constant rise in the proportion of the national income which is devoted to defense. In these circumstances the result of technical progress may be simply to enable nations to devote an ever-increasing proportion of their resources to war. This trend is unquestionably apparent in modern history. It is doubtful, for instance, whether any of the wars of the eighteenth century involved more than 5 per cent of national incomes; the Second World War absorbed up to 50 per cent of the national income of the major belligerents. It is a remarkable tribute to the rapidity of technical progress in the Western world that we have been able to witness so enormous a rise in the proportion of national product going to war and still enjoy a rapid increase in standards of living out of the remainder. The race between war and plenty, however (in spite of the spur of military necessity to invention), has usually been won by war, which has been perhaps even a greater destroyer of economic progress, looked at in the long view, than population increase.

The fruits of economic progress can also be dissipated in unemployment. This is a disease which is peculiarly characteristic of rich societies. In poor societies consumption is always pressing on the heels of production, and the problem is never under- but overconsumption. In rich societies, however, productive capacity may be so great that with the existing institutions the capacity and willingness of the society to absorb its output, whether in consumption or in willing accumulation (investment), is insufficient to take care of the great volume of output which results from full employment. When this is the case, full employment will be unstable, for it will result in a volume of accumulation greater than the society is willing to accept. Firms will attempt to reduce their unwanted accumulations by cutting down output, and unemployment will develop until output has been reduced to what the society is willing to absorb. Fortunately this is by no means an insoluble problem. It can be claimed, indeed, that the intellectual and technical problems of unemployment have been largely solved, though the political problems involved are still difficult.

There is no law, however, which says that the attempt of man to improve his worldly lot will always result in the swarming of population, or in the waste of pomp or arms, or in the lethargy of underemployment. Economic progress has taken place in history. It has brought with it improved food, houses, clothes, education, health, not merely for the few, but for the masses. It has resulted in a great increase in leisure, and a lifting of the burden of heavy labor. The hopes of mankind do not have to be confined to another world. A human society is conceivable in which the evils of poverty are completely eradicated, and in which there is sufficient production of this world's goods to enable everyone to live in health and decency. This is the proximate end toward which economic progress moves. It is not a sufficient end, as every religion testifies. But even if the chief end of man is to know God and enjoy Him forever, the enjoyment of goods is surely not inconsistent with the enjoyment of good, and God is better served by a race whose capacities are not stinted by inadequate food, clothing, shelter, education, or health.

II

Economic progress is not in itself an ultimate end of human activity, nor is it a universal criterion for passing judgment on societies. Nevertheless it is a significant partial end, and in making any assessment of the weight which should be given to it other possible ends or criteria of judgment should be considered. Some of these may be in competition with economic progress; others may be complementary to it.

OTHER ENDS OF ECONOMIC ACTIVITY

Economic progress consists in the increase in human power to satisfy human needs. Our evaluation of it therefore depends in considerable degree on our attitude toward power on the one hand, and toward wants on the other. It is by no means a foregone conclusion that an increase in power is desirable. Whether it is desirable or not depends largely on what people want to do with the power. It is probably better for a man who wants to drive down a crowded street at a hundred miles an hour not to have a high-powered car. The problem of the *nouveaux riches* is a familiar one —the people whose debased desires did them little harm as long as they did not have the power to satisfy them, but who rapidly went to the devil when they had the power to do so. There is some case for the suggestion that our whole society is a *nouveau riche* society, and that the result of our economic progress is to enable us to go to hell at a thousand miles an hour instead of at five.

It is perhaps this lack of confidence in the human will that has turned many prophetic figures to "holy poverty" as an ideal in itself. St. Francis immediately comes to mind, as in the delightful story about the novice who wanted a psalter (*The Mirror of Perfection,* Chapter 4). St. Francis reproved him, saying, "After you have a psalter, you will desire and wish to have a breviary. Then you will sit in your chair like a great prelate, and say to your brother, 'Bring me the breviary.'" The saints have usually seen clearly how the power to satisfy desire—of a worldly sort—itself increases the desire, and so power runs a continually losing race with desire, and satisfaction seems ever farther away. There is much wisdom in this prophetic criticism of the quest for riches, whether on the part of an individual or a society.

Nevertheless there is something also to be said on the other side. The idealization of poverty has never proved stable, especially in Christendom, and even the Franciscans were corrupted by the "world." In America the ideal of holy poverty has seemed unsuitable to a rapidly expanding economic universe, and only small groups, such as the Catholic Worker movement, have cherished it. It is hardly represented in Protestantism at all, least of all in the liberal Protestantism of the "social gospel." This is not merely the perversity of human nature and original sin. The power to satisfy existing wants can also be a power to criticize them. The new rich eventually become the old rich. The change of taste which power brings is not always in the wrong direction. And the power to fail is also sometimes the power to learn.

The way of renunciation is the attainment of satisfaction not by expanding our power but by curtailing our wants. It is perhaps more characteristic of the religions prevalent in the East than of Christianity. In a formal sense, if what we mean by economic progress is an increase in the ability to satisfy wants, the way of renunciation would seem to fall under the definition of economic progress just as the way of power. The West gets out its bulldozers and brings the mountain to Mahomet, the East takes things more quietly and Mahomet betakes him to the mountain; but the end result is the same—the mountain and Mahomet are brought together. Indeed, if the satisfaction of desires is really the end in view, the way of renunciation of desires is probably the answer.[4] In Western culture, however, there is little desire for "being" as opposed to "becoming," and the art of static contentment with little is not much regarded.

Another end which frequently rides counter to the objective of economic progress is that of *equality*. Economic progress has gener-

[4] "The Hindus thought this question of happiness through to the end long ago and reached the inevitable conclusion—Nirvana—just enough life to enjoy being dead" (F. H. Knight in *The Ethics of Competition*, New York, Harper & Brothers, 1935, p. 32).

ally arisen not from a concerted effort on the part of all to raise the general level, but by the efforts of individuals to "better their condition." An enforced equality is therefore highly inimical to economic progress—as the Russians, for instance, have discovered in spite of their strong theoretical prejudice in favor of equality. On the other hand, economic progress itself, by raising the general level, makes inequality less necessary. The relations between progress and equality are so important that we must examine them further.

The concept of economic justice—i.e., justice in distribution—has different connotations if we are considering a stationary society or one that is progressing in wealth. In a stationary society in which total capital and income are constant, economic competition reduces itself to what in the theory of games is called a "zero-sum game"—i.e., an affair in which what one gains is gained at the expense of others, the total of gains and losses being zero. In such a society one man's accumulation can be made only at the cost of another's decumulation, or if one man increases his income it can be only by decreasing others'. To an astonishing extent the exponents of the "social gospel" seem to believe that the actual economic system is in fact stationary. Thus Thornton Merriam writes in his famous discussion with Frank Knight: "Modern man wants to do the work of the world in ways that do not require that he put his neighbor out of business at the price of his own success. With all its gilded façade of freedom that is what the free market really means ethically."[5] The assumption here that nobody should ever be put out of business is staggering enough (presumably the railroads should have been taxed to the point where stagecoaches could compete with them), but it is quite evident that the idea that anyone could raise his own level of living without lowering anybody else's is foreign to Mr. Merriam's frame of reference.

In a progressive society, however, economic competition is not generally a zero-sum game but is a positive-sum game, in which the activity of the players results in an increase in the total to be divided, so that my increase is not taken from somebody else but is a

[5] *The Economic Order and Religion* (New York: Harper & Brothers, 1945, p. 271).

net addition to the total pot. The moment this is recognized, both competition and accumulation are seen in a different light, and much of the moral objection to them disappears. Perhaps one of the main contributions which the economist as a technician can make to the moral philosopher in this regard is to render explicit those conditions under which the action of an individual to increase his own net worth results in an addition to the total capital of society equal to, or even greater than, his own accumulation. In contrast are those conditions under which accumulation by the individual results in an increase in the total capital of society less than the increase in his own net worth, and in which therefore the accumulation of one individual is made, at least partly, at the expense of someone else.

One question which must be made explicit by the moral philosophers is the relative weight which they give to the evils of poverty and inequality. They frequently write as if these were the same evil, and as if the way to abolish poverty were to redistribute income more equally. Against this proposition the economist must raise a serious protest. In a poor society even if all incomes were made equal the poverty of the poor would be relieved hardly one whit. There is no avenue to the abolition of poverty save through the increase of productivity. Indeed, even inequality itself is the result to a large extent of the failure of certain groups or societies to raise their productivity as fast as others. America is rich and China poor not because of "exploitation"—not because the Chinese produce a lot and the Americans take it away from them! America is rich because her productivity has been increasing faster than that of the Chinese for the past two hundred years or more.

Even within the United States the great inequality in the distribution of income—the difference between the North and the South—is not due to exploitation; is not due to the North's taking away what the South produces. It is due to the low productivity of the South, which in turn is due to its low rate of economic progress. This is not to deny, of course, that exploitation exists. There is the matter of differential freight rates. There is the matter of immigration restrictions. There is the matter of race prejudice restricting the economic opportunities of Negroes. There is the matter of trade-union restrictions and protective tariffs and Agricultural Adjustment Acts. But all these things placed into the balance together do not add up to one tenth of the causes either of poverty itself or of the unequal distribution of income.

It is arguable, of course, that inequality of income is itself an evil so hideous that considerable sacrifice of other objectives may be justified to attain equality, and that it would be better to have an equalitarian society in which everyone was equally poor than an unequal society in which nobody was poor but some were rich. If such is indeed the objective, it must be stated clearly. Even if this objective is held, however, the difficulties of achieving equality must be taken into consideration. Methods of achieving equality which involve leveling up rather than leveling down, which involve raising the levels of the poorer without lowering the levels of the richer are much more likely to find social acceptance than methods of forcible redistribution. Certain methods of forcible redistribution—e.g., progressive taxation—are entirely feasible and desirable within limits.

Even these methods, however, will meet much less resistance in a society which is rapidly increasing its wealth than in a stationary society. Indeed, it is a defensible proposition that whether we look at the matter from the side of ultimate objective or of ways of achieving those objectives, only a rich society can afford to be equalitarian. If the level of productivity in a society is so low that almost all the resources of the society are needed to maintain its supply of bare necessities, the very existence of any kind of civilization depends on the development of wide inequalities. That is why ancient civilizations all rested on a basis of slavery—which is genuine exploitation—and why only modern civilizations have been able to dispense with it. In a poor society, unless the vast mass of men are ground down to a bare minimum of subsistence, there is no possibility of the development anywhere in the society of the arts of civilization; the very existence of "peaks" necessitates vast and dismal "troughs." The equal distribution of income, even if it were technically possible without lessening the total product of such a society, would result only in an infinitesimal improvement in the lot of the poor and in the complete disappearance of any outstanding human achievement in the physical world.

It is not to be inferred that achievement in the spiritual world would not be possible in such a society of equalitarian poverty. Indeed, much of the preaching of the Hebrew prophets, for instance, is directed at this point—to glorify the "righteousness" of the simple, equalitarian, pastoral society of the hill country as against both the wickedness and the splendor of the cities of the plains. Both the ineffectiveness of their literal recommendations and the effectiveness of their spiritual message, however, point in the same direction—toward the redemption of riches rather than their abolition.

It may well be that in the long view of history inequality must be viewed as a protracted process of transition from the primitive society of equal poverty to the ultimate goal of a society of equal riches. In the long climb from the slough of equal poverty to the plateau of equal riches, certain individuals and groups lead the way, leaving others behind, and inequality develops. But because we are all roped together in the nexus of social and economic relations, the climbers cannot help pulling others after them and the whole level rises. Those who insist that we must all rise together or not at all may be actually condemning us forever to the slough of poverty. And the view that nobody can rise without pushing somebody else down is true only in a stationary state, and is quite foreign to a state of progress. There may therefore be more than mere Scottish optimism in Adam Smith's dictum that "the progressive state is in reality the cheerful and the hearty state to all the different orders of society. The stationary is dull; the declining, melancholy" (*Wealth of Nations*, Book I, Chapter 8).

Equilibrium versus Progress

The neglect of economic progress on the part of the moral philosophers and social gospelers has implications that are even more fundamental than those raised above. The neglect of progress is part of a quite general neglect of *process*. The very expression "goals," so beloved of the moral philosopher, is a striking indication of the basically static nature of his thinking. The term implies that there is some "right" way of organizing the affairs of men and that anything is "wrong" which does not conform to the ideal system. Such an approach may be useful in arousing moral emotion, and as such may have a real function, but it is not useful in the attempt to analyze the real processes of society, nor in the search for the most powerful levers of social change.

The economist himself, likewise, must be accused of neglecting process in favor of static equilibrium. There seems to be more justification for the economist, in that at least his static-equilibrium theory throws some real light on the processes of society. The very success of economic statics, however, has led economists into deriving from their theory more implications than it can justify—the implication, for instance, that distribution according to the equilibrium of perfectly competitive markets represents "commutative justice" (everybody gets what he produces; see Knight and Merriam, *op. cit.*, p. 111), or the implication frequently made in economic theory that there is something sacred about the system of prices set up by perfect competition. The introduction of process analysis (dynamics) into economics creates havoc with many of the cherished allocational ideals of the economist, as Schumpeter (especially in his *Capitalism, Socialism, and Democracy*) showed with great vigor. The case against monopoly, for instance, is much weaker in a dynamic setting than it is in a static one.

In any attempt to sit in judgment on society, however, which is presumably the ultimate task of the economist acting as moral philosopher, society must be judged as *process*; not by how far it falls short of some "goal," but by how rapidly it is moving in "right directions." It is possible to judge directions without knowing where movement will ultimately lead. Indeed, we know nothing about the ultimate fate of the human race. History must be regarded as a process of ecological succession in the great "ecosystem"[6] of society. Men, methods, ideas, processes, organizations, institutions, constitute a highly complex system of interacting "populations," some species rising and some falling, some perhaps stationary for awhile, closely analogous to the dynamics of a pond, forest, or prairie. Man

[6] Biologists use the term "ecosystem" to describe the totality of living things, together with the relevant environment, that occupy a single habitat and form an equilibrium of interacting populations. "Ecological succession" is the process by which one ecosystem gives place to another, under the influence of the cumulative and irreversible processes of the ecosystems themselves; e.g., as a pond fills up, or soil accumulates.

is not a passive constituent of these systems, however, any more than he is passive in regard to nature. Once he is past the food-gathering stage, man intervenes actively in nature, producing field crops, raising domestic animals, and so on. Indeed, agriculture may almost be defined as the process of extreme distortion of the natural ecosystem in favor of man, making grain grow where once grew forests, and cattle flourish where there were once only wild animals.

The task of the "policymaker," whether he is the preacher making policy for the individual lives and conduct of his congregation, the teacher making policy for the thoughts and lives of his pupils, the bishop or the trade-union official or the executive making policy for his organization, or the statesman making policy for the state, is essentially the task of "social agriculture." It is to distort the "natural" system of society and the "natural" forces of ecological succession in society, also in favor of man. If there is to be a division of labor between the social scientist and the moral philosopher or the theologian, it is surely here. The business of the social scientist is to throw light on the *effects* of various policies on the significant *kinds and rates of change* in the society. It is the business of the philosopher and the theologian to throw light on what is in favor of man; what changes, therefore, should be speeded up, if possible, and what slowed down or reversed. These changes are not, of course, measured in homogeneous units. Any evaluation of them, therefore, involves "valuation" in almost exactly the same sense that the calculation of a price level or of real income involves valuation; i.e., it involves assigning a "weight" to the various changes —some of which will be complementary and some competitive one with another. In any such weighting I would urge that economic progress deserves to be weighted high, not only for its own sake, but because it is complementary to so many other desirable ends.

THE OPTIMUM RATE OF PROGRESS

What we are searching for here is some concept of an "optimum" rate of economic or of technical progress. It is impossible to define such a concept exactly. Nevertheless, it is possible to imagine a rate of progress so rapid that it destroys itself and the society in which it takes place. Very rapid growth may produce internal stresses and dislocations which the society cannot survive, just as the 2-4-D weed killer destroys plants by making them grow at a rate faster than they can "take," or the forcing of a child may produce revolt and personality disintegration. On the other hand, there is nothing to be said for stagnation at low levels of living.

The critical question is the evaluation which we place on the "social cost" of economic progress at various rates. If there were no social cost—i.e., if no other good ends had to be sacrificed in increasing the rate of economic progress—there seems to be no reason why indefinitely rapid rates should not be desirable. It is probable, however, that beyond a certain point the social costs of progress rise with increasing rates of progress.

The formal condition for the optimum rate is that at which the benefits of more rapid progress are just balanced by its cost—both capitalized in some way to the present. This is simply an application of the principle of marginal equality familiar to all economists. It is not, of course, sufficient to inform us as to the exact rate of progress we should strive for. Nevertheless some important conclusions can be derived from it—notably the conclusion that the lower the (marginal) cost of each rate of progress, the more rapid the optimum rate will be, assuming that these marginal costs rise with an increasing rate. Any change in society, therefore, which lowers the cost of progress is an almost unmixed blessing.

The human cost of progress depends mainly on the immobility of men. This immobility has two sources: the *unwillingness* to change which is part of the structure of character, and the *inability* to make changes which is imposed by law, custom, or physical circumstances. Both these sources of immobility are susceptible to attack: the one through change in the moral habits of individuals, the other through change in the institutions and equipment of society.

In this connection the economic significance of the Protestant Reformation needs to be thoroughly reassessed. The responsibility of the Reformation for the rise of capitalism has been fairly thoroughly explored, though not enough attention has been paid to eighteenth-century and later developments. Too much emphasis has been laid, however, on the exploitive aspects of capitalism, which are not so significant quantitatively as is its aspect as an extraordinary movement of economic progress.

The progress has taken place not merely in mechanical matters: the progress in techniques of organization, in skills of government and education, and in the art of human relations has almost been as phenomenal as the developments in the techniques of production and transportation. The Factory Acts and social legislation are as much a part of the miscalled Industrial Revolution as the spinning jenny and the railroad. The "technical revolution" through which we are still passing is a revolution in ways of doing almost everything.

A strong case can be made that Protestant and evangelical Christianity, by its stress on conversion, on individual enterprise in religion, and on the minor virtues of industriousness, punctuality, thrift, honesty, truthfulness, and so on, has played a key role in this whole revolution. By its stress on the conversion experience as a radical change in the character of the individual it gives a positive value to change as such which carries over into all spheres of life. By its emphasis on the individual's responsibility to make his own peace with God in an unmediated religious experience it gives a positive value to enterprise as such in all spheres of life. And by its emphasis on personal integrity it has made possible a vast extension of interpersonal relationships in the system of "finance"—a system which, while it may be deficient in charity, at least is based firmly on faith and hope!

Unfortunately Protestantism, and especially liberal Protestantism, has suffered a grave loss of nerve in the past few decades. It has become defensive, ashamed of its own tradition, and even completely unaware of any history or historic mission. Its own scholars and theologians are in considerable measure to blame for this state of affairs. They have accepted much too easily criticisms of capitalism (e.g., the Marxist criticism) which are not for the most part valid, and they have not been able to put their finger either on the significant positive contribution of Protestant capitalism or on its real failings.

More than any other single factor it has been the instability of output and employment in a highly progressive market economy that has undermined its intellectual and moral support. In part, though only in small part, this instability is part of the cost of progress and must be accepted as such. In large part, however, this instability is unnecessary and can be avoided if government is prepared to accept its proper responsibility as a "governor" or stabilizer. Were this difficulty to be cleared out of the way, Protestantism should once more be able to shoulder its prime historic mission as the promoter of enterprise in its best sense, the search for constantly better ways of doing everything. This does not commit it either to "public" or to "private" enterprise—indeed, this distinction is no matter of principle, and the choice among various forms of enterprise should be entirely pragmatic. But it does commit it to economic progress as the most fundamental task of any economic system.

III

Economic Values in Cultural Perspective

by Clarence H. Danhof
Former Professor of Public Affairs, Princeton University, now on leave

Human societies are complex, many-faceted organizations reflecting the multifarious interests of the individual which comprise them. Each society includes the same essential range of human activities and relationships.[1] But great differences exist in the relative importance attached to the different activities pursued, in the methods employed and the supporting institutional organization, and hence in the nature of the various components in societies. It is these differences which give character and individuality to human culture throughout history and over the globe.

Economic activity is a function conducted and organized in some form by the members of every society. Everywhere there exists a set of more or less complex relationships involving the production and distribution of goods available only in limited supply and then only as a result of that form of human effort called work. All men are consumers of scarce goods in some quantity, and all must of necessity secure in some way a supply to satisfy as much as they can of what are felt to be their needs.

Only in some of the most primitive of historic human societies have the difficulties of securing a supply of economic goods adequate for the elementary needs of survival been so great as to require virtually all of man's time and energies.[2] In most societies,

[1] For a summary review see George P. Murdock, "The Common Denominator of Cultures," in Ralph Linton (ed.), *The Science of Man in the World Crisis*, New York, Columbia University Press, 1945, pp. 123-142.

[2] Such people as the African bushmen, the Tierra del Fuegans, the Tasmanians, Haiute Indians, and Malayan Semangs are among the best examples.

84

under normal conditions, man has been able to satisfy his minimum physiological needs by the use of a fraction of the time and energy available to him. Within the possibilities of even simple technologies he has assured himself of survival with energies left over.

Though economic activity, organized in some form, is a function performed within every society, the importance attached to it varies greatly. While in some societies economic matters may be of such importance as to seem to dominate the thoughts and actions of all members, in others economic activities will be deemed of little importance and may be assigned to a subordinate group—perhaps women and slaves—while the dominant group devotes its time and energies to matters considered more vital.

This does not mean that in such societies economic goods were available in abundance. A high degree of interest in and attention to noneconomic affairs is not a function of the relative abundance of the supply of scarce goods or of a high level of consumption. It does mean that the members of such societies, or of groups within them, under the influence of the values of their culture, looked upon their own time and energies as possessing such values when applied in other directions that only limited attention could be given to the problem of increasing their economic well-being.[3] The elaborate artwork, the great variety of ceremonials and lavish festivals, the devotion to warfare and sports to be found in many societies not blessed with high degrees of certainty of food supplies,

[3] Carle C. Zimmerman suggests that "it seems evident that a large part of the total population of the globe is interested principally in securing most of its standard of living, other than bare necessities, through intangible satisfactions of a non-economic nature." "Ernst Engel's Law of Expenditures for Food," *Quarterly Journal of Economics* 47 (Nov. 1932), p. 100. And Prof. M. K. Bennett, after summarizing the level of living of the various peoples of the world, observes: "A low consumption level need not imply a low degree of satisfaction of felt wants, or high level of discontent. Perhaps an understanding of the relationship of consumption level to consumption standard, still better of level of living to standard of living, in the various nations of the world would prove more fruitful in study of political and economic change than appraisal of disparities in consumption levels. Certainly the argument that low consumption level leads to discontent to revolution to aggressive war carries little conviction in spite of the fragment of truth in it." "International Disparities in Consumption Levels," *American Economic Review* XLI (Sept. 1951), p. 649.

comfortable shelters, and other current measures of a high level of living, are illustrative.[4] The fact that in twentieth-century America such noneconomic activities are classified as "leisure" pursuits reflects a basic characteristic of the prevailing value system.

DIFFERING GOALS OF ECONOMIC ACTIVITY

Economic activity is directed to the satisfaction of men's needs for those goods and services which are obtainable only by the application of labor to the conversion of scarce resources into forms which satisfy certain needs. There is, however, need of a more adequate answer to the question, What are the goals of men as they engage in economic activities? than the assertion that the purpose is the satisfaction of wants, needs, and desires for goods. There remain such questions as, What are desires? and, How do such desires come into existence? Phrased otherwise, one may ask, What are the sources of the values which govern those activities relating to the acquisition, possession, and use of economic goods?

The assumption of economists that the wants of men for scarce goods and services are dynamic and insatiable is useful for certain special purposes in analyzing the economic life of contemporary Western civilization. It is, however, descriptive only of a given social milieu; it does not apply to all historical societies,[5] nor is it necessarily a description of the inherent nature of man, if there be such. Such an assumption is applicable only to societies where it is made true by general acceptance and where this way of life is enforced upon individuals by social pressures.

All human activity is goal-directed, though the ultimate goal may be hidden, even to the participant, by immediate objectives. In the economic area, men do not accumulate, without some purpose,

[4] For general descriptions a good source is George P. Murdock, *Our Primitive Contemporaries*, New York, Macmillan Co., 1938.

[5] As, for example, the many "backward" countries whose people resist being brought into the market economy of Western industrialism. *Cf.* E. E. Hoyt, "Want Development in Undeveloped Areas," *Journal of Political Economy*, LIX (June 1951), pp. 194-202; W. E. Moore, "Theoretical Aspects of Industrialization," *Social Research*, XV (Sept. 1948), pp. 277-303; Ruth Benedict, *Patterns of Culture*, Boston, Houghton Mifflin Co., 1928.

large quantities of goods over and above their own visible ability to consume. If the purpose is not ultimate consumption it is then some other: perhaps as demonstrating skill and achievement; perhaps the enjoyment of power that inheres in possession; perhaps to give away, thereby enjoying approval of another sort; or securing the objective of self-enhancement by some other socially approved method.[6] In our society the individual whose accumulation of quantities of economic goods cannot be explained in terms of a socially recognized objective will be considered as a hoarder or a miser; he who acquires less than he might is an ascetic; both are thought of as irrational and eccentric. The continuation of gainful economic activity far beyond the point at which the producer can himself consume has as its objective the accomplishment of something which the individual believes will enhance his social position.

Little familiarity with the history of human societies is required to recognize that economic needs and desires have themselves a geography and a history. Economic needs and desires are from time to time and in various places redefined. Such redefinition occurs, within the limitations of the technology and changes occurring in it; of changes in the knowledge and accessibility of resources; in the institutions which comprise the economic system; and in value judgments as to what is right and proper both in the production and in the consumption of economic goods. It is, of course, true that there exists for all human beings a minimal level of needs. But what is conceived of as a minimal level varies greatly between societies not only historically but also contemporaneously,[7] nor is the concept one that is easily subjected to objective scientific analysis.[8]

At any given time such minimums may fall well below the capacity of the productive order to provide—capacity conceived of as rationalized according to some standard of efficiency. The consumption pattern prevailing may be substantially below the resource potential. For in most historical societies a choice has been

[6] Francis L. K. Hsu, "Incentives to Work in Primitive Communities," *American Sociological Review*, VIII (Dec. 1943), p. 641.

[7] C. A. Bouglé, *The Evolution of Values*, New York, H. Holt & Co., 1926, particularly pp. 102 ff.

[8] M. K. Bennett, *op. cit.*, p. 637.

possible. Men might devote more of their time and energies to activities other than the economic, such as artistic, religious, warfare, and the vast variety we may group as social, or they might continue to apply themselves to the production of more goods and an increase in the supply available for consumption. Most commonly men have chosen some compromise between these two alternatives. The important consideration is that when goods become available in a volume above the biologically required minimum, numerous questions as to values appear. Social attitudes expressive of values then play a central role in the determination of the pattern which is actually operative. Neither rationalization of activities nor efficiency in production need be important among such values.

The scarcity of both the time and energy available to the human individual requires that he select from numerous alternatives those courses of action to which he will devote his thoughts and energies. An individual who is a member of a society possessing only a simple technology and a primitive economic organization must necessarily, it would seem, give a large proportion of his time and energy to the tasks of acquiring control over the necessities of life—a relatively small group of commodities. But the time so devoted is not necessarily a function of the simplicity of the economy. Over history, as societies have become increasingly productive through the increase of specialization and exchange, as the knowledge incorporated in the technology has expanded, the individual has become theoretically more free to exercise his powers of choice and to select from among alternatives those to which he wishes to devote his time and energy.

THE DESIRE FOR ACCEPTANCE

This freedom to choose is, however, more nominal than real. As a member of a family, of various subgroups, and of his larger society, the individual is from birth subjected to a wide variety of suggestions, pressures, and inducements which guide his actions and serve to define narrowly the area within which an effective exercise of freedom of choice remains possible. The values by which men live are not worked out by the individual in isolation or developed as abstractions. Each human being, in the course of his development from infancy onward, slowly works out for himself, under the influence of his environment, a set of assumed objectives or guides as to what is real and important to him. These determine his behavior, his choice of activities, the areas of his interests and thoughts.[9] Such values or standards give focus to human activities; it is through them that we develop our relationships with other humans—in seeking enhancement of our own personalities on the one hand and defending ourselves from doubts and uncertainties on the other. For each individual these guides of conduct constitute the method by which he can express himself as a member of his social group; these standards hence are in a general sense necessarily those of the group.

The place which any given activity holds in the sum total of activities which are engaged in by the individual member of any society is determined by his subjective interpretation of the values widely accepted by the society. Men prefer to do those things which stand high in the scale of values held by the group, and avoid applying time and energy to those things held in low esteem. This they do because, in the process of selecting the objectives to which they will devote their time and effort, they give great weight to the attainment of a desirable position in the eyes of their fellows. For, next to prizing life itself, the human individual is vitally concerned with the opinions held of him by his peers.[10] Belonging to a social group is a human necessity. Such belonging is achieved through acceptance obtainable through conformity and participation.

THE PURSUIT OF STATUS

The consciousness of the attitudes of the group's members and the desire for their esteem produce strong desires to avoid actions that will threaten full membership and stimulate actions that will

[9] For an analysis of this process in the modern United States, see Allison Davis, "American Status Systems, and the Socialization of the Child," *American Sociological Review*, VI (June 1941), pp. 345-354.

[10] "A man's social Self is the recognition which he gets from his mates. We are not only gregarious animals liking to be in the sight of our fellows, but we have an innate propensity to get ourselves noticed, noticed favorably by our kind." William James, *The Principles of Psychology*, New York, H. Holt & Co., 1890, Vol. I, pp. 293 ff.

enhance the feeling of belonging. This means not absolute conformity but adherence to certain standards. To many, and perhaps to most individuals, conformity alone is unsatisfactory, since merely to conform is to be a nonentity (except as the prestige of the group reflects upon himself in contacts with other groups). Thus the desire to be well thought of as a member of a group guides the individual into such courses of action (some method of excelling within the limits of group-approved activity) as will command positive esteem. These are guides which operate in all aspects of human living.

The members of any given society are then motivated in their actions by their own interpretation of the values recognized by the society of which they are members. These are values which both stimulate and restrain; they encompass every phase and aspect of life. To achieve a favorable opinion in the minds of others, to be highly or at least well thought of, men seek to differentiate themselves by superior performance in activities which are acknowledged as yielding such desired opinions. Skill in the performance of some act demonstrates to the viewer the relative prowess of the doer, and is undertaken in part, at least, in the hope of commanding respect. Almost any area of human activity may yield to the doer prestige within a special group. To command widespread respect it is essential that superiority in performance be easily recognizable as well as that the activity be considered as of some importance by at least a significant part of the population. Acts in which most or almost all individuals engage and in which little differentiation in the quality of performance is recognizable command little respect and are consequently not significant sources of enhancement of group memberships.

The Variety of Prestige Systems

The conditions governing admittance to a group and the routes to the attainment of superiority differ widely as between societies. Each social system possesses its own pattern of values, or rather complexes of value relationships, which designate and classify the desirable avenues of activity. The terms of entry into the competition for reputation, the terms of continuing membership, the rules of rivalry, and the nature of the rewards likewise differ. Taken together these constitute the society's prestige system: the objectives, the ways, and the means by which the individual can secure for himself the favorable appearance of himself in the eyes of others.[11]

In simple societies in which the relationship between individuals is characteristically face to face, superior performance will be directly witnessed and will be measured in specifically appropriate terms. In societies of large populations, substantial geographic spacing, intricate functions, and individual relationships which are predominantly distant (secondary rather than primary), prestige systems of a significantly different character will develop.[12] The evaluation of claims to achievement by means of the measurements applied in a face-to-face group becomes inadequate when the group is substantially enlarged. The large, complex society requires a system of prestige standards which can measure differences in achievement with some uniformity, measurements which can be clearly understood by the entire population so that all can appreciate the claims of persons not personally known to them. The qualitative measures used under the simpler conditions continue to be employed by small, special-interest groups. For the society as a whole, the transfer of valuation of small groups to those of larger size requires that increasing complexity of relationships and activities must be offset by simplification and abstraction of values and qualification of measurements. Symbolism, always of importance, becomes increasingly so.

Generally, in any given society, a relatively few areas of activity are recognized by all as the primary sources of prestige. The occupations, the standards and symbols of performance, and the achievements of prominent individuals will be known to all. In addition there will exist many other areas of activity which will be of secondary importance, yielding limited prestige. Some of these will

[11] L. Leopold, *Prestige*, London, Unwin, 1913; G. Landtman, *Origin of the Inequality of Social Classes*, Chicago, University of Chicago Press, 1938.
[12] On this, see Karl Mannheim, *Diagnosis of Our Time*, New York, Oxford University Press, 1943, p. 21.

receive qualified recognition by the social group as a whole; other areas of performance will be understood, recognized, and valued only by segments of the society.

Economic objectives and motivations are only one, though a very important group, among the large number of value areas which go to compose such a prestige system. It is, moreover, important to note that in many and perhaps in most historical societies economic activity plays only a minor role in yielding prestige. Some types of economic activity have historically been associated with distinctly inferior status; the routes to high status have frequently been through such noneconomic activities as the military, religious, political, and, more rarely, literary or artistic fields.

Aside from the prestige which accrues from superiority in actual performance in some field of recognized activity, there exist a number of other important methods through which an individual can less directly but quite as assuredly enhance his social standing. In most societies the acquisition of property or power, or some combination of the two (since property implies power while power implies a superior opportunity to secure property), yields status. These may be obtained by adroitness in activities recognized as acceptable, but they are legitimately obtainable also through transfer from another, as by inheritance, marriage, or political means. Similarly status may be obtained by securing membership in a group or an institution which commands esteem.[13] This is to say that status may be determined vicariously, by nomination and election, by appointment, inheritance, marriage, and similar arrangements which involve the transfer of prestige by another individual or by a group which possesses such recognized and enforceable powers of selection.

The distinction between prestige competitively achieved and that vicariously received is a particularly useful one, even though it cannot be clearly defined. Societies differ fundamentally in the degree to which they permit members to compete for status and also in the degree to which status can be transmitted by the action

[13] For an analysis of prestige as it related to the British government and nation, see Harold Nicolson, *The Meaning of Prestige*, Cambridge (England), The University Press, 1937.

of a single or a few individuals from one person to another. In some societies birth and subsequent inheritance is the major form by which status passes between individuals; in others, inheritance of property is accepted but limited and hereditary rank is not recognized, the inheritance of property or reputations serving the more limited function of giving the inheritor a somewhat superior opportunity to achieve a desirable status.

As the values to which status is attached differ widely, so also are there wide differences between societies in the manner and the degree to which status may be pursued and achieved. At the one extreme a society may possess a rigid structure which classifies all individuals at birth and denies them mobility within the structure by prohibiting or at least seriously inhibiting them from seeking to attain a different status through social, political, or economic channels. Even in such a society some flexibility in certain areas, particularly in religious, literary, or artistic activities, while perhaps not encouraged is nevertheless accepted. The range of such mobility is, however, not great and is primarily horizontal—within the class. At the other extreme a society may refuse to recognize distinctions of a hereditary character and may permit and encourage everyone to compete to attain prestige through superior performance in a field chosen from a number of acceptable alternatives. Where there are no formal restrictions upon horizontal mobility, however, one area of activity will usually be recognized as producing prestige superior to that attainable in any other area, even though it may be understood that the various possible areas of activity are not truly competitive or comparable.

To illustrate the preceding discussion, it is useful to analyze the character of a few historic status systems. We may begin by distinguishing between those societies in which individual status is rigidly identified with that of the group, and the pursuit of individual enhancement is effectively prohibited, and those in which the individual is more or less free, possessing the opportunity to move between groups of different prestige levels in finding his place in society.

The identification of the status of the individual with that of the group of which he is a member is universal among historical cultures of any significant degree of complexity. Variations, however, are great. The extreme form of emphasis upon the group submerges the individual within it and denies him status except in terms of the group of which he is a member. It is the most rigidly stratified form of society and is illustrated in its highest development by the caste system as it has operated among the Hindus.

THE RIGID CASTE SYSTEM

The Indian caste system is a hierarchical layering of the population, each of the numerous layers identified with a specific occupation.[14] Membership is hereditary, and is obtained only by birth. Marriage takes place only between members of each caste. There is thus neither escape from one group nor the possibility of entrance into another; the concept of social mobility simply does not apply to the individual and an elaborate structure of controls serves to prevent it. Since the individual is inescapably tied to his caste, any changes in his position vis-à-vis the larger society can come about only through a change in the status of his caste. Thus the castes engage in a variety of maneuvers both of spontaneous and of rationalized organized forms, seeking to enhance their position and to defend their own status by preventing any encroachment on their prerogatives.[15] Differentiations of substantial magnitude achieved within a caste may take the form of the development and recognition of subcastes.

This system of individual relations enforced by custom and law is given the powerful support of religion since the caste theory is an integral part of the Hindu doctrine of reincarnation. It is in the religious area that a concession is made to the individual: the promise that performance within the laws of the caste system will determine the caste level of the individual upon later reincarnation.

[14] The 1901 Census identified 2,378 castes and tribes, Census of India, 1901, No. 1, pp. 537, 557; J. N. Bhattacharya, Hindu Castes and Sects, Calcutta, Thacker, Spink & Co., 1896; Mason Olcott, "The Caste System of India," American Sociological Review IX (Dec. 1944), pp. 648-657.

[15] Mohandas Gandhi, Young India 1919-22, New York, Viking Press, 1924, p. 482; Olcott, op. cit., pp. 655-657.

The sharp lines drawn between the castes as to occupation and marriage extend actually to every phase of life.[16] Caste determines through taboos the food consumed and its method of preparation and similarly controls every aspect of consumption. Caste determines rigidly the deference to be expected from lower groups; the debasement practices to be offered to higher groups; the services to be received as well as the obligations which must be carried out.

Economic activity occupies a neutral role in individual differentiation since neither by productive nor by consuming activities can the individual hope to secure a change in his status. The level and character of consumption is predetermined by the caste structure and is without provision for alteration; production is likewise controlled within the caste while no significant incentives exist to stimulate changes. Insofar as changes do occur, the higher castes will seek to absorb them and to resist participation by the lower castes. The whole system operates to reduce the incentives to the individual, particularly as they might operate through the economic structure.

FEUDALISM IN EUROPE

In the Western world there have existed in the past two millennia a wide variety of systems of human relationships. The differences that now exist between such countries as the United States, Great Britain, France, and Germany represent in part at least different degrees of development from the same common basis and along the same historical pattern, some current systems retaining much greater elements of the past than do others. Our immediate purposes will be served by a brief review of the relations of the economic and status systems in the societies which are immediately antecedent to our own. We may begin with the reorganization of society which was forced upon Western European peoples as they lost the peace and security enforced by imperial Rome.

As the Roman imperial power faded under the impact of the

[16] See W. H. Wiser, *The Hindu Jajmani System*, Lucknow Publishing House, Lucknow U. P., 1936; J. H. Hutton, *Caste in India*, New York, 1944.

Barbarian invasions, the resultant social disorder extended to the breakdown of the elemental function of society in providing for the protection of persons and property. Such protection, no longer available by right of citizenship, now became something to be achieved at much lower levels of organization and by whatever arrangements might be possible in any given situation.[17] The system which developed to supply the need for protective services was that of feudalism,[18] the patron-client arrangement whereby protection was provided through the personal and eventually the hereditary relationship of protector and protected. The process of disintegration did not exempt economic activity. Commerce and industry declined sharply with the replacement of the imperial by local authority. The largely self-sufficient agricultural unit with its small group of artisans—seigniory, manor, or villa—became the characteristic form of economic organization.[19]

Out of the collapse of the institutional fabric of Roman culture, the Christian Church emerged virtually alone as a universal institution, attaining institutional prestige of an unsurpassed character with the conversion of Constantine.[20] The Church utilized its religious influence as well as its institutional prestige to gather to itself such power that lack of membership was tantamount to being a social outcast.

The society that emerged was one of lords and vassals divided into three major groups: the aristocracy of temporal lords; the clerical lords, composed of Church officials; and the peasantry, including artisans and comprising the great mass of the population. A fourth group, not easily identifiable nor closely integrated into the

[17] A. Dopsch, *The Economic and Social Foundations of European Civilization*, New York, Harcourt, Brace, & Co., 1937.

[18] Excellent general sources are James W. Thompson, *An Economic and Social History of the Middle Ages*, 300-1300, New York, The Century Co., 1928; and Henry Pirenne, *Economic and Social History of Medieval Europe*, New York, Harcourt, Brace, & Co., 1937.

[19] P. Vinogradoff, *The Growth of the Manor*, London, G. Allen & Unwin, Ltd., 1911; *Cambridge Economic History of Europe*, I, London, 1941, Chaps. 1-6.

[20] Shirley Case, *The Social Triumph of the Ancient Church*, New York, Harper & Brothers, 1933, Chap. 3.

structure of society, included the residents of free towns, merchants, small groups of others including such non-Catholics as Jews, and eventually the artisans.

These divisions of the population were not classes as the term is loosely employed in contemporary usage; they are more properly to be conceived of as estates.[21] Each division possessed its own hierarchy of grades, which were hereditary in the case of aristocracy and peasantry, bureaucratic in the case of the clergy. The estates differed also in their legal positions since each subject to its own set of laws.

Status was enforced by the control exercised by the aristocracy over the law and the courts, by their military strength and through their rights, though qualified by responsibilities as expressed in custom and law, over the major productive resource, the land. Though the teachings of the Church served to moderate the relations of the various groups, it supplied in those teachings powerful religious and moral justifications for the existing status system, upholding the doctrine of a proper station in life for every individual. In preaching an other-worldliness, and in demonstrating in some of the monastic orders an ascetic way of life, it may have served to sterilize the earthly aspirations of many individuals by focusing their attention upon the rewards to be obtained in the life hereafter. The Church supplied, also, an important element of stability in the institution of a celibate clergy which required a constant recruitment of priests and monks, this constituting a most important channel through which ambitious individuals might lift themselves out of the lower estates.

Within the estates there existed wide differences in rank: gradations from slave to freeman, *vilain serf* to *vilain libre*; from knight to king; from novice priest or monk to abbot, bishop, cardinal, and pope. The mobility between ranks, however, was low; greatest, for obvious reasons, in the Church.

Though the aristocracy and the higher clergy vied for power and property, they were not truly in competition for prestige except as

[21] Max Weber, *Wirtschaft und Gesellschaft*, Tubingen, J. C. B. Mohr (P. Siebeck), 1925, pp. 677-680, 631-641; Oliver C. Cox, *Caste, Class, and Race*, New York, Doubleday & Co., 1948, pp. 123 ff.

the clergy stepped out of its religious role. With respect to both, the peasant gave recognition of superior status through a variety of debasement practices; homage was an essential symbol of the lord-vassal relationship. Sumptuary customs and laws served to preserve the symbols of superior status from degradation by common usage.

The competition between individuals was restricted then to those within the estates and largely to those within each rank.[22] Members of an aristocratic rank, such as the knights, might freely vie among themselves in sports or military prowess, intrigue, or marriage. Peasants might compete, though, existing closer to the level of bare subsistence as it was currently defined, their competition took the more bitter form of great energy in production and parsimony in consumption, the savings used to purchase greater freedom. The competition within the clergy was undoubtedly of the more subtle form to be found in a bureaucratic organization, but it cannot have been the less real. That craftsmen competed with one another is well attested by the abundance of guild regulations as to quantity of goods, days and hours of work, and the terms of employment of apprentices and journeymen.[23]

The relationship of this status system to the economic order was one of passivity. In the case of both the aristocracy and the Church, prestige rested upon power. Power was determined by the number of men under arms, that number being determined by the volume of the product of the land which could be claimed from the peasant by his lord. Thus the number of agricultural villages over which lordship could be claimed was a key to power. In the case of the peasantry, social standing was determined by the acreage which an individual had the right to cultivate and the share of the product which it was his right to retain for his own use. For the peasant, then, an increase in his land, in the means to work it, and in his rights to the product were the fundamental methods of improving himself.

The aristocracy received revenues from its lands in kind or in

[22] Max Handman, "War, Economic Motives, and Economic Symbols," *American Journal of Sociology*, XLIV (Mar. 1939), p. 631.

[23] P. Boissonade, *Life and Work in Medieval Europe*, New York, A. A. Knopf, 1927.

services in return for military protection, and had of necessity to expend them in large part for such purposes. Resources judged to be in excess of needs for maintaining armed strength were characteristically considered as available for securing more land, not, however, by purchase, but by warfare or marriage. It is true, of course, that the aristocracy was under the necessity of maintaining a high level of consumption as a symbol of its position. Such consumption was more likely to take the form of extensive retinues than the form of goods. Nevertheless, to the degree to which merchants could make them available, the aristocracy was interested in exotic goods and readily broadened its standard of living to include them. Such goods were purchased from revenues obtained from feudal dues. The desire for them did not at first stimulate to any great degree an interest in expanding the production of goods for sale.

The system so cursorily described, modified in various ways, functioned to control men's actions and guide men's aspirations for many centuries over most of the European continent. It proved sufficiently effective and resilient to survive over a long period of time. Yet, in the face of a number of far-reaching changes which touched many aspects of civilization, the feudal pattern of human relationships proved inadequate. It was undermined, becoming in one geographic area after another increasingly merely a façade behind which developed a more vigorous pattern of motivations, methods, and objectives.

Forces Undermining Feudalism

The *raison d'être* of the feudal system was security for the individual. It is almost, though not quite, literally true to say that, to the extent to which that security was achieved, the system encouraged the growth of forces which were foreign to its structure, and which forced it either to take repressive action or to accept modifications. The repressive tools available to European feudalism were, however, of limited strength. Feudalism differed basically from the Hindu caste system not only in lacking powerful religious sanctions but also in the fact that individuals might, when opportunities arose, seek to change the terms of this feudal security, usually for greater individual freedom. As early as the eighth or ninth century, men were securing freedom or partial freedom from feudal dues. As towns developed, their populations came to comprise groups of free or freer individuals surrounded by, but not part of, feudalism. Increasing freedom might be expressed by the less-restrained pursuit of enhancement within the feudal structure, but as time went on aspirations were increasingly directed to objectives outside of it.

Though the feudal system was one of distinct estates, it was also a system of relationships between individual members of each of the estates. Even the least-free peasant retained his individuality; he was under no compulsion from his own group to refrain from improving his situation if he could do so. There did not exist within the feudal system either political, religious, or social sanctions adequate to prohibit such efforts.

The feudal world, which was born out of the great disturbances of the barbarian migrations and which absorbed successive waves of alien conquerors, faced later a different series of events which introduced elements of instability of a different kind.

The Crusades, feudal in objective and organization, nevertheless had the effect of broadening the perspective of men, expanding their wants, and slightly increasing commerce. The revival of learning, begun within the feudal organizational pattern of patron and client, further expanded man's knowledge of earlier cultures and of his own world, emphasized a pattern of consumption inconsistent with feudalism's economic base, and suggested areas of work and aspiration—e.g., the learned professions—which made men restless in the feudal mold. The growth of the national states served to undermine the feudal aristocracy by depriving it of its basic functions, making it directly subservient to central authority, and drawing it into the luxurious consumption patterns of royal courts. At the same time, central governments required financial and administrative techniques foreign to and inconsistent with the feudal pattern. The great explorations drew attention to opportunities which the feudal world tried but failed to maintain within its orbit. The religious revolutions similarly emphasized the inadequacy of the feudal value system, released men from the confines of orthodox doctrines, and gave sanctions to new avenues of individual expression and aspirations.

None of these events stood alone. Each developed in partial response to the others. Any one of them alone might well have been absorbed by the feudal structure. Taken together they provided the objectives, the ways and means toward and by which a new system of human relationships was to develop.

ECONOMIC ACTIVITY EXPANDS OUTSIDE

A most important factor remains to be mentioned—the expansion of economic activity, the growth of commerce and industry, the spread of exchange involving the use of money and an accompanying pecuniary-mindedness. Such changes were not, of course, elements independent of those mentioned above but interrelated with them in a most complex stimulus-response relationship. The development of money exchange and the accompanying practice of evaluating an increasing number of goods and services in money terms were, however, of peculiar and critical importance in the appearance and rapid acceptance of a new and different status system. For at the core of the evolution of the medieval into the modern society and reflecting all the other factors was the rivalry of two systems of evaluating and exchanging property and services and hence of measuring power and prestige—in real terms (in kind), and in the symbolisms of money.

Though the feudal economy was largely one of small, semiself-sufficient units, important areas of specialized production persisted and the local unit exchanged through traders some of its products (so-called surpluses) for supplies of essential commodities as well as luxury items. Trade increased in volume under conditions of peace and security; shrank when lawlessness increased. But after the Crusades the secular trend was distinctly upward. Towns serving as centers of trade increased in number and population, while some became centers of production as well.[24] Though industrial pursuits remained rigidly controlled, usually by the organized producers themselves, the trader, especially the itinerant merchant, led a relatively free, competitive life in which the objective was economic enhancement obtained through profits expressed in mon-

[24] Henri Pirenne, *Medieval Cities*, Princeton, Princeton University Press, 1925.

etary terms. It was the merchant who explored and uncovered areas of relative advantage in production and who applied, when opportunity arose, new techniques—in organization and in method —of production. Insignificant, perhaps, in volume, such exploratory work was to prove of crucial importance in supplying opportunities when conditions were propitious.

The merchants were consistently a group operating outside the ranks of the feudal system. Wholly approved by neither lay nor Church aristocracy, they were essential to both and found encouragement not only in their patronage but in the development of merchant law favorable to their activities, and in the further development of free cities and of trading privileges. As commerce expanded, the aristocracy readily accepted intraclass rivalry in terms of the possession and consumption of exotic goods, obtainable by travel or as gifts, but far more readily by purchase from traveling merchants and at the fairs. Such patronage of the merchants required the possession of money funds. To secure funds, the aristocracy came to look increasingly favorably upon commuting the feudal services due them into money and upon increases in the supply of goods which merchants were willing to accept in exchange for their stocks.

State and Church Contribute to Money-Mindedness

The development of the national state was facilitated by pecuniary-mindedness—essential to increasing concentration of power and to mobility in its use. The weakening of the position of lesser lords was most readily accomplished by placing them on the king's payroll and drawing them to the king's court where they could be more readily controlled and utilized. The development of kingship over a national state required further that the king develop military forces owing allegiance directly to him rather than indirectly through a lower lord. This was most readily accomplished by the development of the paid soldier and the standing army. In addition the national state involved administrative occupations which required the development of a bureaucracy, paid perhaps more often in privileges than by salary but, in either case, in money. These and other activities of the state required funds, which were raised by a variety of tax devices, some of which long continued to be paid in kind or services but which were increasingly commuted into money payments. The handling of funds necessitated that banking institutions be employed to the profit of merchant-bankers, particularly the Jews, who were unhandicapped by the Church's restrictions.[25]

These developments brought the aristocracy of the national state into conflict with the lesser nobility, conflicts won by the states, and, sooner or later, to the great advantage of the groups most deeply involved in the expansion of pecuniary-consciousness, the urban populations whose interests centered about commerce. The peasant also gained, though more slowly, since the state tended to give him its support in his battle with the lords to obtain freedom from feudal services and obligations. All these gains were made easier by the expansion of rivalry within the aristocracy in terms of economic goods. For the lack of commercial-mindedness of the nobility threw it into bankruptcy, and while merchants were not infrequently ruined in that process the net result was that noble estates and titles were increasingly available for purchase. Noble titles thus became an article of commerce at the same time when the functions which the titles represented were disappearing under the impact of the growth of the state.

The Church, the great central institution of feudalism, was also in the forefront in developing pecuniary-mindedness. For the power of the papacy was in no insignificant way dependent upon its ability to gather together substantial resources which involved transporting large sums of money to Rome. In the process the Church developed a pecuniary-minded bureaucracy and also encouraged the development of the important institutions engaged in transferring funds by banking methods. Services of this nature rendered to the papacy and to the national and imperial governments were instrumental in building some of the earliest large money fortunes.[26]

[25] Werner Sombart, *The Jews and Modern Capitalism*, London, T. F. Unwin, 1913.

[26] Such as the Fuggers and Welsers. Richard Ehrenberg, *Capital and Finance in the Age of the Renaissance*, London, J. Cape, 1928.

At the same time, the Church was feeling the effects of the intellectual Renaissance. The revolts of Huss and Luther were symbolic of inadequacies in the feudal value system and of Church doctrines and practices. It is of interest to recall that Luther's revolt in its initial phase was a critical attack upon the pecuniary-mindedness of the papacy. It was, however, the doctrines of John Calvin which broke completely with medieval Catholicism and the feudal value system. It was Calvinism which gave to pecuniary-profit-mindedness and hence to economic activity a religious justification of profound significance.[27]

ECONOMIC CHANGES QUICKEN

Important as these developments were in their own right, their greatest significance in the history of prestige values lay in the fact that they removed barriers and stimulated changes elsewhere. Freed from the inhibitions of medievalism, some individuals with an active and effective curiosity about the nature of physical things contributed in a variety of ways methods by which man could increase his understanding, control, and manipulation of his environment, specifically in the technology of economic production. Beginning slowly and spasmodically in the medieval period, with many false starts, customary methods by which production was carried on were replaced at an accelerating pace with far more rewarding techniques in agriculture, industry, and transportation.

In agriculture, improved techniques developed slowly, partially as a rediscovery of classical knowledge, thereafter as a result of experimentation. The newer techniques, and the institutional reorganization of agriculture following upon the decline of feudalism, resulted in an expansion in productivity sufficiently great to support large increases in the urban, industrial population. To assure an increase in the supply of fabricated goods of desired char-

[27] An extensive literature on this subject has developed around Max Weber's *The Protestant Ethic and the Spirit of Capitalism*, New York, Charles Scribner's Sons, 1930. See Ephraim Fischoff, "The Protestant Ethic and the Spirit of Capitalism, the History of a Controversy," *Social Research*, XI (Feb. 1944), pp. 53-77.

acteristics, the merchant developed the putting-out or domestic system of production; and these and further changes in organization and techniques made it possible to visualize and eventually to employ machinery and artificial power, organized as the factory and staffed by wage earners.

The needs of both the merchant and the government combined to stimulate the building of roads and encouraged the application of steam power to both water and overland transportation. These developments served to minimize the transportation costs which had restricted markets and hence the degree of specialization in production which was economically justifiable. Transportation improvements served to make it possible to physically integrate large areas and populations into single social, political, and economic units. Society came to be supplied by large, specialized production units intimately related to each other, to the sources of materials, and to consumers through the pecuniary exchange relationships of the market.

The merchant was the central, dynamic figure in these changes. It was he who effectively introduced and eventually brought to dominance the industrial method of producing goods; who reorganized human relationships to the requirements of the factory and the market; who visualized the opportunities that lay in his form of control over economic resources; and who, in developing market outlets, hastened the conversion of all economic relationships to a pecuniary standard. He himself specialized. From the merchant emerge the functions of banker; industrialist; wholesale, retail, and foreign trader; or, collectively, the businessman.[28]

The businessman, whose position under feudalism had been one of sufferance, now becomes of such importance to the state that an identification of his interests with those of the state becomes more and more characteristic. This is true because the state requires economic power to overcome the remnants of feudal power as well as

[28] N. S. B. Gras, *Business and Capitalism*, New York, F. S. Crofts & Co., 1939; Miriam Beard, *History of the Businessman*, New York, Macmillan Co., 1938; Werner Sombart, *The Quintessence of Capitalism*, New York, 1915; Karl F. Helleiner, "Moral Conditions of Economic Growth," *Journal of Economic History*, XI (Spring 1951), pp. 97-116.

to carry out its functions; at the same time, the businessman needs the protection and the cooperation of the state. Economic power leads to political influence and power. Such influence extends to other areas as well because the businessman has become the center of the society and his power is of direct importance to every phase of life.

The activities of the businessman center in pecuniary transactions, involving the purchase and sale of goods and the hiring of workers. His immediate objective is that of wealth accumulation primarily, and only secondarily that of wealth consumption. Under his leadership important changes occurred in the function of the consumption of goods as a symbolic differentiator of status. New production methods had enlarged the supply of goods formerly scarce; moreover, businessmen aligned themselves on the side of equalitarianism in consumption. The newer mercantile leaders had achieved their position partly because of voluntary restrictions on their consumption in their need to accumulate capital. In the process of acquiring preferential status they typically did not adopt the consuming customs of the aristocracy but established for themselves standards of consumption generally significantly below their ability to support. This did not prevent them from adopting certain aristocratic habits, such as the maintenance of large estates. But they tended to continue their habits of work, applying themselves to the accumulation of economic wealth well beyond their needs as measured by their consumption habits.

In the countries of northwestern Europe, the status systems that emerged as a product of the forces that have been mentioned constituted various combinations of the old and the new. Value systems change only slowly, and, though the feudal system as a functioning political order had been engulfed, vestigial elements remained everywhere to a greater or lesser degree. In most areas remnants of the aristocracy remained but with continually diminishing political powers. Equalitarianism before the law developed rather quickly but full citizenship in political affairs developed more slowly. As political privileges and disabilities disappear, society becomes one of classes rather than estates, with a marked increase in mobility.

The individual's position in society is now no longer determined solely or even principally by birth and inheritance, but is a result of achievement, particularly in effectiveness in the buying and selling of goods and services for money. Income is measured in money rather than in rights to products and services; consumption is predominantly in terms of purchased goods, purchases which are motivated in some degree so as to display the class level achieved by the individual in the contest for position. Since the pecuniary standard dominates, social status follows from success in those areas of activity which are most readily measured in those terms. This is not to say that pecuniary matters are the exclusive concern of all the individuals involved; there are many other values of importance. But it does mean that pecuniary considerations are central; that considerations of income, wealth, and property penetrate everywhere and permeate everything else. Control over monetary resources has become the means to status, and the symbols of status are appropriately economic in character.

BUSINESS VERSUS BUREAUCRACY AS SOURCES OF STATUS

Though economic activity became increasingly important as a source of prestige, it did not everywhere achieve the position of dominating the social-value system. It has been noted that the expansion of pecuniary-mindedness, of trade and industry, was paralleled by the growth of the national state. In northwestern Europe the state was made subservient to the needs of business and to the business prestige structure. Elsewhere the growth of the state encouraged the development of another prestige system, one which had its roots more deeply in the pre-business period and which was quite different in the spirit with which it approached its activities. Over large areas this prestige system, built up around governmental activities, achieved a higher position in the public esteem than did the economic.

The development of the national state was accomplished by means of paid, standing armies commanded by a military bureaucracy. Its widening sphere of activities was carried on by a bureaucracy of civilian officials. Membership in such bureaucracies offered not so much opportunity for high income, though that was possible, but primarily the exercise of control over persons and property, privileges in using state-owned resources, and opportunities to influence state activities and to create situations favorable to personal aggrandizement, pecuniary and otherwise.

In the bureaucratic society the status of the individual is determined by his position in the hierarchy of officialdom.[29] Admittance to the hierarchy is limited by a variety of devices. Enhancement involves the acquisition of influence to secure promotions involving higher pay, more desirable titles, and greater influence. In such societies the bureaucrats are more leisured, more highly educated, more powerful, and more prestigeful individuals than those who engage in commercial or industrial activities.

The bureaucratic culture pattern is far older and remains today a pattern covering a larger portion of the earth's area and inhabitants than does the pecuniary-economic pattern of the Western world. The conquest of government by the leaders in economic activity and the eventual acceptance of equalitarianism in both law and political life in some countries subordinated the necessary bureaucracy of those governments to an inferior position in the value system.

Among European nations the prestige value of membership in the bureaucracy was probably least in such countries as Great Britain, the Low Countries, and, as industrialism proceeded, in Scandinavia. It should be noted, however, that in some societies the administration of colonial empires involved the bureaucracy in the exercise of considerable powers and likewise in opportunities for personal promotion.

Until the rise of state socialism in the nineteenth century it seems to be true that the bureaucratic prestige system played a dominant role only in those countries which had not fully developed out of an agrarian economy and a feudal or semifeudal political structure. The persistent control by feudal institutions over

---

[29] On bureaucracy, see H. H. Gerth and C. Wright Mill, *From Max Weber, Essays in Sociology*, New York, Oxford University Press, 1946, pp. 196-244; Talcott Parsons, *Structure of Social Action*, New York, McGraw-Hill Book Co., 1937, p. 506; W. C. MacLeod, *The Origin and History of Politics*, New York, J. Wiley & Sons, 1931.

such areas as eastern Germany, Austria, Hungary, the Balkans, and Spain was accompanied by extensive bureaucratic development.[30] In Latin America[31] the bureaucratic scheme of values remains dominant, as is true also of large parts of Asia and Africa. In Russia, the Communist revolution involved the displacement of a feudal scheme of values by one highly bureaucratic in nature. In the past decade or two the bureaucratic pattern has been strengthened throughout Europe and shows signs of increasing importance in the United States.[32]

THE AMERICAN STATUS SYSTEM

In the United States the business prestige pattern which originated in northwestern Europe has been developed in its purest form. A variety of ideas as to the values to be served by the society which was being established was brought to the North American continent by European emigrants. Among these, freedom of the individual to make of himself what he would was perhaps the most nearly universal. Attempts to establish patterns which would restrain individuals were unsuccessful; efforts to establish political systems which limited participation in the political organization to an elite likewise proved unacceptable. The major exception was the development of a Southern society based on slavery: a system which possessed strong aristocratic characteristics but which was also pecuniary-minded, a caste system blending capitalistic production and ostentatious consumption patterns.[33]

Unencumbered by the older institutional forms which continued

[30] Thorstein Veblen, *Imperial Germany and the Industrial Revolution*, New York, Viking Press, 1939.

[31] On this see Max Handman, "The Bureaucratic Culture Pattern and Political Revolution," *American Journal of Sociology*, XXXIX (Nov. 1933), pp. 301-313; W. W. Pierson (ed.), "Pathology of Democracy in Latin America," *American Political Science Review*, 44 (Mar. 1950), pp. 100-149.

[32] P. A. Sorokin, "War and Postwar Changes in Social Stratification of the Euro-American Population," *American Sociological Review*, X (Apr. 1945), pp. 294-303.

[33] See, e.g., Harnett T. Kane, *Plantation Parade, the Grand Manner in Louisiana*, New York, W. Morrow & Co., 1951.

to persist in the Europe of the time, the American prestige system emerged slowly from an agrarian society characterized by a deep interest in maximum production and restraint in consumption, based on free land ownership, political democracy, and social and legal equalitarianism. In the nation's earlier history the outstanding symbol of prestige was ownership of the major production resource —land. Since a high degree of self-sufficiency in production was imposed upon the population by transportation difficulties, proficiency in many skills was valued and admired.

As commerce and industry came to claim an increasingly important part in the nation's economic life, the basically agrarian values came into conflict with those which were more meaningful to an industrial-urban society. The complex society which evolved has produced an equally complex prestige structure which rests upon a high degree of what is conceived to be individual freedom in political, social, and economic life. Its status system recognizes a great many types of activity as possibly productive of status. Because of this diffusiveness it cannot easily be described,[34] though it is probably true to say that it is the degree of achievement rather than the area of activity that is the determinant of prestige.[35] It is, however, unquestionably true that economic activity holds the central position in the system; it is the route followed by more individuals than any other; and success in business as measured by the acquisition of pecuniary wealth is a major avenue to desirable status.[36] But success in wealth accumulation is by no means the only route to the higher levels of status; it is probably true that the highest esteem is reserved for the achievements of individuals whose activities

[34] For an interesting effort to do so see Florence Kluckhohn, "Dominant and Substitute Profiles of Cultural Orientations: Their Significance for the Analysis of Social Stratification," Social Forces, XXVIII (May 1950), pp. 376-393. A useful bibliography is included in Harold D. Lasswell, Daniel Lerner, and C. Easton Rothwell, The Comparative Study of Elites, Stanford, Stanford University Press, 1952.

[35] Cf. D. W. Brogan, American Themes, New York, Harper & Brothers, 1947, pp. 37-38.

[36] More recently, however, with the development of the giant corporation together with high income and inheritance taxes, emphasis is turning more to the power exercised over economic resources rather than outright ownership of wealth.

are outside of the economic, as in such fields as science, education, or public affairs.[37]

The symbols of achievement are democratic and economic in character in that anyone with sufficient funds can obtain them. No generally recognized differences of a class character exist to control freedom in choice of consumption. Rapidly changing fashions in consumption, such as vogues in women's clothing, do serve to increase somewhat symbolic differentiation on the basis of income.[38] But, though status is measured in part by money as a symbol, it is more elaborately evaluated by evidences of achievement, which may include besides relative income such factors as occupation, character and location of residence, make and age of automobile owned, organization memberships, college and university affiliations, ability in sports, and influence in group activities, to mention a few. Such factors are elements in the differentiation of American society into classes.[39] These classes are levels of achievement, measured heavily but not solely in economic terms. Though such classes are frequently classified as upper, middle, and lower, they are non-hierarchical in character, each one of the numerous class groups blending imperceptibly into the groups above and below. Though American classes defy precise analysis their existence nevertheless must be acknowledged.[40]

Since class membership is determined in large degree by eco-

[37] See R. K. Merton and Daniel Lerner, "Social Scientists and Research Policy," in Daniel Lerner and Harold D. Lasswell (eds.), *The Policy Sciences*, Stanford, Stanford University Press, 1951, pp. 286-287.

[38] Thorstein Veblen's *Theory of the Leisure Class*, New York, Viking, 1924, an unsympathetic satiric study, remains the most important survey in this area. See also Lewis Mumford, *Technics and Civilization*, New York, Harcourt, Brace, & Co., 1934.

[39] The most extensive studies of American classes are those of W. Lloyd Warner and Paul S. Lunt, *The Status System of a Modern Community*, New Haven, Yale University Press, 1941; and Warner, Eells, and Meeker, *Social Class in America*, Chicago, Science Research Associates, 1950. For reviews of the literature see Edward Shils, *The Present State of American Sociology*, Glencoe, Ill., 1948, pp. 12-25; and Genevieve Knupfer, *Indices of Socio-Economic Status: A Study of Some Problems of Measurement*, New York, published by author, 355 East 50th Street, 1946.

[40] Cox, *op. cit.*, p. 467. *Cf.* R. H. Tawney, *Equality*, New York, Harcourt, Brace, & Co., 1931, pp. 67 ff.

nomic and occupational considerations, freedom to enter and change occupations is a fundamental characteristic of the American prestige structure.[41] Mobility in this respect, if somewhat less than equalitarianism of opportunity would call for, is nevertheless substantial.[42] Such freedom of mobility is enforced by widespread educational opportunities and is supported by legislative regulations limiting the inheritance of economic power and hence weakening the transmission of prestige by inheritance.

The prestige system includes also a wide variety of values of secondary importance. In the case of the political system, substantial prestige has attached only to the highest offices, though more recently both elective and appointive governmental positions seem to have risen in public esteem.[43] It remains true that reputations achieved in the business world are important considerations in appointments to high offices in governmental administration, particularly in times of crisis.

The growth of science, stimulated by the same forces that produced the businessman, has not only aided in the democratization of consumption but has developed a number of professions offering important prestige opportunities. However, scientists and experts— the professional classes generally[44]—work for the benefit of society in large part through the businessman, and in large part by business methods. Hence, except for those whose achievements are extraordinarily great, their role is one which commands less prestige than does business.

The development of large corporate enterprises in industry,

[41] With the important qualification that Negroes are more or less excluded. In this respect, the American society has some important characteristics of a two-caste society. Allison Davis, Burleigh B. Gardner, and Mary R. Gardner, *Deep South, A Social Anthropological Study of Castes and Class,* Chicago, University of Chicago Press, 1941.

[42] On this see P. A. Sorokin, *Social Mobility,* New York, Harper & Brothers, 1927.

[43] See Leonard D. White, *The Prestige Value of Public Employment in Chicago,* Chicago, University of Chicago Press, 1929; and *Further Contributions to the Prestige Value of Public Employment,* Chicago, University of Chicago Press, 1932.

[44] See Talcott Parsons, "The Professions and Social Structure," *Social Forces,* XVII (May 1939), pp. 457-467.

trade, and transportation presents problems which involve adjustments in the prestige system. The inadequacy of money-income incentives to workers in mass-production industries, particularly those engaged in highly repetitive operations, has been recently recognized.[45] This is a problem which arises from the lack of adequate machinery for socially differentiating between individual workers in a situation where work requirements and incomes are virtually identical. At the same time, the large corporation has required the expansion of the bureaucratic pattern of control in American business.[46] Both of these constitute developments which have not yet made themselves fully felt upon the prestige system.

The identification of the prestige and economic systems has produced a society which places paramount importance upon more or less unrestrained production for a free market, involving continuously increasing intensity of resource use, a vigorous expansion of knowledge, rapid conversion of such additions to knowledge into applied technology, unrestricted participation in the exploitation of opportunities and the use of the products. The result has been a continuing rise in the level of living, a rise giving reality to earlier increases in desired living standards. These changes have been facilitated by the nation's very effective communication system—both the formal educational structure as well as such informal devices as advertising.

Much of the rapid economic progress made in the United States rests upon the fact that its prestige system has encouraged change and ingenuity. The prestige structure has served to attract a large proportion of the most able members of the society, under the strongest impulses, to the task of expanding the volume and variety of goods available, with the knowledge that "consumer acceptance,"

[45] F. J. Roethlisberger and W. J. Dickson, *Management and the Worker,* Cambridge, Harvard University Press, 1941; Elton Mayo, *The Social Problems of an Industrial Civilization,* Cambridge, Harvard University, Division of Research, 1945; Wilbert Moore, *Industrial Relations and the Social Order,* New York, Macmillan Co., 1946.

[46] An excellent theoretical analysis is that of Chester I. Barnard, "Functions and Pathology of Status Systems in Formal Organizations," in William F. Whyte (ed.), *Industry and Society,* New York, McGraw-Hill Book Co., 1946.

if not spontaneous, is subject to powerful techniques of influence.

Viewed historically, the level of living achieved under the system of values described has been phenomenally high. The attainment of a desired level of living and its replacement by still higher standards seems to be an unending process. But it has not produced any readily apparent shift in the attention given to noneconomic values. While it is true that an increase in leisure—nonworking hours— has been part of the rise in the achieved level of living, a large part of that time is devoted to activities strongly economic in character. This is to say that leisure is predominantly commercialized; it involves to a high degree the purchase of services and goods. High production levels have made possible longer periods of education for youth, a process which includes their exposure to a variety of noneconomic values. By and large these noneconomic values have retained their secondary status. As many a fledgling A.B. has discovered when he has undertaken to find a job, greater knowledge of the variety of values in life does not readily enable him to participate in the society he finds outside of academic halls. Thus the educational process, though it is conceived of as possessing a variety of end values, is in fact largely a preparation for the prestige struggle, principally in the arena of business.

ECONOMIC ACTIVITY A MEANS TO A SOCIAL END

If Americans have attained a high level of freedom of choice, as of occupation, and in both quantity and quality of consumption of economic goods, they have not thereby attained within themselves freedom from preoccupation with economic matters. The expectation that they should so free themselves is without foundation if the structure of the society is understood. For the individual is caught in a pattern of values and motivations which leads him and forces upon him a continuing concern with economic affairs. At the same time this concern is not exclusive; there is room in the structure for those who prefer to express values which rank low in the society's scheme of things, though frequently requiring the acceptance of levels of status somewhat inferior by the prevailing standards.

If in the United States economic activity is the principal preoccupation in life, it is not therefore an end in itself. Its importance lies in the place given to it as a means of achieving other values in the totality of human relationships.

Among the institutional components of every society are to be found those relationships by which economic activity is carried on and those by which the status of the individual is determined, measured, and expressed. These two institutional structures are in some societies interdependent; in others they may be intricately interwoven, with the economic structure functioning not only to supply needs but also as an important and sometimes the most important part of the prestige structure.

With reference to both systems it is pertinent to raise the question of their adequacies to human requirements. In the case of the economic system this is a relatively simple matter, widely indulged in, of setting standards and appraising performance accordingly. The judgments, which will be largely in quantitative terms, usually deal with such considerations as the certainty of the supply of goods, their adequacy as to quantity and quality, and the justice with which income is distributed among the members of the society. These standards and judgments will be in terms of the accepted scheme of things or will be based upon the critic's personal concept of proper values, almost invariably derived from an oversimplified analysis of the nature of human needs and the organization and functions of society.

Since, however, the status system determines in large part what will be felt as economic wants, and likewise strongly influences the concepts of justice applied to distribution, the analysis is essentially superficial from the point of view of the goals of life served by economic activity. A critical analysis of the status system deals with far more fundamental considerations. Such a critique is, moreover, far more difficult, for here we have no base of quantitative measurement. We are dealing with such matters as the capacities of individuals, their aspirations and achievements; and while capacities may be relatively fixed, and possibly measurable, aspirations are neither. Until vastly more is known about such characteristics of human beings, we must abandon subjectivism and take refuge in the more objective question of the availability to the individual of opportunity to exercise his capacities, and express his values, whatever they may be.

We are then driven to questions such as these: Is the status system adequate?[47] Does the system give to a maximum number of individuals the opportunity to find satisfying expression of themselves as individuals and a worth-while place in the larger society? Does it not only permit free entry into the standard channels of prestige pursuit but does it also encourage the development of those aspects of life which make for maximum expansion of the individual personality? Are individuals who fail to exercise their opportunities prevented from becoming obstacles to others? And, of a different character, we may ask, Is the training given to the young of such a kind that the role of the various activities in life and their relationship to basic ends and values are adequately understood?

To these questions a tentative answer may be suggested. Though some historic societies of small populations, simple relationships, and primitive technologies may have stimulated their members more effectively, none among the larger and more complex societies of human history has permitted or encouraged as extensive an expression of individual values as has the twentieth-century United States. To this conclusion there are many qualifications of great importance—e.g., as to the importance attached to the individual, the worth-whileness of the specific values pursued, and imperfections in the operation of the system as evidenced by difficulties in entry and the partial exclusion of some groups such as the Negro. There may be those who will reject outright such a conclusion. The final judgment rests, of course, with the nature of the society that will emerge in the future out of the present, and the character of the values which future historians will apply to it.

Meanwhile, in the process of building that future society, it is

[47] "Among the ills of German society in the Weimar period was, centrally, the absence of a unified elite operating a homogeneous structure of symbols and sanctions which commanded a consensus of loyalty among the citizens. The social process fluctuated without central purpose and governing direction in its movements." Daniel Lerner, *The Nazi Elite*, Stanford, Stanford University Press, 1951, p. 36.

essential that critics of the present order recognize that the economic structure is only a part, though an important part, of an integrated whole with which it is inextricably intertwined. It must not be forgotten that, aside from the organization of the tasks of production and distribution of goods, the economic system functions also as the channel through which noneconomic values of the most personal kind are sought. Changes in the institutions of economic life which may be appealing as beneficial to society at large will be so in truth only if they fully recognize the multiple function of economic activity. To the enhancement of the role of the individual, as producer and as consumer, must be added his need for fuller participation in the prestige structure, with adequate opportunities to secure for himself that position in society which measures his capacities.

IV

Comparative Economic Systems

by EDUARD HEIMANN
Professor of Economics, New School for Social Research, and Lecturer in Christian Ethics, Union Theological Seminary

1. PREMODERN SYSTEMS

Economic life and economic systems in the modern sense of the word did not exist prior to the rise of modern society. Economics was and remained what it had been since Aristotle, a chapter in applied ethics, because economic activities were part and parcel of social life and could be satisfactorily understood as such. However closely what we call capitalism may have been approached in antiquity, there are decisive differences. Max Weber never tired of emphasizing that the quest for profit, ubiquitous as it is, does not suffice to constitute capitalism; what is required is the calculation of profit on the basis of cost accounting, and that is impossible without a labor market and a land market to determine the cost of labor and land services which go into the production of goods. Both labor and land markets, however, were in a rudimentary condition throughout the ancient world, which to a large extent operated on the basis of slavery. As for the brilliant and dynamic 500 years of the later Middle Ages in Europe, which founded more than 1,000 new cities and developed architecture, handicraft, and commerce to continent-wide bloom, its economic system was certainly not governed by the modern standard of efficiency in production.

Speaking in positive terms, premodern society controlled economic activities by keeping them directly embedded in social life. That is, production, both urban and rural in different forms, was strictly regulated and coordinated and geared to socially desired ends. This was possible only because consumption was, in turn, strictly regulated. In modern society production is a mere means to the end of consumption, either from the private point of view where the worker works for a wage, which is a ticket of admission to consumption, or from the social point of view where rising productivity is invariably accepted as good because it raises standards of living. In premodern society work was, on the one hand, a means to consumption; but, on the other hand, it also was an end in itself, as part of the creative process in which man, in Biblical dispensation, realizes his power and dignity, or, in a different turn of thought, his vocation, his calling. Modern technology has immensely enhanced the power and often—unawares—the dignity of work, but it allows, in principle, the consumer's interest in higher productivity as the means to higher consumption to suppress the producer's interest in the dignity and human character of his work. Premodern society was intensely awake to the conflict and strove to define and redefine under always changing conditions the balance between the opposing interests, sacrificing whenever necessary the goal of productivity to the goals of dignity and satisfaction in work. Likewise, the land was not a "factor of production" in the market; it was the home, property, and burying ground of the successive generations and was regulated for such durable use rather than for a market period, and vested with semireligious sanctity.

Commodity markets there were, but strictly regulated and segregated—markets, not a market. Their regulation served precisely the desired balance between producer's and consumer's interests, the preservation or gradual transformation of the standards of stratified community life as sanctioned by tradition, and, naturally, the interests of the regulating authorities, the exponents of such community life. Inasmuch as there was capitalism in the sense of free unregulated enterprise for profit, its natural reservation was in the gaps between the areas of local controls, outside their technical reach; that is, primarily in international, transcontinental, and transmaritime commerce, navigation, and finance. These branches of economic activities had always been in existence, although with changing importance; only in the navigation acts of Cecil and Sully, Cromwell and Colbert, they were characteristically drawn into the sphere of jurisdiction of the aggressively expanding political power, the rising absolute state.

It is ironical but logical that this "rational" (efficiency-minded) political power, by subjecting everything to its own control with a view to developing rational methods of production and organization and rational forces to practise these methods, ended up by making itself superfluous. (This is a kind of bourgeois analogy to the mysteriously expected withering away of the Marxist dictatorship into an all-proletarian rational society.) For so long as economic activities are directed to serve social ends they must be firmly integrated in the social and moral structure of life and guided to the appointed goals, which are outside their own automatic movement; but as soon as they are allowed and expected to pursue their own inherent tendencies, toward profit through efficiency, no more guidance is needed, in principle. Guidance and control are still needed historically for the transition, the redirection of the economic forces away from the social ends they were accustomed to serve to the release of their own dormant energies regardless of social motives. One should not deny that historically the drive to power of the state was in the lead in the transition; it was the state which redirected and developed the economic energies for the sake of its own power, either by establishing its own profitable enterprises to pay for enlarging bureaucracies and armies or by helping the bourgeois to enrich themselves and sharing their wealth through taxes. Needless to add, this combination of political and economic goals is far from dead.

2. ECONOMIC RATIONALISM

We shall speak of "economic rationalism"—not simply rationalism—in the specific sense of a system in which economic activities are more or less exclusively geared to providing people with "bigger and better" supplies of goods and services, and the money incomes necessary to buy them; or, in other words, the agents of such activities tend to regard themselves as exempted from other norms.

This definition covers the uninhibited use of modern technology, no matter what this may do to producers during the workday. But the definition covers something even more fundamental. It cannot be decided without a common denominator, nor in absolute terms, which of two alternative techniques of production—e.g., either more workers and less equipment or less workers and more equipment—is preferable; this depends on the "relative scarcities" of the human and material resources needed for the two alternative techniques. To ascertain these "relative scarcities" is the job of the anonymous labor, land, capital, and other markets in terms of the independent denominator, money.

Again, these scarcities of labor, land, capital, and other resources are "relative" to the strength of the demand for the many products into the making of which these resources can be drawn. The demand for the products is expressed in terms of the purchasing power which people acquire by contributing to the making of the products their material properties or their personal labor, and which they themselves can spend or use in different ways and for different goods. It is between this "effective" demand for the products and the supply of the scarce factors of production that the costs of production and the prices of goods and services are determined, and the most desirable directions and techniques of production selected accordingly.[1] That is, those techniques will be chosen which use the relatively less scarce, cheaper resources rather than the scarcer, dearer ones. This determination of directions and techniques of production is the content of economic rationalism.

There are two systems which incorporate economic rationalism in this sense: capitalism or free enterprise or laissez faire, and communism.

[1] This is an adaptation of Max Weber's extremely difficult concept of "rational capitalism"—"oriented toward market opportunities"—as distinguished from "irrational capitalism," the quest for profit by piracy, etc., from which "no rational system of organization of production could ever result." *Wirtschaftsgeschichte*, Duncker & Humbolt, Munich & Leipzig, 1923, p. 286. (*General Economic History*, translated by Frank H. Knight, Glencoe, Illinois, The Free Press, 1950, p. 334.) The concept is fundamental to Weber's thinking and is spelled out at great length throughout his main works, which are now appearing in English. The word "rational" in this use has asserted itself in German and French literature but seems to be untranslatable into English, although Frank Knight, in his translation of the book, translated it literally. Equally untranslatable is Sombart's equivalent word, *Rechenhaft*.

The dominant academic doctrine[2] to the effect that in our economic system the ends sought are undetermined—maximum satisfaction of any kind, including the satisfaction derived from maximum incomes, but any other as well—is untenable. As Adolph Lowe has pointed out,[3] no market economy—least of all the dynamic capitalist market—can function with ends other than maximization of income; the self-regulation of the system strictly depends on the economic units', in their overwhelming majority, being bound to this and no other end. For if a rise of price expresses a relative shortage and a fall of price a relative glut, the former is supposed to attract more producers so as to overcome the shortage, and the latter is supposed to deter producers so as to relieve the glut. But the system would break down, nay, it could never have been recommended or enacted, if producers stuck to their traditions, thus persisting in producing what is no longer demanded and refusing to produce what is demanded. Hence our economic system, and a correctly defined science of economics, includes a concrete set of values, called "rational" and "autonomous" in the narrow technical sense suggested above, where maximum monetary income is what counts but tradition does not count positively nor effort negatively.

Likewise in communism the consumer's interest in highest technical productivity (that is, in maximum income and consumption) outweighs the opposing interest of producers in the human character of their work. To Karl Marx and his followers to this day it has never occurred that there could possibly be in socialism a conflict between the interest of the workers as producers and as consumers; the collective universal interest in maximum consumption would always override what would be opposed to it as a mere group interest; individuals and groups would have simply to accommodate themselves. To hamper technical progress would be denounced as a "petty bourgeois," "reactionary" measure by both capitalism and communism, the hostile twins. Karl Mannheim, although sharing

[2] Lionel Robbins, *An Essay on the Nature and Significance of Economic Science*, London, Macmillan & Co., 1932.

[3] "A Reconsideration of the Law of Demand and Supply," in *Social Research*, November 1942; *Economics and Sociology*, London, George Allen & Unwin, 1935, Chapter III.

many illusions of this age, has brilliantly formulated this ignored problem as the derationalization of the individual by the rationalization of the economic and social process.[4]

In economic history the difficulty the rationalist behavior encounters is almost humorously epitomized by an observation of Frederick II of Prussia, one of the latest representatives of enlightened absolutism, who, as late as the American Revolution, complained that he had to "drag the mob [i.e., the bourgeois] to their profits by their noses and ears." What we see here is the clash of two value systems, the "rational"-minded monarch representing the system required later to operate a self-regulating economy, while his bourgeois subjects stuck to the other. Whatever name we may choose, a distinctive name obviously is needed to designate the nature of so unnatural, unknown, and unheard-of an economic system as the "rationalist" one.

Needless to say, an economic system designated to satisfy, among other things, the need for the dignity of human work or to avoid extra exertions is in no way less rational than ours. A specific reason why our system appears rational is the special inclination or bias of modern science to regard as worthy of scientific attention only such things as are tangible and measurable or at least reducible to terms of weight and length. With the ambition of science reduced to quantitative analysis rather than insight into qualities, it is clear that maximization of income appears as "rational" and regard for the dignity of work does not.

After Max Weber and Sombart, Karl Polanyi[5] has done most to elucidate the changing role of economic activity in the life of man. He finds the turning point in the emergence of the labor and land markets; this is the dissolution of society and its absorption into an economic life which did not exist before. Society, in this context, can be defined as men working in and on nature, under norms which regulate life as a whole. As men seek employment in a labor market regulated by demand and supply, they may gain many things, e.g., emancipation from serfdom, and lose others, e.g.,

[4] *Man and Society in an Age of Reconstruction*, 2nd ed., New York, Harcourt, Brace, & Co., 1940, pp. 58 ff.

[5] *The Great Transformation*, New York, Rinehart & Co., 1944.

the minimum of shelter which traditional society provided. And as nature became the object of land deals and speculation, the possibility of enormous strides ahead in the technical utilization of the land was opened and the age-old concern for future generations was destroyed. Demand and supply are rapidly changing forces; the market is mobile, flexible, and controlled by short-run considerations. But however great the significance of all these major changes in the economic position of man and nature and in the general outlook, they all follow from the even more fundamental fact that society has relinquished its former control of economic activities and has, in turn, been made into an appendix to that which is now constituted as economic life.

The conforming of social habits and institutions to the requirements of an autonomous economic system is the historical event which was generalized by Karl Marx into his economic interpretation of history. What he said is that social, political, and spiritual life is ultimately determined by, or at least accommodated to the requirements of the autonomous economic development. But generalization is not proof. The fact that society gave up the control of economic life and was, in turn, annexed to economic life, proves nothing beyond its own necessity in a purely causal sense, as one specific event in quite specific conditions; as society gave up the control of economic life it can, in principle, resume it. The surrender of our freedom would be an act of our freedom even if we decided to let it be its last act. The life of society, as distinguished from that of an organism like plant or man, is capable of creative renewal, as the historians Rosenstock[6] and Toynbee[7] have shown against Spengler. And even defeat is something totally different from fatalistic submission to a speculative law.

But the science of economics as constituted today hinges on the assumption that strict laws govern economic activities. While the Marxist law of development and transformation is far more ambitious than the laws of academic economics, which are only for

[6] E. Rosenstock-Huessy, *Out of Revolution*, New York, W. Morrow & Co., 1938; *Die Europaeischen Revolutionen*, Jena, E. Diederichs, 1931.

[7] *A Study of History*, 6 vols., New York, Oxford University Press, 1936 ff.

short-term use and not interested in a more distant future, the denial of human freedom is fundamental to both. Strangely enough, the irreconcilability of freedom and scientific law is, for the most part, ignored, and it is felt that people's freedom to decide between spending and saving, to invest where they please, and to buy what and from whom they please is precisely the assertion of human and democratic freedom in the economic sphere. In the same breath, however, the scientist says that maximization of income and consumption in the frame of given circumstances is the law which governs the short-term decisions. And this is where Marxist science takes over by way of elongation and concludes that the resulting deadlock of apparently "free" private decisions is to be resolved on the plane of what Schumpeter[8] calls "higher rationality," where the individual short-run quests for maximum income are merged into a unified and permanent collective quest for the same goal. Rationalism is law; it is not freedom.

It is true that our submission to this law does not refute our essential freedom but confirms it; and we can resume our freedom. But it is also true that, unless we decide to resume it, we are strictly subject to the law we have freely chosen. We can transcend determinism by a creative action which would set a new beginning outside the appointed course of events. But in the absence of such action events will run their appointed course, which we have freely chosen to follow. Deterministic economics and Marxist theories are wrong ontologically because they deny man's freedom; but they are right and will be proved right if man does not make use of his freedom. And they do their utmost to have him forget his freedom by teaching him that it does not exist. We need not drift, but we do.

Everything then hinges on that historical fact, the overthrow of society by its economic forces, which denied man's essential freedom, created an autonomous economic sphere subject to a quasi-mathematical law of necessity, and soon raised it to the dominant position. The West has known rationalist economic society only in the form of capitalism. The commercialization of society, the an-

[8] *Capitalism, Socialism, and Democracy*, New York, Harper & Brothers, 1947, 2d ed., p. 196.

nexation of society to commercial life, can be seen not only in the commercial organization of production, that is, the subsumption of human work and nature under commercial standards, but also in the commercial organization of political, cultural, and spiritual activities, which are, in the great majority of cases, controlled and sifted by profit-guided newspapers, radio stations, concert agencies, theaters, art galleries, and publishing firms. Capitalist free enterprise is an adequate name for all this only if it is clearly understood to include the supreme control of the cultural ends by the economic means. The perversion of the means-end relationship is more fundamental than mere capitalist production; it is what we call economic rationalism.

3. CAPITALISM[9]

Much in our discussion of economic rationalism has anticipated the discussion of capitalism. Capitalism is a system of production for private profit regulated by the forces of demand and supply in

[9] As we develop capitalism from rationalism, it is difficult to establish how much of the system of capitalism is still with us. Political democracy has at long last caught up to capitalism and has created the structure known as liberal democracy, in which the business organization of capitalism is combined with banking and fiscal measures and governmental directives to steady employment, social reforms in the organization of labor, agricultural policies to rebuild the land, taxes to even out the inequalities of income, etc. Hardly any of these measures can be credited to democracy; they all had come into being pragmatically, under different forms of government in different countries, as safeguards against the ravages of rampant capitalism. But now it is these surrounding reforms which attract attention and draw it away from the central fact that we continue to be nourished by capitalism. The apologists of capitalism, on the other hand, continue to this day to explain it as the structure of pure rationality, the pure application to economic life of the formal theory of freedom of choice. But capitalism is a peculiar and unique structure of rationalistic power, and it is only in this light that we can understand its role in past and present. Growing up in a symbiosis with older structures in the older Western countries, it became the first form of the new American society and continued to shape and almost exclusively to rule it until the great crash of 1929. It can and must be described and weighed as the system that it is before the modifications introduced from 1933 on can be described and weighed in the next section.

the market. It is a system of production, not simply of trade; the labor and land markets are essential to it. It is a system of production for profit and is regulated by demand and supply. The making of the supplies is guided by the desire for profit, which can be satisfied only by rendering real or supposed services to demand. It is in the making of supplies that people earn the purchasing power which then appears on the demand side of the market, and the special places and directions of their contributions again are guided by the quest for the most profitable available opportunity.

It has been pointed out that the process presupposes a distinct, historically unique psychological structure. This psychological structure would never have had a chance if it had not been for the extreme forcefulness of Puritan education toward activism, frugality, and honesty. In the absence of such education even the most favorable external conditions, as in Spain in the sixteenth century, did not suffice for capitalism to germinate, or the seeds faded away after a brief period of lusty flowering, as in North Italy and South Germany. Only on Protestant soil did capitalism become the dominant and lasting system of production, and only then could it spread to other areas.[10]

Among the institutional data of the process is the distribution of properties, which determines who can and who cannot contribute material factors of production, and how many units of such services he can contribute. This is not to deny that the autonomous process itself constantly modifies the distribution of properties by revaluation, and new properties emerge in the autonomous process itself through the saving of earnings and through technical innovations. Far from freezing the class structure, capitalism is a highly fluid system of economic and social stratification. But if this important experience is generalized into the theory that our economic stratification simply reflects a stratification of skill and frugality, thus making wealth the just reward of virtue, this ideological attempt miserably fails in its clash with the known facts of economic history regarding the ways in which landed and capital properties have

[10] To the present writer the above seems to be the real conclusion to be drawn from the controversy around Max Weber's proposition on the connection between Protestantism and capitalism.

been grabbed both before and under capitalism.[11] As for the various degrees of personal skill in contributing to production, they too are only partly determined by natural endowment; much depends on the stratification of the educational opportunities, which has been closely geared to the inherited social and economic stratification and is slowly being modified by history as it resulted from history.

In the competitive race for profit, technological innovation becomes the decisive weapon seized by the pioneers and forced on their rivals under penalty of bankruptcy. The often-heard contention that monopoly, by weakening competition, is actually weakening the progress of technology is untenable. On the one hand, there is hardly any one absolute monopoly of any consequence, since even completely monopolized industries may compete with one another through their products; that is, such products as serve approximately the same needs and can be substituted for one another. Examples are the various methods of transportation or lighting or heating, etc. On the other hand, no economic system of the world, however authoritarian and monolithic, could ever apply fully all technical innovations as soon as they become available; the heavy and costly installations they require today cannot be afforded if they are to be scrapped tomorrow. Capitalism has shown and is showing a fantastic power of technical progress, and technology running wild would wreck any system. In point of fact, the opposite objection, that capitalism over and over again permitted itself to be brought to the brink of disaster by unregulated technical progress is easier to justify. Nor is there any sense in contrasting the technological hesitancy, if any, of capitalism with the unbridled progress achieved in Soviet Russia. The Russian crises of progress, even more severe than those of the West, were solved by the use of actual violence in forcing the excessive pace of technical transformation upon the people. Here it suffices to stress the unexhausted technological dynamics of capitalism.

[11] Schumpeter argued that "the ultimate foundation on which the class phenomenon rests consists of differences in aptitude . . . with respect to those functions which the environment makes socially necessary . . . at any given time," *Imperialism and Social Classes*, New York, Augustus Kelley, 1951, p. 210 (first published in 1927). This will be seen not to be incompatible with the above presentation.

But whatever the opportunity for profit afforded by technology, the dynamic motivation itself is furnished by the insatiable quest for profit. At this point the analysis given in our discussion of economic rationalism must be continued and refined to fit the case of capitalism. It does not suffice to say that the market requires people aspiring to the specific satisfactions from maximum profits or maximum consumption rather than to purely psychic satisfactions of other kinds, with smaller material returns. The market can function that way, but not the capitalist market, unless it be added that the profit is not primarily for consumption but for investment as the alternative to consumption. And this is paradoxical and has been misunderstood even by Karl Marx. His theory of exploitation suggests the impression that the entrepreneur eats and drinks at the expense of his workers and reinvests his profit only in order to exploit still more workers and eat and drink even better, and, in dynamic competition, with more assuredness in the end; investment would no longer be needed in conditions of monopoly.

But consumption, however luxurious, is limited physically, and it is most doubtful that the quest for maximum consumption could motivate unlimited entrepreneurial efforts. In other words, the law of diminishing utility applies to consumption but not to profit; this and this alone is why the system can grow, expand, and multiply its plant, equipment, and energies at the pace we have known for generations. The alternative to consumption in the use of profit is investment, which can be understood as the purchase of power over men and things; the insatiability of the quest for profit is perfectly logical in terms of the drive to economic power.

A rationalist philosophy suspects power as "irrational" and is not prepared to admit the existence and strength of the power motive in its system. The force and stratification of power in industrial society is explained by both capitalism and communism in identical terms of the rational necessity of establishing discipline in large-scale production. Yet it is not simply reason, intelligence, mind, which build the immense structure of industry, but the power, drive, and vitality behind reason and guided by reason. Capitalism is distinguished from any other known system of power as providing a private avenue to power (Sombart). The independent individual, through ability, industry, vision, initiative, cunning, or ruthlessness, or through any combination of these qualities, can make his way to the top. He may also fail and lose whatever wealth or reputation he may have attained before; no one can safely predict the future course of a system engaged in stormy piecemeal reorganization and transformation. That is why Professor Knight[12] wisely links profit to risk, the dark side of the quest for profit, of unknowable but immense quantitative importance, even though the risk to the victims of entrepreneurial failure is not counted, and not compensated for by a share in the profit. The willingness to stick out one's neck is essential to success in capitalism.

The proud sense of independent individual achievement is the best part of capitalism and the specific content of its form of power. So true is this that even profit, the material reward of such achievement and the source of power for further achievement, may be skipped when a still more direct avenue to power can be found. This is the significance of the capital market and the modern corporation, that the capital power of the enterprise becomes independent of the private wealth and profit of its central figure and grows through the contributions of outsiders, nonbusinessmen, big and small savers, who invest their money in industrial stocks and bonds. The dispersion of ownership titles thus promotes the concentration of production and of power over production; many billions of "other people's money" (Adam Smith) finance private economic power.

In principle, there is nothing astounding or appalling in the fact of power, which is ubiquitous and identical with life; nothing good can be accomplished without power and nothing bad without the abuse of power. Power fundamentally is just another name for freedom or life and just as ambivalent between good and bad. But any attempt to ignore power can result only in making its temptation irresistible. For we can meet and avoid a danger only by firmly envisaging it; the surest way to succumb to it is to try to argue it away.

Capitalism is not conscious of being a structure of power. Both the positive and negative qualities of power unleashed and unreg-

[12] *Risk, Uncertainty, and Profit*, Boston, Houghton Mifflin Co., 1921.

ulated can be seen in the heroic-tragic development of capitalism, its immense achievements and its immense failure. The failure is in both the economic and social fields. Productivity is bought at the expense of stability, since the former depends on more and more specialized fixed capital and the latter on adaptability to ever more rapidly changing conditions. Price, an efficient regulatory mechanism in a flexible system, does not control the long-range effects of long-range, fixed investments. On the social side, the private drive to power puts the financially and socially weak persons, classes, and races at the mercy of the strong, thus creating a new class division after the destruction of the feudal system, or merging the new with the old one. In sum, neither order nor a just order is the automatic by-product of individualism, which is the unregulated drive to private power.

4. Social and Economic Reforms

Commercialization subjects human labor to fluctuating market conditions. Adam Smith had assumed that they would gradually develop in favor of labor, and they did. But they did not do so steadily, and the severe ups and downs of employment brought home to the workers their degradation to mere means for commercial ends, kept them all, employed and unemployed, in uncertainty and fear, and made a mockery of their self-responsibility. The remedy to all this, the idea of social security, originated in the German universities in the 1870s, and materialized in increasingly comprehensive legislation in imperial Germany in the 1880s, in Britain in 1911, and in America in the 1930s.

Moreover, market conditions were so unfavorable in the beginning that the market mechanism itself was put out of operation. It can work only if and as supply moves in the same direction as price; but below a certain minimum of the real wage a further fall will force women and children into the labor market to supplement the inadequate income of the breadwinner and will thus inaugurate a vicious downward spiral. In all countries the government, barred by classical liberalism from economic jurisdiction, had to intervene and stop the gap in the structure of the market through labor-protection laws.

A parallel and no less serious defect is known in the agricultural market, where crops tend to be enlarged in response to a fall of price. Commercialization did not fully assert itself in the old countries, where feudal and cooperative traditions had kept alive the sense of long-range requirements in dealing with the land; but in young countries, primarily the United States, the ravages were permitted to continue almost until our own day before public enterprises of the TVA type taught the people, and helped them, to rebuild the land. Labor and land are stores of value which can easily be drawn upon and depleted in an emergency at the expense of their long-range health; this is the reason for the necessity of public intervention in their markets. It has been mentioned before that long-range fixed investments, because they are fixed, cannot be adjusted to changing market conditions in the short run and may therefore wreck the market. It is still doubtful how far liberal democracy can go in applying over-all long-range controls to the private, piecemeal, uncoordinated expansion of production which is the essence of capitalism.

Liberal democracy has at its disposal, however, a wide margin of possible social reform to attack the economic and social effects of modern technology in collectivizing human labor. Within capitalism's own philosophy the problem could be expressed in the words that a fair operation of the market, a fair result in terms of incomes, presupposed some degree of equilibrium between the two sides of the market; but the large-scale enterprise represented in itself a coalition on the demand side of the labor market, to which the workers as isolated competing individuals on the supply side were inferior in economic strength; the balance could be restored only by an association of the workers to unify the supply. The main result is the recognition of the labor unions as bargaining agencies to integrate the workers collectively in, and have them share in the benefits of, bourgeois society. "Free labor unions in a system of free enterprise" is the perfect formulation of the program, even with the sinister connotation that both are "free," under the principle of self-responsibility, to withhold their contributions from production, in order to improve their respective shares in the reduced total income. Veblen went so far as to say[13] that both business and labor are agencies for the sabotage of production.

An appraisal of the labor unions in market terms alone is inadequate, however. Through them comes a new turn, the beginning of a new principle, in opposition to both the capitalistic market and communism. The dignity of human work can be restored neither by reorganizing the labor market on the basis of monopoly nor by completing the degradation of work in communism and making it a mere appendix to the vagaries of large-scale technology, which must be left supreme because on its progress depends—supposedly—the final salvation of all men. The new principle, introduced through the legal recognition of the labor unions and the accompanying legal stipulations, is that of the dignity of human work, the dignity of the worker as a person. For the new labor law clearly rescinds the treatment of labor as a dead commodity by reserving to the seller (or his representatives) a right in the use of the commodity sold, by giving him a voice where he had been mute. This is a notion impossible in commercial contract, even though the business ideology pervading the unions has so far prevented the new potentialities from fully materializing.

In Soviet Russia, characteristically, the independent voice of the unions has been silenced again and they have been made into administrative agencies of the government, officially in charge of promoting productivity. This Communist theory of labor unions, then, is the utter negation of their historical significance, which is not simply in opposition to capitalism, but, more fundamentally, to economic rationalism; their place is not in the dialectic between capitalism and communism, but between both and the new society to be born.[14]

To sum up: capitalism restrained by liberal democracy is a far cry from the classic capitalism of the McKinley and Coolidge eras. But it is not socialism either. The sometimes used phrase "mixed economy" is not too happy a name because it leaves the question of the

---

[13] *The Engineers and the Price System*, New York, Viking Press, 1921.
[14] For a fuller presentation see my *Soziale Theorie des Kapitalismus*, Tübingen, J. C. B. Mohr, 1929.

possibility of such mixture open and is silent on the sociological structure. Both the remaining distance and the positive relation between pragmatic American liberal democracy and emerging pragmatic European socialism are illumined by the Marshall Plan, which would not be the creative achievement that it is if the two were identical, and would not have been possible if they were too different.

5. COMMUNISM

Much of the discussion of communism has been anticipated in our discussion of capitalism. Economic rationalism with the ensuing emphasis on technical productivity; the dialectic of individualism at the top of the structure, and expanding collectivism of technical and social patterns at the bottom; and the malfunctioning of individualistic decentralization in the market, necessitating some degree of over-all control—these are the starting points of Marxism. The technical difficulties and human sufferings in capitalism— "contradictions" in Marxist parlance—drive to a unified collectivist organization, in which they will be fully resolved, according to Marxist doctrine. The economic reason on which modern man stakes his social destiny drives, they say, from individualist decentralization—good for tentative exploration—to the complete unification which is the adequate and final application to society of the one system of scientific truth.

In this connection, Marxist political sociology assigns a unique function to the Marxist party. It is true that, according to Marx, the great instrument which dialectical world history forges for the attainment of universal collectivization and rationalization is the working class. Deprived as they are of private property, the workers, and they alone, are delivered from the narrowing and distorting influence which private property invariably has on man's perspective and vision, and are enabled to see the world in its correct proportions. That is, they see the dependence of their own personal welfare on the welfare of everybody else in the worldwide division of labor. But if the workers are essentially rational, even they are only potentially so in the world as it is. Socialism depends on them for its realization, but lack of intellectual training prevents them from comprehending it and allows them only the program of "trade unionism," a junior partnership in dying capitalism. Hence the workers must be put under the strict guardianship of the Marxist party, those equipped by Marx himself with the "correct understanding" of the workers' "real class interest" in the homogeneous, conflictless society of an all-inclusive proletarian socialism.

The members of the Marxist party, priests of a reality higher than the empirical world, a reality which cannot be refuted by experience, use all means to lift the workers to their own level of understanding and transform all people into workers. However atrocious the means employed, the scientifically assured final result of eternal bliss is supposed to justify and demand them. In the end this stage, the "dictatorship of the proletariat," which is the dictatorship of the Marxist intelligentsia in the name of the "real" interests of the proletarians, will "wither away" for lack of a function into the predicted homogeneous society of perfect rationality. For the time being, however, the program calls for a unified economic system under the strict supervision of the Marxist party.[15]

Marx had expected that capitalism would be the force to unify the world market and drive ahead toward socialism on a world basis. Faced with the unexpected differentiation of the world between countries advanced and those lagging behind in capitalism, Lenin, representative of a backward country and an exile in advanced countries, discovered the chance of the backward countries to anticipate the Marxist revolution and skip capitalism. He advised them not to leave the irresistible weapon of mechanized methods of government and administration to capitalist use but to seize them and through them the country for socialism. This is not a denial but a real development of Marxism; without the opportunity to study the tendencies of advanced capitalism in the advanced countries the backward countries would never be able to skip right into socialism. But it is this discovery by Lenin which shifted the center of Marxism from the advanced countries—where liberal democracy prevented its victory and revolution would be impossible anyway

[15] These observations are from an unpublished book of mine.

against the modern methods of government and administration—to the unorganized backward countries.[16]

It is true that this development immeasurably complicated the difficulty of the transition and multiplied the fury of the dictatorship. In the older version the dictatorship was meant to be the socialist roof on an economic society which capitalism itself had socialized technically and sociologically, while now the Communist government has, as it were, to build the house of socialism from the roof down, creating its own industrial and social substructure. On the other hand, as communism set out to destroy the prerational societies of decaying feudalism instead of waiting for capitalism to do this, communism honestly assumed the role of emancipator. As certainly as liberty has no place in the final Communist utopia, it has a vital place as the proximate goal in the prospects that communism holds out to the backward countries; liberation from concrete and oppressive abuses by landlords and tax collectors is promised to the oppressed, and this is what attracts them. The Communist program can be expressed as meaning liberation from irrational disciplines with a view to establishing the rational discipline of industrial life in its supposedly final form.

The economic interpretation of history teaches that once socialist institutions are firmly established in the economic substructure, the rest of the Communist program is sure to follow. The Five-Year Plans which have succeeded one another since 1927, except during the war, represent this program and are supervised in execution by members of the monolithic party, who are in managerial functions in the factories and on the collective farms. It is natural that under the Five-Year Plans industry should be forced ahead at an almost superhuman pace, regardless of sacrifices, in order to provide means for further industrialization, strengthen armaments, and—not least—collectivize and rationalize the people.

The parallel collectivization of agriculture, however, while certainly promoted by the fixed Marxist dogma of the superior productivity of large over small-scale production, has clearly been forced upon the recalcitrant peasants for purely political reasons of direct

[16] See my *Communism, Fascism, or Democracy?*, New York, W. W. Norton Co., 1938, pp. 108 ff.

control and collective training, against the evidence of productivity rising more in the small than in the larger individual farms.[17] The horrors of the battle for the collectivization of the farms ended in a compromise which, in 1934, gave the peasants individual homesteads on the collective farms and the right to private sale of their surplus products. On the other hand, the principle of the collective farms is accepted because it is only through them that modern machines were introduced and now appear as ingredients of communism, in accordance with Lenin's shrewd definition of communism in his backward country: "Communism is Soviet plus electricity."

Hence, the organizational forms are differentiated, not quite monolithic. Industry was given, right from the beginning, what may be called the orthodox form of state ownership and management, soon completed by an elaborate system of accounting with the state bank as the representative of the owner and recipient of the profit. Even while the rural collectives do not own the land, which is nationalized, they still are co-owners, in an interesting organization copied in the main from an early theory of Karl Kautsky.[18] The underlying idea is to split up the various functions and rights which are lumped together in the absoluteness of capitalist private property. The state receives a fixed return on the land; the remaining profit goes to the collective for collective use or partial distribution. The peasants, hence, are not employees as are the industrial workers; they cannot be fired; they have a right not only to this particular job but even to leaving it to their children, or to an indemnity if they abandon it to follow the call into expanding industrial work. Not being private owners they cannot, on the other hand, sell their shares or their individual homesteads; their rights are strictly personal, not marketable. The monolithic state is represented by two strategic functions: the manager is usually a party member, and the machines are not owned by the collective but lent to it by special state-managed machine stations. These two provisions are not found in Kautsky's draft.

[17] See the extensive discussion of socialism and agriculture in my *Communism, Fascism, or Democracy?*

[18] *Die Agrarfrage*, Stuttgart, J. H. W. Dietz, 1899.

Industry and agriculture, both under strict orders from the central plan, do not develop spontaneously, of course, as they do in an unguided market; they are strictly correlated by the plan. The rise in agricultural productivity, whether or not attainable only through collectivization, sets manpower free for the expansion of industry, which in turn is required for the technical improvement of agriculture, among other things. The more rapid the planned industrial expansion, the more central to the plan is the formation of capital. Private savings out of wages and salaries are perfectly legitimate in any socialist system as long as they are deposited with, and invested by, the state bank; what the principle of socialism precludes is private investment in means of production, not private saving so as to facilitate public investment. But the amounts thus made available in Russia are insignificant, despite the incentive of a high interest on savings, because of the low level of incomes. Hence the principal source of "socialist accumulation" is the profit of the socialist enterprises themselves.

Now, if according to Marxist theory profit were nothing but the fruit of exploitation, it ought not to arise in a socialist system; and its justification as a fund for socialist accumulation is not a theoretical explanation at all but only states the purpose to which the fund shall be put and could be used to justify profit in capitalism. In principle, of course, there is no difficulty here; capitalism and socialism differ, not in the existence or nonexistence of capital and profit, but in reserving the formation of capital and the use of the profit therefrom either to a separate class of private people or to the community, however organized politically. But this definition becomes useless in the Soviet practice where prices and costs, and the difference between them, which is profit, are planned. It is not the principle of socialism but that of planning which makes the theoretical category of profit inapplicable in Soviet Russia and brings what is called profit close to a sales tax.

By differentiating the planned levels of profits between the main branches of production, one of them was made to pay the fund for the expansion of the other; agricultural prices were held low while industrial products for consumption or use by rural people were made very expensive. This is the policy known to statisticians as the "scissors" in the graphs representing the statistical development of agricultural and industrial prices, and to Soviet theorists as "political economy," the planned exploitation of the relatively backward section of the economy in favor of the one considered strategic for building up socialism. If the premises of the entire argument are accepted, the policy of the scissors would in the long run work for the benefit of the presently exploited as well. The related technique of the sales tax has been vigorously used in more recent years to curb the vast inflation which had vitiated all Soviet accounting. It was an effect of the reluctance of Soviet economists to heed the teachings of the despised bourgeois economists on investment as a source of inflation (likewise, on value and capital).

·The Soviet system, whatever avoidable or unavoidable technical defects may remain, is based on a full range of positive and negative psychological incentives, which make it a workable system. The profit motive is used in a subordinate but still effective way, both through an often exorbitantly graded piece wage for manual work and through bonuses for managers in proportion to "extra profits" derived from lowering their plants' cost of production below the planned level. But in the main the capitalist sense of independence is here replaced by the sense of membership; freedom of the individual, by security under the collective. This contrast implies the contrast of the sanctions: bankruptcy and starvation—now mitigated —in capitalism, forced labor in communism—a sanction applied on a millionfold scale against suspected political unreliability rather than against economic inefficiency. The strategic place and driving power of the profit motive in capitalism, as the private avenue to power, are here replaced by the ambition to rise in the Soviet hierarchy—an end in itself for experts—and to contribute to the building of Soviet power, which is an end in itself for nationalists while for Communists it is the supreme means to the supreme end of mankind's salvation.

That this is a workable system can be neither proved nor refuted by comparison with the United States. What such popular comparison invariably attributes to the differences of the systems is attributable, for the most part, to the difference of age between the two systems. Productivity, although rising, is still low. Industrialization of a vast country is a hard and painful process and cannot be completed within the span of one generation, even though the very example of the advanced countries, in which it has taken four or five generations, permits shortening the procedure considerably. Living standards are still lower than productivity, although rising too; what they now are is difficult, and how they have developed is impossible, to ascertain, owing to the distortion of income statistics by the inflation and, even more, owing to a long-continued practice of severe rationing, where many groups of unknown numbers had relatively higher or lower rations. On the other hand, the absence of unemployment was a triumph for Russia twenty years ago, when unguided capitalism all but wrecked the American economy; but it does not prove the superiority of Russian planning methods over those which are now being tried out in varying ways and degrees of intensity in most countries of liberal democracy. For the more a country is lagging behind, the more unexhausted investment opportunities it has at its disposal; a prolonged building period is a period of full employment under any system, and its danger is inflation rather than unemployment.[19]

6. Economic Society and Christianity

Both rationalist individualism and rationalist collectivism miss the dialectical unity of person and community by making either the strong individual supreme and making society a derived value, a means for ends of individual welfare, or making the collective absolute and treating the individual as a means which may be used or destroyed as expediency suggests. What makes the individual a person and the collective a community is the power of love, which transcends the cleavage and possible conflict between them by creating the person as a loving and loved person and the community as a community of persons rather than of atoms. This fundamental Christian proposition has no place in the logic of either one of the rationalist systems.

But although in essence and intention both systems are anti-

[19] The observations of this paragraph are taken, with the permission of the editors, from my article, "The West and the East," in *Social Research*, March 1949.

Christian, there is between them the difference that rational individualism—despite the French Revolution—implies toleration and collectivism repudiates it. Individualism does not inquire into motives but regards them as strictly private and tolerates, among others, Christian motives. Historically its power of social cohesion has been sustained for generations and centuries by the long-surviving unofficial inheritance of Christian morality, which is precisely what gave rationalism the illusion that people can live without religion. Now that the danger of final disintegration looms large, the attempt is made to draw upon Christian moral reserves for reintegration of capitalism by equating Christianity with laissez faire, and the sermon on losing one's soul in order to save it with the doctrine of the "supreme value of the individual" in search of "self-realization."

Meanwhile Sovietism restored, after almost twenty years of bitter persecution, the Orthodox Church to its ancient splendor, to strengthen the loyalty of the profoundly Christian Russian people and exploit for its own political purposes the fifteen-hundred-year-old tradition of rivalry between the Eastern and Western churches. To the Soviet itself the concession appears harmless because the economic interpretation of history teaches that the religious superstructure of irrational institutions will soon crumble away once socialist institutions have securely laid the economic foundations of atheism.

Neither an economic system nor a form of government can possibly be Christian in itself; essentially both are mere technical functions of society and equipped by it with special powers and sanctions. What we call society is the spontaneous association of people held together by common moral convictions, which become natural to the members of the society, including those in charge of the governmental and economic functions. Neither collectivist governmental power nor financial economic power can be expected to exercise self-restraint so as to shrink back from encroaching upon the dignity of man; what is required for the dignity of man and the ensuing freedom and equality of men to be secure is that society believe in them and put every self-respecting member under obligation to conform. That is, economic and governmental power must be under the moral control of society, which is the strongest and only reliable control; those powers, since they are surely not limited from within, must be limited from without and above. Society, controlled by common moral convictions, is the place through which religion can influence institutional history; it is society which can and should be Christian.[20]

But the revulsion from late medieval clericalism—clericalism is the abuse of religion for the power of its human servants—has dechristianized society, weakened its moral controls, and thus made possible the ascendancy of the subsocial forces of government and finance. They are massive and tangible and hence considered "rational," while religion is denounced by rationalism as "irrational"; the "rational" rather than the "irrational" forces are called upon to organize the life of society. The destruction of the rich, complex, "irrational" fabric of society and its absorption into the efficiency-dominated life of governmental and economic power are the way to totalitarianism. This proposition is not refuted by the decentralization of power in laissez-faire capitalism, as is currently assumed; the trouble is that the very decentralization holds modern large-scale industry under the constant threat of the economic crisis, and industrial life thus seems logically to demand centralization. On this, men like Marx, Cortez, and Spengler, for all the worldwide differences between them, saw eye to eye, while laissez faire has no theory of history at all to fortify its position. The decisive event thus was the destruction of society's controls, and the decisive event in our time, if there is to be a future, will be the restoration of society's controls.[21]

7. SOCIALISM

Modern socialism, as conceived by its pre-Marxian founders and suggested by its very name, means control of the economic and governmental functions by society. Socialism thus is essentially the

[20] Control by society, of course, does not guarantee morality, since society itself and its "moral convictions" may be deeply immoral, swayed by passions and lusts. Our quest is not for a guarantee but for the possibility of social morality.

[21] These suggestions, as many others throughout this article, are systematically developed in my unpublished book mentioned before.

third and higher alternative to the two rationalisms of economism and statism, as previously defined: capitalism and communism. So thoroughly, however, have economism and statism done their job that socialism itself has learned to deny its own mission and to understand itself as a mixture of economism and statism. This, of course, is due to the overpowering influence of Karl Marx, who, by virtue of his striking and revealing socioeconomic analyses, confused social democracy into labeling itself Marxist. The practice of social democracy naturally belied its theory in all countries. It had drunk too deeply from the cup of Western civilization not to regard personal and political liberty as a perennial and invaluable treasure, and it found this belief so natural that it read it into Marx. Only gradually does social democracy begin to realize that it cannot hope to retrieve its own nontotalitarian version of Marxism from the letter and spirit of too many passages in Marx himself, which it had chosen not to take seriously.

Anyway, social democracy is now forced by history to rediscover the genuine idea of socialism. On the one hand, the old social democratic parties must, under penalty of death, clarify their position on liberty in opposition to Marxism. On the other hand, social democracy has long been in the process of transformation from the name of a party to a broadly conceived direction of many diverse political efforts and tendencies; in this sense, and in this sense alone, the word is used even in the United States. Furthermore, and still more important, the rise of the British Labour Party has focused the light of international attention on this unatheistic and unrationalistic party, which has always, despite a brilliant half-Marxist wing and the invaluable scientific work of the Fabians, regarded as its strongest weapon the appeal to the conscience of men, more often than not the Christian conscience. In sum, people become increasingly aware that for liberty to be immune it must be anchored in a spiritual foundation rather than in supposedly rational economic and governmental institutions or in the financial or bureaucratic or class interests which create them.

Hence the institutional system of socialism differs in style and conception from the rationalistic systems of individualism and collectivism. The institutional system of socialism is already discernible with some degree of clarity. It must not be all in one style because it is not totalitarian, and it need not be all in one style because its coherence is in common moral beliefs rather than in the institutional structure of property and power. Its gravest internal peril is that socialism may again misinterpret itself as meaning political control of things economic. The problem is in the proper use and delimitation of that centralized power without which modern industries cannot be made steadily to interlock and sustain one another.

Fortunately, insofar as the problem of stability arises from the destabilizing forces in industrial progress itself, the stabilizing measures can be kept strictly within the framework of the market. The routine production of current consumers' goods needs normally no regulation but that by the free market within a strictly regulated flow of purchasing power, since it is expansion which threatens to unbalance the system; but it is the means of expansion, steel, coal, and credit, whose prices and outputs must not be determined by momentary demand and supply but must be manipulated with a view to steadying the expansion and transformation of industry as a whole.

But there are in addition the external disturbances which demand planned intervention: the ravages of war and the far-sighted creation of new political and economic bodies. The question whether a market, if left alone, could work smoothly is purely academic, because the market in this age of social and international turmoil is not left alone and would crash if it were not deliberately steered on a somewhat safe course. Laissez faire can work only in a somewhat stable market, where independent businesses find enough reliable prices and costs to serve as data for their precalculation; that is, for that minimum of assurance without which they will not go into investment. In times of crisis they need guidance, advice, and help from a centrally located authority. That is why in many countries, after the war, governments more or less committed to laissez faire were forced to adopt planning measures and why, as these measures succeeded in establishing a new, tolerable equilibrium, they could gradually be withdrawn. This shows the present need for some degree of central control as part of the new "socialism," with the spiritual forces providing cohesion in a diversified system of institutions, if a collapse into totalitarianism is to be avoided.

Socialism and capitalism as organizers of the units of production, on the one hand, and planning and the market as alternative techniques of economic integration, on the other hand, do not coincide in principle, although they did in the past phase of history, where the market was a capitalist market and planning was the instrument of a degenerated socialism gone totalitarian. A socialist market would be one which is not controlled by autonomous economic forces in search of profit but is, in this sense, "decapitalized;" that is, turned over to the forces of society organized in as many different forms as possible: consumers' cooperatives and producers' cooperatives; municipal and state enterprises; autonomous corporations, such as TVA and BBC, financed by the government but responsible to public opinion rather than to the government, and foundations like the Zeiss Optical Works; independent family farms supplemented by cooperatives to let them partake of the advantages of large-scale enterprise; and, last but not least, private enterprise, where competition, labor law, and the public control of the means of expansion put limits to irresponsible power. If democratic society means anything, it means responsibility of power; its enemy is not property but irresponsible power, whether private or public.

The irresponsible power and social inequalities springing from too great wealth are not compatible with the democratic spirit, even though arithmetical equality is neither possible nor desirable. Intolerable degrees of inequality are diminished by the spread of education, which makes the higher qualifications and functions accessible to more aspirants and thus lowers the pyramid of skills and incomes. The remaining inequalities are wisely limited by undramatic taxation rather than by unequal, more or less sadistic expropriations. This mixed system combined of nontotalitarian planning and a noncapitalist market is not a halfway station between capitalism and communism because its institutional pragmatism stands outside their economic rationalism.[22]

[22] For a fuller presentation of the economic ideas of this section see my article "On Economic Planning," *Social Research*, September 1950.

8. OTHER PROBLEMS AND POSSIBILITIES

A significant experiment in socialism on a small scale is being presented to the world by the young state of Israel. The conditions of the experiment are unique and cannot be duplicated anywhere else, but one lesson may set a beginning to vast new developments. The pattern that seems to emerge after a surprisingly short period of heroic deeds is, roughly speaking, a mixed economy generally controlled by the production department of the labor organization. It is the socialist wing of this mixed economy which offers new ideas in two regards.

In the first place, its historical center of gravity is in agriculture, contrary to any socialist tradition or theory.[23] In the second place, agriculture is organized either in traditional family homesteads fortified by their village cooperatives for purchasing, marketing, education, etc.; or, for the major and most spectacular part, in a new type of collective villages comprising up to some hundred families, jealously democratic in the formation of the common decisions and jealously egalitarian-collectivist in pooling all their work, distributing in equal shares all food and manufactured goods produced in their self-sufficient system, avoiding altogether money payments within the community, and going to different extents in reducing or even abolishing the family home. This form is flexible and, owing to its perfectly voluntary basis, adaptable to changing needs of members and recruits; most recently family homes are restored while the work remains pooled. Whether the uniqueness of the human material prevents imitation elsewhere remains to be seen. But the general idea of a socialist commonwealth based on more or less self-sufficient rural communities cannot fail to acquire great influence as the nonwhite races emerge from colonialism and decaying feudalism and move toward some form of modernized and democratic life.

To help these old and young countries in their new start and promote the rise of living and health standards is an urgent necessity,

[23] Franz Oppenheimer was alone among economists in demanding, in a vast theoretical structure, a regeneration of democracy through cooperative rural settlements.

both moral and political. The American Point Four program and the more concrete British Colombo Plan are designed to serve this purpose. Should they be somewhat successful, it is safe to predict that the world will see new economic forms emerge in the near future, mixed products of European and American experiences and Oriental traditions. This, however, implies the solution of grave problems. It implies that those ancient countries be modernized by Western industrial methods without having to pass through the Industrial Revolution which was the price paid by the Western nations for their industrialization. If modernization were avoided and ancient abuses were permitted to continue at a time when the victims know that misery, sickness, and abuses are not an unalterable fate, they would turn to communism for their emancipation; this much China has taught us. But there also is the opposite way to communism, through the misery of an industrial revolution which would deprive them of their traditional pattern of life and throw them into the arms of economic rationalism. Modernization without industrial revolution is the program.[24]

That it is possible to raise an ancient country to a high level of economic efficiency, even in the absence of favorable natural conditions, by integrating modern forms of industry into traditional patterns of life, is demonstrated by the remarkable, not enough appreciated, example of Japan. Equally remarkable and still less known is the example of Switzerland, where a small nation without much of a domestic market has built up some of the leading industries of the world and has strictly prevented the rise of any large city of an industrial-proletarian character (the shame of all the other industrial countries). If these examples show that industrialization can be kept under control and guided into desired channels, the problem ahead of us is no less staggering for this reason. What one can say is that with a vast oversupply of labor and undersupply of capital, capital-intensive heavy industry and labor-saving devices are not indicated; and that, for this reason and the sociological reasons discussed above, heavy industry will be avoided and light consumer-goods industries will be integrated into a modernized, cooperative rural life.

[24] For a wealth of material see Wilbert E. Moore, *Industrialization and Labor*, Ithaca, Cornell University Press, 1951.

V

Goals of Economic Life:
An Exchange of Questions between
Economics and Philosophy

by WILLIAM VICKREY
Associate Professor of Economics, Columbia University

THE ETHICAL CONTENT OF ECONOMICS

Economic theory, in its purest and most abstract form, can be treated as a system of logic, having no more immediate ethical content than a proposition in Euclidean geometry. And even with applied economics, it is possible to approach the study with the detachment of an entomologist observing an anthill. Yet no scientific investigation, however abstract or detached, can entirely escape the probability of having ethical consequences, remote though this possibility may at first appear. Roemer's observations of the eclipses of the moons of Jupiter, remote as they may have seemed at the time from human affairs, eventually proved to be not without relevance to the development of the atom bomb. No investigator in any field can entirely escape the possibility that his results may come to have ethical implications.

But while Roemer can hardly be held accountable for Hiroshima, somewhere down the line of the pursuit of knowledge there comes a time where the results cease to be purely abstract information and begin to have ethical implications. In economics this point is reached much sooner than in many other disciplines. Economics, as a social science, deals with human beings directly, rather than with inanimate objects or even the lower organisms whose development can be considered of relatively negligible intrinsic significance. Economics studied in complete abstraction from all human values would be an insubstantial discipline, for economics is pivotally concerned with values. And even though an economist restricts himself to the values of the market place as distinguished from the more fundamental ethical values of the philosopher, these values of the market place usually reflect these more fundamental values, in spite of frequent cases where the market values stand conspicuously at odds with ethical values.

Thus while it is possible for an economist to maintain an Olympian aloofness and declare that he is merely studying the techniques of adapting limited means to multiple ends, without in the least concerning himself with the source or justification of these ends, such economics is likely to prove limited and sterile. Whether he consciously admits it or not, the economist who goes far toward using his discipline as a means for recommendations, or who even steps beyond the stage of building abstract logical structures in a vacuum, must develop some scheme of ultimate values as a criterion for his judgments.

To be sure, an economist, like any other specialist, can abdicate his responsibility as a citizen and moral being, and offer his talents to the highest bidder, letting his employer determine the goals toward which his abilities will be applied. Or, engaging directly in business, he may act with an eye single to his own selfish interests. In economics as in other disciplines, in spite of much effort in a higher direction, far too much emphasis is still placed on training for material success in a "devil-take-the-hindmost" world. In this case ethical considerations become irrelevant, except as one would need to consider as data the customs, mores, and prejudices of the world in which one is to operate. But to the extent that his discipline is more closely associated with values, the economist who thus fails in moral responsibility is even more culpable than the engineer or chemist who works on in indifference as to whether his product is to be a vehicle or a juggernaut, a therapeutic drug or a harmful adulterant.

Values in Normative Economics

Thus no morally responsible economist can get far, and no one who wants to make policy recommendations concerning economic matters can get anywhere, without at least implicitly calling upon some set of ultimate values. For some limited fields of economic decision, the values necessary may seem to be so clear and universally acceptable as hardly to need explicit expression; it is usually assumed that nearly everyone would agree that it is better for individuals to be well fed and clothed than to be hungry and naked (though even here a few masochists and ascetics may be heard objecting). But the interesting economic decisions, involving such matters as the distribution of income, methods of organization of economic activity, or the freedom of the individual, do involve matters of ethical values for which there is no obvious and unanimously accepted scale or ranking.

Latent and Implicit Values

But it is only recently that economists have begun to probe into the systems of values that underlie their discussions, and indeed in many cases the judgments are implicit, rather than explicitly stated.

When they have been specific about the ultimate goals that they are using, economists have been prone to specify their values in such a way that they lend themselves to economic treatment, with a tendency to ignore or subordinate those values that are less susceptible to quantification and analysis. This is justifiable only if the values so emphasized are treated as approximations and it is kept firmly in mind that conclusions are to be later modified so as to give effect to a more complete set of values. Unfortunately, it is easy to forget this supplemental process and to elevate the proxy values set up, because of their tractability to the level of ultimate values valid in their own right.

Individualistic Values

The most striking example of this tendency is found in the individualistic approach of most modern Western economists. Here we find that the satisfaction of the desires and preferences of individuals comes close to being considered a final value. In the more extreme form of this approach, the world is represented by a model in which each individual exists in an isolated cell connected with the rest of the community only through the exchange of goods and services. The welfare of the individual, or his state of satisfaction with his circumstances, is supposed to depend solely on the kinds and quantities of goods and services that he provides for the rest of the community, and the kinds and quantities of goods and services that he receives in exchange. On the basis of such a model, perfect competition finds justification as the system that most nearly meets these desires and preferences.

But even the economist himself, when he gives it his attention, finds that such a formulation of final values is faulty. In the first place it is inadequate, in that even on its own presuppositions such a formulation of values is incapable of providing criteria that will yield answers to questions that involve a redistribution of income. Economics cannot supply from within itself a generally applicable and acceptable rule for comparing the merits of the degree of satisfaction achieved by different individuals. Thus, when asked to advise on a choice between two policies that involve different distributions of income, an economist as economist must be mute for lack of the appropriate value basis. If a judgment is tendered, it must be based either on an inadequate foundation of ultimate values, or on more or less unrecognized values which are held by the economist as an individual, and concerning which the economist can claim no greater knowledge than any layman.

THE DISTRIBUTION OF INCOME

One of the first requests that the economist makes of ethics, then, is for a criterion for the making of interpersonal comparisons, or for judging choices of policy that involve the distribution of income. This is not a simple demand, and it may be one impossible to fill completely. The problem cannot be reduced to a mere matter of determining the best pattern of distribution of a given total aggregate "income" among a number of individuals, for the manner of distribution may and probably will seriously affect the total amount to be distributed. The economist may be able to determine or at least to have an expert opinion concerning the relation between aggregate income produced and the degree of inequality permitted in the society that produces it. At one extreme, complete equality may be held to produce a low aggregate output, whether from lack of incentives or for other reasons. At the other extreme, there is presumably some degree of inequality that would give the maximum total product. Perhaps few egalitarians would be so extreme as to insist on equality regardless of the degree to which this would reduce the total product to be shared, and perhaps few rugged individualists would insist on the maximum total product (assuming this can be defined!), regardless of how unequal the corresponding distribution. This is an ethical problem on which individuals have differed widely in their answers, and perhaps no universally acceptable answer is possible. But the economist hardly knows even how to go about finding an answer, or how to start to appraise the merits of alternative answers.

Equality versus Productivity

Of course, if it were possible to assert that complete equality could be achieved without impairing output, as through developing new incentives outside those of the market place or through developing altruism or social responsibility, then the issue would not arise. But the question here is not what the facts may be concerning the relationship between inequality and output, but rather, assuming that a conflict exists between these two objectives, how to determine the proper balance between them.

To be more concrete, if we have ten high-output farmers A and ten low-output farmers B, and if we allow each farmer to keep all he produces, each A may produce 300 tons per year and each B only 100. If we decide to give each an equal share in the total produce, then each may receive 200, but only if the removal of the direct incentive does not affect the effort of each farmer. This indeed may happen if social motivation is strong. But if a "dole" psychology is created, production may fall off sharply, so that the A farms yield only 100 tons and the B farms only 50, each farmer gets only 75, and everyone is worse off than before.

But of course it is not necessary to go so far. We may allow each farmer to retain half of his own product, and put the rest in a pool to be shared equally. This leaves some incentive to effort, and we may suppose the A farms to produce then 200 tons and the B farms 80; they keep 100 and 40 respectively; the balance is shared out 70 to each farmer, so that the A farmers get 170, the B farmers 110. As compared to the individualistic case, the A farmers get 130 less, the B farmers 10 more. The ethical question is then whether the 10 more that the B's get should be considered to outweigh the 130 less that the A's get, by reason of the fact that the B's are poorer. To be quite comprehensive, allowance should be made for the greater leisure enjoyed by both the A's and the B's under the redistribution plan than under the individualistic plan, but the essence of the ethical question remains unchanged.

It may not always be true that a redistribution reduces the total product. If each A under individualistic conditions produced only 300 tons because that was all he had much use for, but could without much additional effort produce 340, and if each B continued to produce 80, then the process of redistribution might actually induce each A to produce the 340 in order to retain 170 plus his share in the pool, which would now be 105, leaving him with 275 and each B with 145. Such extreme cases may not be entirely unrealistic; it is often asserted that heavy taxation of large inheritances may make productive workers out of heirs who might otherwise have been content with unproductive leisure. And to the extent that such cases arise, the ethical argument is virtually all on one side.

Ethical Auras of Income Sources

In many cases one is tempted, in making an ethical judgment, to look to the nature of the source of the discrepancy in income. That is, some sources of higher income are conceived of as having a greater merit than others, and redistribution of such income as being less desirable. Thus if the superior output of the A farms was due primarily to the fact that the A's had inherited superior farm lands, some might urge that redistribution of the product should be carried farther than if the differential were due to the superior skill of the A's, or to greater effort on their part. "Earned" differentials are often considered to be entitled to a higher respect on ethical grounds than inherited or accidental differentials.

However, here seems to be a point where an attempt is often made to substitute a spurious ethical notion as a basis for a judgment in place of a perfectly adequate economic criterion. On ethical grounds it is hard to see why an individual who has inherited a high I.Q. or a green thumb is more entitled to preserve for himself, as a matter of moral right, a larger share of the product of that capability than the person who has inherited a particularly fertile piece of land.

Economically, the two cases are different in that it is ordinarily possible to transfer some of the land of the A's to the B's, while it is not possible to transfer skills in this way. If the land is thus transferable, it may be possible to redistribute the land between the A's and the B's, with an effect quite different from that of redistributing the product. The economist views inequalities in inherited wealth as different from inequalities in inherited or native ability only because transfers of either the wealth itself or its product differ, as to ease or as to consequences, from transfers of the product of ability. If, for reasons of technology or tradition or other overriding considerations, it were impossible to transfer land from one farmer to another, then the economist would have no reason to treat differentials derived from property any differently from differentials arising from ability. It is thus the transferability of the unequally distributed factor that should govern how it or the products attributed to it are to be treated, and not any spurious ethical aura that may become attached to the factor in one way or another. Ethical notions misapplied in this way can be seriously misleading.

The necessity for setting up some sort of basis for placing an ethical value on equality cannot be avoided merely by postulating some method of organization, or some all-pervading conversion to a more social motivation, that would maintain output without the aid of the incentives that become possible only when inequality is admitted. Even if everyone should become willing to work just as hard for the benefit of the community as a whole as for himself, complete equality would not solve the problem of the distribution of income. Inequality may be essential for maximum output for technological reasons wholly aside from any matter of incentives. Out of a community composed of equally endowed and equally worthy individuals, it could conceivably become necessary to select a small number for strategically important posts; and perquisites or other differentials, such as shorter hours, better food, more comfortable working conditions, might have to be provided to enable the incumbents to work effectively; wholly aside from the provision of incentives, complete equality would then be impossible. Or, at least, if complete equality were insisted on, it could only be at the expense of a lower total output, regardless of how willing the members of the community might be to put forth their whole effort without individual reward; nor would it always be possible to equalize matters by a rotation of the strategic posts, or by an adjustment in the distribution of other goods, without some sacrifice in total output.

Here it is possible, at one extreme, to put so high a value on equality as a social aim as to maintain equality even when the allotment of added income to the strategic few would "pay for itself" in added output. The individualist, finding all his values in each distinct individual, would doubtless reject such a "dog-in-the-manger" type of social choice. Nevertheless, when equality as a social value is reinforced by, or perhaps rather used as a stalking-horse for, administrative convenience, we do get examples of this general nature. For example, in times of a shortage in a public water supply we may find that an edict against sprinkling of lawns or washing of automobiles is invoked even against those with their own ample private water supply, though in these circumstances enforcement may be rather perfunctory.

But in general we would expect the problem to resolve itself into a compromise between the objectives of output and equality, with the balance not going all the way to maximum output regardless of distribution on the one hand, nor to the point of unconditionally minimizing inequality, or perhaps maximizing the minimum share, on the other.

Equality, Tastes, and Resources

Yet even here the problem ultimately becomes more complicated than merely reconciling the conflicting aims of maximizing the quantity of some homogeneous output and providing for the equal distribution of this similarly homogeneous output. Neither production nor consumption is homogeneous, and to specify that equality should also mean a regimented uniformity would be repugnant to almost everyone. In a population containing vegetarians as well as carnivores, it is not at all obvious how one should measure the degree of equality or inequality between the two groups. An economist would tend to do it in terms of relative quantity of resources used, assuming that these also would be reduced to a common denominator. But this means necessarily that equality is relative to resources, and that for example an outbreak of some cattle pest would cause a redefinition of the relative states of the two groups.

All of which merely indicates that if an attempt is made to define values in terms of needs, there must be set up some kind of criterion for arriving at some kind of relative value judgments concerning meeting the needs of vegetarians as compared with those of meat eaters, or, for that matter, of smokers as against nonsmokers, or drinkers against abstainers. If we cannot do this, then we are driven back to defining distribution in terms of resources, according to which rule one might have the paradoxical result that equality might mean that meat eaters starve while vegetarians are surfeited, or vice versa.

Fortunately, perhaps, most decisions do not require so precise a formulation of values as would be required to resolve the various conundrums that might be propounded. But the conundrums are still useful in bringing into sharper focus some of the essential issues involved.

WHERE INDIVIDUAL PREFERENCES FAIL AS CRITERIA

Thus even the most individualistic economist is compelled to go beyond the mere preferences of each individual in society if he is to make any but the most restricted recommendations as to policy, either individual or social. But even where decisions are to be made that do not involve interpersonal comparisons, the neat reliance on the preferences of the individual concerned as the ultimate test of values fails at many points. When these failures occur, new criteria will have to be found. There is, moreover, a need for determining when individual preferences can be properly overridden by other considerations.

Incompetence

There are fairly well-recognized special instances where by common agreement it is considered proper to disregard individual preferences, even when only the one person is directly concerned, and to impose choices from without. A child's preference for hopscotch over arithmetic, the suicide's preference for self-destruction, and the addict's preference for drugs are almost universally dishonored in most concepts of the good society. While these instances are recognized, it is not clear on just what basis these instances are excluded from the values to be determined by individual preference, nor how far it may be justifiable in principle to set aside such individual preferences in other less clear cases.

Changes in Taste

Another and more pervasive difficulty with the individualistic valuation scheme, one that the economist requires help to deal with, arises when individual preferences shift, become inconsistent, or, because of inadequate information, are untrustworthy. For some types of shift we can perhaps assume that we are justified in appealing from Peter drunk to Peter sober, or from John ignorant to John informed. But in some cases it is of the essence of the service sought that the purchaser is not the best judge of how much he needs or wants; for example, medical or legal advice. And on what basis, if any, can we say that the preferences of the person who has just been converted to vegetarianism, or to an aversion to nakedness, are to be considered more valid than his former preferences? In an earlier, less rapidly changing era, such questions were less likely to arise. In smaller, more homogeneous communities, individual tastes and patterns tended more to cluster more closely about rather widely accepted norms. But in a rapidly changing environment, with a wide variety of specialized patterns of preference in existence at one time, the implications of changes in tastes are of much greater importance.

Propaganda

Not only do we have the problem of reconciling conflicting preference patterns that arise spontaneously in succession in individuals, but far more seriously we have the problem of evaluating activity specifically designed to change preferences. Such activity ranges all the way from fraudulent misrepresentation, at one extreme, to informative advertising, education, propaganda, and missionary enterprise. To misleading advertising one can perhaps give short shrift, almost by definition, although any practical measure for the curtailment of such activity raises, in borderline cases, serious questions of how to distinguish between fraud and mere overenthusiasm.

Concerning informative advertising and related activities, the economist wants help in determining how much they are really worth. If one could think of advertising as merely informing individuals how they can better satisfy a given fixed set of preferences, then perhaps it would be possible to compare the cost of the advertising with the cost of obtaining a comparable degree of satisfaction with a larger aggregate of goods chosen with less discrimination. But advertising almost inevitably does more than this and produces changes in the fundamental preferences of the individual himself. Even though this were interpreted as merely bringing nearer to the surface some latent preferences considered to be inherently present in the background, it would still mean that a measurement of the value of such advertising with the accepted tools of the economist would be virtually impossible, even conceptually.

Informative advertising shades over imperceptibly into propaganda, education, and missionary activity in the broad sense. What is the place, in the broad scale of values, of activity designed to change the opinions, preferences, and ideals of individuals? We can hardly rest content to leave the decisions, as to how much effort is to be devoted to various kinds of educational and propaganda effort, to be determined by the financial support of those who are interested, either commercially or emotionally. This would imply that the ability of an idea or a program to command financial support would be the prime measure of the importance attached to its propagation. Such a proposition seems morally indefensible as an absolute standard, and defensible as a practical standard only in the absence of alternatives. But no alternative seems available, unless it is to lump this with other social values to be determined in part or in whole by methods outside the sphere of economics.

Satisfaction and Wantlessness

Another difficulty in appraising informational and educative activity lies in the fact that values may lie in the relationship of individuals to their environment and not merely in the degree to which the environment suits the individuals. We may have one group of individuals who are satisfied with their condition because they know of nothing better; others may be better off than the first group but nevertheless dissatisfied because they know of better circumstances that for one reason or another they are unable to attain for themselves; a third category may be fully aware of other possibilities but reconciled in one way or another to their present condition. Is the second condition ethically better or worse than the first? Assuming that the third condition of knowledge and reconciliation is better than the first condition of ignorance, is it possible to achieve it without passing through the second, and if not, is it worth while to make the passage?

Here we meet a dichotomy between the popular materialistic

philosophy characteristic of much Western thinking and the more contemplative philosophy of the East. Economists of both cultures may formulate the goal of economics as one of bringing about a closer agreement between human wants and their satisfaction. But the Western economist takes wants as given (at least in a latent sense) and conceives of economic activity as providing more and more goods to satisfy these given wants. On the other hand, the Eastern economist is prone to consider also the possibility that wants and resources may perhaps be equally well reconciled by restraining wants to those which can in fact be satisfied. The pragmatic result of the Western philosophy is a dynamic urge to material progress, while the Eastern philosophy tends more to traditionalism and stagnation; but this is not necessarily in itself a sufficient basis for judging the ethical merits of the two approaches.

Ends and Means

Nor can we confine our attention solely to the avowed or apparent goals, and the degree to which they are approached, without regard for the means. Often enough, if we examine the matter closely, we find that the means are as important as the goal, and indeed may form a part of the goal. Many things that are thought of as ultimate aims derive their value in large measure from the fact that their attainment is evidence of obstacles overcome, and the removal of the obstacle often removes the value of the goal. If the satisfaction derived from the game of golf, for example, could be completely described in terms of the degree of success obtained in driving a ball into eighteen holes in succession, one would be driven to conclude that the golf-course architect who insists on installing traps is an antisocial character (a judgment possibly concurred in at times by frustrated golfers!).

The Meaningfulness of Processes

Such instances taken by themselves might be classed as trivial, were it not that they merely point up more dramatically an important and pervasive aspect of economic activity too often overlooked.

In nearly all economic activity, satisfaction derives from the process of overcoming the obstacles as well as from reaching the goal. To some extent, to be sure, the economist can include the direct satisfactions of work in his pattern by merely treating them as another by-product. But to do this the economist has to ignore or gloss over the fact that such satisfactions are greatly influenced if not almost wholly conditioned by the social environment. Plowing a field behind a team may be exhilarating if done in a pioneer environment in which this represents the best technique available; it becomes drudgery if in the adjoining field there is a man with a tractor performing ten times the work with less effort. Or the satisfaction derived from the work may derive from the worker's realization of his role in a larger scheme, and may vary greatly according to whether the job is unique or merely one of a large mass. There is the classical story of the gang of laborers who were ordered (during the days when "made work" was prevalent) to dig a series of trenches, then to fill them up again and dig in another place. The workers grew disgruntled and finally quit in disgust at what looked like fruitless work, but resumed cheerfully when it was explained to them that they were looking for a buried pipeline whose location had been lost.

Social Values

Finally the individualistic economist must recognize that some values are social in their very nature. Over and above individual satisfactions that may be provided for collectively, such as postal service, and over and above the dependence of individual satisfactions on the environment in which they arise, are satisfactions inherent in the social structure itself, in the degree of equality, opportunity, freedom, range of choice, not only of a given individual but of individuals in general. There is satisfaction derived from being a part of something larger than oneself, from realizing that others likewise have their roles, from all the intangibles that go to make up a culture. And even though the economist cannot directly work these values into his nice theoretical framework, they nevertheless affect the values attaching to the more tangible economic goods and services, and the way in which the more purely economic objectives are achieved will greatly affect the values in the social structure.

Indeed, some economists have gone so far as to focus their attention on their conception of these social values, almost to the exclusion of the individualistic values. However, their writings have usually been outside the normal range of economics, tending to deal in vague social generalities rather than in the details of the day-to-day economic process. Such comments or recommendations as they have had to make concerning specific economic measures and activities have often not been too closely connected with their expressed ultimate values. In some cases the ultimate values are almost exclusively concerned with a remote future to which the present is to be completely subordinated. An extreme form of this is Marxism, in which almost any present means is acceptable if it can be claimed to promote progress toward the ultimate stateless communistic utopia.

Another type of approach is to consider the entire economic and social system as an organism in which the whole is supposed to have a motivation, purpose, and ultimate goal that transcend the purposes of any of the separate parts. All individuals become expendable where this would serve this organic purpose, as completely as a white corpuscle or a fingernail paring is expendable where the health or well-being of a human being is concerned. However, such a concept, at least in its pure form, is so repugnant to the traditions of freer countries as never to have gained much hold; and even where such a concept has served a temporary purpose as one of the apologiae of tyranny, the role has been an apologetic one rather than one of guidance.

Yet there is a sense in which some transcendent value must attach to the society as a whole. This becomes apparent when the economist is asked to determine what policy should be pursued with regard to the heritage to be passed on to future generations. To what extent should the present generation stint itself or exert itself to provide a greater heritage of resources for future generations? This is a topic concerning which little is said directly by economists. Yet their underlying attitudes toward this question distinctly color a great deal of their thinking. On the other hand, many conflicts of opinion in this field turn out to be founded on misapprehensions which it should be the duty of economists to clear up.

The laissez-faire economist tacitly proposes that this problem should be solved by accepting that provision which individuals make for their heirs as the proper one. It is not always recognized, however, that in addition to property passed on by gift and bequest, there must always be a substantial creation and transmission of the aggregate wealth of a society wholly aside from what we usually think of as inheritance. Even though every individual consumed all his wealth during his years of retirement, the process of saving during his productive years, holding wealth for a while and dissaving during retirement, would, through the overlapping of generations, constitute him a member of a sort of relay team by which wealth is passed on and even accumulated over the centuries.

But this individualistic answer seems hardly enough even to determine a specific over-all policy, let alone to command acceptance as the right criterion. Inheritance is greatly affected by the laws of mortmain, which are even more clearly a social artifact and have even less title to claim the status of natural law than have, say, the system of free exchange and other elements of property rights. The degree to which society will respect and even enforce adherence to the wishes of the deceased concerning the disposition of their property involves primarily ethical values, but also has profound influence upon the economic system as a whole.

But increasingly the social heritage is being influenced by collective decisions, many if not most of which are taken without conscious reflection of their effect upon the relative interests of the present and the future. The choice, for example, of whether to curb inflation by a proper combination of low interest rates and a relatively large government surplus, or instead to achieve the same end by higher interest rates and a smaller surplus, is a choice that should be made not merely in terms of current effectiveness but also in terms of the effect on the social heritage. Election of the low-interest-rate alternative, whether it is recognized or not, will tend to increase the social heritage, other things being equal, and will impose a correspondingly higher degree of stinting upon the current generation. Similar considerations are in order when the problem is one of preventing or reducing unemployment. And of course decisions are always being made concerning the expenditure of public funds that have profound influences on the social heritage. Public funds may be spent in ways that benefit primarily current generations, or in ways that benefit future generations, even though such distinctions are not ordinarily reflected in public account books.

CONSERVATION

The most obvious and specific clash of the interests of the present and of the future, and the one that attracts the most attention, is in the area of conservation. Yet to the economist it often appears that the manner in which such issues are presented involves a misconception of the issue. We often hear about the wastage of such natural resources as timber, oil, gas, land, and the like, the implication being that the present generation is selfishly squandering these resources and leaving nothing for the future. It may be true that these resources are being wastefully used, but in many cases this waste arises not from an excessive preference for present gain over possible future benefits, but rather from a specific malfunctioning of our laws concerning rights in certain types of property. The fact that the effects will be felt only in the future seems to polarize attitudes toward the wasteful activity. Some tend to ignore the waste because it is not immediately apparent, while others seem to lay special emphasis upon it because of a special importance attached to the future, even to the point of belittling the actual consideration that the interests of the future receive at the hands of even the least socially minded exploiters.

To the extent that the form of property rights is responsible, ethics, tradition, and economics may come into apparent conflict, but it should be possible to resolve that conflict if the issue is properly understood. At this point it can probably be said that economists have on the whole failed to expound adequately the economic principles involved.

Competitive Seizure

For example, one of the most flagrant examples of wasteful exploitation of natural resources occurs in the development of an oil pool, where the oil lying beneath an area has been held to belong to whoever can first pump it out of the ground. Traditional concepts of property rights failed to provide for this case: the treatment in the early years of oil exploitation was derived conceptually from the law concerning the capture of wild game. Important differences were, however, overlooked: one who overhunts his own property is by no means sure that his stock will be replenished by migration from his neighbor's land. The man who pumps out an oil well may be fairly confident that the oil will flow from under his neighbor's land to his. And game replenishes itself to a certain extent while oil pools once exhausted do not grow again.

Thus the traditionalistic attempt to solve this situation by analogy to precedent has produced disastrous results that had to be modified, not too successfully, by *ad hoc* regulations. It is not certain what the philosopher attempting to provide a solution to such situations on an ethical basis would prescribe. Assertion by the community in the form of the state to paramount title to such underground wealth seems quite logical, but if this leads to lease under a royalty, it is not at all clear that present and future interests are likely to be properly weighed. Indeed, it would certainly be possible for such a royalty to be set so high as to impair the social heritage; more oil would be left for the future, but possibly the curtailment of present consumption of oil would impair current productivity and result in less capital of other kinds being left for future generations.

A similar class of problems comes up where existing institutions concerning the use of a natural resource are such that private possession is secured by seizure or discovery from a common pool. The traditional staking of claims by prospectors is an example. A somewhat more difficult case is that of ocean fishing, in which there is not only the matter of preserving a natural resource, but of settling international conflicts. In a practical situation, it is not at all clear how one should decide how far the need of present-day Japanese for fish from the Aleutian area should be stinted to ensure a plentiful supply for future Americans.

Where important "neighborhood effects" exist, the problem can perhaps be treated more nearly in terms of economics: problems of soil erosion, flood control, waste disposal, and stream pollution, for example, are problems of bringing home to the responsible persons the injury they may cause to values that would not ordinarily appear to them in terms of profit or loss. The problem is not so much one of balancing present and future interests as it is of comparing values that are ordinarily not adequately represented in the market place.

Some values affected by "conservation" are somewhat esoteric, and may be beyond the capacity of the economists' techniques of assessment: the extinction of the passenger pigeon, the preservation of the "scenic spectacle" of Niagara, or of virgin wilderness. The relative place of material progress and sentimental nostalgia in our scale of values is a real problem, though its quantitative importance may not be great.

The Possible Effectiveness of Private Property

If, however, we strip the conservation issue of all of these side effects and look at the bare issue of consuming a specific resource now or saving it for later on, it becomes not so clear that private property is incapable of doing a reasonably adequate job of saving the kinds of resources most needed by future generations aside from the question of the aggregate volume. Thus, if a mineral deposit is reasonably well delimited and incapable of flowing away or being seduced or seized by interlopers, and if there is some expectation of a future shortage of this mineral such as would tend to drive its price up in the future, or if there are prospects of better and cheaper methods of extraction being developed, the economist can at least imagine the owner deferring its exploitation as long as such deferment will result in an increased ultimate recovery from the property by more than the return that could be earned on a comparable investment elsewhere. If the owner makes a reasonably accurate forecast, there will be no serious discrepancy between the choice made in his own interest and that which would be in accord with social welfare, provided the general rates of profit and interest adequately reflect the relative claims of present and future. And to the extent that they do not, the problem is a general one and is not peculiar to conservation of natural resources.

Of course, when we look at the way in which decisions are actually reached concerning the exploitation of natural resources, we find that most of the time attention is paid only to current costs and prices, or those of the relatively short future, and the possible circumstances of the remote future seem to get very little attention. Is this then to be taken to mean that the theoretical analysis of the economist is irrelevant to the real world, and that in fact decisions regarding exploitation of natural resources are in general made in a way inimical to social aims? Perhaps, but such a conclusion should be arrived at slowly. It may be that the lifetime of the individual, or even of the heirs to whose interest an individual owner would defer, is short compared with the period over which conservation would yield its returns; but this does not of itself imply that individualistic decisions are biased against the conservation of resources. Even though an investment might not yield its full return for centuries, an individual can, given an adequate market, recover for his own use the fruits of his careful custody by selling his property.

Even if in fact individuals seem to pay little attention to values that would be realized only in the distant future, it is still possible that there are socially valid justifications for this behavior. If, for example, rates of interest are so high as to reduce values for the remote future to insignificance when discounted to the present, this is likely to be a general phenomenon not confined to the heritage of natural resources. If the threatened scarcity is so uncertain that it appears to be a bad risk for the individual to hold his resource off the market in the hope of a better price, it may also be a bad risk from the point of view of society. Shortages have a habit of appearing in other places than where they have been expected; new methods of extraction, substitute materials, and completely unforeseen developments have a habit of upsetting predictions. Before assuming that private interests necessarily make inadequate allowance for the future, one would have to inquire whether in fact the property owner's crystal ball, polished as it is by self-interest, is any cloudier than the one being used (possibly more casually) by the conservationist.

There remains, however, the possibility that future developments may rob the individual of the fruits of his abstention and foresight in a way that does not entirely destroy their value to society. The individual who postponed exploitation of his resource runs the risk of expropriation, onerous taxation, or private depredation. Political instability is thus inimical to conservation, or at least to conservation through the institution of private property. Excessive political stability on the other hand is inimical to progress and to many important values. At this point an extremely wide range of values conflict.

POPULATION

Another topic on which economists and philosophers need closer collaboration is population. Economists are often prone to take population as one of the given variables. In spite of Malthus and diatribes against the "dismal science," too little attention has often been paid to the effect of economic decisions on population. Moreover, once we turn from maximizing in some way the satisfaction or fulfilling the desires of an existing or at least an externally determined population, much of the economist's elaborate structure of welfare economics falls to the ground, or at least needs revalidating. For in spite of the fact that a surprising amount of economic writing ignores questions of population, a wide variety of economic measures have a substantial effect on population trends and distributions.

Transcendental Standards

What are the goals of economic life, if we admit the possibility of differing population patterns and aggregates? Do we, at one extreme, allow other-worldly considerations to dominate, and consider the aim as the production of the maximum possible number of saved souls for eventual admission to Paradise? Such a goal might be interpreted as having for corollary objective the maximum possible population consistent with some minimum standard of living needed as an environment in which to practice salvation. Or should population be considered to be determined by an Act or Acts of God which it would be impious either to interfere with or to try to influence? Or, if interference or influence is permitted, what types of interference or influence are morally admissible?

Or, if we return to a more materialistic level, one might at the other extreme set up as the objective such an adjustment of population as would provide the maximum real income per capita, or highest possible average standard of living. Even here, again we are confronted with the conflict between the present and the future. A population conducive to the highest average standard of living now or in the immediate future may not be at all the same as the population conducive to the highest standard of living in the more remote future. And should we look primarily at a moderately remote future, or at the distant future almost over the horizon of our powers of anticipation?

Or, taking a more organic point of view, should we aim more at the maximum possible development of "culture," which would depend on and to some extent include the growth of technology and capital, as well as art, literature, and other more directly cultural phenomena, either currently or in the remote future? Conceivably this point of view would support measures tending in the direction of a larger total population with a greater concentration of resources in the hands of an elite, in order to promote the accumulation of capital and the diversion of resources to cultural pursuits.

Indeed the whole question of equality of distribution is bound up with both the question of heritage and the question of population. Unequally distributed incomes up to a point may lead to a greater social heritage than complete equality, and indeed one could argue cogently that this is what has happened in history. Now that a greater degree of social organization has been achieved and measures for maintaining or increasing the social heritage have developed that do not involve individual inheritance of concentrated wealth, inequality may not be so important a factor in determining the social heritage as it has been in the past; yet the redistributive techniques are still not perfected to the point where it is irrelevant.

Inequality and the Malthusian Hump

On the other hand, the degree of inequality and the steps taken to mitigate it may affect the rate of population growth. Inequality may keep the bulk of the population near the subsistence level and limit its increase, while the elite attain a standard of living that fosters a low birth rate.

Here we may find two important sets of values in poignant conflict. Insistence on equality, even if not carried to the point of serious interference with incentives for production, may spread any improvement in total product so thin that it is merely absorbed by an increased population. It may be that the escape of much of Europe and the West from the Malthusian treadmill was made possible only by the persistence of a high degree of internal inequality, coupled with an even higher degree of international inequality through which the West was able to secure for itself almost the entire economic benefits of the Industrial Revolution and the opening up of new continents. It is possible that had there been greater internal equality, and had the benefits been spread more widely internationally, the spell of the "dismal science" might never have been broken.

In terms of current problems, the economist is thus faced with a dilemma for the resolution of which the philosopher has thus far not provided the tools. In extending aid to "underdeveloped" areas, whether under Point Four or any other program, how far should the allocation of assistance be based on current need, and how far on the prospects that in any particular instance the benefits of the assistance will not be swallowed up by the increase in population which it stimulates? Indeed, should one go further and single out some groups which are small enough so that with the resources available they can be raised rapidly over the Malthusian hump and brought to a standard of living at which they will no longer dissipate the added resources in proliferation, meanwhile leaving other no less needy or worthy groups to struggle along in squalor while waiting their turn? Should one actually condemn indiscriminate aid in the form of medical, public health, and sanitation services, on the ground that in spite of their striking immediate results they may in the long run defer the time at which the population can be raised to a stable and adequate standard of living?

Calculation versus Impulse

Even if some sort of calculated compromise or balance can be produced along these lines, the results may still be subject to attack from another angle. Is, after all, calculated philanthropy entitled to as much esteem as the generous unpremeditated impulse? There is, after all, something less attractive, from some points of view, about an oversystematic, oversophisticated economic process than about a more human, less coldly calculating, and even erratic approach. The economist by nature tends to be much more of an "economic man" than his neighbors; possibly the philosopher has something to add toward the correction of this bias, even if the economist has managed to stop short of complete obsession by an "irrational passion for dispassionate rationality."

Spurious Ethics

But if the economist has some searching and fundamental questions concerning ultimate values to put to the philosopher, he is also prone to chafe considerably under many of the value judgments that have been urged upon him in the name of ethics.

"Just Price"

Most prominent of these is the general attitude toward trade which can be summed up by the term "just price." In its original setting, the notion that each article had a "just price" which truly represented its intrinsic value had as a corollary the notion that in trading articles at the just price neither party gained or lost, while any departure from this just price involved a gain to one party at the expense of the other. As long as circumstances changed slowly, this idea did much to prevent exploitation in potentially monopolistic situations. But it has persisted in a world where the rapidity of underlying changes makes the rigidity of the just-price notion unsuitable.

Insistence of economists that an exchange freely entered into involves some gain to both parties, else one would demur, has overcome a good deal of the attachment to this notion, but some of it seems to persist, carrying with it a spurious ethical sanction that often does much to interfere with the functioning of the price mechanism. Thus when a considerable period of normal supply and demand has established a certain price in the minds of buyers and sellers as being proper for a given commodity, there is often a great resistance to raising such a price in a period of scarcity. The issue is often confused by the fact that in many cases there are other perfectly adequate reasons for adhering to a customary price, such as difficulties of communication, effects of price change on the distribution of income, or the like, coupled with unsatisfactory performance of price change in stimulating supply or allocating use in the specific instance. But even where these other valid reasons do not operate, a policy of adherence to the established price is often followed with approval in spite of undesirable consequences, such as the waste through queues, gray markets, the intervention of speculators, and uneconomical allocation generally.

The "just price" notion spreads its congealing influence even where no element of unexpected emergency exists. Many prices are, from the point of view of the economist, inadequately responsive to such peaks of demand as result from holidays, special events, seasonal factors, and the like. A premium is thus attached to making plans and reservations well in advance and a corresponding penalty attached to last-minute arrangements that unduly hinder the attainment of flexibility. The fairness of "first come, first served" is at best only superficial; at worst it can be both arbitrary and wasteful. The price system has its faults, but the traditional antagonism between ethical values and the values of the market place should not be allowed to interfere with permitting the price system to function in those cases where it does function reasonably effectively.

Business "Ethics"

Another area in which a spurious ethical sanction is allowed to support practices of doubtful value is that of "business ethics." To a large extent, to be sure, the practices or restraints supported by business or professional men as "ethical" are praiseworthy and in the public interest. But in many cases they constitute more nearly a sort of "honor among thieves" representing an attempt to preserve the interests of a narrow group to the detriment of the public good. Perhaps nowhere else is this quite so prominent as in the "fair trade practices" acts in effect in many states by which manufacturers are supported in attempts to eliminate price competition among the retailers handling their products. It is barely possible to argue for such provisions on the ground that they promote order in marketing, but this should be done on economic grounds alone, rather than pretending that the acts protect the more virtuous from the unscrupulous competition of competitors. "Free competitive enterprise" must include price competition if it is to live up to what is claimed for it.

In a wider and more pervasive sense, the concept of ethics tends to be distorted by a kind of provincial bias in the practice of altruism. Many people find it easier to practice the golden rule toward persons in their own class or of their own culture, with whom it is easier to identify oneself and whose feelings and wants it is easier to imagine, than toward persons of greatly different status. Not only is it easier to put oneself in the other's place, but there is often a certain likelihood of deriving reciprocal benefits more or less indirectly. Thus, motorists may be more polite to other motorists than to pedestrians, and merchants more considerate of other merchants than of their customers. In many instances there may be much good and little harm in this, but it is something that must be watched lest it develop into an economic caste system, as some saw threatened at the time of the NRA. And even though no overwhelming damage is done, a subtle bias is introduced in the patterns of competition that should not be further consolidated by wrapping it in a mantle of "ethics."

ETHICS, ECONOMICS, AND THE INDIVIDUAL

But while these searching questions are basic to any determination of public policy, they seem remote to the ordinary layman seeking to find out how he can uphold his ethical standards in the complexities of modern economic life. In a primitive economy, where the effects of a man's actions spread over only a limited area, ethical conduct and the practice of the golden rule had a clearer meaning to the individual. Such clarity did not lead to the millennium, however, and with the growing complexity of economic life, more and more of the decisions of the individual were wrenched from their moral moorings and left to the free play of self-interest. It is perhaps one of the essential miracles of our civilization that in this process the frequency with which morality and self-interest come into direct conflict has been kept as low as it has.

Economic Motives as a Relief of Moral Strain

From where we now stand, it seems clear that it is no longer possible, if it ever was, for an individual, in each decision he is called upon to make, to determine what is the correct choice, directly in terms of ultimate ethical values. Time for deliberation would be wanting, if nothing else. More important, for the average person there are limits, varying from one person to another, to the extent to which he can submerge his own interests in the interests of society as a whole. For some decisions, at least, a less demanding basis must be found, both in terms of sophistication and in terms of the powers of self-abnegation.

Fortunately our economic system has so developed that in a great number of cases the choice to be made on basic ethical grounds coincides with the choice that is made on the basis of self-interest, or at least so that the selfish choice is not materially incompatible with the achievement of the ultimate goals. In an appropriately organized economy, a choice between a new hat and a new pair of shoes, and indeed most choices among alternative types of consumption, can usually be left to individual self-interest without compromising any fundamental values.

This property of our economy has indeed been so remarkable that the temptation has been strong to assert that it works universally, and thus that everything can be left to the workings of the "unseen hand." In its extreme form, of course, this notion leads to the absurdity of denying that ethics has anything to contribute to the determination of proper choices. The obvious failures of the automatic workings of self-interest at a great number of crucial points are, however, sufficient to discredit any proposal that ethics should thus abdicate in favor of a complete laissez faire, even if it were possible to tolerate such a denial of all necessity for morality.

The Domains of Altruism and Self-Interest

In any actual world there will be, for the individual, cases in which he can give free rein to his personal predilections, and others in which it will be hoped that he will draw upon his moral resources and act in accordance with ultimate ethical values rather than indulge his own preferences. The initial problem, for the individual, will be one of learning how to distinguish readily between these two cases; the subsequent problem will be of finding out what decision to make where it has been determined that self-interest is not to be allowed free rein. One of the sins committed by the glorification of economic freedom has been precisely that it has tended to confuse individuals as to where the boundary between the two cases lies. And one of the great defects of our economic system is that its very complexity makes it difficult for the individual to see just when he is expected to look farther than his own self-interest, and that on those occasions when he is expected to do so the consequences of his acts have become so difficult to trace that in many cases the individual may still find it beyond his capacity to discover the ethical course of action.

Assisting the "Unseen Hand"

One of the chief aims of public policy, therefore, should be to so organize the economic system as to make it easier for individuals to see in what respects they should attempt to look beyond their own interests, and easier for them to trace the consequences of their behavior in such cases. One of the most important ways of doing this is to establish institutions which increase the extent to which self-interest is compatible with ultimate values. In effect, where the unaided unseen hand seems to fail, society should establish institutions that will help it out. By thus placing more of the individual's decisions in the noncritical self-interest area, even the most altruistically inclined individuals will be able to concentrate more attention on the socialization of their remaining decisions, and thus do a better job of approaching the satisfaction of the ultimate values.

The Capacity for Altruism

But further, it may be argued that in many people the capacity for altruistic behavior is limited, and that the smaller the demands made upon this capacity the better will be the performance. To be sure, the opposite contention is also possible, that virtue grows by exercise, and that reducing the area in which altruism is to be exercised may stunt the development of this capacity. There may indeed be a point at which this would be true. But considering the world as it is, one can perhaps hazard the guess that we do not appear to have reached, nor does there appear to be any serious likelihood of our ever reaching, a situation in which there is a shortage of opportunities for the exercise of altruism. And if there is anything to Toynbee's thesis of progress being made through the challenge that strains but does not break, one may hazard the further guess that there will always be plenty of strain of this kind for individuals willing to take it on. Reducing the demands made on the resources of altruism seems more likely to reduce the casualties among those whose resources might be strained too far than to stunt the growth of the morally stronger.

DEVELOPMENT OF THE MORAL SOCIETY

This does bring us, however, to the searching question of how far our economic system is in its nature and philosophy conducive or otherwise to the moral development of mankind. At the extreme we have those who reject Western capitalism on the ground that no system relying so heavily on self-interest for its functioning can possibly bring out the best that man is capable of becoming. Possibly there is truth in this view. However, no large-scale high-productivity society has yet been successfully operated that has not relied to a large extent on self-interest as an organizing force. Perhaps a way may yet be found; and perhaps this way can be found only after having gone through the state we are now in.

As yet it is not possible to deny categorically that we may have bought material progress at too high a moral price. All that we can observe is that those who believe this strongly enough to attempt themselves to return to the primitive, small-scale, self-subsistent mode of life are but a minute minority. And, in any case, such a regression is out of the question for the world as a whole, short of an elimination of a large part of the present population. Our best hope is probably to make the self-interest-powered part of our economic system as smooth running as possible, so that more and more of our conscious effort can be directed toward the solution of those problems that cannot be resolved without explicit ethical considerations.

PART II

Our Economy in Democratic Perspective

VI

Government and the Goals of Economic Activity

by Robert Morrison MacIver
Lieber Professor Emeritus of Political Philosophy and
Sociology, Columbia University

Individual Activities and Social Goals

If we want to learn what ends men seek, what values they cherish, we run into a swarm of difficulties. For men vary one from another and every man is changeable and sometimes inconsistent. Each acts under the impulsion of immediate conditions, immediate wants, and immediate opportunities. Thus in times of crisis their behavior may be unlike the responses they give to ordinary situations. Two men may have broadly the same values and yet act differently, because one is more far-sighted than the other. All men seek many different things and in the turmoil of their tangled activities the scale of their values may be hard to discern. Men do some things not because they want to do them but because they are in the net of circumstance. The act of a competitor, for example, may impel them reluctantly to take similar action. Or, on the other hand, they do things because it is socially expected of them, though they would themselves have chosen a different course.

These remarks, which could be greatly extended, are made as a preliminary caution against the simplifications that so glibly sum up the values or goals of the "economic man," or of the "capitalist" or the "worker," or of capitalistic society or socialistic society.

More particularly, they are intended to suggest that we cannot adequately assess the values or goals of a group or a whole society by focusing attention solely on the activities of its individual members. There may indeed be an inconsistency between the values genuinely accepted by a group and a considerable part of the behavior of the members of that group. Each man may tend, under the incentive of private advantage, to ignore considerations of public good to which he fully subscribes. He may not realize that his individual deviation matters much. He perceives readily his own private gain, but the hurt to the public welfare is nebulous and seems so small. In these everyday affairs how little, he may feel, he can do for the advancement of the social good, and how much he can do to better his own chances. Consequently his average behavior may not adequately express his sense of values.

This kind of discrepancy between values and behavior is not the only one, but it has a relevance for our theme. It occurs in every type of society and is in no way peculiar to what is described as capitalist society. In the capitalistic type, however, there was developed a pleasant formula of reconciliation. The laissez-faire doctrine maintained that the private interest of individuals, in their economic pursuits, worked out for the economic good of all. The doctrine lingers on, but the experience of the early days of industrialism destroyed its potency. It could not overcome the evidence that the uncontrolled pursuit of private advantage meant the exploitation of the weak and the aggrandizement of the strong, with serious consequences for social well-being.

The discrepancy between the larger values and the momentum of the everyday pursuit of private gain persists now and always, no matter what form the economy takes. In the mitigation of this discrepancy government has always a role to play. Our task here is broadly to assess that role. We shall not be concerned with the disparity between men's *ideals* in a larger sense and men's behavior. The values we are concerned with are accepted values, values that men do not merely pay lip service to but which they on the whole recognize as their own, values they regard as capable of realization in our present society. Some of these values cannot be attained without concerted action, without institutional controls, without an established code—in short, without government.

THE ROLE OF THE CITIZEN IN POLITICO-ECONOMIC ISSUES

We are concerned in this statement with the formidable and far-ramifying question of the role government can or should play in forwarding the goals of economic life or, somewhat more explicitly, in advancing that whole area of human welfare that depends on economic activity and on the manner in which this activity is organized. Around this question major political conflicts have raged throughout modern history, and now the issue in its most aggravated form resounds in the international arena, where a system of government that abrogates all forms of private economic activity militantly opposes all other systems as outworn and inherently exploitative.

We could not pretend to deal here with the whole range of so vast a theme. Various aspects of it inevitably receive consideration in other contributions to the series. Our interest here will be focused on the question: What are the primary objectives in the light of which the policies of government will be determined if, in its exercise of controls over economic activities, it is animated by the desire to make these activities as serviceable as possible to the goal of human well-being?

We shall seek to set out these objectives without the qualifications that are involved in various situations within which governments must operate. For example, we pass by the conflict between the requirements for national security and the requirements for greater social advancement, or again the conflict between the conditions making for the greater prosperity of one's country and those making for the general economic well-being of other countries. The second of these conflicts may be on the whole and most of the time an illusory one, because most of the time what we do to restore the economic well-being of other countries redounds in the longer run favorably to our own prosperity. The first is inherent in the present state of world order or disorder, but theoretically it raises no problem of practical alternatives, since if national security is really imperiled the diversion of resources to the economically unproductive costs of defense must be regarded as an elementary form of insurance.

We shall limit in another respect the treatment of our theme. Government must act in situations involving many complexities, in situations in which, aside from other complications, the direct and indirect advantages of a given program must, at least roughly, be weighed against the direct and indirect repercussions of its implementation; not only so, but government is subject, in all its economic operations, to the pressures and counterpressures of various interest groups. It is therefore out of the question to affirm that the functions of government in the furtherance of economic well-being are such and such; or even that, no matter what the situation, they should be such and such. The functions of government, under a democratic constitution, are those that the people sufficiently approve by voting for their representatives. We shall therefore put our question in the form: What values broadly accepted in the community are specially relevant for the guidance of the citizen on politico-economic issues? Can we set down any simple propositions expressive of these values as general criteria that he should seek to apply, with due regard for qualifying conditions, when particular measures involving governmental action in the economic field are under consideration?

Problems of economic policy, as they actually present themselves in the political arena, are complex and tangled. They rarely appear as *purely* economic problems. They are bound up with questions of group liberties and group controls, of group advantage and group disadvantage, and beyond these lie the larger questions of the impact on national solidarity and on the creative cultural life of a people. Even the economic gain or loss can rarely be calculated, since there are so many intangibles that may make the longer-run results different from those of the partly calculable shorter run. No important problem of economic policy would ever be solved if we had to wait for a conclusive scientific demonstration that this or that solution would have precisely these results.

In a democratic society most governmental policies contain some measure of compromise. What is significant is the trend. The trend reveals the deeper tides of public opinion, responsive not merely to the changing situation but also to the changing ethic of socio-economic life. The spirit of the times is more important in determining economic policies than is the prevalent doctrine of the economists, and not infrequently has been at odds with it. The role of the citizen is decisive. He is not likely, by and large, to be concerned seriously with economic analysis (though possibly giving attention to polemic presentations of "economics in one lesson" or oversimplified analyses in a one-page advertisement or a fifteen-minute broadcast or a basic-English editorial or a cartoon). But he can be influenced by leaders who assess the trends and give more conscious direction to the underlying ethic and show its relevance to particular problems where it is obscured by group interests. It is therefore in this area that the churches can play a significant part, given enlightened leadership. It is not easy for them, and may indeed be unwise, to take sides directly on the economic issues that continuously agitate the political arena. But they can align themselves with the economic ethic that lives and moves in the community and help so to express it that it is disembarrassed from the specious pleading of private interests.

Two Primary Principles

If we ask what principles we can derive from broadly accepted values to guide the economic activity of government we must be content, unless we are rash enough to turn our particular predilections into universal premises, with certain simple propositions. There is, however, a wide consensus, in effect an agreement, among men of good will, no matter what their differences on questions of policy, on certain fundamental desiderata. They agree in thinking that a well-ordered economic system should serve certain broad ends and should be so constructed that it will not sustain, for the mere production of wealth, a system of economic relationships that grossly subordinates the interests of some to the interests of others. For our present purpose it will suffice to adduce two broad propositions that are in accord not only with the Christian ethic but also with the judgment of equity accepted by the great majority of men and increasingly revealed in the trends of legislation.

1. *All men should enjoy the minimum economic conditions and opportunities requisite for a decent and healthy life.*

It is only in recent times that this principle has received general recognition. In earlier times two factors stood in the way. One was the class-bound character of society, where a demarcated upper class exclusively controlled the means of production. The other was the relative poverty of all societies that depended, as nearly all did in the main, on a simple agricultural economy. It was only with industrial advance that the principle of the minimum standard became practically realizable. And, while on the one hand the resources to maintain it were now becoming available, on the other hand the need of it was made more urgent by the precarious dependence of the wage earner, who could no longer in times of distress find refuge in the patriarchal shelter of the agricultural kin-group.

Today the principle is accepted generally in all industrialized countries, and it is the basis of the various forms of socio-economic legislation that have increasingly become a charter of security against the hazards of capitalistic society. When we say the principle is now accepted we must add that without the organized political power of the classes that need it most, the mere recognition of the equity of the principle would not have sufficed to bring it into operation. The extent to which it is made effective varies considerably in different countries. Our own has been one of the slower to recognize the need for it. And there are still important limitations and qualifications against its full implementation.

The principle is obviously one that depends on governmental action for its adequate application. Voluntary schemes for the protection of its members are partial, insufficient, serviceable only for the more privileged groups, and least likely to be available where the need is greatest. Only government can establish an all-inclusive and impregnable system.

The principle covers the physical well-being of the individual, so far as it depends on protection from the hazards of modern social life. It includes therefore, besides proper nourishment and decent housing, medical care, insurance against accident and unemployment. It includes access to educational opportunity and broadly to a kind of work for which a man's capacities fit him. It includes protection against economic privation in old age.

On some aspects of this program Americans have still to make up their minds. Acute controversy rages around any extension of it. It is important that the citizen should learn to distinguish between the self-interested pleas of special groups and the genuine advantages, the real costs, and the proper limits of socio-economic security. In some quarters the cry of "socialism" and "communism" is raised whenever it is proposed that disadvantaged groups be given elementary protection not only for their own sake but for the sake of all. Those who raise this cry are blind to the fact that the chief danger to the system they uphold comes from the haunting fears and corrosive insecurities in which multitudes still live. If they could imagine themselves in the place of the unprotected, if they could envisage what life means within the shadow of this fear, they would be wiser as well as better citizens—and they would falsify their own fears as well.

The principle can be defended on several grounds. The ethical ground is intrinsic and prior. A community, a state, may be thought of, in Aristotle's terms, as a partnership in the good life. In order that citizens may live that life they need this elementary protection. The modern state provides general education for its citizens, for all of them whether they can pay for it or not. It is precisely the same ground that justifies the provision of general protection against the hazards that otherwise would defeat and frustrate the fulfillment of life. All men owe everything they become to the heritage of their community. The individualistic spirit that assumes its own capacity to succeed, its self-made superiority, is mere arrogant blindness. Men differ endlessly in qualities, but all men, whatever their potentialities, are utterly dependent on the nurture they receive. Only where all men are given the opportunity to achieve can difference of achievement be assessed in terms of merit. But achievement is not all that counts. And the basic argument for our first principle is that it vindicates alike the primary brotherhood of man in community and the potential worth and dignity of man himself. It is thus a primary expression of the essential Christian ethic—and indeed of the ethic of all the great religions. The principle can be defended also on narrower grounds. As has often been pointed out, the price of incapacity, like the price of disease or the price of discrimination, is paid by the community. The wastage of human resources is a community loss—just as much as the wastage of manpower in warfare.

In a country with ample and still-developing resources, such as the United States, the argument is trivial that the cost of protection by social insurance would be an undue burden on the taxpayer or on the economy. We do not grudge the cost of new highways, because we know that in one way or another they yield more than compensating returns. Even less should we grudge the cost of this protection, nor would we if we had the imagination to see the far greater returns, returns not merely in an enlarged economic prosperity but even more in the advancement of the solidarity of our democracy and in the evocation of the human qualities of those who still live within the shadow of a great fear.

One of the primary distinctions we need to make today is that between the so-called welfare state and the socialistic state. The confusion, often deliberately fostered, is most prejudicial. Whether we approve or disapprove of thoroughgoing socialism is here irrelevant. Socialism as a doctrine advocates the nationalization of the means of production. This is a different proposition from the advocacy of an inclusive system of social insurance. Its objectives are different and its methods are different.

Our first principle has a wider range than we have so far indicated. It includes the opportunity to develop and utilize capacity as well as the mere protection against economic hazards to life and health. It implies therefore the establishment of certain fundamental freedoms. It implies, for example, that no irrelevant barriers be allowed to close the avenues to achievement against any class or group within the community, against any ethical or racial or religious or economic or ideological group—an implication limited only at the point where any such group in turn seeks to deprive other men of the same right and opportunity.

Here our principle appears as a simple principle of equity. Government alone cannot guarantee its implementation, but government alone can establish and sustain the universal standard, provided the goal is given reasonable recognition within the society.

It is not—or at least it should not be, as we shall seek to show—the function of government directly to define or to pursue the goals of living, but only to establish the conditions under which men can more fully and more freely seek their goals. Our first principle is concerned with one great system of requisite conditions. Our second points to another such system, one that is complementary to the first. The first depends on the exclusive prerogative of government, that it alone can establish standards that apply alike to all the members of a community. The second depends on another exclusive prerogative of government, that it alone is invested with the final right of coercive power.

2. *Economic power must be held continuously in check, so that it does not exploit individuals or groups, exalt private interest against public advantage, restrict access to opportunity, suppress the liberty of opinion, or otherwise dominate the creative life of the community.*

This broad function of government views economic resources and economic relations in their second aspect. Economic means are at once equipment for living and power to command service, which in effect is power over other men. When economic means are highly concentrated in private hands the aspect of power becomes of major importance, and those who exercise this economic power, while they seek to control government itself, can in turn be controlled only by government. Such political control in turn requires, under democratic conditions, the constant alertness of public opinion. Under modern conditions economic power, concentrated in great corporations, in cartels, in financial syndicates, in trade associations, in political lobbies, and so forth, is elusive and works quietly in many directions with the great resources at its command. Another form of economic power, that of the great trade unions and trade union federations, has developed, possessing the formidable weapon of the strike, a weapon which can bring the whole economy to a standstill when employed without restriction. This latter form of economic power is at times opposed to the older forms, but at times it in effect makes an accommodation with them, as when price increases follow wage increases in the spiral of inflation.

On every side, then, there is need for control over the encroachments of economic power. It is primarily the task of government to prevent these encroachments, by setting limits to price agreements, by curbing tendencies to monopoly, by broad regulation over credit and banking, by preventing the destructive waste of natural resources through competitive exploitation, by intervening when the strife of worker and employer threatens the public welfare, by setting up standards and limits of various kinds in the public interest, and so forth. There is always the danger that economic power will in one way or another, directly or indirectly, hold up the public. There is always the need for political power to counteract this danger. In brief, given a sufficiently enlightened public opinion, the function of government will be properly exercised in harnessing economic power to the conditions that make for the general weal. It is an endless and endlessly difficult function.

Our second principle has a further implication. If we call on government to curb the use of economic power by private organizations, to control tendencies to monopoly, and to regulate or even, it may be, to take over those areas of economic activity the nature of which makes competition impossible, extremely wasteful, or socially undesirable, it is because economic power, thus concentrated, is a dangerous thing and the only resource to control it is the overruling authority of government. In a so-called capitalistic system, which is of course in fact always a socio-capitalistic system, economic power and political power remain distinct at important points—they are not merged into a single type of centrally operated power, which is the political form. But in a totally socialized order they are wholly fused. One of the final questions of social organization is whether, under such conditions or any near approach to them, our fundamental liberties could survive the pressures and persuasions that so complete a monopoly of control might entail. If economic power must be vigilantly held in check when it is in private hands, the need for the curbing of that pervading and secretly moving power does not cease when it is exercised by government instead, even though the power may now be formally responsible and ostensibly no longer secret.

Our two principles, taken together, conceive government as providing a framework of ordered liberty and opportunity within which men can more fully and more freely make the economic means serve the goals of living. The goals themselves are not, under these two principles, determined at all by government. It is highly important that primary goals should not be determined by the fiat of government. To see why, and to conceive more adequately the relation of government to the economic life, we must restate some elementary propositions regarding the nature of government, the nature of the economic system, the relation between them, and the relation of each and of both together to the goals they serve or can serve.

THE POLITICAL METHOD AND THE ECONOMIC METHOD

Government is a way of regulating the affairs of a community, through the laws and administrative rulings of an authority exclusively invested with final coercive power. This power may or may not be limited by a constitution. It is a system for the ordering of the relationships between men, as a condition of the satisfaction of the great variety of human needs or objectives. It is, thus viewed, apparatus for the provision of conditions required for the pursuit of human goals. Whatever the ends men seek, whether private ends or common ends, they need an established order within which to seek them, and in any complex society this order is assured and developed by government.

The primary function of government is regulation—regulation not as a goal in itself but as a condition of the pursuit of goals. We do not want regulation for the sake of regulation, as something to enjoy, as something to live for. Take any governmental operation, the work of any office, department, bureau, board, commission. What is its product? Not something men live for, but something utilitarian in the proper sense. Take, say, the work of the Interstate Commerce Commission or the Federal Reserve Board. What it provides is a way of ordering the relations of men in a particular area of activity. It does not prescribe the goals of action—it merely defines the conditions under which people engaged in that area of activity may do what they want to do. It is of primary importance that government regulation follow this principle. As soon as it goes farther it employs the alien means of coercion to determine what goals men seek. This is the road that leads to totalitarianism.

The only position consistent with man's fundamental liberties is that which was well expressed by T. H. Green when he declared, in his *Lectures on Political Obligation,* that the state should not prescribe any actions the value of which depends not on the external doing but on the spirit, the attitude, of the doer. If government imposes a way of thinking, a way of believing, a way of writing, a way of feeling, it is destroying the very meaning of what is thought or believed or felt or written. This is the final tyranny that invades the very citadel of personality. Sometimes well-meaning religious people move down this dangerous road when they ask government to support their moral code. Government should never legislate morals as such. It should limit itself to prohibiting actions that do overt and ascertainable harm to others.

That is what we imply by speaking of government as a system for the provision of means to human ends. Every form of government, it is also true, is the expression of values either of the ruling party or of the community as a whole. Democracy is based on a sense of human values, but democracy in particular rests on the realization that it cannot, without betraying itself, impose by coercion the endorsement of its values by any minority—or majority.

If one great utilitarian apparatus is the political, the other is the economic. Both orders provide or ensure the *conditions* under which men are enabled or equipped to pursue their ends, as individuals or as groups. Some of these conditions only the political means can assure, such as the establishment of a guaranteed contractual basis for the dealings of men with one another, the enunciation of standards universally binding over the community, and so forth. Some of these conditions the economic means can assure much more flexibly than can the political, such as the exchange of goods and services on the basis of accepted medium of exchange, the adjustment of supply to demand within a market structure, and so forth. But the conditions under which a considerable number of man's wants are met may be determined alternately through the political mechanism or through the economic mechanism. Thus wages or prices or the conditions of work or the rates of interest or the rewards of enterprise may be settled by the "higgling of the market"—by some combination of competing and bargaining between individuals or between groups—or by political regulation. Indeed, a major issue of our times is precisely how far the one way should be employed and how far the other. For while the economic way has limits to its potential application, there is no limit to the range of the potential application of the political way.

Before we go further we must, however, define what we mean here by the economic way. Let us suppose a total communism were set up. Let us imagine that everyone gave according to his capacity and received according to his needs—raising no questions about how capacities are adjudged and how needs are assessed. In this utopian world the economic way of settling things, as described here, would have ceased to exist. In the actual "communistic" states we know the political way has over great areas superseded the economic way, but the economic way is for certain purposes still found quite necessary. One can within limits rent a better apartment if one can afford to pay for it. One receives higher wages if one works more efficiently—and so forth.

In a more capitalistic society there is of course a much greater area over which the play of economic forces, apart from any centrally regulative machinery, is determinant. This play of economic forces, as they mesh and clash and adjust themselves without overall regulation, constitutes the economic way. Wherever it operates there is, so far, a self-regulating system, in the sense that the results of its operation are responsive to the interrelations of the economic forces themselves and not directly to the everruling will of any planning agency or authority. Prices move according to the changing demand and supply. Unemployment increases when inventories mount up, and so on. The results of the system can in degree be controlled by various kinds of manipulation exercised by powerful economic groups. But that is because they are in a position to increase or diminish one or other factor in the price equilibrium, not because their word is law. This kind of "self-regulating" system is the antithesis to a politically regulated one.

One difficulty in understanding the role and the relation of the two systems arises from a certain confusion that tends to haunt the term "economic." If we understand by economic activity all such activity as is concerned with the acquisition or the manipulation of the means of production, distribution, or exchange of marketable goods and services—any roughly corresponding definition will equally serve here—then there is much economic activity that falls within the political sphere. All governments inevitably carry on numerous economic activities. They buy and sell, they employ labor and pay wages, they compete in the market for goods and services—aside altogether from the particular forms of production that they operate themselves. Some governmental operations take goods out of the market area altogether, as when they convert private land into a public park. But not even nationalization of property puts an end to economic activity, as above defined, in the management of that property. Every organization, whether political, educational, religious, or anything else, carries on economic activities. In short, economic activity is not exclusive to what we think of as economic organizations.

And there is no demarcation to be drawn between political activity and economic activity. The line is between two *methods* of doing things: one the political method, which directly regulates, through laws, decrees, administrative orders, and so forth; and the other the economic method, which employs the specific economic means of competing, bargaining, trading, performing all kinds of market operations. The political method, in its full scope, is exclusively carried on by public organizations, in the sense that only such bodies possess the right to make rules coercively binding on all men within their ambit. The economic method is predominantly or characteristically carried on by private organizations or private individuals, for the sake of the private acquisition of economic means.

As has already been pointed out, the political and the economic method offer themselves as alternative ways of conducting any and every kind of economic activity. The question, however, is not which of the two should be employed but how much, how far, of this method and of that. Our two principles are in effect statements of broad considerations that on any particular issue might give us reason to choose one or the other.

Another confusion, closely related to the first, besets the use of the term "economic." It occurs when we draw a hard-and-fast distinction between the areas of economic and of noneconomic activity. The greater part of human labor is occupied with the making of a living or the acquisition of wealth in some degree. In a capitalistic order the means thus provided accrue in the purely neutral form of money—wages, salaries, interest, rent, profits—purely neutral in the sense that a dollar is a unit of a medium of exchange that can be converted at will into an equivalent amount of goods and services of any available kind. Obviously, however, not all goods and services are money-commanded, nor again can money command the spirit in which services are rendered. Money commands the means prerequisite to our satisfactions, not the satisfactions themselves. In its developed form the economic system is a means-apparatus, a means of providing the means to satisfactions.

The only direct qualification on this statement is the inverted economic activity that finds its satisfaction in the acquisition of means *as such*, divorced from the satisfaction arising from the prospective utility of the means thus acquired. The classical example of this inversion is the case of the miser, who has completed the process in which the intensive pursuit of means tends to blur and then obliterate the perception of the goal to which it was primarily directed. This is a situation entirely different from the common one in which the pursuit of the means to a satisfaction is itself satisfying as a process of accomplishment in the skillful or successful adaptation of means to ends. One charge not infrequently brought against the industrial system is that it so often fails to provide this kind of satisfaction.

Our main point here, however, is a different one. All our goals require some means, some equipment, for their pursuit. To carry on that pursuit, no matter what it be, we must at the same time receive an economic return for so doing or else we must depend on the means that have been already provided for us by other or previous activity of ours or of others. That is equally true whether our activity is preaching the gospel or writing poetry or making shoes or bringing up a family or running an empire. What then shall we call economic activity—how shall one limit its range? One man makes a living by preaching, another by driving a taxicab. Is the latter to be called economic activity and the former not? One man earns money by doing scientific research and uses it to support a family; another earns money by digging ditches and also thereby supports a family. Is the latter economic activity and the former not? Carry the argument further and it appears there are no such things as *economic* wants and economic needs or desires. Any kind of activity can have an economic aspect and most kinds do have one.

If there are then no economic wants there are, properly speaking, no economic goals, but only economic means to any goals. Indeed, the economic means as such are means to the means to goals. We make no genuine distinction when we call food and protection and apparatus and books and a home or any other thing we need for our goals, no matter what they be, economic goods. Why should butter and eggs be economic goods and museums and, say, codes of law, noneconomic? To obtain any of these an economic cost has to be met, a price has to be paid—as one aspect of the process of getting them. In a modern society we cannot obtain even fresh air or sunshine without some economic provision of some kind.

Our analysis here must be left incomplete, but we may have gone far enough to make our initial distinction clear. We started from the point that the economic system and the political system constitute two great means-structures or agencies through which the conditions or means required for the goals of living may be secured, and that to an important extent they offer alternative ways of doing so. The economic way uses the mechanisms of our economic system, the political way the mechanisms of government. Economic activity is, properly considered, a means-seeking operation, and so also, properly considered, is political activity.

One last point must be made on this topic, since our conclusion that economic activity is properly and strictly a quest of means may seem at variance with the position taken by other contributors. Economic activity is, as we understand it, merely an aspect of a totality of behaving. An author writes novels; he is interested in marketing them and takes steps accordingly. In his actual writing the marketing aspect may be more or less influential or even determinative. But no novelist worthy of the name thinks of that alone. He makes use of the economic way and so far is thinking of the means he can acquire for further ends.

But what, it may be said, of the man who spends his whole working time in market activities? It is of course a matter of degree. Market activity as such remains a means to means. But human beings do not live in separate compartments of their personality. Their other interests are not excluded when they work in or for a market. Other attitudes enter into their activity. There is companionship, there is some consideration for the needs of others in the process, there is the sense of workmanship or of the quality of achievement where opportunity is offered to it, and so forth. Utilitarian interests are in this respect like utilitarian goods. An automobile is designedly a means of transportation, but the people who make and use automobiles want them to be something more as well. The utilitarian requirement is made the opportunity for the fulfillment of requirements of a different kind.

Economic activity involves at the same time economic relationships, but again when a man enters into economic relationships he acts as a social being, not merely an economic one, so that certain satisfactions of day-by-day living arise in the processs of maintaining relationships that were primarily entered into for economic reasons. One of the major problems of a modern society is the establishment of an effective rapport between the economic aspect of a man's work and its other aspects. Indeed, it might be said that the burden of the contributions to this series is to explore this whole problem.

The Economic Way and the Political Way as Alternatives

The means to many of the goals of living may be sought by enlisting for the purpose in hand either the mechanism of government or the mechanism of the market. One or the other way or some combination of both may be chosen, and the particular choice is nearly always a matter of controversy. Take, for example, the provision of medical care within a community as a whole. In any modern society that provision is not left solely to the free play of the market. There are rules determining who shall be permitted to be medical practitioners and under what controls. These rules are in the last resort dependent on the sanction of government. The profession thus officially sanctioned in turn makes rules concerning the practice of medicine. It has, for example, rules prohibiting advertising and other competitive practices on the part of the doctors. In the last resort the sanction of these rules depends on government. There are again a great many provisions concerned with public health that are prescribed by government and carried out with the aid of the medical profession.

At present in this country there is a lively controversy over the question whether a further great expansion of the political method is or is not here desirable. Should medical service be provided for the people as a whole by state action or should we rely in general on private practice together with such devices as group health insurance, voluntary arrangements for hospitalization needs, and so forth?

Here is one of the multitude of issues that arise concerning the desirable range and limits of the political way as against the economic way. The controversy over each of them is continuously confused by irrelevant arguments. Special interests on one side or the other dress their appeals in the garb of sacred principles. In weighing these arguments our own biases and our lack of knowledge of the processes of implementation often prevent us from being logically determined by a sincere consideration of the merits of the case.

We have set out two broad principles that, if we could sincerely and knowledgeably apply them, would at least orient us properly in coming to a decision. But the application is never simple. Any change from the economic way to the political way or vice versa is likely to involve both a gain and a loss. If you choose one alternative you are likely to incur the loss of some value associated with the rejected alternative. Which way lies the net gain to the community at large? Exaggerated statements of the gain on the one hand and of the loss on the other are likely to be made respectively by the proponents and by the opponents of change.

To take our example, the establishment of a socialized or national medical service limits the freedom of doctors to practice as they please and it confers on government a new responsibility and with it a new power. On the other hand it brings medical service more adequately to those sections of the population who are least able to pay for it, and by giving them greater protection may help to raise the health standards of the whole people. There are also of course other considerations to be adduced on both sides. Which then is more significant, the gain or the loss? How great is the loss? How important is the gain? We can never fully reckon the alternatives. We must use the best judgment at our command.

In doing so, there are certain types of argument we should discount. So far as may be, we should attach more weight to the arguments of those who have, to the best of our knowledge, no special or private interest whichever way the decision goes. Special-interest groups may honestly feel that they are pleading not their own benefit but the general benefit, yet we all know how exceedingly hard it is to be unbiased when our own advantage or our own prestige is, or is thought to be, involved.

Again, we should beware of arguments that sweepingly prognosticate the direct consequences from any new intervention by government in economic affairs and denounce any change, no matter what its manifest benefit, as heralding "socialism," "communism," the "servile society," the "road to serfdom," or what not. Every modern society, at least outside of the Soviet block, is sociocapitalistic, some kind of combination of the economic way and the political way. It is inevitable that it should be so. There is no reason to suppose that measures of social insurance and other forms of welfare services are significant of a trend to communism. There is good reason to believe that the provision of such services, removing as they do the primary defect of a capitalistic society, the economic insecurity, the sense of unprotected detachment that undermines the foundations of social solidarity, is a safeguard against and not an invitation to communism. Communism has never succeeded in winning freely to its cause any society that was not shaken to the depths by economic and social despair. Even in those cases it has succeeded only during war-generated crises, when it could seize on government by the violence and cunning of its trained revolutionaries.

With such cautions and distinctions in mind we can weigh more adequately the alternatives when we are presented with one of the ever-arising problems regarding the choice between the economic way and the political way. Sometimes the assessment may be difficult; often, if we keep our primary principles clear, it should not be hard, at least where our particular interests are not involved. To take a simple case, there is, say, a program of forest conservation that requires governmental control over the wasteful activities of lumbermen that are out for short-run profits. The cry is raised that such control would be undue interference with private enterprise or with the rights of property. Any such objection is obviously using as a screen against the public interest a laissez-faire doctrine that has no relevance to the real issue.

We *must* use the political way as well as the economic way, and the problem for the good citizen is to try to assure, so far as his vote or his judgment counts, the best services of both. It is interesting in this connection that the economic way, the way of private enterprise, the way of the free market, if unchecked by government, degenerates through the operation of its own forces into an array of greater and lesser power systems that within their limits stifle the very freedom of enterprise whose banner they fly and become pseudopolitical entities of aggrandizement and exploitation. In short, the free market is not self-maintaining. It needs government to keep it so. Like all other free things its freedom requires the restraint of the forces that would control it, from within or from without. One of the hardest tasks of modern government is to keep within proper bounds the various monopolistic forces, the expansive organizations that subdue competition and can thus dictate their terms unless they are held in check by a vigilant political authority. In the elaborate interdependence of a modern economy any inclusive organization, or even informal combination, that has control over the supply of any one of a hundred commodities or any one of a vast number of services can, if not subjected to the over-all regulation of the state, hold up the community until its demands are met.

Every industrial society is all the time a kind of great laboratory engaged in experimenting in ever-changing combinations of the political way and the economic way. So long as a society is free it is bound to experiment, in response to changing conditions and growing experience. And here we come to the final challenge of alternatives, that between communism, a system that on the ground of an inherited dogma rules out the economic way altogether, and the mixed economy of all other systems. The challenge, incidentally, is never one between communism and capitalism, since pure capitalism does not exist and never has existed, but between a rigid system that closes down one of the alternatives and a flexible system, sociocapitalism, that operates with both.

There is often, however, a misunderstanding as to the nature of this final challenge. We must not confuse the threat of communism, as a power system animated by a dogma concerning the inevitable processes of history and having aggressive designs to make the dogma come true, with the challenge of communism as a creed, as a system of values. Communism has won its major victories only under the former aspect. Under the latter it has never won the allegiance of a people that was free to choose. It has never won the verdict of a democratically governed people. It has never yet been chosen freely on its merits.

The reason is not far to seek. Soviet communism cannot offer itself as an alternative in a democratic fashion. Its proposition is always "all or nothing." It rejects with scorn any proposition except its total fulfillment, brought about in a single cataclysm that "destroys the machinery of the bourgeois state." It can proceed only by the road of revolution, with the violent suppression of the whole pre-existing order of things. Even if its party were greatly in the majority it could not suffer any minority that dissented from its creed. It is thus through and through antidemocratic and it is animated by a virulent hatred of those who resist its tenets. The proponents of other forms of socialism are ready to advance by degrees to their goal, and those who believe in private capitalism accept varying mixtures of socialism. Communism ridicules all such doctrines and has no mercy for their advocates.

Now in a democratic society there is always a choosing between alternatives, but the alternatives are always some change in the established ways or no change in that particular respect, always more of this or more of that, always a shift toward the left or toward the right. Public opinion moves in this direction or in that. There are trends of change and thus some preparedness for the next move, whatever the direction may be and whatever controversies may rage over it. The all-or-nothing alternatives that alone are congenial to the rigid Marxist mind are thus wholly alien to the spirit of democracy.

A free society is a flexible society, always experimenting, always, so far as it is also intelligent, seeking to adjust its conditions to its changing needs. It enthrones no dogma, it surrenders to no power system. Whatever mistakes it makes it never binds its own future. It uses the economic way but with some recognition of the need for limits and safeguards. These limits and safeguards are provided by the political way, but in turn a democratic society recognizes that limits and safeguards must be vigilantly assured against government also. For the danger is always the unguarded power of men over men, whether the power be economic or political. Some kind of equilibrium must always be sought.

The citizen cannot leave the decision to the experts or to the authorities. The choice of alternatives is always presented afresh. Being neither an expert nor an authority, he must bring to bear instead the principles of equity, the spirit of the good citizen, with whatever enlightenment he possesses. And in the longer run, whatever mistakes he may make in the process, it is only so far as such principles prevail that any society can advance toward the goals of living.

The alternatives continually present themselves and the citizen cannot evade the choice. He does not make the alternatives; he has only to choose between them. Nor can he take the line offered by one of my colleagues in this symposium and say: "There is something I approve and something I disapprove in both the alternatives presented; I shall accept the best compromise or balance between them." This principle is good and applicable when a question is up for discussion, when we are in a position to formulate a policy or to offer amendments to a program, when we are seeking to educate ourselves—or others—respecting the merits of a case. But in the political arena the choice is between alternative candidates, or sometimes between the acceptance or the rejection of a particular measure or policy. These are the alternatives out of which action results. These are the decisions that make history. These are the vital choices we have to make in the practical business of living. In these conjunctures we are not faced with opposing principles that are *equally* valid—for us. In the light of our judgment we have to choose between the better and the worse. The choice of the second best, when the best is not the other alternative, is the choice of the best. If we stand aside and refuse to choose, we are either indifferent to the issues or by our inertness are aiding the worse to win. In every important choice there is assuredly the need for balance, but it is the balance that weighs the gain against the loss.

VII

Conflict of Values:
Freedom and Justice

by FRANK H. KNIGHT
Professor of Social Sciences and Philosophy,
University of Chicago

This chapter will attempt to contribute to the discussion of goals in economic life by offering a brief survey of one aspect of the problem. The general theme is the relations between conflicting "goals." All problems of conduct arise out of conflicting alternatives, and social problems out of conflict between individual interests, or behavior, and interests of other persons, or of "society." Any discussion looking toward reconciliation and agreement obviously must run in terms of "values" in a sense distinct from mere individual, subjective desires, i.e., from values in the economic meaning.

Freedom, for the modern liberal mind, is to the individual both a desideratum in itself and a means or condition of achieving other ends; and—again in modern liberal thought—it is also a value in the more objective meaning, a thing essential to full human status, which men ought to want, and which in a sense they may properly have forced upon them. Manifestly, these relationships are complex and subtle, and their treatment calls for some orientation on the use of such terms as freedom, economic, and value, and also, as we shall see, truth and discussion.

The ultimate assumption here is that social values and political norms are real and discussible, hence objective, superindividual. It must provisionally be taken on faith that this chapter itself is intended as discussion. It is neither an effort to put over purely personal predilections by some psychological sales technique of persuasion nor a proclamation of absolute truth from a source superior to ordinary intellectual communication between truth-seeking human minds.

A main issue, as to the nature of virtue, and specifically political virtue, was raised early in the history of thought. Socrates-Plato took the intellectualist position (in one form) that virtue is knowledge, hence teachable; but we must expressly say discussible, since teaching is another ambiguous term. The poet Ovid and the Apostle Paul (the father of Christian theology) are the familiar references for the opposed view (or one such view) that it is a matter of will; that men know what is right but choose wrongly (Paul thought because of inherited moral corruption, original sin). The concept of discussion as opposed to "preaching," in particular, commits this essay to an intellectualist point of view, though, as already suggested, examination will soften the antithesis into a concept of intellectual morality or conscience, as opposed to a pure voluntarism.

The position here is that the differences between men which give rise to serious conflict root in differences of opinion about rights rather than mere clashes of individual "selfish" interest. Deliberate evil, ill will, "sin," is real, of course; but it is not the main source of social problems. Men in general are "sincere" in putting forward their claims as rights. Indeed, the more sincere they are, the more serious the conflict. It is grounds of belief, propensities to believe, and the opposition between intellectual and other grounds or causes that need both examination and improvement for the promotion of a better social order. "Prejudice" is a phenomenon which may serve to bridge over the crude antithesis between sin and error. Intellectualism is in a way "pagan," and runs counter to our older inherited ethical tradition, which is Pauline and came to be the official "Christian" view. Several aspects of this opposition between intellectualism and moralism will be examined, within the allowable compass, in an effort to clarify the ethical axioms or presuppositions which underlie modern liberalism and define its main problems.

The primary or central "value" in modern liberal thought is freedom, as the word "liberal" implies. This must be clearly related to truth, in the modern liberal conception of truth, as the objective in *free* inquiry, investigation, and discussion. But it is moral-political truth, truth "about" values in this field, that is in question. These are ethical values, and a point for special emphasis is the categorical difference between such truth or objectivity and that of (natural) science. Hence there are sweeping limitations to applying the conceptions of science to man and social-political problems, "factual" (positive) as well as "normative," though the two conceptions of truth are not unrelated.

The value conflict of particular concern is that between freedom and justice. Freedom is closely related to efficiency and progress as values. Justice, unhappily, is also variously defined, and in particular the relation between equality and merited inequality admits of question-begging yet plausible formulation. The term equality itself is highly ambiguous. And definition and careful use of words are a large part of the general issue, of intellectual morality, and one of the hardest and most repugnant tasks to the undisciplined mind.

FREEDOM AND ITS LIMITATIONS

The expression "goals in economic life" should itself call to mind the issue between individual desires and ends or norms for social policy, and also the central place of freedom and its limitations. Social action is called for because the "free" activities of individuals—directed by some mixture of personal desire and various ideals (or "prejudices")—lead to conflicts, of kinds recognized as undesirable. All will agree that literal individual liberty must be limited by law, by enforced law. We need not here debate against anarchism; nor, we should hope, against the view (though held for many centuries by official Christianity) that laws and governments "would be" superfluous if men were not sinful. A pure personal-relations ethic, of whatever form, can hardly furnish rules for such activities as international trade, or any dealings with people too numerous and remote to have reality for us as individuals, with the unborn, or for the future of cultural values; in fact, any rules for organizing work or play.

It is a familiar contention that law increases freedom rather than limits it. And this is undoubtedly true—up to a point. But the question is, "What point?" and here there are conflicting answers. One is that of extreme nineteenth-century individualism (Mill and Spencer) that men should be free as long as they do not injure others, or interfere with their equal freedom. Another, sharply opposed, answer would be that all inequality involves unfreedom, exploitation, and that social action is called for as long as this condition exists. Doubtless no one whose opinion is to be taken seriously will really advocate policy in accord with either of these extremes. The issue illustrates the danger of appeal to "principles" in any strict interpretation, overlooking other principles which are always to be found that would support an opposite conclusion. The question is always one of the best compromise, of enough and not too much; and that is the case with law and freedom.

In any accurate analysis, equality as a concept is in conflict with freedom, not a form of freedom. Much of what is said about freedom and exploitation, specifically by advocates of more state interference in economic relations, involves a confusion between freedom and power. It is true that without power freedom is empty; but nonetheless the two are distinct factors in voluntary action, and must be kept distinct or confusion results. This is not only a matter of correct analysis; the implications for policy are entirely different. And freedom is also relative to wants. It must be defined in that negative way which is commonly so repellent to economic reformers; freedom is the absence of interference in doing what one wishes to do and can or could do. It presupposes both desire and capacity. (The reformer is usually guilty also of the fallacy of thinking that the form in which "capacity" or ability is at issue is simply that of ownership of property; in fact, personal capacity is in essentially the same position.)

Freedom is thus the opposite of coercion and, in particular, is not the opposite of determinism. With the free-will "squabble" we are not at all concerned. Freedom in the metaphysical sense cannot be denied without asserting it; a mechanism does not contend that it is not one, and does not make mistakes or judgments based on prejudice, as must be the case with one side or the other in this dispute itself. The qualifications should go further, to include "moral error."

Coercion is "arbitrary" manipulation by one of another's terms or alternatives of choice—and usually we should say an "unjustified" interference. Metaphysically, one choice is as free as another, even that of "Your money or your life" presented by the brigand. Properly, or ideally, as already intimated, persuasion should be included under coercion, as should all effort at "influencing" others' beliefs, except through intellectual argument, which tries to enlighten, not even to convince, much less persuade. And to be truly free, even information and reasoning should be given at the behest of the other party, or at least with his full assent. Another problem is the extent to which free choice requires knowledge of the alternatives; certainly misinformation, or deliberate withholding of information from another to his disadvantage, is interference with freedom.

Freedom in society means association by mutual assent. It cannot mean freedom to coerce, in the overt sense, or to deceive. If the parties are competent to manage their affairs, free association implies mutual advantage. However, the liberal philosophy in no way implies that all human interests are mutual; it implies only a presumption that relations freely entered into benefit both parties, including promotion of whatever ideals or causes either chooses to promote. Whether the advantage will be "fairly" distributed is a harder question, answer to which requires examination of the whole mechanism of free association, from an ethical point of view. Liberal advocates of freedom have not been anarchists and have been clear as to the necessity of law to prevent force and fraud, where "conscience" and social pressure prove insufficient.

The really hard problem in defining freedom and coercion arises where authority—or anyone in a position to use power or chicane—deceives or "persuades" so completely ("makes him like it") that the victim follows the manipulator's will unknowingly, thinking he is acting from his own free choice. This is done to adults by "appeal to emotion" in contrast with "reason," especially when they form a crowd; but the victims are ordinarily too ready to be put in such a position and so "intoxicated." The extreme case, and the most common, is that of indoctrination from infancy, which will be noticed presently as the regular deliberate policy of churches, as custodians of what is "sacred" and must be protected from rational examination or questioning. And modern secular authoritarian "parties" act on the same principle. But it is also the process of "acculturation" in general, or social heredity, by which the ideas and attitudes of any society, good, bad, or indifferent, are implanted in the oncoming generation. Most of any adult person's mental furniture, even in a liberal society, is largely derived from this source; and it could not be otherwise, biological man and the physical world being what they are.

The difference between a liberal and a traditionalist-authoritarian society is that in the former what is established or ordained is always *open* to questioning and criticism, and subject to gradual change by agreement reached through free and honest discussion. This amounts to saying that no concrete detail of belief or of the culture pattern is "sacred," but only the principle and method of orderly change, with the limitations it implies. Similar considerations apply to the mature individual also; freedom must at best be quite limited; for the ultimate freedom is that of changing *oneself*, and can affect only a narrow "fringe" around what one already is.

Thus the real and crucial freedom is that of the mind, and the nature and scope of causal mechanics affecting the mind is the essential mystery. Even more formidable is the problem of the public mind, the formation of a group will and group decision through intercourse between individual minds. This process of "discussion," of free intercourse between free minds, continually comes into view as the meaning of democracy—in accord with Lord Bryce's familiar definition "government by discussion." Mental freedom is crucial; any dictator or despot must make the first point in his policy the control of communication and expression and the formation of a favorable public opinion and attitude, or at least the prevention of the opposite condition. The danger to freedom where it exists is the failure to maintain a fairly unified public mind, and so allowing the growth of interest groups, partisanship, factionalism, or some other form of class struggle, to a point where in desperation large numbers incline to accept any leadership that promises to create unity even by force, as the alternative to chaos.

Thus free society is ultimately defined by the subtle difference between free discussion (including education) and "thought control," the latter involving some combination of tradition and authority, both of which must be placed beyond effective criticism. The simple way to achieve this immunity is that they be covered with an aura of sanctity; but modern dictatorships have, rather surprisingly in the light of history, been able to impart this quality to an ethnic or class concept, with the self-selected and self-perpetuating party as its priesthood, without overt appeal to supernatural sanctions. At the same time, any ruling clique must keep its policies fairly representative of any common interests of its people which it cannot effectively direct or create.

The practical problem of social freedom is set by the fact that discussion must lead to agreement, but debate or the "arguing" that takes place when people act "freely" often tends to exacerbate opposition and degenerate into conflict. The nature of what passes for discussion, and its relation to "true" discussion, are undoubtedly the central problem of democracy as free society; but "discussion of discussion" is a task too formidable to be undertaken at any length here.

The necessity of agreement seems to imply that discussion must aim at "truth"—political discussion, at truth with respect to "right," and specifically as to what constitutes "improvement" in a given institutional complex. (We have already observed that ethics in the sense of personal "goodness" in relations with other persons is only indirectly to the point.) Now the meaning of truth, moral-political truth, about norms for judging cultures or civilizations, is a question which here can only be called to attention. A vital aspect of this question is the conflict between truth and other values. Freedom, in our context, must mean primarily the free pursuit of truth, in a cooperative quest, implying complete toleration of honest and reasonably competent disagreement, i.e., exclusion of all dogmatism.

But free intercourse must have a place for much else. Truth, objective accuracy, often does not harmonize with esthetic quality of expression; and figurative language, wit and humor, romantic fiction, finally ironical expressions which mean the opposite of what they literally say, all have their place in human intercourse. Spontaneity, defiance of rules and authorities, and in general sport and "fun" are also qualities of the good social life, which commonly get left out in formal philosophical treatment of the problems—especially when conducted under the auspices of our Hebraic-Puritanical religious tradition. Further, what is said and the manner of saying it must take account of various "effects," i.e., of ethical considerations, as well as effectiveness in a pedagogical sense.

The Long Struggle of Freedom versus Authority

Before turning to the specific theme of the conflict of freedom with other values, and principally with justice, in the economic aspect of social life, the general picture of free society may be pointed up by the use of contrast. The practically perfect contrast lies at hand in the medieval society out of which our liberal culture evolved in the historically short period of a few centuries. Some delineation of this contrast, a virtual antithesis, is appropriate not only for exposition but for the value of a historical approach to the study of any culture situation.

If it is possible to learn from history at all, as we must surely hope is the case, it is a sobering fact that society based on individual liberty and self-government is unique and recent, and still locally restricted; indeed, it has lost ground heavily in the past generation instead of rapidly conquering the world as was expected only a short time before. Other cultures have rested on tradition and authority—the former perhaps predominating in "primitive" groups, the latter in the "civilized," and rather more so as civilization has advanced and the units have increased in size to "empires." Ancient city-states, even Athens, are hardly examples to the contrary, as they were not at all democratic in our sense, had the size of rather small towns, and usually were quite short-lived before being absorbed in some kingdom or empire (even if a city-state became capital of the latter, as was Rome for some centuries).

But very nearly the limiting case, as the antithesis to liberalism (i.e., as a society based on tradition and authority, sanctioned by religion, rooted in a dogmatic and intolerant religion and hence in spiritual despotism), is found in Western Europe in what we now call the Middle Ages. Out of this system came the only liberal culture known to history. It came through the most profound and sweeping spiritual revolution known, a short series of changes involving a sweeping "inversion of values." The heart of it, to be expected in view of what we have said above, was a revolution in the conception of truth and of the way in which truth is to be found and known.

It will be said that one should not use the expression "medieval culture," or "system." No doubt one ought to write at least a thick tome, with dozens of chapters treating of different times, places, and aspects of medieval life; and from a tome on up, without limit. And similarly for the periods of change in which medieval gave place to modern, particularly the two periods most commonly referred to, the Renascence (and Reformation) and the Enlightenment. Yet, for the purpose in view here, which is not to write history, it will be useful and need not be misleading to sketch a few of the great contrasts and changes, by way of clarifying our present situation and problems.

It is proverbial that history knows no beginnings, and the disintegration of any notable culture complex is usually visibly under way—at least to hindsight—before it has reached its full development. So it seems to be with the liberal economy, and so it was with medievalism. The classical civilization, specifically the Western Roman Empire which is our concern, "declined and fell," in what Gibbon's familiar words call a "triumph of barbarism and religion." It was anything but democratic; but it did practice a high degree of religious and even philosophical and scientific toleration. (The requirements of the state religion were really a gesture symbolic of political loyalty.)

The system which replaced it was equally authoritarian, but with a notable difference. Based on dogmatism ("orthodoxy"), compulsory acceptance of a creed interpreted by a hierarchy, government was ecclesiastical more than political and the Church as much a political as a religious institution. That all this was completely alien to the thinking of Jesus or his immediate followers, according to records accepted as sacred truth by the Church itself, does not change the facts. Much was, indeed, preserved from original Christianity, established by the Apostles, especially Paul. It was a mystery cult, one of several highly similar, competing for recognition at the time. The essential thing was "salvation," by initiation; but Christianity put overwhelming emphasis on "believing." What was to be believed became more and more elaborately formulated, but always consisted of theological propositions having little if any relation to conduct, and presently amounted simply to accepting the absolute authority of "The Church." Naturally enough, and in common with the "pagan" mystery cults (and post-Socratic philosophies), Christianity preached a rather ascetic personal morality; but the practice depended on one's position in society, in the Church itself on a par with other careers (except for some enforcement of celibacy).

What is essential in the medieval system is salvation by believing. (Originally, "faith" should in the present world remove mountains and provide for the ordinary wants of life, specifically food and raiment; and anyone who sacrificed anything for the Gospel's sake should receive a hundredfold in this life and in addition eternal life beyond.) This made believing a specific formula a moral duty and also a thing to be brought about in any possible way. Particularly sanctioned and regularly employed were indoctrination and ritualization, from birth, designed to prevent doctrine from ever being questioned by impious and presumptuous intellect. Ordinarily, this "worked"; in the exceptional case of obdurate adults, recourse was had to torture and execution by torture.

It must be understood that all this was logically inevitable, given the basic claims of the Church to a divine authorization and commission to save men's souls through formal acceptance of a creed and performance of certain ritual. It followed, too, that the social ideal was "static" and the social order one of status, of classes, to which the term "caste" is not inapplicable. The duty of man was to work out his lot in the station to which he was divinely called by birth; to try to "get ahead" was sinful—except in the Church; and, interestingly enough, politics and war were more honorable ways than trade or other productive activities. (Some accommodation to reality was made by the dualistic ethic, monastic asceticism as the ideal, by a system of "precepts" alongside that of the "counsels.")

From far back in the Middle Ages many "ferments," streams of change, historical causes, were at work undermining this order, even before it was fully established, as we have noted. Serfdom, which had displaced slavery after the fall of Rome, itself disappeared through the influence of a resurgent, somewhat strangely "free," town life. Contact with the more civilized East (Byzantine and Moslem, including North Africa and Spain) worked directly and indirectly to arouse curiosity and stimulate ambition. Geography itself was a new interest, compared with classical antiquity. Numerous technical innovations appeared, partly imported from the East by way of Islam. The "Arabian" mathematics (from India) is doubtless most important in the long run, as the basis at once of modern science, technology, and business. The most immediately potent was the lens, specifically the interesting case of Galileo's discovery of satellites of Jupiter. The Church had become committed to quite primitive ideas of cosmology—in fact two different systems, from Genesis and from Aristotle (who was in some respects a reactionary in Greek science). A small impulse toward objective inquiry or critical scrutiny must demolish this structure and undermine the claim to eternal and immutable divinely revealed truth in other areas. Increasingly, too, the magnates of the Church adopted ways of living in sharp contrast with the example or teachings of the founders of their religion; and, as the records became accessible to a wider public, revolts and "heresies" appeared (even before the advent of paper and printing) in a series of increasing scope and determination, until—under changed conditions —the "Reformation" was able to survive.

The main change in "conditions" was the concentration of feudal power in the hands of monarchs, in a rivalry of power with each other, and with the Church as a power, and in a tacit alliance with the money power of trade and finance and developing industry. At first, "Protestantism" stood in an uncertain degree for religious individualism. But the result of the whole movement, after more than a century of "religious" wars (with political and economic motives more and more involved), was less an advance toward liberalism than simply the replacement of the unitary ecclesiastical absolutism with a number of political ones, monarchies by divine right, which were quite as sweeping in their claims. Religion itself was in effect "nationalized," even in Catholic Spain and France, as well as in the northern lands which became Protestant. However, the fact of change tended to destroy the sanctity of the established; and fragmentation made way for further change.

In particular, as the rivalries took a military form, war stimulated adoption and growth of new technology and science. The money power, the "bourgeoisie," and also the newer intelligentsia, more or less aspired to enter the old aristocracies, but tended rather to become a new pseudo-class, the "third estate." They could not be a real class, with ranks sufficiently closed to new upcomers, and the majority were generally opposed to monopoly and genuinely in favor, on the whole, of freedom of opportunity. Both trade and industry and science seem to be bound up with freedom and the spirit of freedom. At the bottom of it all was a general psychological shift in attitudes, one of those mysterious groundswells of historical change characteristic in particular of Europe and Western Europe. Men ceased to believe in theology and lost interest in it; and if not in Salvation itself, at least in the rituals through which it had been promised and sought. They swung toward concern for values of the present world, and for solving its problems as the most hopeful approach to those of any life that may lie beyond.

We habitually think of two great revolutionary changes, or stages in the transformation, the Renascence and the Enlightenment. In fact, a "break" perhaps as important had occurred in the thirteenth century, with the replacement of a Neo-Platonic Platonism by Aristotle as the official philosophy of the Church. The Renascence spirit, developing in the next three centuries or so, was not individualistic in the modern or democratic sense. It may be regarded as a Nietzschean inversion of values (*Umwertung*), i.e., from the exaltation of weakness (more in theory than in practice as to both ecclesiastical and temporal magnates) to the open exaltation of power. Liberalism, the spirit of freedom for all, is a product rather of the Enlightenment (which flowered in the eighteenth century, after the English Revolutions and John Locke). Its root may be found in a new faith, faith in man, in reason and human reasonableness and generosity—the antithesis of the doctrine of Original Sin. (The period is also called the Age of Reason, but was about as conspicuously one of feeling, of humane sentiment.)

In a deeper view, the cultural revolution consisted, as we have said, in a completely changed conception of truth and the way to knowledge. Dogma, with belief a moral attitude, engendered by early conditioning and supported by ruthless coercion, and with questioning a mortal sin, was replaced by the skeptical approach, questioning as a virtue, and truth to be reached by testing and submission to the final test of open discussion. In other words, truth came to be an intellectual category instead of a moral-religious one.

The new attitude may be said to have come from the field of science and technology, with trade, followed by industry, an influence second in order. The basic freedom, that of the mind, came as a by-product of terrible wars over religion, but not over toleration, which the main protagonists did not want and in fact abhorred. The real touchstone of liberalism is in the field of education—the "indoctrination" of the young to the attitude of questioning and testing as the basis of knowing the truth, and not to unquestioning loyalty to particular dogmas. This revolution in ideals came gradually and in part by a roundabout way. That is, education was progressively secularized, and at the same time "religion" was reinterpreted to harmonize first with the indisputable findings of science and then, gradually and more or less, with open critical discussion of moral and political issues.

Involved in the two movements, toward freedom of the mind and freedom in economic life, was the third, toward political democracy or responsible government through representative institutions, the last to be achieved. The drive for democratization was at first negative. It had the aim of preventing governments from doing things opposed or not wanted, rather than their use to achieve positive ends. The particular motive was control of the public purse—by the main taxpayers, naturally enough. Gradual extension of the suffrage to working people and finally to women is a matter of nineteenth- and twentieth-century history, along with the further liberalization (and some commercialization) of the intellectual life (education, the status of churches) and various changes in attitude toward trade and production.

The growth of freedom as "Individualism" in turn, characteristically, went to an extreme, and provoked a reaction which, characteristically again, can be traced in some respects before the movement itself reached its climax in other respects. Industrialization led to (or was accompanied by) "abuses," which were felt to be intolerable and, specifically in England, its main original home, prompted such action as "factory legislation," national assumption of responsibility for poor relief, and other social reforms. Governments also came to be loaded with more and more positive functions, along with policing and defense. Among these, early felt as requisite to effective individual freedom itself, was provision at public expense of at least elementary education, as well as sanitary and health measures, both positive and negative.

This new reaction had made considerable headway in advance of the classical doctrinaire formulation of the extreme principle of individual liberty by Mill and Spencer. Central to the new movement was dissatisfaction with the results of reliance on the free market for the organization of economic life, and specifically the "cry for justice" against the extremes of wealth and poverty which at least continued to prevail, and for which the new conditions took the blame. (Accusation of personal insecurity and economic instability would have been more to the point.) Meanwhile, labor unions were growing apace, and also the socialist movement; the *Communist Manifesto,* as will be recalled, appeared in 1848, contemporary with Mill's *Political Economy* and eleven years prior to his *Essay on Liberty;* and it was another decade or two before Spencer attracted attention.

The drive for economic reform through the agency of the state naturally had repercussions in the field of government itself, and even in that of education, the intellectual life, and religion. The socialist movement, at first politically democratic, soon gave birth to an offshoot of growing strength—later distinguished as communism—advocating an interim "dictatorship of the proletariat," represented by the Communist parties. This was to re-educate men for the new noncompetitive, purely scientific, classless, and stateless social order, essentially anarchism. Communism swept to power in Russia and later in other lands. In reaction against it, the nationalistic stateisms of fascism and national socialism took rise and won control in Italy and Germany, followed by imitations in Spain and Portugal. Also, the medieval Church itself has been more or less reactivated, in opposition to liberalism as well as, more overtly, to the menace of a totalitarianism not under its own control. Not being sponsored by a foreign power which is aggressive in the military sense, it works through political action; it seeks especially control of education and its use for creedal indoctrination. The forms of political and of economic organization it would establish if in power are left too vague to admit of effective criticism, especially within brief compass. And indeed, the specific question is of minor importance apart from that of what *any* dictatorship would probably do.

Even in a democracy men in power do mainly what they hope will keep them in power—under prevailing rules and the machinery of responsibility to the electorate, nominally the majority. A dictatorship would differ in not being subject to any rules, since it would make its own, at will; and different metaphysical pretensions (theism versus materialism) would certainly make no substantial difference. Nor, of course, would specific promises given in advance as to policies to be pursued or results produced. An authoritarian government based on a "blank-check" commission from God to bind and loose, lock and unlock at will, could hardly be expected to regard or consult the wishes of the people beyond necessity or more than would one professing any other justification for its position of power.

RISE OF THE ENTERPRISE ECONOMY

We come to the last and main part of our inquiry, a brief survey of the situation in the field of economic activity and its organization, with respect to the conflict between freedom (and associated values of efficiency and progress) and other norms, especially justice. The task calls for a survey (within the allowable compass) of the nature of the enterprise economy, from the standpoint of this conflict, and of what would be involved, from the same point of view, in the political action that is agitated for by way of remedying real or supposed evils.

The main general statement to be made about the enterprise economy is that, in the theoretically ideal form described by pure economics, it is the embodiment of complete freedom. In the perfect market, no one has any arbitrary power over anyone else, since every trader faces a number of substantially equal trading offers. Economic freedom must be defined by all that has been said earlier about freedom in general, especially that freedom in society means association by mutual assent. This implies freedom to choose those associations which are offered or accepted on the most attractive terms—what is called "competition," unfortunately, since no rivalry is implied. Freedom to emulate or surpass others holds the same position in the market as in other associative conduct. And freedom, of course, includes the alternative not to associate but to "go it alone."

Economic association is that which is motivated by the desire to use means more "economically" to achieve more fully whatever ends are in view. These may be satisfaction of "material wants" or the pursuit of "ideals," high or low. It is requisite only that they are freely chosen by the individual or any group actually functioning as a unit. (The family is the minimum real unit in social life, and "familism" would be a more accurate designation for what is called individualism; and there are other organized units of all degrees of importance.) Such cooperation, carried out on a substantial scale, takes the form of exchange or buying and selling, in markets, of goods and services produced with this intent. Production for sale, for "money" to be used in purchasing other things, is in effect merely indirect production of the things finally bought. It is done when, and to the extent that, it is thought to yield a larger or more desirable result than direct production or self-sufficient economic life. That is, the individual member of a market economy gains an almost incalculable increase of efficiency through specialization (of machinery, etc., as well as personal activities); he gets a manifold greater yield of his resources, without any constraint on the purposes or ends for which he chooses to use them.

In order to understand the essential nature of the modern enterprise economy and the ethical and political problems which it presents, one must bear in mind that specialization is now carried to an extreme degree, involving more than one "stage." To picture the current situation, it is useful to think again of its development, under the form of history, much simplified as usual, in comparison with what actually happened. But it is not misleading to say that an early form of specialization involved only the creation of a distinct product by each individual or family unit. These would be exchanged or sold in the market and the proceeds used to buy the great variety of products the individuals required for their consumption. That is, we picture first and in idealized form a "handicraft" economy. What is notable is the negative fact that people get their money income as the sale price of goods produced, so that there is no such thing as the forms of income familiar today—wages, rent, interest, and profit. Nor is anyone even superficially in the position of "working for" anyone else, unless it is the consumers of his special physical output.

All this is changed and the familiar relationships arise when specialization is carried a step further, when each person (as an individual worker or through the productive wealth he owns) performs particular detailed operations in the making of some product, which may involve an indefinitely large number of such contributions. This consequence of modern technology carries with it the organization of production in large and highly complex and articulated units, employing perhaps hundreds or thousands of minutely specialized workers, and tools and machines, requiring close coordination. It presents a striking contrast with the individual worker in his shop, aided perhaps by members of his family and one or more "apprentices."

It works out that for the most part the way to get such a productive unit to function effectively is to have the organization as a unit, the "enterprise," hire the personal and property services required in its operations and pay for them with money. Thus arise wages as payment for the labor, and rent and interest as payment for the use of property. (Whether it will be rent or interest depends on whether the property is leased from owners or bought with borowed money; the difference is important but more or less a matter of detail too intricate to describe briefly and not essential for the present argument.)

But the arrangement involves another specialization, giving rise to "profit," which is very important and not generally well understood. For it turns out to be expedient also to have the bulk of those who work in an enterprise (or furnish the use of various property items) not to be responsible participants in the management of its affairs, but simply to sell their services (personal or property) for an agreed compensation and leave the control to one person or a limited group. The "members"—roughly speaking, the holders of common stock—formally "own" the enterprise, but may own any fraction of the assets used in it, or none, or their interest may be a net liability. They are not paid a remuneration stipulated in advance but take their chances on something being left over after such agreed compensation is paid to the others. This "residuum" is, of course, "profit," or loss, if negative, as things may work out. Thus the owners combine the functions of making the responsible decisions as to production and bearing the "risk," which is connected with the "uncertainty" of the return, in advance of final realization on product and on assets.

What is important for our argument is that this organization involves no restriction on freedom, but results entirely from the free choices of the parties concerned. Anyone who will and can may hire whatever services are required, on terms satisfactory to the parties concerned, and conduct any industry or business which seems to him to promise more remuneration than he would get by himself hiring out to someone else; or he may choose to do the latter, whichever promises more or has the greater appeal, depending on his faith in his powers and his taste for adventure or security. Nor is there anything to prevent the entire group from organizing democratically as a "producers' cooperative" and managing the affairs of the concern in any way they like—say, by town-meeting methods or hiring agents for a salary. Or again, the "workers" alone could set up the enterprise and hire the capital and the management.

The role of the enterprise owner or "entrepreneur" (now usually a corporation, in form a cooperative, under representative government), who formally pays the other participants and himself receives a residual income (profit or loss), is merely a matter of efficiency and convenience. In the large, it makes an uncertain difference in the distribution of the product, since there is no evidence that profit is on the whole a positive share (the losses quite likely equal or exceed the gains, if all the costs are counted). But the arrangement makes an enormous difference in men's ideas, giving rise as it does to the groundless belief that they are working to enable a "capitalist" to make a "profit," and not for themselves, as they are in fact. Each merely works for himself more efficiently by producing under specialized direction products to be consumed by others, which are converted by exchange into the things he himself wants. In the individual case, the effect of the entrepreneur's intervention on the distribution of income may be great, since the concentration of risk gives rise to returns either large or small, zero or negative. The element similar to gambling that is involved in the conduct of production is greatly intensified for the entrepreneur and correspondingly reduced for those who supply the labor and property he employs.

Apart from this fact, or with the really minor qualification that it introduces, the enterprise economy has in theory the result previously indicated: it enables each participant to employ his resources in the way in which they have the largest possible yield, and gives him what they do yield as his share in the total. That is, each gets the maximum fruits of his activity, subject to the condition that all exchanges are free, equal values being given and received by each party. Anyone's income may be more or less than his economic product only by the amount of any gifts received or made, voluntarily or otherwise. Any two or more persons are always free to cooperate on any terms other than the market values of their respective services, on which they may agree, on ethical grounds, or for any other reason; but such divergences amount precisely to gifts.

It is a proposition of elementary economics that ideal market competition will force entrepreneurs to pay every productive agent employed what his cooperation adds to the total, the difference between what it can be with him and what it could be without him. This is his own product in the only meaning the word can have where persons or their resources act jointly. As to justice, it embodies the "natural" relation, that acts are compensated by their consequences, or "what a man soweth that shall he also reap." That is what anyone would get working alone; his product is merely multiplied by the vastly greater efficiency of organized effort. It is also what any group or society as a whole must get. It exemplifies freedom, correctly defined, in the sense in which a Robinson Crusoe is free. Possibly we should qualify—insofar as freedom is supposed to mean "rational" freedom. Modern society, with large-scale organization, impersonal relations, and interdependence of specialists, does set serious limits to the possibility of knowing the alternatives between which one chooses; but we must choose between "business" and some other organization, presumably "politics." As in the case of some other admitted evils, the chance of improvement from such a change is the practical question.

FREEDOM VERSUS JUSTICE IN ECONOMIC ORGANIZATION

The enterprise economy is the organization in which freedom is carried to the possible limit—remembering those functions of the state which have never been in dispute by serious advocates of freedom, or "laissez faire," such as Adam Smith; and remembering also the freedom of any and all to give and receive and to cooperate in any other way on which they can freely agree (including giving and receiving counsel or buying and selling it). It follows that its weaknesses are those of freedom, as a principle of social life. They center in the accusation of injustice.

In a brief survey, these issues may be considered under two heads. The economic system may be criticized because it does not "work" in accord with the pure theory of the economists, or because it does.

1. Mechanical Weaknesses of the Enterprise Systems

What needs to be said under the first head can be indicated, for present purposes, in a few sentences. The most important observation is that this line of criticism is grossly exaggerated in the popular mind and in general discussion, to the neglect of the other, and in fact, while it presents hard practical problems, it does not raise serious intellectual issues. For the most extreme advocates of freedom have never contended or imagined that the theoretical picture of "perfect competition" is descriptively accurate in detail. And they have not opposed, in principle or in practice, political measures effectively designed to make the reality conform more closely to the theory, to "make competition work." At present, at least, there is no serious opposition to quite sweeping measures going farther, to supplement and even counteract the workings of the market where there are grounds for believing that this is needful and practicable. Examples are, first of all, provision of education and many other "amenities," as well as relief of destitution and distress, at the public expense; that is, out of taxation levied in accord with some accepted measure of ability to bear the burden. And this principle is extended to levies expressly imposed to mitigate the twin evils of excessive wealth and extreme poverty. There is disagreement and opposition only as to the details of such measures and how far it is wise or just to carry them.

There are admitted "mechanical" weaknesses more or less inherent in the free economy. The two obvious cases are monopoly and the tendency to more or less regular or cyclical oscillations, boom and depression. The latter cause widespread unemployment and distress, particularly among the poor, who are primarily wage earners or independent farmers.

As to monopoly, it is hardly needful to point out that the evil has always been recognized both by economists and by most businessmen; and measures effectively promising to reduce the evil, as far as practicable without creating worse ones, have been approved. The public has most exaggerated ideas of the scope of monopoly as really bad and remediable, and talk of "abolishing" it is merely ignorant or irresponsible. There is no clear line between legitimate and necessary profit and the monopoly gain that presents a problem for action. Every doctor or artist of repute has a monopoly, and monopolies are deliberately granted by law to encourage invention and other creative activities. And, finally, most monopolies work in the same way as "patents," etc., and are temporary and largely balanced by losses. Moreover, by far the worst monopolistic restrictions are those organized by wage earners and farmers with the connivance or direct aid of government and with public approval. With monopoly, also, it is not principles but only matters of degree and the details of measures that are seriously in dispute.

A far more serious problem, in reality, is that of the "business cycle." It is too large and complex to permit going into in detail here. The main fact is that no important sector of society—and particularly of "business"—makes anything out of depressions. Hence, again, all that is or can be at issue is the nature and extent of remedial action that will be more beneficial than harmful.

We may add two observations: first, that the difficulty centers in monetary policy, and is extremely hard to deal with—probably impossible to correct adequately—without destroying the essential freedoms of economic life, for the ordinary citizen as well as for business itself; and second, the measures on which economists are in fair agreement as beneficial arouse no popular enthusiasm, but rather encounter popular support for the special interests that oppose them. The essence of the matter is inflation, and the public seems to think that all selling prices should constantly go up; and since the selling price of one is the buying price of another, the obvious result is public pressure for inflation of all prices, or at least opposition to any effective contrary measures. Somewhat the same can be said of monopoly; most people are directly or indirectly interested in some monopoly, which they regard as in the interest of "justice," and oppose restrictive measures—notably the labor unions and farm organizations already mentioned.

2. *Conflicting Moral and Social Ideals*

The really serious "evils" resulting from economic freedom are those which fall under the second head. Under theoretically perfect free markets alone, natural forces make for injustice between individuals, as defined by the moral standards of individualistic liberalism itself. The sole function, and in that sense the objective, of free economic association is to increase the effectiveness of the use of means, through cooperation, specialization, and organization. The meaning of freedom, to repeat, is open opportunity to do what one will and can—completely respecting the equal freedom of others—hence cooperation on the terms most satisfactory to both or all of the parties directly concerned in the individual case. Freedom is relative to wants and to the means at the command of individuals or other free units. If the wants are "bad," or if means are wrongly distributed, the results must be bad accordingly. Individual liberty cannot in the nature of the case do much to correct such evils.

The main source of conflict and of dissatisfaction is the way in which income is distributed. The distribution of income, insofar as effective competition prevails, simply reflects the distribution of economic "means" (always treating personal capacities on a par with "property"—contrary to a prejudice which we cannot discuss here). The distribution in preindustrial societies is more unfavorable to labor than in our own, and the division of income and relative standards of living are more unequal; reformers ignore such facts, but the problems of other societies are not at issue here. The point to be made is simply that (qualified by mechanical difficulties also not really at issue) the enterprise economy enables given individuals, with their various economic resources whatever they may be, to cooperate to their mutual advantage, as far as their interests actually are mutual in the judgment of the parties themselves; and, equally important, enables them to do it without arguing. By the same token, this form of organization will not solve any other problems. Specifically, it will not make people want what they ought to want and will not redistribute productive capacity to accord better with the ideal of equality, or "just" inequality, or any other ideal.

The market system remunerates its members on the basis of "productive contribution," which depends on the economic value of the productive services furnished. This value is determined by the free choices of purchasers of the product, whose tastes are also "given" and whose purchasing power is a matter of *their* incomes, determined in the same way. This is to be qualified for a large element of "luck," particularly in the case of the profit incomes of entrepreneurs. What to do about luck is one of the major problems of justice; but, again, freedom must mean freedom to take chances, which also someone has to do if society is to be progressive. The free economy not only will not work toward equality (apart from voluntary charity) but actually works in the contrary direction. Goods have to be produced before they can be distributed; and an even more neglected fact is that the means of production also have to be produced before the goods can be—again not excepting either personal capacities or, in the long view, what are called "natural" resources.

But the possession of economic capacity by an individual is determined largely by the position in society into which he is born— or by biological heredity—and only to a limited degree by his own efforts, or factors subject to his control. And the fact that productive capacity is itself produced—that of "workers" as well as of owned nonhuman agents—obviously means that those who at any time possess more of it are in a better position to add to what they already have. And social institutions, particularly inheritance through the private family, tend to carry this tendency to cumulative growth of inequality forward through the generations (and to aggravate it insofar as the well-to-do divide the inheritance among fewer heirs than do the poor). We have said, it is true, that inequality does not seem to have actually increased under industrialism; if not (the evidence is vague), it is because the "tendency" has been roughly offset by such remedial social measures as we have already suggested. It may be that the principle is in some way sociologically self-limiting at some point; if so, the point represents a degree of inequality and extremes of wealth and poverty which the liberal sense of justice will hardly accept.

We here confront an evident and extreme conflict of rights rooted in incompatible ideas of justice itself. The "right" to the fruits of one's own acts logically includes the right to accumulate and to pass accumulated fruits on to one's heirs, natural or of one's own choice. But every person also has a "right" to an equal or fair start in life—and beyond that has some claim to a decent human scale of living, regardless of ability to make a sufficient productive contribution to provide it. In fact, there can be no question that the strong (and/or fortunate) must help to bear the burdens of the weak (and/or unlucky).

This is not only moral idealism; society could not otherwise survive. It is most obvious in case of the completely helpless, or not gainful, who as individuals and at any given time include a substantial majority of the population—children, the aged, many of the women, and all who lack usable or salable productive capacity for any reason (lack "enough to live on"). But helplessness is a matter of degree; and if we reject the principle in the extreme case, we seriously weaken it in general. Even in the abstract, remuneration in accord with capacity furnished is ethically dubious, except as the possession and use of the capacity are connected with previous conscientious effort by the same person, or have some adequate moral ground. However, if we are to reason about ethics in such connections at all, it may seem better to accept the unalterable facts of life, and concede that legitimate possession of productive capacity confers some rights, and try to define these and the corresponding obligations rather than set up ideals which merely defy reality. As to the moral factor in productivity, the mode of acquiring "capacity" just referred to, there is no difference in principle between internal or personal powers of body or mind—"labor power"—and external possessions or what is "property" in modern law.

The final root of the issue here is that any literal individualism is untenable, absurd, and monstrous. Society is not in the main made up of responsible individuals at all—still less equally responsible. The individuals who function in society have been chiefly the product of society, only in small part their own creation. And this also gives pause to proposals to have society drastically remade —by its members living at a particular date in history. What we know, have, are, and "can" are mostly the creations of antecedent individuals and of culture processes not fully analyzable into individual acts or, especially, responsible acts. We are all helpless in our first years—in fact are not, properly speaking, "members" of society or any action group, even the family; and this is usually so again at the end of life, and a fair amount of the time even in our "prime." And many "human beings" are never in any other state.

From a historical (backward-looking) point of view or that of policy, looking forward, it would be about as near the truth to say that the individual is a myth, that we are but evanescent bearers of a culture, as to say that society is an organization of individuals.

But the freedom principle takes individuals as given, particularly in the economic view, as regards their wants and income-earning capacities; and these factors underlie and condition the principle of remuneration by productive contribution, giving it content. As a possible basis of distribution it is subject to the sweeping limitations mentioned above (the majority of individuals are not "productive"—the family is the minimum effective unit in the long view), and in ethical terms is of much more limited validity.

3. *Conflicting Values Must Be Compromised*

Freedom is the basic value of liberal society, and our most precious possession. We have won it in war and suffering, and fought repeatedly to preserve it, and will fight again, if need be. But it has limitations, as adamantine as the value itself, both in the unalterable conditions of life and still further in other and conflicting moral values, which may be summed up in the vague term "justice." Consequently, he is no real friend of freedom who attempts to treat it as an absolute principle or a cure-all for moral and social maladies and discontents. One of the most ominous symptoms in present-day life is this sort of antagonism between those who clamor for freedom and those who clamor for justice. It is at the bottom of the "iron curtain" situation, cutting off discussion between liberalism and communism. For the Communist position is logical; if justice is to be an absolute, some absolute authority must be set up for its definition and enforcement. (The "Catholic" position is the same on this, the essential issue.) In our liberal culture itself, too, freedom versus justice is the issue between radical reformers and those now called conservatives, for justice calls for political action. But it is alike indefensible to set up either freedom or justice as an absolute principle; so taken, the one means anarchy, the other despotism.

The question of policy that confronts us is on which side the greater danger lies. The climate of opinion is now in another reaction, away from liberty, in the direction of centralized political authority, and again threatens to go too far. The questions raised are vast, and we can only list a few "high points."

Our position is that the choice between the open-market economy and governmental interference is not one of either-or but of how far, and in what ways. If "the economist" inclines to stress the dangers of political action, it is not because he is on the "side" of business or property, in favor of economic as against political power, *per se*. Rather, he sees so many ways in which political measures already adopted are demonstrably wrong. The main causes for alarm are in the political field. The history of the West is a clear warning of the tendency of reactions from one extreme to go to the opposite one, until there is another turn, or a breakdown. Political power is inherently monopolistic, and otherwise subject to the same evils, especially the tendency to concentration, as economic power; and often to a worse degree, even if formal democracy on a national scale is preserved. Rule by the majority at best means power to tax and to repress and exploit in the hands of whatever political party can carry a national election. It cannot safely be carried very far. A government that undertakes to conduct or to control in any detail the economic life of a modern industrial nation will be virtually compelled to stabilize its authority, i.e., to suppress opposition. Thus the result of any effort to secure an impossible justice will be to sacrifice both freedom and justice by establishing a despotism.

Finally, there is no formula, or principle that can be stated in words, that will indicate definitely how far and how to compromise between conflicting principles; it is inherently a matter of judgment. Formulation should be carried as far as possible, the best way being, undoubtedly, that of case law. But any law will require interpretation in the light of the moral sense of the community. It is the great task of education to train judgment, the ability and the will, to discriminate objectively. The first requisite is tolerance; liberalism might be defined as the antithesis of dogmatism. Yet tolerance has its limits, especially in that the discussion attitude must be mutual. But even where disagreement is rooted in honest and competent opinions, there comes a point where appeal to force is inevitable and right. Then one must fight; and this implies an obligation to be strong.

VIII

Is a Consistent Governmental Economic Policy Possible?

by CLARK C. BLOOM
Associate Professor of Economics, State University of Iowa

In many countries today citizens are being urged to have their governments pursue specific, logically consistent patterns of economic action for the attainment of goals upon which it is implied there is adequate agreement. In many other countries—constituted differently, politically—citizens are being told of government action that is alleged to be carefully calculated to attain ends of the very highest order. In either case the usual implication is that it is obviously possible to know what the desirable end (or goal) is, that there is a single means or pattern of measures best adapted for its attainment, and that all important segments of the population are certain therefore to support the indicated governmental activity.

It is the task of this brief chapter to show the unreality of this simple view. The underlying thesis is that any government will respond simultaneously to various groups urging varying ends upon it, that it will employ many means for the attainment of its multiple goals, and that it will at no time fully satisfy any important group. This thesis will then be illustrated briefly with reference to our contemporary United States economy.

GOVERNMENT ACTION LIMITED BY SOCIAL PRESSURE

Government action must properly be viewed as group, or social action. The political state is formed around the central core of a

231

belief that some organization is necessary if all residents of a given geographic area are to have some common goals realized. This means that governmental policy must be made, and its results administered, within the permissive limits established by the prevailing mores of the community over which it exercises authority. The political state is merely part of an integrated social structure with which it must essentially be in harmony.

The preceding generalization is applicable to even the most dictatorial and autocratic of governments. Even an absolute dictator must figuratively put his ear to the ground to ascertain public opinion and must then either act within the limits the public will tolerate or take action to change that opinion through the use of the various propaganda devices that are open to him. An action taken contrary to strongly held opinions of the citizenry would certainly subject the dictator to penalties. He could expect noncooperation, general lethargy, excessive police or supervisory costs, or—in extreme cases —even open revolt. After all, while the most autocratic of rulers can afford to liquidate relatively small and uninfluential minority groups, he cannot liquidate his whole population. He may bend to the pressures of their opinion or he may propagandize and cajole them to the acceptance of his views—but always he must act within the limits of their toleration.

If political states dominated by dictators must find their sovereignty limited by the views held by their citizens, how much more likely it is that states governed by freely elected executive and legislative officials should be so bound. Here the government's activities can be more quickly and easily influenced, inhibited, modified, or completely changed than is likely under alternative governmental forms. As a matter of fact, the essence of democratic government is the ability of citizens to make their common goals, if any, the goals of the political state, or to secure some action recognizing the goals of various groups. It further implies the ability of individual citizens and groups to make the means they desire for the attainment of their goals the means to be employed by the state.

ENDS AND MEANS

Goals of Government Activity

If the preceding introductory statements are valid, the goals of the political state, at least as they are presented to and are perceived by the citizenry, must be those which are within tolerable limits. There remain, however, two fundamental questions. First, is there a single, well-defined goal for governmental action? Second—and this anticipates the probable answer to the first question—if there are several goals, are they likely to be consistent with one another? Or does the full—or perfect—attainment of one goal likely set limits on the attainability of others?

Goals for any social group—and particularly for the state—are likely to be many and varied. This results fundamentally from the fact that individuals seldom have a single goal—for themselves, their families, or their state—to the exclusion of all others, and from the fact that different social groupings within the confines of a single state are likely to have differing predominant motives and ends. So far as a given individual is concerned, his chief concern, for example, might be with acquiring the maximum possible income and wealth. He would choose as the primary goal of government the maintenance of a climate within which this end could be most fully realized. At the same time, however, he might wish the government to pursue policies designed to ensure peace, increase the volume of foreign trade, diminish or abolish the use of alcoholic beverages, ensure civil liberty and equal economic opportunity for minority groups, and so on. Some of these goals may complement his primary goal and others within the group. Still different ones are undoubtedly contradictory. For example, to guarantee minimum living standards to others, or to maintain full employment, might well require action which would reduce the ability of our individual to acquire a maximum of income, wealth, power, and prestige.

It is not certain that such contradictions in goals will be obvious to our hypothetical individual. He may simply never have methodically and systematically set forth his ends—he may simply favor apparently disconnected policy decisions or actions on a piecemeal basis, generally, as one or another issue arises, without considering their effects on the attainment of other goals toward which he believes society should also move. Or in that circumstance wherein he has carefully listed and considered the many goals he is seeking simultaneously, he may never have ranked them in order of their importance to him. That is, he may never have clearly recognized that he has a marginal decision to make, a decision which involves weighing the cost of giving up a little of "this" in order to get a little more of "that." He may want all of everything—a situation which he would immediately recognize as ridiculous as he moved to allocate his own time among alternative pursuits or his income among alternative employments. Add to these considerations the probability that he may never have rationally considered the consequence of action flowing from each, or may—through lack of adequate information and tools of analysis—have done so incorrectly. The net result is that individuals may find the simultaneous pursuit of contradictory ends not only within tolerance limits but actively to be desired.[1]

If this multiplicity of contradictory ends is possible for an individual, it is even more likely for a government which reacts to the blandishments of not one, but millions, of individuals; to not one, but scores, of organized pressure groups and institutions. These individuals and these organized groups will have differing primary goals, differing subsidiary goals, and may or may not have formally and accurately tested them for contradictions. Yet the goals of most may be tolerable to all—if not necessarily desired by them.

Some of the many goals of individuals and groups within any nation will be intolerable to the majority or to strategically placed groups within the society. It will be impossible to implement policy effectively for their attainment. Many of their other goals, however,

---

[1] This seems certainly to be possible within the framework of the views presented by the project psychologist, Professor Snygg. The individual's "psychological field" need only be incomplete or inaccurate—an almost inevitable situation where most individuals are not trained to examine reality systematically and objectively.

will be accepted as proper ends of government action. They can be implemented, the probability of contradiction and conflict notwithstanding.

Means for Attainment of Ends

Just as there may be many goals for government action to be simultaneously pursued, so also may there be a number of means suggested for the attainment of each. Different individuals and different groups may have selected varying means for the attainment of a certain goal. Or the same individual or group may, with the passage of time and a change in circumstances, advocate the use of a changed method.

Thus, for example, one of the major goals of government *might* be held to be the encouragement of an economic organization allocating the factors of production as they would be allocated in an economic system meeting all of the economists' requirements for "competition." Means suggested to allow the achievement of this goal would today almost certainly include the following: (1) on the assumption that such competition would occur except for government action, get government out of (almost) all economic and business affairs; (2) restrict monopolistic action by decision-makers, in part by persuading government to adopt a vigorous antimonopoly campaign; (3) on the basis of a belief that attainment of such results will be possible only if government functionaries make decisions for individual business entities, the government should own and government officials should operate business units to the prescribed end of achieving essentially the results which would flow from a competitive, privately dominated economy.[2]

Each of these alternatives would be chosen by some of the individuals who agreed that the attainment of results achievable under

[2] It may seem exceedingly strange that government activity is advocated to ensure essentially competitive results. Nevertheless, in an economy where large size and hence, inevitably, monopoly power accompanies the achievement of lowest cost, this is logically inevitable. See Oskar Lange, and Fred M. Taylor, *On the Economic Theory of Socialism*, Minneapolis, University of Minnesota Press, 1938, particularly pp. 98-121.

formally rigorous competition was a proper end. The choice made by individuals would depend upon (1) their knowledge of the nature of the existing industrial structure; (2) their definition of "competition"; (3) their knowledge, or perhaps more aptly their lack of knowledge, as to how each of the suggested means would actually change the allocation of factors; (4) their other goals, the importance thereof, and the perceived effects thereon of the use of any of the means suggested; and (5) their emotional reaction to the state of affairs each alternative suggested to them.

Further, as specific instances looking to the solution of the problem of attaining "competitive" allocation arose, differing answers might be suggested by the same individual or group. For example, we might find the same individual recommending that government "get out of agriculture," demanding dissolution of "monopolies," and asking for government ownership of utilities. And while as a matter of fact these three recommendations may be uncontradictory and represent only objective and rational differences based upon a recognition of varying basic circumstances, there is certainly no guarantee that this will always be the case when such pronouncements are made by untrained, frequently unobjective individuals.

The net result is that means thought to be probably effective are a multiple of the possible ends and goals. More than this, the means may be as contradictory as the ends, since emotional response, inadequate knowledge, or insufficient consideration of available facts and evidence may cause the selection of obvious means inadequate to the attainment of those ends which it is desired to reach.

Many Goals, Many Means

The foregoing analysis suggests the virtual impossibility of having at any time, in a democratic society, a single sharply defined end for government action and a clearly defined and stated means for its attainment. Such a situation would demand either a simple goal or a carefully arrayed hierarchy of goals (with well-defined "balancing" points at which marginal increments of satisfaction yielded by further pursuit of each goal are precisely the same) to which all politically or economically influential groups could adhere. It would further entail a similar common acceptance of the means proper for the attainment of those ends.

To get such common purpose and common action would require that the important groups in society have (1) the same view as to what life should hold for each specific group, (2) the same view as to the state of affairs then existing in the social structure, and (3) the same view as to how—in the given society—the desired ends could be attained. Such unanimity of opinion is, in a free society, most unlikely; in a dictatorship, it is unlikely over any protracted period.

Thus, in a relatively free society such as has existed in the United States for generations, we may expect the simultaneous pursuit of many unranked goals by the use of many different mechanisms. Many individuals, many groups, from time to time impose on the state attempts to attain one or another of their goals. They suggest—and from time to time impose the use of—certain means for this attainment of goals. Previously important groups decline; others rise to positions of influence. They have new goals or new means to offer. They may wipe out the old, they may modify the old, or—and this is quite likely—they may simply superimpose the new upon the old.

With the passage of time we have then a government the policy and organization of which are truly "mixed"—many goals pursued and many means used, at one and the same time.

IMPORTANT GOALS AND THE MEANS FOR THEIR IMPLEMENTATION

In a society wherein government activity having an impact upon economic and industrial institutions is conceived and implemented under the circumstances previously outlined, such activity is obviously not likely to be neat, logical, and consistent. It will not be possible to explain policy in terms of any individual's preconception of what its goals either are or ought to be—indeed, it will not be explainable on any monistic basis.

Despite the foregoing, however, it should be possible to ferret out the ostensible goals of government activity in any society, to ascertain the means offered for their attainment, and to point out the individuals and groups who are most likely to be connected with each. As an example—and as an illustration of competing ends and means—we might use the current United States economy. Here we would certainly find the following major goals of government activity, the following means being urged for the attainment of each, and the indicated groups supporting each.

These goals are not here arranged on a logical scale or continuum, as this would be contrary to the helter-skelter pursuit of a host of contrasting and oddly assorted goals that feature our actual economy. Neither are these objectives and means of achieving them defined with precision, for this too would be at odds with the vague, overlapping, undelimited way in which such definitions are actually formulated.

I. *Minimum Governmental Functions in an Economy of Individual Action*

In Great Britain, Western Europe, and the United States, there was in evidence during the eighteenth and nineteenth centuries a considerable body of thought which reflected confidence in the existence of a "naturally" ordered society—an order that could be achieved through the relatively unfettered action of individuals. This confidence in the existence of "natural law" made fearfulness of positive government action reasonable. When it is held to be true that free individual action usually operates to give the populace the widest measure of satisfaction, government action can frequently only act to obstruct the ordered operation of the system.

This confidence that the individual's natural—and, therefore, presumably beneficent—actions would give satisfactory results was given intellectual respectability by economists who spelled out the supposed workings of natural law and free individual action within the concept of the "competitive system." When directed by "competition," free individual action came to mean rational, deliberate choice (by consumers, factor suppliers, and entrepreneurs) among alternatives of a certain stipulated kind in an economy with certain stipulated institutions. These stipulations notably included (1) the assumption of unlimited wants and limited resources; (2) the basic assumptions of private property, freedom of contract, private business firms, and motivation of individuals to seek maximum personal satisfaction; (3) assumptions that decision-makers take market prices as given, have full knowledge, and find no bars to indicated adjustments; and (4) assumption of the close identification of the owner and manager within business enterprises.

When competition was "perfect"—when, that is, it met all of the qualifications listed above—then economists, using impeccable logic, demonstrated that a very desirable economic organization existed. They demonstrated that—given the distribution of income and wealth—goods most wanted would be produced in the amounts most wanted, that all productive agents desiring employment would be employed, and that all these agents would be utilized in that capacity wherein they would be most productive. Competent economists, of course, realized that these happy results would follow *only* if the assumptions of competition actually described reality— the actual, existing state of affairs. Many other individuals—legislators, businessmen, labor leaders—accepted, however, the conclusions of these economists as being applicable to our society without inquiring as to the nature of the assumptions. It was sufficient for them that the economists required competition (of some kind), that actual competition (albeit of some other kind) was obviously present in our economy, and hence that the ideal organization of industry necessarily resulted.

It should be noted that no important groups calling for minimum government activity actually desire *no* government activity. They will usually call upon the government to (1) protect private property and enforce private contracts, (2) provide a medium of exchange, (3) provide for the defense of the country, and (4) furnish such necessary goods and services (postal services, canals, roads, etc.) as are not profitable or feasible for private enterprise to undertake.

Individuals and groups in the following categories are likely to embrace this laissez-faire view:

1. Those holding to the views of the nineteenth-century liberals that maximum freedom of action in the economic sphere not only

inevitably leads ("naturally") to optimum economic organization but is essential to political freedom and democracy as well. These persons point to the atomization of economic power as necessary if relatively decentralized and democratic political institutions are to be maintained.

2. Those relying on the logic of "perfect competition" either (a) because they do not take note of its assumptions, or (b) because they believe the assumptions descriptive of reality.

3. Those now in a position, or believing themselves soon to be in a position, wherein the maximum exercise of their power requires limitations upon government activity.

II. *Action to Enforce Competition*

The view has persisted that free competition provides a satisfactory economic organization where its underlying requirements ("assumptions") are met. However, most economists, and many laymen, realize that our existing society does not conform to these assumptions. They observe that if these assumptions are to be realized, government action will have to be taken to give us a reasonably competitive structure.

Government action to enforce competition between private decision-makers has taken primarily the forms of (a) antitrust activity, and (b) programs of aiding small business. Such action is probably desired by the following:

1. Economists—and others understanding their position—who do not see as existing or as natural a society conforming to competitive assumptions, who believe antitrust action is sufficient for attainment of a workably competitive structure, and who believe that such a structure would not prevent important efficiencies of large scale.

2. Those who believe that political and social advantages accrue to a society of small firms and individual freedom of action, and who see large units placing important restrictions thereon.

3. Those whose economic status, growth, power, or existence is currently being impinged upon by existing large and powerful units.

III. *Action to Attain a More Equal Distribution of Wealth and Income*

An economy conforming in fact to all the assumed conditions of "competition" will demonstrably afford to individuals an income equal to the value of the marginal product added either through the individual's personal effort or through the use of nonhuman factors owned by the individual. This means, of course, that incomes of individuals will certainly vary with differences in native abilities, training, and ownership of material resources. Further, the magnitude of such deviations increases when certain decision-makers gain monopoly power and increase their incomes and ultimately their wealth at the expense of economically weaker groups.

Since the demand for goods and services therefore emanates from individuals coming into the market unequally equipped with incomes, many have held that the market mechanism is incapable of producing a satisfactory distribution of goods among individuals. Persons of this persuasion call for action leading to a more equal distribution of income (which, of course, ultimately both depends upon and leads to a more equal distribution of privately held wealth), so that all consumers will come into the market equally equipped to demand goods and services from it.

Government action tending to increase equality has taken the forms of support to antitrust activity, progressive personal-income taxation, progressive estate and gift taxes, and expansion of governmentally furnished consumption goods and services, including education (furnished, in part at least, out of the proceeds of the progressive taxes). Advocates of such action include:

1. Those—particularly economists—who are concerned about the ability of the pricing mechanism to afford an optimum allocation of resources.

2. Those who simply see a tax structure based on "ability to pay" as the easiest means of getting the funds to cover increasing government expenditures.

3. Those in lower income brackets who anticipate that they will become better off as the result of decreased inequality.

4. Those who feel that existing inequalities are morally undesirable.

IV. *Action to Restrict the Use of Monopoly Power*

Most groups and individuals within our society recognize that in certain industries firms able to make most efficient use of resources are necessarily large. While there is widespread disagreement as to the number of such firms, where their existence is recognized it is understood that the restraints normally enforced by rivalry or competition cannot be operative and that the dissolutions which might be dictated by antitrust activity would result in important loss in efficiency.

The solution found here is most frequently price regulation of such businesses (usually termed "utilities"). Occasionally solution is found in outright government ownership and operation.

V. *Government Ownership of Material Resources*

Although historically and currently of relative political impotence in the United States, some hold the view that the government should own the material agents of production and operate the producing units. This view will be held by:

1. Economically unsophisticated groups who react against what appear to them to be abuses of the present system by asking for government ownership and operation, frequently simply assuming that government operation will result in higher wages and a disappearance of profits, rent, and interest.

2. Economically highly sophisticated individuals who hold that (a) a more equal distribution of income and (b) an allocation of resources similar to that described by "competitive" theory are effectively attainable only when the government owns the nonhuman factors of production and operates the larger business enterprises. Such positive government action is held necessary to halt the tendency of private ownership of land and capital to generate income inequality. It is also required so that it can be ensured that the prices and outputs of the individual producing units (private firms taken over by the government) will be determined according to

the "competitive" norm (i.e., where the additional costs involved in producing another unit are just equated with the price consumers are willing to pay) without the necessity of an atomistic society.

VI. *Action to Give Monopoly Power to Specific Groups*

In the "competitive" economic system wherein individuals are presumed to act freely to attain their own ends, they are also presumed to be at the mercy of the market mechanism and to act in response to its dictates. Specifically, such a society is presumed to furnish to its constituents amounts equal to the value of the marginal product added either through individual effort or through the use of nonhuman factors owned by the individual. Further, it is presumed that individuals, land, and capital will be utilized at that location, or in that particular employment, wherein the market indicates their return will be the greatest.

There is, of course, no reason to suppose that individuals—or organized groups—would ever be satisfied with their lot under such a system. As a matter of fact, many have not been satisfied with competitive situations and have sought the solution through attaining a monopoly position—and the important, though only partial, relief it brings from the dictates of an impersonal market mechanism. Various attempts to gain monopoly status have been buttressed by positive government action. Business firms have been aided by government-sponsored cartelization of industry in some instances, patent and copyright protection, tariff protection, and so on. Organizations for the monopolistic merchandising of labor's services and of farm products have received government encouragement and asistance in the implementation of their programs. In fact, the general attitude has seemingly been that "everyone should be subject to competition but me."

VII. *Action to Maintain the Proper Climate for Private Enterprise*

Regardless of other governmental actions taken, it seems to many that private enterprise retains two great faults: the first, a tendency to take action considered immoral and dishonest relative to customers, suppliers, and rivals;[3] and the second, a disheartening tendency to sink into protracted periods of low-level activity and painful unemployment.

Individuals and organized groups have, therefore, frequently taken the position that if private operation of business enterprises is to continue such operation must not offend standards of morality and must give relatively stable and full employment. These groups have obtained at least some government action on both counts.

Action to maintain acceptably high standards for business action has been taken under the Federal Trade Commision Act, the Pure Food and Drug Act, the various securities acts, and acts regulating banks and insurance companies.

It is likewise true that governmental monetary and fiscal policies are being more closely scrutinized in order that they may have desirable effects on cyclical fluctuations and employment. In part, this action is being taken pursuant to the general directive contained in the Full Employment Act of 1946 and to the advice of the President's Council of Economic Advisers created thereby.

VIII. *Action to Attain Security Through Government Action*

As we have noted before, a free-enterprise economy does not always reward its citizens as they wish to be rewarded, or as they are able to convince government officials they should be rewarded. They have, as has been pointed out, therefore asked for and received the right to benefit themselves through monopolistic organization.

There are, however, certain goals which even monopoly organization seems unable to achieve for all. They are what have loosely been termed "security" goals—protection against the financial hardships flowing from poor health, accident, unemployment, and old age. The government has taken action—and is constantly being asked to take additional action—designed to give such protection.

[3] Such actions would include (1) actions of corporate officials who might use their powers to enrich themselves at the expense of the corporation, (2) false disparagement of a competitor and his product, (3) the sale of harmful or useless products falsely or deceptively labeled, (4) "rigging" of securities markets, or (5) the hiding of unfavorable information or the presentation of false claims to inflate security values.

IX. *Action to Give Maximum War Potential*

In an economic system geared to produce the maximum output of the tools of war, many of the important functions usually performed by the price mechanism are performed by administrative fiat. Demand is not the total of the effective demands of individual consumers expressed through the market; instead it takes the form of orders by defense officials for armaments and their allocation of available consumer goods to civilians. Business firms do not adjust to changes in market conditions; they produce goods administratively required and are compensated in accordance with their costs. In such an environment, it should be obvious that a bureaucracy is required to turn requirements into orders, orders into goods. Large integrated corporations possess this bureaucracy and obviate in some important measure the necessity for the creation and training of an expanded government bureaucracy. This fact, plus the need for large quantities of standardized weapons, argues for an economy of a few large firms to give a maximum war potential.

Thus important groups, who in peacetime see the desirability of the impersonal market mechanism over administrative fiat in translating consumer demand into orders, who see corporate bureaucracies as luxuries, and who feel that small firms are more sensitive than large to shifts in demand, are disposed in periods of war and active preparation for war to favor an expanded role for large, integrated enterprise.

CONCLUSIONS

This chapter has attempted to indicate the unlikelihood of a comprehensive government economic policy with a clearly defined hierarchy of goals and uncontradictory means for their attainment. The preceding brief examination of the ends which are currently being pursued by government economic action in the United States, and of the means being employed for their attainment, gives a vivid illustration—though, of course, not conclusive proof—of this contention. Many of these ends, as well as many of these means, are obviously ill defined, inconsistent, and even mutually exclusive.

An acceptance of the point of view here espoused will have certain important effects. First, it casts doubt upon the ability of any group, no matter how learned or how powerful, to either educate, propagandize, cajole, or force its program on a heterogeneous society without important qualifications and modifications. This means that the efficacy of a suggested program of action cannot adequately be assessed purely in terms of that program itself. It must instead be evaluated in terms of its impact on the existing structure and of internal modifications necessitated in order to gain acceptance. That is to say, teleological systems can never be adequately judged from the vantage point of a simple examination of their logical consistency or a simple evaluation of the desirableness of their fundamental purpose. Such systems must, instead, be examined in light of their probable place and functioning after their introduction into an operating, organic society.

Second, while it is undoubtedly true that contradictions and tensions inevitable in governmental policy vary inversely with homogeneity in the views of the populace, such contradictions and tensions are inevitable except in a completely stratified society where every individual is satisfied with his assigned role. This means that it is a dubious presumption to suppose that a dictatorship is much better able to implement a wholly consistent policy than a democracy. True, it may on the surface, and for limited periods, appear to resist modifications in ends or means. This, however, must be at the cost of accumulating underlying frustration and tension certain to reduce the needed cooperation of the citizenry. On the other hand, in democratic societies where neither reason nor ideology has been adequate to the attainment of some considerable homogeneity of view, such conflicts may make virtually impossible any effective government action of any kind. Such a result seems close to the situation in France and Italy today.

Third, acceptance of the view presented in this paper points up the difficulties in the way of defining usefully what it is that constitutes a "satisfactory" economy. It suggests simply that an economy—together with the economic activities of its government—will be considered adequate when the influential groups therein consider that sufficient attention is being given their points of view. On this score it is well to remark that what these groups *think* is actually the case is important—what in fact exists is of only secondary significance in the short run. Actual "progress"—in the sense of movement toward a well-defined goal—is therefore not essential to a "satisfactory" economy.

Finally, of course, the thesis here expounded makes it impossible to take seriously statements to the effect that governmental policy has been oriented to any single end or to the use of any single technique.

IX

The Law, the Economy, and Moral Values

by WALTON HAMILTON
Formerly (1928-1948) Professor of Law, Yale University,
since 1945 with the law firm of Arnold, Fortas, and Porter

I

It is easy to assert that the law serves humanity as the instrument of justice. It is hard to identify the law which performs this essential office or to define the justice which it seeks to provide.

For in any society the law is only one among many institutions through which the community exercises its authority over human conduct. Its compulsions are enmeshed in a larger system of discipline which imposes order upon the whole of the affairs of a people. From society to society the law differs in character and office: in the agencies through which it is administered, in the taboos and imperatives which make up its substance, in the place it occupies within the cultural order, in the breadth or narrowness of its orbit of authority. The law has no meaning apart from the culture it serves; it is forever being remade by all the usages of mankind which impinge upon it.

The law, accordingly, appears in the dual role of creator and creature. It has in a Ulysses-like journey down the centuries become a part of all that it has met. Its codes of doctrines and principles and rules are alike durable and flexible. A doctrine lives on long after the sense which it embodies has ceased to be common. A decision gets frozen into a rule which is invoked long after the rationale which called it into being is forgotten. The "web of the law"—a figure of speech much favored by jurists—catches up, preserves for, or imposes upon posterity, many a thread which belonged to a social fabric of bygone times. But, if the law endures, it also changes. Time in its steady march serves up novelties; men in everyday life must adapt themselves to new situations; as the new crowds in upon the old, stresses and strains previously unknown emerge; conflicts in life become actions at law for which there are no precedents. Old concepts are given new contours; old rules are fitted out with "exceptions" which grow in number and eventually cause the rule to be recast or even set in reverse. A doctrine goes through its mutations as it encounters "the infinite variety of the changing conditions of life." At once the law serves with its legacy from the past and with formulae flexible enough to hold the values of the future. Like the culture it serves, the law preserves its continuity with a constant change in identity.

As an active factor in a culture, the law compels. Yet, as it compels, it makes its accommodation. At any time it tends to impress its imperatives upon human affairs; but, at the same time, trends are at work to bring it into accord with the ideas, values, and ways of life of the community it serves. Its connection alike with the economy and with the moral sense of the developing society is intimate and abiding.

The nature of its economy gives character to a nation's culture. Although other codes of usage or cultural factors are often in play, it is its economy which usually resolves a people into income groups or into classes, effects a distribution of opportunity, and in the long run determines how rigid or mobile the social structure is to be. The law appoints and maintains the arrangements within which industrial activities are carried on. Property, contract, the corporations, the cooperatives, and all forms of business associations are legal inventions. The right of a man to sell his labor or to enter the trade of his choice is as good as the law makes it. Licenses, franchises, privileges of one sort or another, are valid only so far as the law accords protection. A monopoly, to be legal, must have the sanction and submit to the regulation of the law. Competition may be the life of trade, but its own vitality depends largely upon the existence of antitrust laws and their vigorous enforcement. The cases which the law is called upon to resolve are largely economic in origin; the impulses which beat upon the law to bring about its restatement come largely from the economy in action. The law is not, and cannot be, isolated from the medley of everyday activities by which people make their livings.

Nor can the law be insulated against the prevailing system of moral values. As conflicts out of life, processed into actions at law, come into the courts, they must be decided. In each a judgment is reached by an application of the relevant rules of law. But the law does not create its own rules out of nothingness. They rest ultimately upon notions of what is worth while and what is not, and where the balance of justice lies. And such notions have—and can have—no other source than the moral sentiment of the community, or of dominant groups within it. To say that the source of "legal justice" is the law's own rules is to state a half-truth. If the rules, principles, and doctrines so easily invoked are traced back to their entrance into the law, the moral values long ago encased in them will be apparent. But, while the law imports, rather than creates, its moral values, the legal is not to be identified with the moral law. For the law cannot always compel where it is good to go. Hence legal duty may be lesser than moral obligation. It is grand to lift the conduct of the whole people to a higher moral plane. But it is imperative to keep their conduct from falling to a plane which is morally intolerable.

II

A trio of concrete incidents will serve to translate the abstractions of the paragraphs above into language which has clearer meaning.

1. Chattel Slavery

The ancient and once honorable institution of slavery attests the interaction of the law, the national economy, and the prevailing system of morals. The slow development of the institution in ancient Rome is in striking contrast with its catastrophic overthrow in the United States.

A number of centuries separate the Twelve Tables of primitive
Rome from the sophisticated days of the Empire. During this
period Roman life and thought, its economy and culture, were
transformed by all the forces which converged upon the Eternal
City. In this extended period of gradual development no institution
could remain intact. No usage of society could for long withstand
the great "historical trends" which beat upon it. As slavery served,
so it moved, with the changing times and mores.

In the Twelve Tables it is written that the head of the family,
the *pater familias*, has the absolute power of life and death over
his slaves. By the third century of the Christian era, the *pater familias*, responding to the rise of a constitutional government and to
the human influences of a world at peace, was no longer a sov-
ereign over a household dominion. The Roman law had raised its
code to limit his rights by regard for the rights of the circle of
others whom his actions affected. A sense of the dignity of the individual had set limits to family authority. The absolute in authority had been converted into the responsible; and the petty tyrant,
whose will had once been his own law, was called upon to answer
in a court of law for acts of injustice to members of his own household which lay beyond the bounds of the community's tolerance.

The usages of slavery could not escape this reiterated beat of history. As Rome fashioned a far-flung economy, new occupations
came into being, and men and women of new and distinctive capacities were called upon to fill them. The fortunes of war brought
a host of intelligent and educated persons to the slave market, and
the slaveowner was much too responsive to the money he had laid
out not to want to get as much as possible out of the chattels which
were his own. So not only the skilled trades but the professions
were opened to slaves; and persons who belonged to other persons
in time came to buy and sell, to execute contracts, and to own property. Where the slave was the equal, or even the superior, of his
master in all save legal status, the relationship of master and servant was hopelessly confused, and in time the compromised status
was recognized at law. In the palmy days of the centuries of peace,
more than one person was at once a *pater familias* in his own right,

a slave of the Emperor, and a ranking minister of state. In so anomalous a legal status eight hundred years of history speaks.

If the history of our South does not tell a like story, it is partly because time had no real chance to get in its licks. The character of Negro slavery in the United States differs radically from that of Rome because its subjects were of an alien race from the masters and because they entered slavery untutored in the industrial arts of Western culture. Here, in contrast with Rome, the acquisition of an alien culture arrested the development of slavery, and the conversion of racial taboos into a system of moral values was a barrier to rapid advance. But far more significant than differences in race and culture was the brief time in which Negro slavery in America had to run its dominant course. Although the Census of 1790 showed a substantial number of slaves, it was not until after 1815 that slavery became "the South's peculiar institution," and as such it had a life history of less than half a century. A similar period in the history of Rome would show hardly any change which was perceptible. For the play of human events in the metamorphosis of an institution, a span of five decades is far too short to signify.

Yet there was change—and rapid change. As soon as "cotton slavery" came to be an institution, it fell under attack. The frontier, which plays so large a role in American history, was for a time its salvation. For slavery immobilized capital, which should have gone into equipment and improvement of the land, into the property values of human beings; and such was the capacity of cotton to exhaust the soil and so wasteful was the labor employed upon it that slavery could be made to pay only upon "new ground." So, from 1820 to 1860, the plantation shifted from the Carolinas and Georgia to Alabama and Mississippi, and by 1860 was unsafely entrenched in several states across the river, whence, as the soil betrayed the system and the crop, there was nowhere else to go. Yet even on fresh plantations, if records had been accurately kept, they would under the best of conditions have revealed losses. In fact, at the beginning of the Civil War, the large estates were heavily mortgaged.

But even rapid mobility was not enough to preserve intact the integrity of the institution. Virginia made Negro slavery pay (that is, as well as it did), not by putting human beings to bondage, but by breeding slaves for the cotton fields now far away. Where commerce intruded, as in Louisiana, mutations in the institution had already appeared. The slave who set himself up as a moneylender in a petty way by 1860 was a familiar figure on many plantations. In New Orleans a number of men whose legal status was that of a slave were themselves the lawful owners of other slaves; and there many a slave, using his own funds or "set up" by his master, was in business for himself. Chattel slavery itself, as the first gun was fired at Fort Sumter, was at the point of the adaptation demanded by survival; many a plantation, as insurance against doom, was experimenting with a system of profit sharing.

What moral values would have been called into play by an economy headed for bankruptcy we cannot say. Nor can we describe in detail the institution into which chattel slavery would presently have been transformed. The course of development, impelled by silent yet mighty forces, was violently interrupted by that excursion into futility called the War between the States. That military struggle did yield, at least on paper, the emancipation.

Freedom, however, came to the black man without adequate preparation for the responsibilities it imposed. It came as an affront to the Southern whites, who, as soon as a Reconstruction which did not reconstruct was over, consigned the Negro to an inferior position in their society. Even as yet the black man is excluded from the full heritage of civil liberties, without which freedom is largely a word. As federal statutes proclaimed a nominal liberty, state statutes by ingenious legal devices established servitude in the guise of punishment for crimes whereof the Negro had been lawfully convicted. The Civil War could not have come fifteen years earlier, for as yet the slave power had not come into its own. Nor could it have been "inevitable" or even possible a decade and a half later; by that time it would have been well on the way toward its own destruction by the forces of decay inherent in it. The glory of that heroic struggle was bought at a fearful moral cost; for the course of events is far more constructive than any wholesale coercion which man can devise.

2. Shall the Employer Answer?

In 1837, the first year of the reign of Victoria, there came before the Court of the Exchequer a "case of first impression." A "servant had been presumptuous enough to sue his master" because of an injury suffered in the course of employment and caused by the negligence of a "fellow servant." The question was whether the court would entertain—and accord a remedy for—so novel and peculiar a "cause of action."

The court had to meet head-on an issue for which there was no precedent; it could not look ahead to see that the suit before it was the forerunner of tens of thousands of its own kind. To Lord Abinger, who presided over the court, the resort to law in a matter of this kind was as strange as the archaic terms of "master and servant" in which it is cast are to us. Since nothing like it had ever been impressed upon the law, Lord Abinger could not draw upon the ponderous leather-backed volumes of the English Reports. He had to draw upon his own common sense, which was the common sense—and reflected the moral values—of the English squirearchy which he honored in his person and in his sojourn upon the bench. The opinion, accordingly, reads like a piece out of Henry Fielding. It is the extended comment on an incident of the day, delivered by one country squire to a number of his fellows.

Few of his class would have doubted the morality or denied the wisdom of Lord Abinger's ruling in the case of *Priestly* v. *Fowler*. It was shocking—and what was the country coming to?—that a servant should have haled his master into court, especially when the master was called upon to answer, not for any wrongful conduct of his own, but for the misdeed of another of his servants. The butcher shop of the master did have its dangers, but Priestly, the injured person, was a male and an adult in full possession of all his faculties. If he went into the butcher's trade he did so of his own free will, well knowing the risks he was taking. If Priestly's fellow servant had habits which enhanced the ordinary risks of the business, certainly the master was not to blame for any accident that ensued. Was not Priestly guilty of negligence himself by his agreement to work with so irresponsible a fellow? And think what would happen if the courts were open to so frivolous a suit! The guest could sue his host for putting him to sleep in a crazy bedstead; the chambermaid could sue her mistress; the footman could sue because of the coachman's negligence. And so Lord Abinger brings his opinion to a close with a "parade of all the horribles"—as they are called in the law schools—known to an English class society.

The law does not create; it merely subdues to its own distinctive process the stuff of life which it handles. It has to get its values, its moral notions, its strict or flexible rules somewhere, and life itself, with its impinging culture, provides the only reservoir in which it can dip. Lord Abinger in *Priestly* v. *Fowler* talked the language of the country gentry. But he brought into the law in unprocessed form all the raw material it required for a doctrine of "employer's liability"—or, more accurately, nonliability—which was destined to outlive, by some decades, its usefulness.

Lord Abinger did not subdue to legal lingo the aristocratic wisdom which he had uttered. The task of applying legal craftsmanship to English common sense fell to Mr. Chief Justice Shaw of the Supreme Judicial Court of Massachusetts. In a beautiful specimen from his judicial workshop which appeared some four years later, the whole opinion in *Priestly* v. *Fowler*, in a neat series of propositions, is assimilated into the august corpus of the common law. Yes, said Mr. Chief Justice Shaw, in a concession which, as it worked, proved to be no concession, the courts will entertain a cause of action by a servant against his master. But the master who is sued is entitled to defend himself.

And, said Mr. Chief Justice Shaw, three separate and distinct pleas may be interposed by the master in his own defense. He may invoke "the rule of assumption of risk"; that is, the master is not required to answer if the accident is due to an ordinary business risk which the servant may be assumed to have accepted in entering into the contract of employment. He may invoke "the fellow-servant rule." And he is not called upon to answer if the negligent act which led to the accident, in whole or in part, was that of the injured servant. In a word, the master could be sued only where he, the master, was wholly at fault. In the words of an ancient adage, dear to the hearts of common-law judges, there can be no liability without fault.

The substance of the two opinions is the same; the languages in which they are written are utterly different. It was the Shaw rather than the Abinger version which, as case followed unlike case in the law courts, lived on. The assumption of the "ordinary" risks by the servant came itself to be assumed. And since trades were unlike and their hazards different, there could be no rigid boundary to confine the risks taken to a limited area. The rule of "contributory negligence" became severe. To invoke it, it was enough to show that the servant had made some contribution of negligence to the stream of events which resulted in the accident. As for the fellow-servant rule, the fact of any fellowship was completely forgotten; it was enough that the servant who acted negligently and the one who was hurt were the servants of a single master. Thus the rules of law, emancipated from time and place by Mr. Chief Justice Shaw, were carried far beyond the frontier where the concrete reasons of Lord Abinger would have arrested them—and probably much farther than Mr. Chief Justice Shaw would have them go.

But the lawful way of escape for the master could not endure. The older rationale of the master's defenses was gone. How could it be held that the servant, now an employee, had quite on his own "assumed the ordinary risks" when there was not a shred of writing to show that any such idea had ever entered his mind? And what of a justice which gave no compensation to a worker for a disabling injury because of some minor act of carelessness on his part, when the employer's neglect of the safety of his laborers was notorious? Why a lingering myth of fellowship between persons who were total strangers to each other, when the only bond was employment by an identical master? And, under the factory system, wasn't it unrealistic to conduct a judicial search for personal negligence, when the cause of industrial accidents lay in the impersonal operation of the machine process? This list of questions, in the front of many a mind alert to a changing situation, can be extended at length. It reveals the growing chasm between the changing facts of industrial life—and changing ways of looking at them—and the rigid legal formulas which in effect made an industrial accident the worker's own private affair.

But changing fact was not arrested at the courthouse door. As brief after brief was hurled against the Shaw-Abinger structure, a set of rules moving to an adverse goal came into being. At last each of the three dominant defenses of the master was matched by a counter-rule which kept the servant's cause of action alive. It was true that the worker assumed the "ordinary risks of employment," but it was equally true that the master was under a legal duty to provide a safe working place. A contribution of negligence by the worker was enough to prevent a judgment in his favor, but the master was under obligation to instruct the worker in the duties of his task. The master could not be held for the negligence of a fellow servant, save when the servant whose carelessness touched off the accident was acting at the time as the representative of the master. When these three counter-rules came to be recognized, as in time they were, the whole character of the suit was changed. Each of the three issues created by the opposition of rule to counter-rule presented a "question of fact," and questions of fact were to be decided by a jury of the injured man's peers.

The Shaw-Abinger rules insured victory to the defense; the contrivance of the counter-rules turned all issues into open questions. They served to "get the case to the jury"—and that was enough. For in general the sympathies of the jury were with the victim of industrial accident, not with the corporation out of whose till the money judgment would come, and sympathy was a mighty force in determining the facts of the case. Juries responded nobly to the new doctrine; not only were they able to see clearly where justice lay, but they saw it in figures so large as to seem excessive to the defendants who had to pay the judgments.

Accordingly the business group which, had the Shaw-Abinger rules remained pure and undefiled, would have fought the rising movement for "workmen's compensation" came to favor it. Rates fixed in accordance with a statute, irrespective of what was the personal responsibility for the accident, were preferable to such extravagant verdicts as juries were rendering. So the insurance principle came to replace the tort law of personal responsibility. Under the new arrangement, in terms of schedules with fixed rates, each employer made a definite contribution to a pool, out of which benefits were paid graduated to the severity of the accident. In the end so sensible a scheme appealed to a majority of the United States Supreme Court, who found the cost of industrial accidents thus distributed to be no more than a necessary cost of production that was passed on in the price of the product.

3. Labor's United Front

A single case may reveal, even more clearly than a succession of them, another legal doctrine in the throes of involuntary restatement. The cause of the Duplex Printing Company against a man named Deering and his brethren in the faith of trade unionism, decided by the Supreme Court in 1921, is a dramatic example. There the growing strength of the labor movement, with the new values and ways of thought engendered by it, opposed its strength to ancient and established law. In a divided court ancient justice and morals again won, but their triumph was marked by impending overtones of defeat.

The opinion of the court, concurred in by six judges, was announced by Mr. Justice Pitney. From "the facts of the case," in an able and well-reasoned opinion, his argument marched to an "inescapable conclusion." The Duplex Company, a manufacturer of printing presses located in the Midwest, had been having trouble with its employees. At the same time, in New York and other cities, the trucks on which printing presses of its manufacture were being delivered to customers were mysteriously breaking down. These breakdowns occurred with a unanimity which accident or act of God was powerless to explain. So the Duplex Company, with an accusing finger, pointed at Deering and other officials of the teamsters' union and asked the court for, and received, a mandate which in effect told Deering and his fellow labor leaders that they had better see to it that the like didn't occur again. On appeal the matter reached the highest court in the land. For the majority Mr. Justice Pitney had no difficulty with so simple a problem. To recite the facts was in effect to dispose of the issue. The parties to the suit were connected by no lawful bonds. To the Duplex Company, Deering and his fellows were utter strangers. The company as innocent victim was therefore entitled to the law's protection against the interference of "strangers" who had no legal interest in its affairs.

For Mr. Justice Brandeis and two of his colleagues the issue was not so simple. They took issue with Mr. Justice Pitney primarily over "the facts of the case"; and, since they viewed the facts differently, it was necessary to invoke quite another legal doctrine. There were in the country—a fact ignored by Mr. Justice Pitney—four companies engaged in the manufacture of printing presses. In three of these, the employees were organized and, to the extent of their power, were insisting upon high rates of wages and a decent standard of life for their members. But progress was slow because the fourth concern was not unionized. Accordingly a determined drive had been put on to organize the Duplex Company's plant, and in this systematic campaign the teamsters, among others, had been enlisted. To Mr. Justice Brandeis and his colleagues, the concept of "strangers" as applied to the parties was unrealistic; the teamsters were allied with the workers in the printing-press industry in a common campaign to guard the standard of life against the efforts of the Duplex Company to break it down. To these Justices, therefore, it was not only irrelevant, it was mischievous for the court to invoke the ancient law within circumstances never within its contemplation. In a situation such as this it was better to let the Congress appoint rules for the game. Until it does, they said, it is better to allow the parties in interest to hammer out a settlement by private combat than for the courts to obtrude with their mandates based upon doctrines from which the wisdom of old has long since departed.

III

Our culture has come to look upon morality as personal. But personal conduct is actuated by the institutions under which men carry on, and if they are to earn livelihoods and to get ahead it is under the duress of the impinging environment. Accordingly, a system of usages is as prone as a person to do the things it should not have done and to leave undone the tasks it should have performed. And of an institution as well as an individual it can be said that there is no health in it. The moral quality of human behavior in the aggregate is the moral quality of the arrangements for life and work which human beings obey.

There is nothing new in appraising an economy in terms of moral values. To the maker of proverbs "the love of money is the root of all evil"; to the Christian fathers "worldly goods" are to be held in trust. By the time of Thomas Aquinas, a Christian norm with the help of feudal land law was elaborated into a doctrine of stewardship. The axiom that "a man can do as he pleases with his own" had given way to the principle that he holds in trust from God and must be held responsible for what he does with his earthly possessions.

Practice was not in strict accord with preachments and, in the discharge of Christian duty, the part was often accepted for the whole. Thus many a monastic charter recites that the donor, in consideration of the affluence with which a benign Providence had blessed him, had decided to set aside "some small part of it toward the salvation of his immortal soul." There were also necessities of the people which could be satisfied only through activities which lay beyond the bounds of tolerance in a Christian society. In view of the prohibition by the Church of the taking of usury, that person was bold indeed who for the sake of a few pennies would surrender his hope of Christian burial. It was far better to have within the community a few persons who were not of the elect—and therefore not subject to canon law—who with impunity could perform an essential and tabooed function. The system of moral values at once arose out of and set bounds to the conduct of persons in an ecclesiastical society resting on an agrarian base and little touched by trade.

That society, with its ecclesiastical discipline, far more exacting than any moral code of trade regulation, is gone. Gone, too, are the institution of slavery, the old interpretation of employer's liability, and the system of law in which the parties to a labor dispute are treated as strangers the one to the other. But the very fact that they are in the past, that they exhibit life histories to which a period has been put, makes them the more valuable for this inquiry. Our interest is not in the concrete stories which they present, but in the things they tell about law as creator and as creature in a changing industrial habitat and within a changing moral climate. And the character of this process stands out the more sharply because time endows with perspective each of the three chapters recited.

It is harder to realize that the process by which the law is remade is ceaselessly going on. As events take their course, impinging circumstance forever demands its response from the law; and when, as at present, everything seems to be happening at once, we become conscious of conflict without certain knowledge of what values will ultimately prevail. Accordingly, to project the law as it is being remade, within the framework of a volatile economy and against the background of a moral order which itself is on the march, is a challenging—and impossible—adventure. It is helped along, however, by a maxim as old as Mr. Chief Justice Shaw and as youthful as John Dewey, that the rules of law are the transient instruments of values far more enduring than the rules themselves.

1. FREE PLAY FOR THE DYNAMIC URGE

A dominant moral requirement in our society is free play for the dynamic urge. The people of the Middle Ages made a virtue out of scarcity and held out this world as a wilderness of woe to be a proving ground for the world to come. As knowledge grew and wealth was enlarged, such severe values had to be compromised or even set in reverse. In time self-interest came to be exalted as a mighty force for good. The eighteenth century found it to be a spur to the "progress" of mankind; Adam Smith insisted that in serving his own interests man is led as "by an invisible hand to promote an end which was not part of his intention." But Adam Smith, unlike many of those who now quote him, was too moral a man to venerate self-interest in the raw, or to endow the joint-stock company with the civil rights of persons. He would pit the self-interest of one against the self-interest of others and, if necessary, have society interfere with its controls to make certain that the pursuit of gain was made to serve a public purpose.

As thus the good things of earth came to be held worth while, a moral obligation on society came to be to see to it that there was enough to go around. Men discovered that there are no such things as natural "resources"; nature serves up only stuffs of one sort or another. What the stuffs are, what properties they possess, and whether useful or harmful to humanity can be determined only by putting them to the test. Knowledge, then, is the thing which converts the sheer stuffs of earth into resources; and those things are moral which allow knowledge to grow. Petroleum was once a nuisance and farmers offered rewards to any persons who would rid their lands of it. The medicine bottle, the kerosene lamp, and the internal-combustion engine in time made of it a different product; and, with an improvement in the art of refining, its quantity is doubled. As knowledge increases, the "useful arts" advance; and with their advance, the catalogue of resources is rewritten. Our wealth today has come into being through bringing an advancing technology to the stuffs of nature. The crux of public policy, therefore, is to advance the frontiers of knowledge, and to enlarge potential resources, as rapidly and as richly as may be.

About the end there can be no quarrel; but men differ as how best the dynamic urge may be given free play. The practical answer which the nation has hammered out is the competitive system. The lawful—note the qualifying adjective—pursuit of gain is the creative urge. If it is to perform its moral office, it must be bridled and directed. The pursuer must, therefore, be pitted against rivals who seek the same rewards. The market, where goods are sold and services disposed of, must be kept free and open. A "fair field and no favors" will crown with success those who produce what the people want. Bankruptcy will remove the laggard and the inefficient from the field. The law was, therefore, invoked to keep all trades open to all men who were willing to tackle their chances. And when experience proved that in many an industry the dominant firms were prone to gang up in order that they might shirk responsibility and claim monopoly profits, the antitrust laws were enacted to compel competition.

As an instrument of the dynamic urge, the competitive system was not cut to plan. It came into being as a by-product of a stream of human behavior. The continent was new; the population was scanty; the gospel of catch-as-catch-can prevailed. No scheme of economic order could have been imposed upon so turbulent a ride into the future; and the spirit of the pioneer was too strong to tolerate so orderly a settlement, even had it been attempted. There was for decades no formal outlawing of monopoly. Only gradually did the improvised competitive system of the new republic come to be set down in the books as if it were a consciously contrived instrument of public policy—or even an economic version of the order of nature itself.

An important support was the common sense—a nineteenth-century common sense—which the competitive system embodied. It rested upon the rational belief that every man was the best judge of his own advantage. The buyer could be depended upon to prefer the cheaper to the dearer price and to demand quality in the article he purchased. The seller, accordingly, was under pressure to meet the exacting standards of informed customers. The producer had the strongest incentive to clip a cost or eliminate a waste, and thereby to put an honest penny in his own pocket. Every man was free to invent new processes and to bring to market new products. If a man cut his cost, his competitors were compelled to imitate or to lose custom. The morality vitalizing the competitive system and the antitrust law was uncompromisingly individual; the authority and orbits of an organized society were to be reduced to a bare minimum referred to as "the prevention of force and fraud." The system, in the thought of the times, opened far more facets to make for progress than any collectivistic state could offer.

But a simple and obvious system of natural competition is one thing; a competitive order, established and enforced by the state in the law court, is something quite different. The ingenuity which the rivalry of businessmen quickens into life can also be employed in devising ways and means for allowing members of an industry to form a more perfect union and still avoid the antitrust laws. The devices for action in concert are alike numerous and wonderful displays of the inventive spirit. A concert of marketing practice can be effected without leaving behind any telltale document or overt testimony which conforms to the rules of evidence. In a search for proof, the courts have been driven to "infer conspiracy" from the sheer fact of coincidence in conduct. But it is only the exceptional case which gets to the point of proof. For lack of funds and manpower, the number of suits which the government can bring is limited. And as for private suits by persons who have been "injured in their business or property," as a result of violation of the anti-trust laws, the sums necessary to prosecute suits to a successful conclusion are beyond the means of the ordinary litigant. After sixty years of law enforcement, the concentration of economic power, so alarming in 1890, has been pyramided in a way undreamed of then.

Here confusion must be avoided in respect to means and ends. The freedom of man, with his latent capacities developed by a rich and varied exposure, is perhaps the ultimate goal. To that end there must be a standard of life which, along with a minimum of worldly goods, insures access to personal opportunity. If the worldly goods are to increase, and if opportunity is to be enriched and enlarged, the dynamic urge must be given full play. The competitive system seems to be the best device which as yet our culture has hit on for releasing and developing the creative faculties inherent in the people.

But the instrument must not be exalted as if it were the end. It seems to operate best in a new industry on its way to a place of rank within the economy. The automobile business was established and came into primacy in American industry by the use of new and ingenious methods at odds with "sound business principles." As a release of the dynamic urge, competition has been least effective where it has been most intense. In an industry marked by a multitude of small firms, such as men's clothing, ladies' garments, gravel and stone, or turpentine, the alertness necessary to survival is so exacting as to leave little time or energy for the thinking and contriving necessary to industrial advance. Nor are the funds essential to research to be had from small firms jealous of each other. The dynamic urge imparted by competition is most manifest in an industry (such as the production of phonograph records) marked by a number of sizable yet not too large firms, with a healthy galaxy of independents whose enterprise and mobility enable them to survive.

The moral values of the dynamic urge and the release of the capacities of men for finding out are inadequately served by a competitive system made mandatory by the antitrust acts. The system should be compromised only where novel devices promise to ensure better performance. It should be abandoned only when it can be replaced by its better. But its shortcomings make imperative a search for amendment or substitute. It may be that the time has come for a divorce of scientific work from the operations of business. It has been suggested that the invention of a new technology is a far better weapon for fighting the concentration of economic power than an antitrust suit. The healthy condition of its use, however, is that the new art does not become the exclusive property of firms which are established. Keeping the dynamic urge alive among the people is a moral value; to contrive an instrument which the better serves the end is a moral question.

2. THE RASH VENTURE INTO REGULATION

The moral quality of competition has long been under bitter attack; and to it have been applied many ugly names. It appeals to the least noble qualities in human nature, embodies a gospel of self-service, induces men who should be brothers to cut each other's throats, and engenders an insecurity in the land which makes the solution of the problem of poverty impossible. But none of the critics has demonstrated that "mutual help" is an adequate substitute for personal challenge or has shown that it is better to annihilate so mighty an urge as the pursuit of gain than to domesticate it to social ends.

The people of the United States have clung to competition as an article of faith, but where it has been demonstrated to have gone astray they have been ready to modify it in detail. It was where the rising humanitarian surge met the institution enthroned as "liberty of contract" that exceptions were first written. Rival business firms were free to compete for labor, but children were not competent to bargain for themselves and an age was fixed by law below which no boy or girl was to be hired. Women are potential bearers of offspring and must not be put in jeopardy by being allowed to be engaged at whatever wage or for whatever hours they are willing to accept. The courts further decided that physically men too were subject to fatigue; it was, therefore, quite right for the legislature to fix maximum hours beyond which their employers were not lawfully free to work them without extra pay for overtime. So the catalogue of items, which in time came to comprehend a labor code, emerged from the "felt necessities" of a human people and at last was blessed by the courts. This code has proved to be the most satisfying and enduring achievement in our venture into regulation. Our satisfaction is due largely to the high moral values upon which it rests. Its capacity for endurance stems largely from the strength which it has imparted to the labor movement in creating an organization within the commonwealth which has a vested interest in its perpetuation.

The ethical limit set to competition is even more sharply revealed in the creation of a code of business conduct. An old doctrine of the law, borrowed long ago from the canons of the church, forbade "unfair competitive practices." In many states, and eventually by the Congress of the United States, this principle was lifted from the common law and elaborated into a telling series of prohibitions. The federal courts were opened to the victims of such unlawful practices for the collection of damages because of injuries done. The Congress which passed the laws had no idea of either abandoning or abridging competition. As Henry Carter Adams, upon whose philosophy the Congress had acted, had stated it, the new laws established "a moral plane for competition."

But legal excursions into morality may themselves go astray. The concept of unfair competition has been transmuted into "fair trade" laws which have been employed to guarantee wide markups on merchandise and narrow the field of competition. At times the trend has offered notorious exhibits in proof of the old adage that eternal vigilance is a requisite of liberty.

A kindred legislative venture involved an even more direct public control of business. It began in the states with a number of industries, the telephone, the water works, the street railway, the provision of light and power, which at first were said "to serve the public utility" and in time were called "public utilities." In respect to each it was argued, more or less plausibly, that the businesses were "natural monopolies" and that a single concern, by a unification of operations, could better serve the community than a number of concerns. The recognition of monopoly meant the abandonment of competition in certain parts of the economy as a mechanism of control. And in its place, by almost universal consent, a system of "regulation" was set up. The theory seems sound and the device of a commission as an agency of control seemed obvious. The utilities were kept under "private enterprise"; the economies incident to a single operation would substantially lower cost; an authority was there to insure adequate service, to hold profits to a reasonable sum, and in general to safeguard the public interest.

As at last the federal government took on the role of public control, it followed the pattern set by the states. In 1887, an obvious move was to set up the Interstate Commerce Commission for the control of railroads; and in several installments of legislation its powers were enlarged. In 1914 the Federal Reserve Board replaced more primitive agencies of control as the regulator of the credit and monetary system of the country. After World War I, an improvised organization to meet a military necessity was remade into the United States Shipping Board, and the shipping industry under the American flag was brought under regulation. In the years which followed F. D. R.'s first inaugural, an alphabetical array of agencies, authorities, boards, and commissions, each laid upon a specific area of the national economy, came into being. Many, but not all, of these agencies were created by Act of Congress. Each was endowed with the authority to create a code of law for, and to enforce its commands over, a dominion of our industrial life.

3. BUSINESS STAGES ITS COUNTERREVOLUTION

It was, of course, too ideal to be true. In the early days of the New Deal, the medley of interests within the republic was too disorganized and frightened to fight measures for so unpartisan a purpose as "recovery." But as time passed and business picked up, business executives began again to do their own thinking. The objective came to be quite simple—if the controls set up by the government could not be destroyed, they could at least be captured. And captivity might serve the purpose even better than destruction.

The very system of control by commission invited attack. The moral purpose which led to the creation of agencies to oversee areas of the national economy was sound. But the device chosen, the regulatory agency, was destined to betray the ethical office of safeguarding the public interest which it was set up to perform. All initiative in ordinary business affairs is left to the concerns which are being regulated. Their method of operation, their various states of efficiency, their financial affairs, are largely their own concern. The commission does not sit in on policy making or administrative decision. At best, sitting apart and without an everyday acquaintance with the business, it makes a belated review, and until a few years ago it operated in the fear of being reversed by a court of law.

But the frailties of commission rule go far beyond procedure. The agency's work is of little special interest to the public. It is of daily concern and vital interest to those who operate in the section of the economy which is being regulated. If an issue is burning, the regulated interest can quickly mobilize and concentrate all its power at the point of decision. The public is highly diffused and lacks the capacity to be deployed to good purpose. If an appointment is to be made the public usually waives its rights by a failure to come forward with a candidate. The regulated interest, however, can put forward not one but a number of qualified men. Nor is it content to leave the matter to the President; it acquaints him with the superb qualities of its selection in a deluge of letters and telegrams from the most reputable of citizens. To say that, under regulation, the consumer is as well off as he would be if seller were pitted against seller for his benefit is to overlook the infirmities which beset the regulatory process.

The moral bankruptcy of an ill-chosen agency of federal regulation is exhibited in the oldest of them, the Interstate Commerce Commission. At the beginning it was staunch in the public service; but as years have passed, moth and rust have overtaken its establishment. In fact the rates are made, not by the Commission, but by a series of private rate bureaus through which the railroads decide for themselves what they will charge the public for carriage. Although the Commission has power to set aside rates, or even whole schedules of them, as unjust or unreasonable, it exercises its prerogatives in only the smallest fraction of instances. The Congress, of course, must share responsibility for the gross miscarriage of administrative control. A man's business must not, under our system of law, be delivered into the hands of a competitor; yet the Congress has placed the trucking, motor-bus, and river-barge industries in the hands of the Commission, which itself is responsive to the interests of the railroads. An old adage of the law—and, I take it, of justice and morals as well—is that no man shall try his own case.

How far the counterrevolution has gone it is impossible to say. An answer awaits a detailed study and appraisal of agencies of public control, a venture which is well worthy the attention of the National Council. But any old Washington hand stands ready to recite a multitude of instances. The Federal Trade Commission was once taken over by the interests it was set up to regulate. But it was presently recovered; and its domain, almost as broad as the economy, makes it hard for men of many trades to act as one and gives sane protection against lapse from moral duty. Its dominant vice seems to be an inability to distinguish between things which are important and things which are not. The Reconstruction Finance Corporation was set up to promote industrial progress by providing the necessary funds to long-time ventures which were sound but which the investment bankers would not touch. But by being set up as an "independent agency" it was cut off from the administration whose public policies it was its purpose to instrument. It was further diverted from its task by being entrusted to professional bankers who, in the making of loans, operated much as if they were still sitting at their old desks. If the Tennessee Valley Authority has stuck to its job and kept its integrity, it has been due not to the lack of pressures upon it, but to an unusual personnel which has stood up where the ordinary agency is accustomed to yield.

But instances are too varied and numerous for real presentation here. The common law is the law of the folk; and although the detail of its statement must be rewritten as the changing circumstances of society demand, the values which over the centuries it has served have an amazing capacity to endure. In his *Medieval Mind*, Henry Osborne Taylor measures the conduct of the age against its ideal and calls the result "the spotted actuality." The common law has always recognized "the spotted actuality." It admits that conduct cannot rise above a reason which is human, and accordingly sets tolerant bounds for the acts of the "reasonable man." But if it refuses to command the impossible, it is uncompromising in the essentials of justice.

The system of competition invites mistakes as well as sound judgments; it tolerates waste in its welcome for progress. But, as we drive into the future and seek to enrich life with products now unknown, we cannot tell before the event who is wise and who is foolish. Competition has the great advantage over regulation that it has a mechanism for throwing off the obsolete and does not allow error to become vested. This distrust of all that is established gives health to the common law, and its exacting rule that a man must not sit in judgment in a matter in which he has an interest is as close to the verities which are eternal as our age with its belief in relativity is likely to come.

The twin evils of decadence and captivity are evils of the first magnitude, often heightened by the disposition of the Executive to cheapen performance by shoddy appointments. An appraisal of the operation of our federal regulatory system in terms of adherence to or lapse from the duties they were set up to perform is a public necessity. A crusade to bring the activities of the several agencies back into accord with the exacting standards which are the very spirit of the common law is today the great moral task of the body politic.

IV

All of this, I trust, speaks for itself and demands no extensive gloss to establish relevance. A wise jurist has said that no one can see further into general statements than the concretions in his possession allow; and if the discussion here has run off into slavery and employer's liability, into the promises and wastes of competition, and into the attempts of agencies of government—in defiance of the demands of justice—to serve two masters, it is because the law has significance only within its habitat. For the law neither exists in isolation nor is "a brooding omnipresence" which in terms of "there shall" and "there shall not" issues its mandates from the skies. It is a creation of the folk, maintained as an instrument of justice; and its worth must be assessed by its capacity to do justice amid the rough affairs of the everyday lives of countless men and women who have not yet attained human perfection. In the light of the instances set forth above, it is thus possible to set some general propositions which, without the previous illustrations to give them reality, would be quite without meaning.

1. Our law, the law which the courts administer, is in essence the "common law." It hails from the age, and reflects the spirit, which has found expression in such terms as the village common, the common inn, the common callings, the book of common prayer, and the communion. Where it has gone astray from its office of providing a common justice for the common people, it has betrayed its trust.

2. The common law is an instrument flexible enough to do justice in many ages and in a variety of cases. Its dominant drive is to the redress of injuries done; but, with recognition of the need for prevention, it has borrowed "equity" from the law of the church. It can thus not only punish crime and assess injury but also issue decrees which in effect say to the wrongdoer, "Go and sin no more." Although for centuries equity and the law were separate instruments of justice, they have at last been merged to its more perfect administration.

The ideal of the common law is to secure a justice which is that of the layman. Thus the legal standard of behavior is that of the "reasonable man," one which allows conduct to be assessed—and differently assessed—by the mores of the community and the age. The jury, made up wholly of laymen, is accorded an important place in the administration of justice; the judge must be a jack-of-all-trades. A series of courts, specialized to the distinctive tasks they are set to do, is abhorrent to our system of law. The court must be kept broad enough in its view, and varied enough in its experience, to come to grips with the diversity of conflicts—and situations— which life constantly serves up. A rigid code by which all conduct is to be measured would betray the very purpose of justice for which the law is invoked. The facts, as was revealed in the *Duplex* case, are "the facts of *the* case," by virtue of which the law is in-

dom, and the integrity of the judges into whose trust it is given. It cannot be made to reflect the more objective view and the higher moral standards of a community it never knew. The charges which can be lodged against the shortcomings and the backwardness of the law—and their number is legion—and its lapses from the service of justice can be laid at the door of many another institution. The law departs no farther from the moral code than does the culture whose creature it is.

On the contrary, the intellectual process by which the law is revised operates in a more critical fashion than do most of our other social controls. For the court which, through its handling of cases, remakes the law works neither in isolation nor in secrecy. The lawyers for the contending parties explore the facts, present and analyze the issues, cite the authorities which are relevant, and work under the strongest incentive to correct each other's mistakes. The judge who tries the case usually finds himself compelled to give his reasons, and he must answer before an appeal court for any errors he may make. If more than one judge sits, a decent respect for the court and for the parties demands an opinion from the dissenting member of the bench. No other institution hedges in the integrity of its process with such safeguards.

The cases which the law handles are created by, or have their setting within, the national economy. The ultimate values by which these cases are resolved are derived from the moral order. If the law, amid the tangled and conflicting conditions of an industrial society, is adequately to fulfill its office as an instrument of justice, all who have a part in its administration—litigants, lawyers, judges —must be alert. If the law is to be a responsible institution, it must be shaped by the moral values which converge into the thing called justice. With the law, as with all which is precious in our culture, eternal vigilance is the condition of life.

PART III

Our Economy in Other Perspectives

X

The Biological Foundations of
Ethics and Social Progress

by Alfred E. Emerson
Professor of Zoology, University of Chicago

Introduction

The question has often been asked whether the methods and principles of natural science can be applied to the study of ethics—or, indeed, to any of the subdivisions of the humanities and social sciences. Although sciences are divided according to their subject matter, they all use a logical method for the attainment of self-correcting knowledge, and the method may be applied to a great variety of fields of inquiry. The essential principles of the scientific method are observation by means of sensory perception; classification of related facts; determination of causes and effects and the formulation of theoretical interpretations in conformity to the facts and their relations; the verification of facts, relationships, and interpretations through reobservation and accumulation of relevant facts; and, finally, the reporting of the facts, relationships, and interpretations in order that others may criticize, modify, and correct the data and the conclusions.[1] Scientific logic is itself an aspect of the philosophy of knowledge.

There would seem to be no valid reason why ethics cannot be studied by scientific method. It is true that science is based upon

[1] The facts and theories of biology used as a basis of this chapter will be found more extensively discussed in W. C. Allee, A. E. Emerson, O. Park, T. Park, and K. P. Schmidt, *Principles of Animal Ecology*, Philadelphia, W. B. Saunders Company, 1949.

objective data, while ethics may arise in part from subjective feelings, but subjective data may be objectivized and analyzed. Psychologists constantly treat subjective emotions scientifically. The origins and the effects of subjective attitudes may be studied by the objective methods of social science—in large part the same methods that are used in natural science. Subjective concepts and emotions give rise to behavior in both animals and man.

There are some who feel that so-called cold-blooded scientific analysis takes away the response to beauty and the aesthetic delight inherent in art and religion. The philosophy of aesthetics is still in a crude form. However, there is some reason to think that the recognition of order and harmony in thought and ideas as well as in nature and in the works of man may give rise to emotional pleasure akin to that derived from other forms of beauty. The motivation from aesthetic emotions stimulates the scientist and the humanist alike.

Many scientists would not agree with some of the above statements and would take the position that ethics, values, and beauty are not valid problems subject to scientific investigation. The contention of this chapter is that a partial understanding of value systems is possible through the scientific method.

Man tends to rationalize his subjective attitudes. Ethical statements often are used to cover up more basic motivations and feelings. For the purposes of this essay, this conscious or unconscious hypocrisy is not examined in detail. It is thought best to confine the discussion to ethics as it initiates and controls human behavior and social coordination. The secondary psychological aspects of ethics are important but are left for further analysis to the psychologists.

Because of the complexity of society, we may expect to find the scientific methods used in biology to be more applicable to the social sciences than are those used in the physical sciences. Biology handles intricate data and concepts. Neither biology nor ethics can ever become an exact science with rigid mathematical formulation or prediction. If a few factors influence a repeated event and these can be quantified, mathematical formulation and prediction are possible. In biology and in the social sciences, however, a great many factors usually affect any given event, and these are seldom completely known or evaluated. In spite of the complexity of the subject matter, biology has made great advances in understanding and in controlling life processes. Progress in agriculture and in medicine demonstrates the applicability of basic biological science to complex activities and events. There would seem to be no intrinsic reason why social science, including much of the humanities and ethics, may not be expected to advance and to find applications in some measure commensurate with the rapid development of the biological sciences.

We should not expect to find absolute truth by means of the scientific method. Unproved and possibly unprovable assumptions are fundamental for scientific method—for example, the validity of sensory perception in bringing us into contact with reality. Relations of sensory experience are basic to the logic of science, and all scientific truth is therefore relative. So, likewise, any scientific knowledge of ethics will remain relative and will never become absolute.

Certain biological principles are found to be transferable to social science. Biology and anthropology have clearly demonstrated that man has evolved directly from the higher mammals. Not only do his body and mental faculties show relationship to his primate relatives, but his society is based upon mammalian group behavior —particularly family group behavior. These comparisons may assist us in understanding fundamental principles of societal coordination.

There are many unique characteristics of the societies of man, particularly those associated with language. Biology does not deal directly with social phenomena that are dependent upon symbolization. But these unique qualities do not prove the lack of fundamental connecting principles between the social and natural sciences. Probably the study of the great bulk of human social activities will remain within the fields of the social sciences, and biologists will only assist in laying foundations upon which the social scientists can build.

PHILOSOPHICAL CONSIDERATIONS

If we agree that scientific method and concepts as used in the complex biological sciences may be applicable to the study of ethics, we must validate the use of analogy. No biological group with the exception of social man possesses an ethics based upon the communication of symbols. Therefore the comparison of ethical man to any other living system is through analogy.

There is much controversy concerning the use of analogical comparisons. We may briefly state that comparative resemblances are classified into three types—fortuitous, homologous, and analogous.

In the case of *fortuitous resemblance*, the correlations of observed facts indicate no incidence beyond that expected by chance, and no cause-and-effect relations can be established. Sympathetic magic[2] and astrology may be cited as widely held beliefs of causation with little or no indication of any significant correlations beyond those that may be attributed to chance.

Comparisons of *homologues* are used frequently in biology and are fundamental to much of our knowledge. Homologues are similar because they possess the same intrinsic cause-and-effect relations. For example, the eyes of a gorilla, a chimpanzee, and a man are considered homologous. Illustrative homologous characters usually have only a proportion of identity that seldom reaches 100 per cent. In consequence, differences occur associated with homologous similarities, and complete identity of compared organs is rare.

In the study of ethics, we may apply the concept of homology to similarities of ethical practice with the same origin under the same guiding forces and passed from one individual to another by means of the same symbols with the same meanings. For example, similarities of ethics in different Christian sects may be considered socially homologous if they can be traced to the same historical source.

Biological *analogy* refers to functional resemblances arising independently of each other through the action of natural selection on different genetic systems. Analogous similarities are neither fortuitous nor homologous, but they appear through the action of similar extrinsic or environmental guiding forces. For example, the eye of an insect and the eye of a man have similarity in their image-perceiving function, but there is no evidence that any genes initiating eye development are the same in these two forms. An-

---

[2] Sympathetic magic may be illustrated by the attempt to injure a person by injuring his image. "Hanging in effigy" is a related modern custom.

alogues in biological systems are the result of convergent adaptive evolution—a principle that will be briefly mentioned later.

A complex structure or process may have both homologous and analogous traits at the same time, and these may be difficult to separate in all cases. On the other hand, homology and analogy may be easily separated in certain instances.

Much of biological science is founded upon comparisons of analogues. It need only be stated that many genes are analogues: different hormones in the vertebrate body are analogues; sex determination mechanisms in trees, insects, and man are analogues; the multicellular individual sponge, vertebrate, and plant are analogues; and the societies of termites, ants, and men are analogues.

Only general resemblances between analogues should be expected. Significant analogues often lack close similarity of detail. Because of the expected limitations in the degree of identity between analogues, extrapolation from one analogue to another has definite restrictions. One cannot presume that two analogues necessarily possess common traits or principles of organization without comparative facts and significant correlations. But the possession of similarities in independently derived systems substantiates the concept of analogy and stimulates inquiry into the causes of the resemblances. The more distantly related the compared phenomena are, the more difficult it is to recognize shared causation, but at the same time the more fundamental and important is the discovered principle.

Critics of analogical reasoning are concerned over its use for certain false conclusions. It is true that there are many examples of naïve associations and even dangerous thinking resulting from false analogical comparisons. The danger is real that scientists will rationalize their prejudices by the use of false analogical reasoning under the guise of purported scientific method. It is hoped that this danger has been avoided in the present discussion.

The pitfalls of analogical reasoning may be avoided by a scientific investigation of the meaning of terms. Verbalisms and euphonious metaphors may often prove to be false analogies. Analogy is valuable in scientific comparisons, but only when true functional resemblance can be demonstrated.

A comparative study of ethical patterns and systems may be expected to reveal fortuitous, homologous, and analogous similarities, and these may be objectively studied and measured. Significant resemblances between ethics and any biological process are largely if not wholly analogous.

Analogy between Ethical and Biological Systems

The reason why ethics is confined to humans seems obvious. Man constitutes the only species that has attained communication through learned symbols that can be transmitted from one individual to another and from one generation to another.

Biological inheritance is made possible through the transmission of genes. Genes are considered to be self-duplicating protein molecules, each different one distinctive in its enzymic action. Human social or cultural inheritance is made possible through the transmission of symbols—usually spoken or written language. Social contact and continuity are necessary for social inheritance. Germinal contact and continuity are necessary for biological inheritance. Biological and social inheritance are analogues with fundamental differences in mechanisms and fundamental similarities in their hereditary function.

Duplication and the repeated initiation of homologous activity are not the only functional analogies between genes and symbols. Symbols are also analogous to genes in their ability to become modified and to pass on the modification to other individuals. Modification of symbolic meanings seems to be a necessity for the progressive social evolution of man. A rigid invariant system of symbols passed from one generation to another would be social inheritance but would prevent progress. Any attempt to establish a fixed and unchanging pattern of symbols and ideas is consequently unprogressive. Here we may begin to discern an important difference in emphasis between democratic and authoritarian political philosophies—between freedom of expression and inquiry as contrasted to a stereotyped ideology. Freedom of the individual is the basis of criticism and new adjustments, and no political regime has lasted long which has so restricted individual freedom that it has negated the possibility of reform.

Gene mutations are nearly always haphazard in the adaptive direction of their effect. In contrast, modification of symbols by means of human intelligence and reason often produces a directed adaptive response. Humans not only intelligently direct the change in symbols, but they create new symbols to express new meanings and initiate new directional responses. There would seem to be little question that a part of the uniqueness of human social evolution rests upon this important difference from biological evolution. The difference in the rate of the two types of evolution is largely to be explained by this principle.

The two functions of genes—one the repetition and duplication leading to inheritance, and the other the capacity to mutate—result in a compromise between the two. Too much change would destroy inheritance and result in the loss of accumulated adaptation. Too little change would prevent evolutionary advancement. Genes have evolved toward a balance between these somewhat opposed functions. This balance is termed "mutation pressure" by biologists. Have the analogous functions of symbols also tended to evolve toward balanced equilibrium? The question needs exacting study.

Genes have a unitary property that includes a degree of individual independence. Each gene may be naturally selected and sorted independently according to the efficiency of its function.

One gene may have numerous effects in different physiological settings. It seems obvious that symbols also vary in their effect in different combinations with other symbols and in different social settings. The differences in the meaning of the same word in different contexts is a simple example of this principle as it operates in a cultural system.

Characters of organisms are dependent on many genes. Functional symbolic systems also are dependent upon multiple symbols, each of which can also function in several directions.

Recombination of genes into new patterns is a basic cause of genetic variability. Recombination is the main function of sex in plants and animals. Organized recombination of symbols may also profoundly influence the evolution of symbolic systems including ethics. The science of ethics will probably find some significant analogy to sexual fusion. Our common use of the term "cross-fertilization" is indicative of such an analogue.

We may predict that changes in patterns may produce novelties in both gene and symbol systems. The concept of emergent evolution emphasizes new properties emerging from new associations. As a matter of fact, it is hoped that this book will produce some emergent concepts from the cross-fertilization of science and ethics, science and economics, and ethics and economics.

Individual organisms are integrated by a variety of biological mechanisms (biochemical and biophysical) that are predominantly dependent upon protoplasmic continuity or contiguity. Intraspecies populations are integrated by genetic continuity, by biochemical agents, and especially by sensory reaction and behavior. Population integration is not dependent upon protoplasmic contiguity except for the reproduction of individuals.

Behavior may be learned or instinctive (genetically initiated). Learned behavior is predominant in humans and learned symbols are practically unique. Ethics is an important aspect of learned symbolic communication integrating human populations and groups. Learned ethical behavior is both one of the causes and one of the effects of human social unity.

Biological organisms and populations show development in time (ontogeny, embryogeny, or life history) and evolution in time (phylogeny). Genes and gene patterns may have sequential effects in the life history of the individual. Distinctive adaptive traits associated with age may evolve in animals or plants. Populations often exhibit life cycles of the group as a whole (malarial protozoans, tape worms, aphids, etc.) with physiological and psychological functions distinctive in the different generations within the population.

Both individual and population characters have evolved through time with genetic modification during phylogeny. Ethics, as a primary integrative mechanism of human populations, may be expected to have these time dimensions. One may expect a development of ethical concepts from childhood to maturity, and a different ethics for children compared to adults. Not only is there an individual development of ethical attitudes, but there is an evolution of ethics through racial experience and cultural transmission from one generation to another.

Functional Relations of Organismic and Social Systems

Efficiency demands a degree of specialization, and all life now existing exhibits specialization of function among the parts. Division of labor is found among individuals in population systems, particularly in truly social animals. Natural selection sorts more efficient mechanisms for survival and the less efficient may be eliminated. The result is a general increase in division of labor during both development and evolution. The psychological division of labor within human society resulting from the learning of special skills shows a relation with the time factor of both individual and group development and evolution.

Division of labor and integration are reciprocal principles and are always associated. Specialized function has no utility if the parts are not brought into coordinated relationship and incorporated into a larger unit. And this unit is the result of the interaction of the parts.

Various levels of integration with division of labor among the parts are found among living systems. In all levels of interaction we find parts functioning toward the coordination of the more inclusive unity. Many types and gradations of mechanisms leading toward integration may be found. These mechanisms are often analogous in different organismic systems—for example, in cells, in multicellular organisms, in intraspecies populations, and in interspecies associations.

In human society, integration is attained by numerous devices including aesthetics, ethics, religion, economics, government, and education. The social institutions and customs are used to enhance, develop, and channelize the basic virtues of love, loyalty, mutual sympathy, and constructive competition. Destructive competition, hatred, and social vices may also be increased through social integration, but in the long run inefficiencies tend to be eliminated and functional efficiencies tend to be perpetuated.

Division of labor and integration are not ends in themselves. In order to evolve progressively, they must produce greater functional efficiency. The control of the necessities of life at optimal values for efficient existence seems to be a universal evolutionary trend. This self-control, regulation, and maintenance of many important conditions of life within the organismic system has been termed *homeostasis* by the great Harvard physiologist, Walter Cannon. Homeostasis within the human body includes the regulation of water, sugar, salts, and temperature, to mention only a few examples. Equilibrium within narrow ranges of variation and balanced compromise among multitudinous activities are characteristic of homeostasis. Homeostasis may be a delicate regulation with subtle mechanisms as well as a grosser and more obvious control.

Homeostasis is not static but is dynamic. Functional differentials and unbalance may be homeostatic. For example, the nerve impulse is a wave of depolarization of the nerve membrane. Depolarization is rapid, thus maintaining functional capacity of the nerve. The maintenance of polarization in this case is the homeostatic establishment of disequilibrium. Optimal conditions of life and existence often require differentials, asymmetrics, and variation, rather than uniformity, symmetry, and stability. Homeostasis is the regulation, control, and maintenance of conditions for optimal existence.

Homeostasis of population systems is also characteristic of animal groups. It may be observed in the activities leading to group protection from predators, stabilization of food resources, and shelter construction. What appears to be individual competition and combat may be group homeostasis. Survival of the species may depend upon efficiency in spacing the feeding and mating activities, so that we find animals fighting in defense of mates, nesting sites, and feeding territories. The size of the group in relation to the efficiency of biological activities is important and is often controlled and regulated.

Homeostasis within human society includes the social regulation of physical and biotic conditions of human existence toward more optimal values by means of architecture, industry, transportation, agriculture, public health, and economic exchange—to mention only a few aspects of social balance and control.

We may conclude from the accumulation of great quantities of evidence that the trend of all organic and social evolution is toward increased homeostasis, and that ethics and economics are important portions of the process in human social evolution. Many terms and phrases carrying implications of homeostasis indicate that this concept is old. These include such words and phrases as "well-being," "human welfare," "security," "harmony," "equilibrium," "the good life," "prosperity," "balance," "self-sufficiency," "the greatest good for the greatest number," and "the pursuit of happiness." Many of these terms also have ethical connotations.

Innumerable aspects of social life may have optimal values. These values, at least in part, may be measured and partially determined. Although the more obvious regulations are used to illustrate the principle—for example, the control of temperature in buildings, the control of the food supply through agriculture and business, the control of mobility through transportation, and the control of health through medicine—there is no doubt that a large number of social variables may become homeostatic. Social research will doubtless discover many subtle aspects of balance and dynamic equilibrium in multiple social interactions. The roles of music, art, literature, and entertainment have not been fully evaluated in terms of advancing civilization, but there is good reason to believe that a balanced life includes a proportion of time devoted to many activities—physical, aesthetic, intellectual, social, and relaxing. Humor seems to assist in personal and social integration and balance, but its function in human coordination is only vaguely understood. Much investigation of psychological and social control and balance is needed.

Organic and Ethical Evolution

The three fundamental factoral complexes that combine to produce progressive organic evolution are genetic variation, reproductive isolation, and natural selection. In the evolution of any social system we must also expect social variability, a degree of social isolation, and selective assortment of the most efficient social characteristics producing homeostasis.

In organic evolution genetic variation occurs by means of mutation and sexual recombination. In social evolution, it is suggested

that new discoveries and new ideas are roughly analogous to mutations, and that new arrangements and organizations of ideas and
concepts are analogous to biological recombination.

In its initial appearance, variation is likely to be unbalanced and
is often deleterious in its effect. To arrive at functional adjustment,
other factors must operate.

Organisms and social systems are too complex ever to expect perfection of adjustment either now or in the future. There is always
room for improvement and new adjustments are always necessary
to meet the constantly changing environment. Therefore, any restriction of evolution by means of a gross limitation of variation and
creativeness results in retrograde motion relative to other freer competing systems.

We now begin to detect the role of individual freedom in the
evolutionary advance of society. Freedom of opportunity, freedom
of speech, and freedom of inquiry are essential forms of controlled
variability necessary to social progress. Individual enterprise may be
a necessary trial-and-error mechanism with commensurate reward
for ingenuity, initiative, and skill in business or in other human
activities—for instance, in scientific research and in the creative
arts. Individual enterprise in social exploitation, however, is not
ethical if it rewards cleverness directed toward antisocial objectives.
Social pressures that inhibit or prevent such "individual enterprise"
are ethical if the result of freedom is a decrease in social health and
social homeostasis, a waste of human energy, and an economic exploitation of the ignorant. Initiative and cleverness are not virtues
in themselves. They may be deemed virtues only when they are
directed toward individual and social progress.

In organic evolution, reproductive isolation (lack of gene flow
between groups) is the dividing factor. It results in the branching
of the phylogenetic tree. Through its effect upon inbreeding, isolation also effects the establishment and perpetuation of gene patterns—a process of prime importance inasmuch as functional
characters are usually the result of gene combinations rather than
the effects of single genes.

It seems probable that cultural isolation analogous to the reproductive isolation within and between species of organisms has an
important bearing upon social evolution. Social isolation has not

been explored sufficiently to give us an adequate understanding of its role.

Complete reproductive isolation in organic evolution separates species, but also there exist numerous types of partial isolation separating portions of species populations to some degree, and this partial isolation profoundly affects the characteristics, adjustments, and survival of the intraspecies groups.

Humans are one species. There is not only gene flow between all human groups with quantitative variations in its extent and rate; there is also a horizontal (spatial) and vertical (temporal) flow of ideas, concepts, and symbols with variations in the degree and rate of flow.

Complete or partial isolation probably has a highly important effect upon diversity and upon fixation of patterns in both organic and cultural evolution. Diversity and fixation allow whole integrated systems to be selected as units. Partial isolation enables parts of the system to affect other parts.

In human society, there is partial isolation between geographical groups, between language groups, between racial groups, between national groups, between religious groups, between professional groups, and between economic groups—to mention a few. There is also partial isolation between repeated unit institutions within these social groups—for example, between churches of the same denomination, universities, and business firms in the same business.

Accompanying the numerous partial isolations, there is communication between all of the groups and subgroups within the species, so that there is a degree of coordinated unity for human society as a whole that even transcends the lines of conflict in war areas.

It is obvious that one individual may belong to a number of partially isolated social organizations. On a much more simple level, there are parallels to this situation in the biological world. For example, a worker honeybee may sequentially take part in various hive activities and field work. A single human individual may have different social relations and serve different functions in each organization in which he is included. Each of the cultural units to which he belongs tends to develop balance and coordination in time. Progressive social evolution is in part dependent upon both cultural diversity and pattern fixation, and rapid progress is dependent upon partial isolation. Either extreme isolation or extreme interchange would slow adaptive evolution, if it be granted that the biological analogies are applicable to social evolution. Individuals in their multiple group relations exert a control over both extremes. The fluctuating degrees of isolation and interchange may themselves become homeostatic.

The guiding factor in organic evolution is natural selection. The unfit are eliminated and the fit perpetuate their fitness. Genes established in different pattern combinations are sorted by natural selection with resulting increase in adaptation and homeostasis.

It appears that selection is also the guiding force in social adaptation. The processes are strictly analogous because selection operates on genetic variation in organic evolution, while it operates on cultural variation in social evolution. If, however, the analogy between genes and symbols has some validity, the analogy between the forms of selection may have significance. It is admitted that there are intricacies in the analogy between natural and social selection that need investigation and clarification.

It would seem probable that social evolution has moved toward increased adjustment and homeostasis by means of a sort of natural selection of more efficient systems and the slow elimination of the less efficient. The economic principle of laissez faire results in a selective sorting through success and failure.

Natural selection has not just favored the strong, the powerful, and the courageous. It has led to adaptation in innumerable directions, including both competitive and cooperative interrelations. Cooperation within the organism and within the intraspecies population often increases efficiency and well-being and is therefore subject to positive selective pressures. This seems to be the real reason for the evolutionary trend toward better physiological and behavioristic integration—mainly physiological within the organism and mainly behavioristic within the population system. By means of cooperation, the group may become more powerful in its competition with other groups and species. But individual power may be self-defeating if it is harmful to the group. Power, therefore, does not always lead to survival. If power is used to augment the long-term well-being of the species as a whole, then an evolutionary trend toward an increase in power may be expected. The relation of strength and power to survival is often misunderstood. Whether or not the strong survive depends upon the use made of strength.

Selection operates on whole units, so whole populations may be selected as entities. Social units are doubtless subject to selection in their entirety without precluding a relatively independent selection of the component individuals. The species as a whole is often the integrated unit. Selection will favor mechanisms that increase living efficiency among individuals composing the species and that increase the adaptation of the entire species to its environment.

Natural selection is based upon the elimination of the unfit and the survival of the fit. This recognition of death as necessary to much progressive evolution is abhorrent to some. Certainly there is no biological evidence to indicate that the prolongation of individual life is a general directional trend in organic evolution. The individual life span may be increased in time if greater species efficiency results. But evolution will lead to a shorter individual life if the species adaptation is thereby increased. With the increase of the individual life span in recent human history, social science must direct much study to this problem.

Elimination of the unfit does not always involve death. For instance, competition between males for a female may prevent one male from fathering offspring at least temporarily, but usually does not result in his death. There are many other cases that show that competitive elimination is not always lethal to the loser, and it should be emphasized that cooperative units may survive at the expense of less cooperative systems and interactions.

When we view survival and elimination as guiding factors in social evolution, we immediately see that death is relative. Business enterprises often succeed or fail in relation to their relative efficiency in meeting human wants, but the life or death of the individuals composing the business firm is not crucial. Symbols and ideas may die or survive within a culture without complete dependence upon the life or death of the individual originating or harboring the concepts. This principle seems to be grossly misunderstood under some forms of government—witness the political purges in Soviet Russia, the murder of millions of Jews by the Nazis, and the numerous executions of "heretics" under the Spanish Inquisition.

The question arises concerning the automaticity of selection. It is true that progress toward increased homeostasis in organic evolution is almost wholly the automatic result of natural selection, but the growth of the learning capacity in man, his conceptual thought, and his ability to transmit symbols have produced a striking change in the processes of evolutionary progress. The social growth of knowledge of factors in the physical and the biological environment enables man to control processes to a marked degree. Artificial selection has taken the place of natural selection in the rapid evolution of domestic animals and plants. There would seem to be no doubt that man controls his own social evolution to some extent, and many social trends are the result of his conscious choice of alternatives.

With the growth of a scientific understanding of the causes and effects of social evolution, man can exercise greater control over his own destiny. The slow evolutionary trends resulting from unintelligent and unconscious processes may never be eliminated altogether, but there can be little doubt that far more rapid progress toward better adjustment will be fostered by conscious understanding and control. The general direction of progress toward homeostasis is the same in the long run whether the selective sorting be natural or artificial, but the relative speed of evolution is vastly different. Control, of course, does not imply force by a dictator or dictatorial clique. Control is by broad social and cultural understanding and skill, made possible only by freedom of inquiry and freedom of speech.

The analytical task of the social scientist is tremendous. It is usually difficult to isolate and evaluate the factors leading to social progress or decay. The biologist has shown that multiple factors may be analyzed in part; and a partial understanding is far better than no understanding, although there are accompanying hazards. Many phenomena are now partially understood and controlled that were formerly considered beyond the capacity of human intelligence. Historically, defeatist philosophies were constantly invoked in the attempt to prevent scientific advance—for example, the philosophy of vitalism that stated that inorganic principles could not be applied to life. Prevalent at present is a philosophy that states that biological principles cannot be applied to social and humanistic man.

To return to the analysis of selection, we find that it varies in its effects with certain environmental periodicities. There is a tendency for selection temporarily to guide a system toward short-term efficiency, but the long-term efficiency in a relatively stable environment ultimately prevails because the systemic unit possesses long temporal dimensions. One can imagine a gene that increases adjustment to a warm climate and that decreases adjustment to a cold climate being positively selected during the summer and being negatively selected during the winter. There are doubtless many instances of fluctuating selection pressures in social evolution also. An individual German could not get a certain job in the late 1930s unless he were a Nazi. But, in the late 1940s, the same individual could not get the job if he had been a Nazi.

In both biological and social systems these fluctuating pressures balance each other or result in compromise solutions. On occasion fluctuations may match environmental periodicities, for example in seasonal activities. Also, on other occasions, asymmetries and lack of equilibrium may be functional, and a homeostatic maintenance of controlled variables may evolve—for example, the accumulation of emergency food in one place either physiologically or socially.

Because both the organism and the social supraorganism are temporal entities incorporating the past and exhibiting adaptation to that portion of the future that repeats the past, selection operates on temporal adjustments, and long-term adjustments tend to survive over short-term adjustments even though the short-term efficiencies may be temporarily greater. Predators and parasites are known under certain circumstances to destroy their potentially permanent food supply by overexploitation. The killing of the goose that laid golden eggs is a parable with many social implications. Strikes for higher wages beyond the capacity of the balanced economy of the business sometimes destroy the livelihood of the workers.

There is a prevalent attitude among biologists that competition and cooperation are opposites and that one prevents the other. Actually there is a fair amount of biological evidence which indicates that competition may have an optimal value, too much or too little both being detrimental to the survival of the group. The studies of W. C. Allee[3] on the social hierarchies of vertebrates show that competitive interaction results in a cooperative organization under some circumstances. It seems plausible that competition among men may be socially beneficial at optimal pressures and that either too much or too little competition might interfere with the growth of cooperative social organizations.

Cause and effect are not always linear in time and much confusion results from the assumption that they are. It can be demonstrated with data from the study of organic evolution that variation, isolation, and selection are not linear in the time sequence of their relations. Genetic variation has often been assumed necessarily to precede the action of selection. But there is much evidence that the mechanisms of variation (for example, sexual recombination) have a function, and that these are consequently selected and evolve in an adaptive direction. The mechanisms of isolation may also have survival value. These factoral complexes have circular and web relations and the effects often influence the continuous or repeated cause. Many problems of teleology are resolved by an understanding of circular causation.

The principle of circular causation is certainly applicable to the factors determining social evolution. In fact, the conscious control of the events of social evolution made possible by scientific knowledge of these events is a clear example of circular causation. It is quite possible for an individual who is the result of a process to influence the future operation of the process and its effects.

CORRELATIVE PHENOMENA IN ORGANIC AND SOCIAL EVOLUTION

If organic and human social evolution are even partially proceeding according to similar forces and principles, one might expect to find certain parallels in the results.

[3] In *Principles of Animal Ecology*, p. 417. Also see W. C. Allee, *Cooperation Among Animals*, New York, Henry Schuman, Inc., 1951.

It has already been mentioned that the dividing factor in organic evolution is reproductive isolation. We certainly find partial cultural isolation dividing social systems, and there is no doubt that evolutionary "trees" may be drawn for numerous social and cultural patterns—for example, the splitting of languages from a common stem and the evolution and branching of forms of art.

We are also aware of horizontal infiltration in addition to vertical origins—for example, the French words incorporated into the English language following the Norman conquest. Horizontal infiltration of genetic components (gene drift) occurs among subspecies and racial groups in organic evolution, always with partial isolation separating the groups. Horizontal infiltration of species is also characteristic of the evolution of interspecies community systems discussed later. Horizontal infiltration is more complicated in social evolution than in organic evolution. Social "evolutionary trees" show numerous intertwinings of the branches.

As natural selection operates upon different organisms in a similar habitat, *convergent evolution* may lead to similar analogous adaptations. In social evolution, symbols may be similar in function but unrelated directly in origin. Money as a medium of exchange and economic value originated independently numerous times. Taboos on incest have originated independently in widely separated cultures.

Adaptation may often become modified so as to perform several successive functions in turn during progressive evolution. In later stages a more recent function may dominate while an earlier function may be lost. For example, among the vertebrates the support of the gills became modified into jaws and portions of the jaws later were incorporated into the middle ear. The function of a basically homologous organ changed from breathing to eating and ultimately to hearing. Changes of function can be traced through numerous social lines. Words often change their meanings in time. Architectural form may change from utilitarian to aesthetic value. Religious ritual may symbolize one concept at an early time and a different concept in modern times.

Former adaptations may be lost, but the genes involved in the growth of an organ may be so woven into the fabric of the system as to be lost with difficulty. We may detect thousands of vestigial and functionless structures in the bodies of organisms. Examples are the vestigial eyes of cave fishes, the pelvic bones of whales, the reduced wings of flightless birds, and the ear muscles of man. It is a simple matter to find such vestiges in our cultural patterns. Examples are functionless details of architecture and clothing. Legal codes are notorious for their inclusion of outmoded laws. The spelling of a word frequently outlives its original phonetic value. Religious ritual often repeats a form the meaning of which is lost in antiquity.

Although the word "degenerate" is often used for regressed structures, the implication is not fully justified. There is always a compensation for the loss of function, often by incorporation into a more inclusive system where inefficient duplications of function are avoided. Although the reproductive function of a cell is regressed in a nerve cell, it is hardly correct to refer to a brain neuron as degenerate. All animals have regressed as they lost the power of photosynthesis possessed by their plant ancestors, but are all animals thus degenerate? It would seem better to recognize regressive evolution as a concomitant of adaptive specialization or division of labor in more inclusive systems and to measure the resultant increase in homeostasis of the whole system. We must be careful to evaluate the complexities of social regressions before we label them degenerations.

SOME APPLICATIONS OF BIOLOGICAL PRINCIPLES TO ETHICAL PROBLEMS

If ethics is correctly conceived as a learned integrated cultural system symbolizing human experience of success and failure in striving for a better life, if ethics is a set of customs pertaining to responsibility, duty, and right, and if right is conceived as conduct leading toward increased optimal living and homeostatic control, we may now study its application to special problems. A basic classification of ethics is proposed as it relates to the integration of various levels of organization.

Individual Integration

Evolution has been guided by means of natural selection toward individual integration. Most individual integration is physiological in its nature because of protoplasmic contiguity. However, particularly with man, behavior and conscious thought also integrate the individual personality, and ethics may function at the individual level. Any controlled behavior that leads toward individual disintegration may be considered unethical, and any behavior leading toward personal balance, control, and greater effectiveness may be considered ethical. Effectiveness through self-discipline, serenity through the appreciation of the arts, health through exercise and diet—all these are ethical. One may say that each person is morally responsible and dutifully bound to strive toward individual health, emotional balance, and personal effectiveness and integrity.

In terms of evolutionary science, we may say that adjustments leading toward individual homeostasis were selected because of their influence upon survival. Before the advent of symbolic thought, these mechanisms of homeostasis were essentially genetic. But with the emergence of intelligent man, symbolic systems could lead effectively toward the same goal with a greater degree of plasticity under diverse environmental and social conditions. So concepts of right and wrong enabled man to control his behavior more effectively. Individual happiness is often given as the goal of human life, but homeostasis seems to be a more adequate goal for both organic and social evolution and has the added advantage of being subject to objective analysis, quantification, and comparison. Possibly individual happiness and individual homeostasis are correlated, but the two concepts are difficult to compare by scientific method.

It is not implied in the foregoing statements that an individual can always control his actions. Although alcoholism is unethical if the individual has the power to direct his own behavior, the addict may be sick rather than morally undisciplined. The same may be said for neurotic and psychotic behavior. In a broad sense there may be no more blame for a person with a psychic disturbance than if he has a bacterial disease. Any individual or social action leading to a cure of such a disease is ethical. Condemnation on so-called moral principles may be unethical if it is based upon a fallacious understanding of the causes, and if it does not lead to amelioration, cure, or prevention.

Sexual Integration

The integration and mutual adaptation of the sex pair was an early biological evolution based upon physiological and behavioral mechanisms. Sex is one of the most obvious examples of population differentiation with division of labor and integration, both leading to increased homeostasis of genetic recombination and many other functions. In the case of sex, it should be noted that homeostatic control over genetic variation was established through selection, thus illustrating circular causation. In later stages of evolution, sex differentiation of individuals itself became genetic.

Much of human psychology and social life is an outgrowth of sex biology, and it is to be expected that ethics and morality will evolve to a marked degree around the sexual relationship. Marriage has become a sacrament of the Church and morals have guided the mores and stability of the marriage relationship.

The sexual pair is a biological entity and it is likewise a social entity. Any custom that integrates husband and wife increasing their adjustment and homeostasis is ethical. Any self-controlled behavior that disrupts the biological, emotional, aesthetic, and social values of marriage is unethical. An infinity of detail is ordered by this fundamental principle that is surely biological in its foundation.

Family Integration

The family unit, like sex, is a socially integrated group with an obvious biological basis. Adaptation between parents and offspring has evolved with an increased control over shelter, food, and defense of the offspring. Specialized organs such as mammary glands have undergone adaptive evolution. The unit of selection is the family group as a whole with its temporal relations. Behavior leading to parental hazards and sacrifices evolved among animals long before the rise of human ethics.

Again we find a behavior system evolving out of the physiological system that integrates the group. Some of the group behavior is genetic, as can also be demonstrated in sexual behavior; but with the human family much of the behavior is learned, intelligent, and transmitted through symbols. The emerging learned behavior tends to evolve in the same direction as did the inherited behavior—namely, toward maintenance of the family unit and more optimal conditions for the development of the young.

Behavior leading toward familial homeostasis has usually been considered ethical and our analysis substantiates this conclusion. Behavior leading to a disruption of family ties, especially during the period with dependent children, is considered unethical. We may also note that parental interference with the establishment of sexual and family relations by mature children is considered unethical even though the parental control may have been ethical during the developmental period of the children. In other words, ethical relations between parents and offspring change as the children mature.

Social Integration

Animal societies are real biological entities established by evolutionary factors. Like other biological units, they exhibit division of labor, integration, and a directional evolution toward increased homeostasis. Most of the attitudes and behavior that we term ethical involve human social relations, and we shall return to this subject shortly for further discussion.

Interspecies Integration

We often find, in the study of organic evolution, that groups of species, each reproductively isolated from the other and often very distantly related, exhibit mutual adaptation to each other. Although genetic continuity integrates the individual, the sex pair, the family, and the intraspecies society, only environmental or ecological continuity, particularly by means of natural selection, integrates interspecies groups. We have seen, however, that the factors of evolution include both internal and external continuities in interspecies systems, so that supraorganismic integration may still appear in interspecies systems as the result of natural selection. Obviously the organism, the intraspecies supraorganism, and the interspecies supraorganism are analogues. But these systems have significant similarities produced by the action of similar forces. And they all show division of labor, integration, and an evolutionary increase in homeostasis. Although quantitative comparisons of the degree of integration are lacking, it seems safe to conclude that the individual organism is likely to be a more tightly knit system than the population group, and that the intraspecies population usually shows a greater degree of integration than the interspecies system.

Without question no species of animal or plant has had such a profound effect upon the physical world and its life as has social man. Homeostasis has not only developed within the society of man, but man has also learned how to control his external environment, including all other living organisms. His rapid development of power over the world, however, has sometimes resulted in harm to himself, and when it does, negative selection occurs.

If man, like other organized living systems, is moving toward increased homeostasis, and this control at optimum values involves other forms of life upon which man is dependent, it seems clear that ethical behavior must include his relations to his domesticated animals and plants and also to the wild animals and plants occupying his global habitat. We must remember also that the interspecies community, like other biological systems, has time dimensions. The human species is part of a larger entity that is temporally integrated. Intelligent conservation of our wild life and natural resources is ethically sound. Wasteful individual exploitation and destruction is wrong and bad. Even harmful species may be studied with benefit to mankind so that a far-sighted ethics may suggest the preservation of the harmful species.

Ethics and Social Integration

Let us now return for a somewhat more extended discussion of our main theme—the biological basis of social ethics.

Races are partial genetic segregates within the species of man. The majority of species of animals and plants have similar subdivisions resulting from partial reproductive isolation and natural selection operating in different habitats. Sometimes, although not always, races and subspecies diverge until they are reproductively isolated and contemporarily genetically discontinuous. They evolve into full species by this process. In the case of the human species, the development of transportation has reversed the trend toward complete isolation of the races, so that we are now witnessing the slow breakdown of ethnic barriers. The human species is already a genetic and cultural unit, and the present indications point to increasing integration and coordination of the system. Ethical relations between species and between races of the same species may have different qualities.

Although competition occurs between individuals within a species, it is noteworthy that combat and drastic elimination are more common between species. The reason for this difference is that the individual is in a greater mutually beneficial relation to other individuals of his species group, and natural selection operates for the benefit of the whole species population rather than only for the benefit of the individual.

It is therefore usually against the long-term interests of society for an individual to kill or harm another of his own species, although it may be to the interests of both the individual and his species population to kill an individual of another species. Also individual exploitation of other individuals within the same species is harmful to the group and will be negatively selected, while cooperation, integration, and division of labor usually result in an increase of efficient homeostasis for all concerned and will be positively selected.

Therefore we find that the concept of the "brotherhood" of all mankind rests upon firm biological principles. Ethics leading to firmer integration and mutual benefit between the races of man is in conformity with biological trends. Behavior toward racial elimination, racial exploitation, and human slavery in all its forms does not lead toward increased long-term homeostasis. The exploiter is harmed along with the exploited, and natural selection of these cultural characteristics tends gradually to eliminate unethical racial practices. Behavior close to that of many stated principles of Christian ethics would seem likely to survive the onslaught of temporarily powerful philosophies like that of Nazism with its fallacious theory of racism.

schools, or different business firms, often seem to view their relations as wholly or largely competitive. An evolutionary perspective upon their social functions, their integration, and their relationship to the more inclusive societal system may bring a better understanding of their role in society. And with this better understanding, better ethical standards may bring about a healthier relationship. What is often termed "good business" may be found to be ethically bad, and selection, both natural and social, may be expected slowly to sort the good from the bad.

When a benefit is gained through cooperation by means of learned behavior, honesty enhances confidence between the cooperating individuals, whether the social unit be the sex pair, the family, or a social system. Honesty is thus ethical, because it tends to establish firmer cooperation between individuals, between business firms, or between nations. Dishonesty tends to be destructive of group homeostasis and is consequently unethical.

Justice, when contemplated from the viewpoint of social evolution, emphasizes individual responsibility to the social system, establishes criteria for the judgment of human conflict, and enhances attitudes of fairness and compromise in human relations. Law based upon justice augments social homeostasis, and it can be seen also that social progress necessitates functional pliability and change in legal codes.

This chapter makes a few suggestions concerning the existence of reciprocal principles in biology and sociology that may be further studied and evaluated. We can now begin to perceive the direction we should follow in our search for ethical truth, ethical wisdom, and methods of increasing human welfare. Not knowing why social evolution has taken place nor whither it is bound, but vaguely sensing its reality and direction, man has often rationalized the process by means of mystical explanations. At present we are only at the threshold of a science of social evolution—a science that can objectively analyze both ethics and economics and thus increase our ability to interpret, predict, and evaluate processes and effects more adequately than is now possible.

XI

An Anthropological View
of Economics

by Ralph Linton
Sterling Professor of Anthropology, Yale University

Since the employment of an anthropologist in a study such as the
present one is somewhat unusual, the writer feels a brief initial
statement of the scope and aims of this science may be desirable.
Anthropology is usually defined as the study of man and his works.
However, for present purposes we need concern ourselves only with
that branch of it which deals with the behavior of human beings
in society. This is also the subject matter of other social sciences
such as sociology, economics, and history. In practice, however, anthropology tends to differ from these both in subject matter and in
techniques. It has taken as its special fields uncivilized societies.
The term uncivilized is here used to refer to groups that have not
yet reached the level of culture complexity involved in city living,
still less in modern mechanized production.

Although such societies differ greatly in many of their characteristics, they have one feature in common. The functional unit is
the small local community, corresponding in most of its characteristics to the *Gemeinschaft* of the German sociologists. Within such a
community, face-to-face contacts are at a maximum and the necessity for formal legal controls of economic behavior is at a minimum.
In such close in-groups, reciprocity is self-enforcing, while the emotional ties established between individuals and the inevitable identification of the society's members with the community and with
each other ensure mutual assistance and the satisfaction of at least
minimal survival needs for all. Only a pathological individual enjoys

seeing someone whom he knows personally suffer from cold or hunger when he himself has a surplus.

Such a situation is markedly different from that existing in modern Western society with its urban centralization and widely extended lines of impersonal economic interactions. The modern science of economics has, understandably, been developed almost exclusively in terms of urban culture, with its socially anonymous individuals, impersonal relations governed by law, and still more impersonal international exchanges of goods and credits. I was interested to note in reading the papers in this volume the extreme infrequency with which the pressure of informal public opinion was noted as a factor contributing to the maintenance of ethical standards.

As a result of its particular subject matter, anthropology has developed somewhat different techniques from those employed by the other social sciences. Since anthropologists have worked almost exclusively with nonliterate peoples, they have been debarred from employing questionnaires or consulting accounts and market reports. In compensation, they have developed the participant-observer technique: an individual establishes residence in the community to be studied and, as far as possible, integrates himself into its daily life. This technique has both advantages and disadvantages. It makes possible an excellent record of actual as distinct from ideal behavior and of individual differences in belief and action. Its disadvantages derive from the unavoidable influence of the investigator's personality and unconscious value system on his interpretation of what he observes, and from the impossibility of reducing most of his observations to forms susceptible to exact measurement or statistical treatment.

The question naturally arises whether the results obtained by the study of uncivilized communities are applicable to modern societies. There are various points at which they obviously are not. However, the comparative simplicity of economic behavior in small, well-integrated, and relatively isolated communities makes it much easier to ascertain the fundamental values and types of interaction involved. It seems safe to assume that any value or type of interaction which is recognizable in all or nearly all uncivilized societies must bear a close relation either to the normal physiological and psychological needs of individuals or to the effective functioning of societies in general. To this extent the results obtained through the comparative study of uncivilized societies may aid in the understanding of our own economic institutions. In a society such as our own, where the necessity of adjusting to rapid and far-reaching technological changes is complicated by the presence of conflicting economic and social ideologies, a knowledge of these fundamentals is vital. Any attempt at economic and social planning which fails to take them into account is unlikely to succeed.

The Anthropologist's View of "Values"

The attempt to ascertain what are the fundamental institutions and types of interaction involved in social living inevitably leads the investigator into the field of values, in the philosophical rather than the economic sense. There seems to be a widespread misapprehension of the position of the modern anthropologist with respect to both values and ethics. The earliest anthropologists judged the value systems and culturally established behavior patterns of uncivilized peoples on the basis of whether these did or did not conform to those of Western Europeans, especially the British. This was followed, as an understandable reaction, by a period in which great stress was laid on the concept of cultural relativity. The possibility of passing valid judgments on the value systems and behavior patterns of any society was denied, and the prescribed scientific attitude toward these may be summed up in the phrase: "Well, some do and some don't."

At the present time few anthropologists maintain this position, which, they feel, was based on a superficial study of cultural phenomena. To make their present attitude comprehensible it is necessary to digress briefly into a discussion of the vague and controversial field of values. Hardly two authorities will agree on a definition of what constitutes a value, but the consensus of opinion would seem to be that a value is "anything toward which the members of a society bear a favorable attitude." The writer would like to amend this to "A value is anything toward which the members of a society bear a *definite* attitude." There are numerous things which the members of any society reject or consider undesirable. Murder and theft within the group would be cases in point. These negative values appear to be closely comparable to the positive ones in terms of their effects upon individual and social behavior. Concepts, behavior patterns, and objects can all be considered values under this definition since they are all "things" toward which the members of the group may share definite attitudes.

It is an observed fact that all cultures reveal by their organization and content the presence of certain concepts which have been called *themes.*[1] This term is derived from literary usage where, in the course of a novel, the same motif, say conflict between father and son, may appear in a number of different contexts or episodes. The themes in any culture are reflected in and instrumented by numerous patterns of overt behavior. Since attitudes attach to both the themes and the behavior patterns which instrument them, we may consider any culture as having *thematic values* and *instrumental values.*

Both the needs of individuals and the imperatives of social existence are much the same everywhere, and there are numerous thematic values which can be recognized in all cultures. Examples of these would be solidarity of the community against outside aggression, the proper rearing and enculturation of children, and the maintenance of health and happiness for the majority of the society's members. The behavior patterns by which thematic values are instrumented are inevitably shaped by practical considerations of materials and skills available and by the conditioning of the individuals who compose the society. Consequently, they constitute an area of phenomena in which the concept of cultural relativity is valid. Unfortunately, there is a strong tendency to confuse the universal thematic values with the instrumental values, which cannot, in the nature of things, be other than linked with particular cultures, and to accord equal importance to both. Thus, when the Pope refused to receive the late Mahatma Gandhi because he wore a loincloth, both parties would have agreed on the *thematic value* of mod-

[1] Morris E. Opler, "Themes as Dynamic Forces in Culture," *American Journal of Sociology,* November 1945, pp. 198-206.

esty as common to both their cultures; but they disagreed on the *instrumental values* of loincloths vs. trousers, each reinforced within a particular culture by symbolic associations.

In summary, the modern anthropologist is fully convinced of the existence of universal values which can be used as datum points in developing ethical judgments. At the same time he believes in the relativity of many instrumental values and that these should always be appraised in terms of their effectiveness in the particular milieu in which they operate. He is critical of economic determinists, since he has abundant proof that the same fundamental thematic values can coexist with a wide range of economic systems. At the same time, he recognizes that changes in technology will inevitably lead to modifications in instrumental values. He does not believe that any institution or pattern of behavior which occurs with great frequency in cultures is necessarily "right" in an ethical sense. At the same time, he feels it is safe to assume that such a culture element must be intimately related to one or more of the universal thematic values, and that social planners are unwise to attempt to eliminate it without careful study of the situation and development of functional substitutes.

The economic life of any people includes activities of several different orders. As a minimum there are always formalized patterns controlling ownership, production, distribution, and consumption. Certain universal thematic values can be recognized in each case with a limited range of variability in instrumental values. In the case of ownership two universal values are recognizable: (1) the value of individual well-being, deriving from satisfaction of the physical and psychological needs of persons, and (2) the value of group well-being. The patterns of behavior by which these universal values are implemented in various cultures are so organized as to maintain a balance between them, although emphasis on one or the other will vary with the time and place. However, to ensure the survival of the group, both values must be adequately implemented in terms of the local conditions. Serious imbalance in either direction is a transitory phenomenon. Either the imbalance is corrected or the society breaks down and ceases to exist as a functioning entity.

Before discussing the patterns of economic behavior usually found in "primitive" societies, it may be well to dispose of the myth of primitive communism. Transient visitors in "primitive" communities are often struck by the way in which the same ornament or garment may appear on half a dozen different individuals on as many occasions, or by the seemingly casual and openhanded way in which a hunter will distribute his bag to others, leaving himself barely enough for a family meal. Closer acquaintance will always show that such practices operate against a background of clearly defined concepts of private property. There may be the same easy, informal borrowing and lending of objects which characterize some of our own small, closely knit social groupings (fraternity houses, for example), but such temporary use is never confused with ownership. As regards sharing of food, investigation usually shows that the distribution follows definite rules and is made in anticipation of return in kind. Since many sorts of foods cannot be preserved for any length of time and since the fortunes of the hunt are unpredictable, the seemingly free distribution is really the safest form of insurance. Communism, in the sense of common ownership of all resources and products, is to be found only in organizations, such as some religious orders, which have a highly sophisticated, civilized background. If it marks any stage in the evolution of economic life, it is a late stage rather than the first one. From the brief duration of most of the attempts at true communism, it seems doubtful whether our species has reached a point in its own evolution where it is capable of the sort of altruism such communities demand of the individual.

OWNERSHIP OF PROPERTY

Ownership of property may be vested in individuals, in families or other kin groups, in sodalities (i.e., groupings formed on the basis of common interest rather than kinship), or in communities as wholes. It is frequently difficult to distinguish between individual and group ownership since it is not uncommon to have the property rights of a group formally vested in its head. This arrangement provides, by a sort of legal fiction, sanction for the exercise of controls designed to benefit the entire group, but at the same time does not entitle the "owner" to dispose of the property without group consent. Extreme examples of this type of fictional ownership can be seen in certain West African kingdoms, such as Dahomey, where not only the tribal territory but the belongings and persons of all tribe members were theoretically the property of the king. From this legal fiction, the king derived his authority to administer justice. If the criminal and his belongings were royal property, the right of the king to impose fines or capital sentences could not be questioned. Wherever Europeans have come into contact with native groups, they have found it advantageous to emphasize individual at the expense of group ownership, since it has always been much easier to purchase land or other significant resources from a chief than to obtain group consent to such expropriations.

The types of property recognized by primitive cultures are frequently more numerous than those recognized in our own legal system. In the absence of a money economy by which all types of property can be reduced to a common denominator, curious, and to our way of thinking, fantastic distinctions may arise. However, certain classes of property seem to be generally recognized. These are: (1) clothing and ornaments, (2) tools and weapons, (3) utensils and furniture, (4) songs, dances, and symbols, (5) magical objects and formulae, (6) food, (7) houses and building sites, (8) land, (9) domestic animals, (10) rights of borrowing, plunder, or veto.

All primitive societies make an initial distinction between men's and women's property, but the point at which the sex line is drawn with respect to any of the categories just listed varies from one society to another. A strict division of activities along sex lines is characteristic of all primitive societies, and the general rule is that property of a given sort is owned by the sex which makes and/or uses it.

Clothing and ornaments constitute personal property in the most emphatic sense of the term. They are almost universally owned by individuals. The principal exceptions appear in those cases (1) in which ornaments which have been transmitted in the family become heirlooms invested with strong attitudes of family pride, or (2) in which the accumulation of ornaments has become a recognized technique for hoarding family wealth. The latter situation is not uncommon and is by no means limited to primitives. Thus, in good seasons, the Indian peasant invests his profits in jewelry for his wife instead of depositing them in a bank and regards this jewelry as a savings account.

Tools and weapons are also, with few exceptions, owned by individuals. As any craftsman knows, no two tools, even in our own standardized culture, are exactly alike and familiarity with a particular tool makes for greater efficiency of production. Where a craftsman makes his own tools or has them made especially for him, the adjustment is particularly close. The continued use of a tool or weapon also leads to strong identification on the part of the owner. Thus, in several of the Australian aboriginal languages, a special gender is used for parts of the individual's own body and this is extended to include his spear thrower, which is felt to be as much a part of him as a hand or foot. Such identification is probably a factor in the common practice of burying a dead man's tools and weapons with him. Inheritance of objects of this class is normally limited to the sex which uses them.

The classification utensils and furniture may be taken to apply to the equipment of a dwelling. Here ownership distinctions are usually even more sharply drawn among "primitive" people than among ourselves. It is an almost universal regulation that in the establishment of a new household the husband's family provides those articles commonly manufactured or used by men and the wife's family those commonly manufactured or used by women. The individual ownershop thus initially established continues throughout life and is extended to children as these are added to the family group. In almost all primitive households every object is individually owned. Only an exceedingly courageous husband will dare to sell a utensil from his wife's sphere of ownership, even when offered many times its value; and the child, from the moment that he (or she) can walk, has his own property and complete rights in its disposal. In the course of making museum collections, the writer has frequently had to bargain with a child of four or five years for some object. The parents might advise, but always left the final decision to the child as owner.

A not uncommon type of primitive property consists of the right to sing certain songs, to use particular masks or other symbolic objects, and to perform particular dances. The initial value of such forms of property theoretically lies in the strengthening, through its use, of the individual's or group's supernaturally derived powers. However, a very real value consists in the social prestige derived from ownership and in the admiration aroused in the bystanders by the performances involving property of this type. The outstanding example of ownership of such rights is found among the Indians of British Columbia where the right to use a particular series of animal forms in decorative art is the inalienable property of particular family lines, while the right to wear certain masks and perform the associated dances is personal property in our own sense of the term and can be sold or given to another individual by the owner without consultation with the family. In the absence of written records the fact of ownership must be maintained by occasional public performances, and the guests who are invited to attend these performances are given gifts in payment for their services as witnesses.

Magical objects and formulae tend to be individually owned but may also be the property of families or sodalities. Thus, a certain type of magic may be transmitted within a particular family like any other sort of skill. The members of the family derive advantages either from the protective power of their magic or from exercising it for fees. Sodality ownership of magic is implied in practically all secret societies, even though this aspect has been allowed to wane among ourselves. An extreme example occurs in the graded secret societies of some parts of Melanesia. In the Melanesian cultures in general, property is of tremendous social importance and the richest individuals exercise the highest degree of power and prestige irrespective of the methods by which the wealth was obtained. The secret societies teach their initiates magical formulae for the protection of property and the increase of wealth. The two are unusually closely linked in this case since every increase in wealth is assumed to have been made at the expense of someone else. Thus, if a man has an abundant yam crop, it is assumed that it is abundant because his magic has lured yams from other men's gardens into his own. Each grade within the secret society has its particular magics and also its antidotes for the magic of the grade below. As a man buys his way upward from grade to grade, he also buys protection of his property from a larger and larger proportion of the community and, with this, the magic which will make it possible for him to draw their property to him.

Returning to types of ownership more familiar to our own concepts, highly complex property regulations often center on food. The most fundamental distinctions here are those between food which has been obtained by the efforts of a single individual and that which is a product of cooperative labor of several individuals. A second almost universal distinction is that between fresh foods which cannot be preserved and foods which can be preserved or which actually are preserved and in storage. Individually obtained food which cannot be stored is usually regarded as the property of the taker, but tends to be freely divided with other members of the family or even community. In this connection, individuals standing in certain degrees of kinship to the procurer may have rights to certain parts of any animal brought in. Under the systems of food taboo it is also quite possible for a hunter to be completely deprived of his kill because the animal is taboo to members of his kin group or age group. However, the individuals who can utilize his kill will be under obligation to make a return to him later of food which he can use. Food which can be preserved and stored tends to become the property of family groups rather than individuals. This is particularly true in the case of agricultural products which have involved the labor of the whole family. In such cases the theoretical ownership of the food store is frequently vested in the wife, who allocates an appropriate amount to each member of the family for each meal. Thus, a familiar sight in native dwellings in Madagascar is a row of small baskets of graduated size used to measure out the rice which shall be put in the cooking pot for each member of the family. The older the child, the larger his measure.

Individual ownership of dwellings is the rule for nomadic peoples who employ portable shelters. Among the Plains Indians, for example, the tepee is everywhere the property of the wife, who also is responsible for its transportation and erection. The question of house-site ownership rarely arises. However, it is a common nomad pattern to have the same village arrangements at each encampment so that each family finds itself with the same neighbors on either side. A disgruntled individual may withdraw from the camp and pitch his tent some distance away, but any attempt of one family to take another's regular place would be hotly resented. Wherever primitive people are settled in villages with fairly permanent housing, both the dwelling and the land on which it stands are normally owned by the family group. Especially at the level of primitive agriculture, this group is frequently a joint family, consisting of a number of related nuclear families of our own type. In the typical joint family the sons, grandsons, and subsequent male descendants of the original founder continue to live together, holding the residential and some other sorts of property in common, and building additions to the dwelling establishment to provide for the new nuclear families set up by successive marriages. Under this pattern, the daughters marry out, taking with them movable property as dowry, but forfeiting all rights in the joint family dwellings and lands. A parallel arrangement also occurs in which the female descendants of the founder keep the establishment while the male descendants join other establishments through marriage, but this is relatively rare.

Although the members of a joint family form a corporation exploiting their common property cooperatively and dividing the produce according to their individual needs, the arrangement does not preclude the accumulation of wealth by certain individuals. Wealth which has been accumulated by the individual through his independent activities, such as trading, practice of a specialized craft, or performances as a medicine man, belongs to him. In societies with the joint family institution, it is the ambition of every individual to become the founder of a new family line. When enough personal wealth has been accumulated, a town lot will be bought from one of the already established joint families, a house built, and the founder's spouse and children moved to it. Such a move does not entail the break-up of the joint family, since the seceding individual will be given the equivalent of his share of the joint family real estate in money or goods.

Although the town lots within fairly permanent settlements are always owned by either individuals or kin groups, the attitudes toward land outside the village limits vary greatly. In general, every primitive society has a clear picture of its territorial limits. Even the most primitive nomadic groups follow a cycle of seasonal movements within a certain territory. This movement brings them back to the same camping sites year after year. They exploit the same territories season after season and resent and punish trespassing by members of other social units. However, the patterns governing ownership of land within the society's territory vary greatly with different societies and different ecologies.[2]

In general, private ownership, whether by individuals or families, is linked with the ability of the territory to produce a regular and predictable yield. Thus, where the main economic dependence is on migratory game, as in the Great Plains in the days of the buffalo, the attitude toward land is normally like our own attitude toward the open ocean with its wandering schools of fish. Since private ownership of a definite area would give no economic advantage, the idea simply does not occur to those who exploit the wandering food source. On the other hand, where game is not migratory, or where a given piece of land has a predictable yield of wild vegetable foods such as acorns or lily roots, concepts of private land ownership tend to emerge. The Northern Forest Tribes of American Indians divided their range into clearly defined family hunting territories delineated by natural landmarks such as streams or divides. Each family knew the approximate number of fur-bearing and food animals of each species living within its territory and practiced conservation, taking only as many of each as could be killed without diminishing the permanent supply.

Where there was heavy economic dependence on the collection of vegetable foods, fruit and nut trees and patches of growing plants were often marked by their discoverers and regarded thenceforth as their private property. Such ownership often involved care

[2] Ecology: The relation of organisms with each other and with the physical environment in their particular region.

of the plants and was actually the first step toward the development of agriculture.

Among the simpler agricultural peoples, it is often exceedingly difficult to differentiate between true ownership and usufruct.[3] Here again, patterns seem to be largely determined by the nature of the crops and the techniques of agriculture. In those areas in which farming is carried on by the process of clearing land, utilizing it until either the fertility is exhausted or weed growth makes further cultivation unprofitable, and then allowing it to lie fallow for long periods, ultimate ownership is rather uniformly vested in either the community or some kin group larger than the joint family. However, during the time that such land is actually in use, the individual or social unit which has cleared and planted the fields has full right to the produce and can punish trespassers. When the land is lying fallow, individual ownership rights are abrogated. The lands are reallocated when they have recovered sufficiently for cultivation to be carried on once more, usually a matter of at least a generation.

Wherever permanent village settlements have been developed by farmers and dairymen whose culture traces from the Southwestern Asiatic center of agriculture, as does our own, a uniform pattern can be recognized. The most productive fields and those closest to the village are owned by families, while poorer and more distant lands are held in common and used for pasturing the flocks and herds of the villages. The cultivated land is normally inherited by the joint family wherever this institution exists, or, in its absence, is divided equally among the sons. The old Western European pattern of male primogeniture is rare among "primitive" cultivators. In case a family becomes extinct, or dwindles to the point where it can no longer cultivate its former holdings, lands left free in this way are reallocated by the village elders. Where irrigation has been developed, both land and rights to water are, with few exceptions, owned by families. The main irrigation works are the property of the community and are kept in order by joint labor, while the intensive cultivation characteristic of irrigated agriculture is carried on by individuals or families.

[3] Usufruct: The right to use a property without the right of disposal.

Natural resources other than land, such as mines, timber, favorable fishing places, etc., are practically always owned by the group, which allows all members access to them. In certain cases, especially if the resource has supernatural powers, the right of access may be extended to several groups, even when these are mutually hostile. Thus, the red pipestone quarries from which a number of Plains Indian tribes derived material for their ceremonial pipes were regarded as neutral territory, and parties from hostile tribes who met there kept a truce.

One last type of property which requires mention is domestic animals. When these are not numerous they are regarded much as we regard pets. The tendency is toward individual ownership of particular animals, with mutual understanding and affection. The domestic animal is in a real sense a member of the family, whose idiosyncrasies are regarded as differing very little from those of the human members. In the case of pastoral peoples who acquire great numbers of animals, they tend to be dealt with *en masse* and family ownership is usual. Herds differ from land in that, through their natural increase, they provided the earliest form of interest-bearing investment.

In addition to the more or less universal types of property hitherto discussed, there are numerous local varieties which need not be discussed in a report of this length. Thus, in several Polynesian localities, the right of a nephew to carry off anything belonging to his maternal uncle might be considered a form of property, since it certainly contributes to the nephew's resources. A second and somewhat more widely distributed right is that of veto over property. Inherited property in particular may be owned by one individual, while its use and sale outside the family are controlled by a designated relative.

At the primitive level, ownership of the means of production is rarely vested in any society as a whole. As has already been mentioned, tools and hunting and fishing equipment are commonly of such a sort that they can be made and used successfully by one man. The main exceptions are in connection with traps for big game and with fishing appliances where the use of canoes and large seines and the building of fish weirs may require the cooperation of several individuals. In this case, the ownership may be by either families or sodalities.

MOTIVES FOR WEALTH ACCUMULATION

Like ownership, the accumulation of property is a universal phenomenon. Even the first men must have felt the necessity for making provision beyond the immediate needs of the moment. Food which could not be eaten at once would be kept and promising bits of raw material hoarded against the time when a new tool had to be made. Today, one finds in nearly all societies accumulations of property in excess of the anticipated survival needs of either individuals or families. The motives of such accumulation are varied and complex. However, the desire for increased comfort seems to be one of the less significant ones. While this may provide an initial stimulus toward accumulation, in most societies it can be met by the possession of a relatively small surplus. There are many "primitive" societies in which individuals at all economic levels eat much the same food, dress in much the same clothes, and enjoy much the same housing. In such societies, differences in wealth are reflected mainly in accumulations of ornaments, which may reach a point where they interfere seriously with the wearer's comfort. Thus, in some African tribes, rich men's wives wear series of brass arm and leg rings which weigh them down almost to the extent of an old-fashioned American convict with a ball and chain. Even in those societies which consciously think of wealth as a means to comfort, the possible ceiling for expenditure for this purpose is set by the technology and by human needs. After all, the individual can eat only a limited amount of food and wear only a limited amount of clothing. Above a certain level, the small house can be made quite as comfortable as the big one, and expensive foods are no more nourishing and often no tastier than cheap ones. Even with modern technology, wealth beyond a certain point can lead only to multiplication of gadgets, not to greater comfort.

The main motives for wealth accumulation at the primitive level appear to be the desire for prestige and the desire for power. In the

order to ensure these, production must reach certain levels in both quantity and quality. These levels are initially established by the local environment. Thus, the minimal production which will suffice for survival is very different for an Australian aborigine and for an Eskimo. In the case of the Australian, clothing is not only minimal but frequently lacking, and is rendered unnecessary by the climate. The same applies to housing. A crude windbreak or other shelter which can be raised in a few minutes suffices for survival. Most food can be gathered by hand or killed with spear and boomerang. Eskimos, on the other hand, must expend a great deal of labor on tanning skins and making tailored clothing which will protect the body from cold while permitting freedom of movement. They must devote much attention to housing, while hunting of the large sea mammals on which they depend most of the year requires an elaborate and ingenious equipment of harpoons, lances, and seagoing canoes.

While the minimal production necessary for survival is thus set by the environment, all societies actually produce more and spend more time and energy on production than simple survival needs would dictate. The values responsible for such excess are primarily social and psychological rather than utilitarian. The motives for the accumulation of property, which provide incentives for the production of economic surplus, have already been discussed. Another incentive for excess production is the desire for novelty. All societies are interested in new experience and, as such, are subject to "fashion changes," which destroy the social utility of display objects, such as clothing and ornaments, before they have lost their practical utility. Although in primitive societies these changes are not artificially stimulated as they are among ourselves, wherever we have adequate records extending over two or three generations for any primitive group, changes in fashion can be recognized. It is interesting to note in this connection that except in rare cases involving materials which are locally unobtainable, such as salt or iron, most primitive trade has to do with luxuries and novelties rather than necessities. The members of a society will produce more luxury objects than they themselves need, for purposes of exchange for luxury objects from neighboring groups. High production *per se* may also serve as a source of individual or group prestige. Competition of individuals or work groups for finishing tasks in the shortest possible time is familiar in most societies. Also, sheer quantity of product, even when carried far beyond the point of utility, may become a source of prestige in itself. Thus, Malinowski has noted that the natives of the Trobriand Islands not only take great pride in the way their yam gardens are planted, kept clear of weeds, etc., but also gain much prestige from a full yam storehouse, even though it is recognized that the crop far exceeds the needs of the family and that much of it will go to waste.

It is obvious that the minimum quality of any product is set by considerations of utility. Tools, weapons, and shelter must be adequate to their anticipated use. They must also have sufficient durability to make too frequent replacements unnecessary. However, there are few societies in which the craftsman is willing to stop at this point. Anyone who studies collections of "primitive" artifacts will be struck by the amount of labor which is frequently expended on fine finish or other nonutilitarian features. Although some of the apparently decorative elements may have use in the sense of imparting magical qualities to the tool or weapon, most of them are certainly applied for aesthetic reasons. While the psychological factors which produce aesthetic response are poorly understood, such responses are universal. People derive emotional satisfaction from the use of objects which are aesthetically pleasing. Also, the hand craftsman, through his identification with his product, acquires added satisfaction from making it beautiful as well as useful. Such activity not only satisfies his own aesthetic urge, but excites the admiration of other craftsmen. The result stands as an enduring witness to his skill and a source of personal prestige.

In general, one feels that, at the primitive level, high quality of any product reflects psychological rather than utilitarian values. One of the greatest social losses involved in our present methods of standardized mechanical production is the failure of such methods to provide any satisfaction for the workmen's aesthetic desires and interest in virtuosity, or for his need for identification with his products. Even the factor of prestige associated with good craftsmanship is now almost reduced to terms of quantity of production.

LABOR AND MANAGEMENT

The interaction of labor, ownership, and management, which is an increasingly important feature of modern production, is of much less significance in primitive societies. Wage labor is comparatively rare and the individual incentive for it minimal, since patterns of ownership of natural resources usually give all members of the society access to them. There are few means of production other than simple hand tools and, when these means exist, they are normally owned by kin groups or sodalities. The worker is a free producer who carries on his activities either alone or as a member of a cooperative group.

It is the nature of the activities themselves which determines whether they shall be carried on cooperatively. Such activities as seine fishing, housebuilding, game drives, and land clearing can be done more efficiently by groups than by single individuals. When, as in the case of building houses or clearing land, the results of the cooperation benefit a single family, the technique is usually that of labor exchange. This pattern is universal among settled agricultural peoples, and can be seen still active in our own rural districts, where threshing and hog killing are carried on by groups of local men who go from farm to farm and take care of the needs of each of the members' families in succession. Another universal pattern, also observable in American rural districts, is that the family whose work is being done by the cooperative group is supposed to feed the workers. An understandable rivalry between wives assures excellent meals on these occasions.

It is interesting to note that primitive societies frequently suffer from a genuine shortage of workers. One finds that the heads of local groups in hunting or pastoral societies frequently compete with each other for the allegiance of able-bodied young people. Thus, among the Plains Indians, band chiefs would make gifts to young men of other bands to persuade them to come over to their own. Even when there are enough workers, most primitive societies have an almost complete lack of hired labor, particularly domestic servants. The problem of assistance in the household is usually met by the institution of polygyny, i.e., plural wives. In this the value of company and the advantage of sharing activities far outweigh, for the average woman, any emotional satisfaction which might come from the exclusive sexual possession of a husband. Where rich men require personal services over and above those which can be performed by wives and children, such tasks are usually taken over by "clients," who thus express their submission and dependence, receiving in return the protection of a strong patron and frequent gifts.

Labor required for the exploitation of individually owned resources, such as improved land or herds, may be provided in various ways. Herding of other people's cattle tends to be an activity of young men by which they acquire property through a share of herd increase and are able to become economically independent in turn. Land is usually farmed on shares rather than for wages. Such sharing arrangements make the employee a partner in the enterprise with consequent personal interest and identification. Moreover, because of the time required to produce returns, the primitive sharecropper or share herdsman is assured of employment and economic support over long periods. As a consequence, he achieves a degree of economic and emotional security quite different from that of the modern urban proletarian or even organized skilled laborer.

The rise of a proletariat in the modern sense seems to have been definitely associated with the change from village to urban living. With the creation of cities, with their combination of added opportunity and need for population, individuals were drawn into them from rural communities. The consequent breakdown of old associations resulted not only in a collapse of extended family patterns but also in expropriation of the former villagers' rights in communally held land or other resources. The urban immigrants became not only landless but kinless. A factor which contributed heavily to the latter condition was the exceedingly high mortality rate of early city life. The peasant migrating to the city lost his extended kin group and was unable to establish a new one. Few family lines were able to survive in cities more than three generations, and even today there appear to be no cities which maintain their populations by the process of natural reproduction. The city everywhere draws into itself raw human materials as it does raw natural materials, and shapes both to its needs.

The differentiation between labor and management, although commonly thought of as a modern phenomenon, is actually an exceedingly old one. All cooperative exploitative activities require direction, and even in the most "primitive" groups labor is found represented by the ordinary workers, and management by chiefs or specialists who direct and coordinate their activities. Such management is necessary for maximum efficiency. At the primitive level it is based on real skill and knowledge and is, interestingly enough, nearly always rewarded with a higher return than that given to labor *per se*. The chief or director of the cooperative work group receives first choice of the products or a larger share than the other workmen.

Before leaving the discussion of labor, a brief statement should be made regarding slavery. The institution is much more characteristic of unmechanized civilizations than it is of "primitive" peoples. "Primitive" slavery, in the rare cases where it does exist, is necessarily light and of slight economic advantage to the masters. The slave can produce little more than he consumes, while the constant chances for escape which he enjoys assure him excellent treatment. Among such groups as the nomadic Arabs, for example, the position of slaves, who are owned only by chiefs or wealthy men, is actually much better than that of many poor freemen. Their owners take pride in giving them equipment as fine as their own, while the slaves in turn pride themselves on their fanatical devotion to their owners' interests. Agricultural villagers can find more employment for slaves and the institution is correspondingly more frequent among them than among food gatherers or herdsmen. However, even here the relatively small size of the community and the constant face-to-face interaction between slaves and masters give them a position in the family not greatly different from that of poor relations.

Methods of Distribution

The distribution of services and products is a necessary accompaniment of social life since all societies include not only specialized producers but also nonproducers. In the simplest societies such exchanges are for the most part socially prescribed and as such are aspects of the individual's social role. Exchanges of this type are universally associated with membership in nuclear families and generally associated with membership in larger kin groups, although the degree to which the latter are involved in economic life varies considerably. At one end of the scale lie such patterns as those of the Australian aborigines, with whom the distribution of food is almost completely controlled by kin ties, relatives of each degree being entitled to a specified part of the kill, while at the other lie patterns like our own in which kinship beyond the nuclear family plays no formally recognized role in economic interrelations. The most significant aspect of distribution regulated by kinship is that it involves no element of individual choice. Relatives must exchange goods and services whether they like each other or not, and there is no opportunity for personal advantage. At the same time, such economic interdependence promotes the solidarity of the kin group.

Voluntary exchanges of services and products are also to be found at all levels of cultural development. The exchange of services in activities requiring massed labor has already been mentioned. In such service exchanges an equitable return to each member is assured by the voluntary nature of membership and the ease of eliminating lazy or uncongenial individuals. Exchange of products occurs in many forms, the least familiar to the European being gift exchange, although even this survives in a minor role in our society. Many hostesses still keep a record of those who have entertained them so that they can return the compliment, and a careful evaluation of Christmas presents with an eye to return gifts the following Christmas is not infrequent. Gift exchange is an effective method for the distribution of products in simple societies. Even though the return of equivalent value for value cannot be openly enforced, failure to make adequate return is punished by loss of prestige and also by exclusion from future exchanges, with consequent deprivation. In keeping with good manners, gift returns are usually delayed for a time. Where gift exchange has been reduced to a system the donor has insurance against future needs, while both parties in the exchange receive considerable ego-satisfaction, not to speak of social prestige. While both sides may understand perfectly that a return is required, nevertheless the donor can indulge in a play of generosity and the recipient in one of gratitude, to their mutual entertainment. Gift exchange operates most successfully where communities are small and their members are in frequent face-to-face contact. Psychologically, it may be considered as an expression of social solidarity.

In contrast, barter and trade with their accompanying bargaining often provide outlets for aggression. Barter, which is the earlier stage of trade, operates effectively not only within a society but also between societies. It is applicable at all levels of economic complexity, as note its reintroduction in recent years to compensate for unstable currency. At the primitive level, we find it employed not only within tribes and between friendly tribes but also between hostile groups. Economic exchanges present so many advantages that even when political considerations might interfere, ways of perpetuating the exchanges are often developed. Thus, at the primitive level, we have the phenomenon of silent trade in which the members of one actual or potentially hostile group leave goods at a particular place and then retire. Members of the other hostile group then visit the place, take the goods, and leave a supply of their own specialities to the same value. Honest dealings in these cases are assured by the same factors which operate in gift exchange. Cheating on either side results in the breakdown of the system with consequent loss to both parties.

In other societies, a similar situation is met by the institution of market truces. Groups who are otherwise hostile agree to meet for trade at certain times or places. Thus, in the Northern Plains, the Mandan and the Dakota, who were hereditary enemies, observed a trade truce during the time that a late fall-flowering plant was blooming. At this time the Dakota freely visited the Mandan villages and exchanged the products of the hunt for Mandan corn. As soon as the truce period ended, warfare was resumed. Similar trade truces are found in many parts of the world. A slight extension of this, the "peace of the market place," is present in most Islamic countries and in many parts of pagan Africa. It was also known in

Europe in the Middle Ages. By this arrangement, persons entering the market place are required to leave their weapons at the gate and to ignore both tribal and personal feuds while market is in session. Any infraction of these rules is punished rapidly and with great severity, the death sentence being common.

Barter is the first form of exchange in which possibilities of individual profit are overtly recognized. Property accumulation through trading becomes possible for the first time and a new psychological factor is also involved. Ego-satisfaction derives only incidentally from the good will and gratitude of the recipient, coming rather from the feeling of superiority and satisfied aggression which comes to the individual who has driven a good bargain. In many parts of the world even today, bargaining and the pleasure to be derived from it are regarded as among the most satisfying accompaniments of goods exchange.

Trade may be distinguished from barter as an exchange involving a common standard of value, i.e., money. The introduction of money not only stimulates goods exchange but also has far-reaching effects on exchange patterns. It results in the reduction of goods and services to a common denominator, and the complicated exchange relations which characterize most primitive societies break down when brought into contact with it. In a money economy all goods and services become interchangeable and are therefore much more readily manipulated for profit. The evolution from barter to money economy can be historically traced in various societies, and the possibilities for profit and wealth accumulation and also for the use of accumulated wealth for power can be shown to have increased at each step. It is only in a money economy that capital invested for purposes of profit becomes functionally important.

Those accustomed to the modern emphasis on profit and capital gain as the main incentives for both production and trade must have been impressed by the minor importance which has been attached to the profit motive in this whole economic discussion. As a matter of fact, in most primitive societies profit in the modern sense is a very secondary consideration. Even in the rare primitive societies, such as some Melanesian islands, where each of a series of tribes has a monopoly of the manufacture of a particular necessary object and could presumably extort heavy profits from the other groups who are dependent upon its product, the trade usually consists in an exchange of objects of equivalent value. This value in turn is controlled by long-established custom rather than current abundance or scarcity. Such tribal specialization results either from knowledge of special skills or from the presence of particular raw materials in a tribe's territory. The advantage consists in obtaining what a tribe needs but cannot produce in exchange for an unneeded surplus of things it can produce.

There are also a number of primitive societies in which one finds patterns of loans with high interest rates and various types of security given, the whole being superficially reminiscent of our own financing arrangements. However, investigation nearly always shows that such arrangements are an aspect of a prestige economy which has little to do with the actual subsistence economy. The individual obtains loans in order to finance his preparation for feast giving or other types of prestige-producing display, and can safely run into debt in anticipation of the returns which he will receive on future occasions when he is a guest rather than a sponsor.

Last among the techniques of distribution is charity, i.e., the giving of goods or services to those unable to make economic returns. Charity may be regarded as essentially a substitute for socially prescribed exchanges. It is rarely of more than incidental importance in societies having a strong extended kin organization. It is also significant that in our own society, with increased centralization of economic power and state control, private charity is steadily being displaced by social mechanisms such as social security. The main incentives to charity seem to be the anticipation by the donor of individual gratitude and social prestige and also the lessening of the discomfort which one inevitably feels in viewing another member of one's society in pain or want. Especially in societies with ethically oriented religions, charity has in the past performed a significant function as palliative to the superego. The functions of diminishing class conflict and making the members of less fortunate groups contented with their lot, important in civilized communities, are not of great significance in "primitive" societies since these are not, in general, class organized.

In general, the values involved in distribution are much the same as those to be found in other forms of economic activity. We have here the desire to satisfy primary drives, the desire for novelty, the desires for prestige, ego-satisfaction, and so forth. The main difference in the values involved in distribution and production seems to be that, in distribution, satisfaction of the aesthetic and virtuosity urges already mentioned in the discussion of production is directed toward the personal interactions involved in the exchange. In most societies bargaining is regarded as an art whose techniques are generally understood and whose results are evaluated and appreciated by everyone. It is characteristic of the reduced attention to human values which is a feature of our own modern culture that bargaining has been largely eliminated at the level of distribution of goods for individual needs. It is still carried on between members of the managerial groups, but there is probably no society in which the small buyer is given as little opportunity for friendly chaffering with the seller as he is in the American economy.

CONSUMPTION PATTERNS

Consumption is the final aspect of economic activity, the one to which all other aspects lead, and is so closely involved with these that most of its features have already been discussed. The main point at which primitive consumption patterns differ from our own is in the almost universal occurrence of what might be termed communal ostentatious consumption. Although such consumption is common enough among ourselves, the unit with us is the individual or the nuclear family, while at the primitive level it is more frequently the entire village or band, with other communities often participating. The larger the group and the greater the consumption, the more successful the occasion. Since surplus created by primitive hand industry or techniques of food production is usually small, the community may voluntarily submit to severe deprivation over a considerable period in order to accumulate the food or goods needed to make an impressive display prior to consumption. Thus, in Polynesia, the chiefs, with full cooperation from the group, would frequently impose a taboo upon food such as taro or coconuts months before one of these communal feasts; while on the occasion of the feast itself the food, prior to cooking, would be displayed on an ingeniously constructed wooden framework which would make it look like an enormous pile.

In a study of consumption patterns, it is more than ever necessary to stress the importance of psychological rather than physiological needs as motivation of human behavior, and the importance of values not directly connected with physical survival. The significance of these two aspects of human existence in any economic system might be expected to vary in direct ratio to the economic surplus which a given society is able to create and distribute. Actually, complex historic-cultural factors seem to be involved. Mention has already been made of the wide differences in standards of comfort established by different societies, and one finds that some "primitive" societies allocate what seems to us a quite disproportionate amount of their time and energy to display activities. Oriental peasants or African tribesmen often seem to be existing on a bare subsistence level, yet they choose to expend part of their limited energies on aesthetic activities and to hoard their meager production surpluses for periods of ostentatious consumption or equally ostentatious hospitality.

Primitive and Modern Societies—Values and Patterns

In summary, a study of primitive economic systems reveals the same thematic values which are to be found in our own. However, the order of importance of these values and the particular patterns by which they are implemented may differ considerably. In all societies the survival values (i.e., those attaching to the satisfaction of the basic physiological needs of the individual and group) lie at the foundation of economic life. However, these values can be implemented (or the needs met) at a level of activity and economic organization considerably below that found in any human society. As technological development progresses, with the consequent increase in potential surplus production, the survival values become less and less significant in the economic picture. The trend may be

toward increasing elaboration of the responses to what were originally the survival needs of individuals, as in the exotic menus of
Roman banquets or in our own plethora of domestic appliances and
frequent fashion changes. These elaborations embody thematic
values of "comfort" and, at least in the case of appliances, "convenience," which are foreign to most primitive societies. Even in
our own case, they are, of course, inextricably interwoven with
prestige values. Conversely, the trend may be toward use of the
economic surplus to reinforce the social values of group solidarity
and euphoria, as in the development of elaborate systems of gift
exchange or reciprocal feasts, or of communal pride, as in monu-
mental construction. The surplus may be expended in pursuit of
prestige or power, these, at the primitive level, usually in terms of
the kin or community rather than of the individual. Lastly, the
existence of a surplus may make possible the diversion of time and
energy into aesthetic pursuits. These would include not only dec-
oration of utility objects or creation of art objects but also the elaboration of social or religious behavior, as in the Japanese tea
ceremony or fetes for local deities.

The most drastic differences between the thematic values involved
in our own economic system and those common to primitive societies in general seem to derive less from the technical developments
which have taken place in our own civilization during the last 200
years than from the lessening of intimate social relations and enduring association which has accompanied these developments. The
extraordinary degree of both social and spacial mobility enjoyed by
individuals during the period of mechanization has resulted in the
breakdown of extended kin groups and in the progressive concentration of populations in cities where opportunities for the establishment of close and continuing social contacts are minimal. A
considerable part of the modern industrial population passes its life
as transients with both the freedom for individual activity and the
psychological insecurity which this condition entails. Under these
circumstances, it is inevitable that those thematic values which can
be most readily associated with individuals, such as power and
prestige, should come to take precedence over all others. Similarly,
the symbols of prestige tend to reduce themselves to objects whose

connection with wealth is immediately obvious, such things as mink coats and big automobiles.

The classical economic concepts of labor as merely one more commodity and of production as motivated only by the desire for profit are valid only for societies in which the interaction of individuals has become depersonalized. They are the products of the lonely crowds, inconceivable where people know each other and feel themselves active interdependent parts of a larger whole. In view of what we know of human behavior in general, it seems highly probable that the present phase of social disintegration will be transitory. In even the current trends in the relationship of ownership, labor, and management, we can perceive a foreshadowing of new patterns in which management will recognize values of social significance and in which individual workers will receive not only economic rewards but also the prestige and aesthetic satisfaction which accrue to the master craftsman in unmechanized societies and which form such an important element in his reward for community service.

XII

The Psychological Basis of Human Values

by Donald Snygg

Chairman of the Department of Psychology and Professor of Psychology, State University Teachers College, Oswego, New York

The Relation of Psychology to Economics

In a rapidly changing society like our own, social and economic situations never repeat themselves exactly. Every situation has something new about it. As a result, no economic, business, or political planning is possible except as the planners have a concept of causation which enables them to make some guess about what people will do under circumstances which have never before arisen. This is true whether we are planning individually as businessmen or consumers or collectively as citizens. The faster the society changes, the more its members have to depend on theory.

One of the major obstacles in the way of getting more dependable concepts for predicting economic behavior is our limited knowledge of psychology. Economic or political behavior is behavior by people. When economists analyze and interpret economic behavior, when they forecast the outcome of this or that economic policy or trend, they are forecasting what people will do. To do this an accurate concept of human nature is essential. Any theories or predictions about what people will do are certain to be inaccurate if they are based on false concepts of the people whose behavior is predicted.

This places economists and other social scientists in an awkward situation. Human beings are complex organisms and there are a great many conflicting theories about them. In choosing among those theories we cannot safely trust our limited personal experience, which may have been with a special kind of people. The social or economic theorist who bases his theories of what people will do on his personal version of human nature is quite likely to get a theory which is applicable only to his own generation of his society or to his own social class. He is in danger of getting a theory which is applicable only to himself.

If he protects himself against this provincialism by basing his economic theories on current psychological concepts, he can still get into difficulties. The conceptual systems of professional psychologists are in the process of development and some of them, including some which psychologists are very hopeful about, are still too specialized to be applicable to the behavior of human beings outside the laboratory. The social scientist who uses a theory of this type without understanding its sources is in danger of building his picture of society on a theory which in its current incomplete form is applicable only to the maze behavior of the white rat.

And no matter which conceptual framework he adopts, he will find many of its concepts unconvincing because they are contrary to what he and his readers have always thought to be common sense.

COMMON-SENSE CONCEPTS OF HUMAN NATURE

One of the main obstacles in the way of our learning more about human nature is the fact that we already "know" so many things about it that are not true. Most people can recognize their ignorance of such subjects as entomology or cultural anthropology or nuclear physics, but few people except professional psychologists feel ignorant about human nature. Psychology, it is generally believed, is just common sense—what everybody knows. Some may doubt that redheaded people are quick tempered, but it is generally held to be "common sense" that *the* basic human needs are for food, shelter, and clothing; that practice makes perfect; and that the way to cure people of bad habits is to punish them. We delude ourselves, however, when we believe that these generalizations are dependable or that we learned them by experience. "Common sense" about human nature all too often turns out to be an author's epigram or an academic theory, now disproved, which was proposed so long ago that our grandparents heard about it in time to teach it to our parents.

The Fiction of Economic Man

One of the most prominent of the "common sense" barriers to better understanding of human nature is the widespread belief that economic motives are the only ones that matter in the economic realm. Studies of employee aspirations in American industry do not confirm the idea that pay is the only incentive or even the most important one. Wage incentive systems frequently result in slowdowns by the more efficient workers, who do not wish to outproduce their associates. Among American industrial workers, desire for group membership and approval has usually proved more potent than desire for money when the two are in conflict.

Katona[1] has recently reported that businessmen have a tendency to aim at increased volume rather than increased profits. He believes that economic motives are changing and lists, among others, professional pride and desire for prestige, for power, and for approbation.[2]

[1] George Katona, *Psychological Analysis of Economic Behavior*, New York, McGraw-Hill Book Company, 1951.

[2] The fiction of complete economic determinism, set up by the early economists as a convenient way of delimiting their field, has been mistaken by a great many people for a demonstrated scientific fact. As such it has had a profound effect on popular thinking about human nature and about our society. At a time when our way of life is under heavy attack, when many of the members of the society have lost faith in its ability to deal with the problems of human need, it is unfortunate that the simplest and most understandable analysis that many educated people are apt to encounter is based on the assumption that our economic system is a mechanism for the satisfaction of greed. Such a picture is not likely to attract converts or to strengthen the loyalty of the present members of the society. Nor does it lead to the effective functioning of the institutions which are caricatured and misunderstood.

Competition as a Motive of Behavior

Another common-sense idea which does not stand up in practice is the idea that people are inevitably competitive. It is quite true that most people measure their achievements by the achievements of their neighbors, and Katona has justifiably concluded that "the more money other people have the more a person wants."[3] As used in many schools and factories, however, competition is a comparatively ineffective way of getting people to work harder. People do not compete actively unless they think they have a chance to win. This causes a large part of any group to withdraw from competition early. These people then exert pressure on the others to drop out of the competition with them. In addition, more people are unwilling to compete when competing means the loss of friends, as it often does. Forced competition, in which people are obliged to compete against their friends, is a threat to the individual and therefore unpleasant. It is not surprising that workers or departments which have been involved in contests frequently drop their output to below normal as soon as the contest is over.[4] As a rule teachers who depend on competition as a means of motivation are able to get the majority of their students to compete only when they "choose up sides" and appeal to group loyalties.

PSYCHOLOGICAL CONCEPTS OF HUMAN NATURE

Although a great deal of progress has been made during the three quarters of a century that psychology has been an experimental science, psychologists are continually reminded of the tentative nature of their generalizations by the fact that competent psychologists may still differ from one another in their preference among the various conceptual frameworks and types of explanation that are used. The truth is that human behavior is so many-sided, so complex, and so variable that there is no single point of view yet

[3] Katona, op. cit.
[4] T. W. Harrell, Industrial Psychology, New York, Rinehart & Company, 1949, p. 280.

discovered by which we can understand it all. The problem is to find a point of view which will enable us to see the whole disorderly mass of phenomena in order and regularity, and, it is hoped, to make it predictable. In looking for a conceptual system which will make human behavior more understandable, present-day psychologists are following a number of different leads.

The Stimulus-Response Approach to Behavior

The most obvious approach is to attempt to explain behavior by the known principles of the physical sciences. Such a conceptual system was made quite plausible by the discovery of the reflex arc in 1832. It was discovered that the stimulation of a given nerve always resulted in the contraction of the same muscles, provided the spinal cord had been severed above the point where the nerve entered it. This fixed stimulus-response unit, which could be explained plausibly by several different principles of the physical sciences, was assumed to be the basic unit of behavior.

Following this assumption, the next problem was to discover how these fixed "basic" reflexes combine and interact with one another to produce the more variable and coherent behavior which is characteristic of an undamaged organism, animal or human.

The most important difficulty confronting this concept of behavior is the problem of stimulus selection. There are in any given physical situation great numbers of physical stimuli to which the organism makes no apparent response. A stimulus which sets off a response in one situation or at one time may have no effect at another time or in another situation. Or it may elicit a completely different response. And the stimulus which does elicit the response is not necessarily the strongest one in terms of physical energy.

This variability is ascribed either to changes in the conductivity of the nervous system or to tensions and imbalances which require (drive) the organism to behave so as to relieve them.

This latter concept has diverted the emphasis in physiologically oriented theories of motivation from the external physical stimulus which "triggers" the act to the internal conditions that determine which of the great number of potential factors present in the physical environment will be selected as the objects of the organism's behavior. A number of these conditions, personified as "drives" for food, water, avoidance of injury, rest, elimination, air, and constant body temperature, have been taken over from physiology.

Since the behavior supposedly motivated by these physiological drives or "needs" is essential to the survival of the organism, they are commonly assumed to be the basic drives from which all other "drives" or "needs" are derived. These physiological drives, at least, operate in all living individuals. They are often considered to constitute a single drive for physical survival or for homeostasis, that is, for the maintenance of the organism's physiological balance.

Homeostasis as an Explanation of Behavior

This is not a mere change of words. The concept of homeostasis enables us to visualize and use a completely different concept of living organisms from the machine concept of the stimulus-response theorists. It even leads to a different system of ethics.

Thinking in terms of the physics of their own day, the physiologists who a century ago adopted the reflex arc as their conceptual unit of behavior were taking a machine as their model. The motive power of their conceptual man was supplied from the outside in the form of a stimulus, i.e., a spur.

The newer concept of homeostasis, which also originated in physiology, assumes, on the other hand, that the living organism is an organized dynamic field and that, like all organized fields, it must behave so as to maintain its organization. Thus the organized nature of our behavior, the explanation of which has caused the stimulus-response theorists so much trouble, is simply an aspect of our nature as living organisms. An individual's behavior, from this point of view, is both the result of his physical organization and the means by which it is maintained. The physiological evidence in favor of this concept is overwhelming and does not need to be given here. The essential thing is that this point of view leads us to conceive of human beings, not as passive machines which have to be pushed into action, but as living organisms actively exploring their environments for the means of maintaining their own integrity. They actively seek the satisfaction of need and, if we consider them as whole organisms, they have free will. Choices between food and water, for instance, are determined by the physiological state of the organism itself.

All of this, so far, is completely in harmony with the known principles of physics and chemistry and fits into the present framework of the physical sciences.

It is too bad that it is not quite adequate. A large part of human behavior and even some animal behavior cannot be explained by or even reconciled with the purely physiological needs. It is not uncommon for people to eat when they have already eaten more than they need or can comfortably contain. It is not uncommon for them to refuse food when they are famished. People drive too fast for safety, they mutilate themselves for beauty, they give their lives as heroes, as martyrs, and as suicides, all activities which are hardly consonant with maintaining the physiological balance. In the wartime experiment[5] on the effects of semistarvation, the thirty-six men who were the subjects lost an average of 25 per cent of their body weight. With it they lost interest in almost everything but food. They dreamed of food; thought constantly about food. Life became, as one expressed it, merely "passing time from one meal to the next." Another reported: "Stayed up till 5:00 A.M. last night studying cookbooks. So absorbing I can't stay away from them."

This extreme preoccupation with food would seem at first glance to be an ideal example of the effect of an urge toward organic homeostasis. But, in spite of the fact that food could easily have been purchased or stolen, only a few of the participants violated their pledge to eat only the prescribed diet. When shopping they did not purchase the food needed by their bodies. Instead they bought cookbooks, cooking utensils, and "bargains." One man hoarded *National Geographic* magazines. Two men stole. But only one stole food. The other stole china cups.

If this is homeostasis, it is not homeostasis in a purely physiological sense.

[5] H. S. Guetzkow and P. H. Bowman, *Men and Hunger*, Elgin, Ill., Brethren Publishing House, 1946.

Even lower animals not infrequently show behavior which is hard to reconcile with a demand for bodily maintenance. The writer once had to remove a white rat from a laboratory activity wheel because of extreme loss of weight. She had been going without food and water in order to keep her cage mates from using the wheel. As soon as she was removed from the cage one of the other animals began behaving in the same way. Homeostasis can explain dominating behavior which results in the individual's getting more food, but when a poorly nourished animal abstains from food and water in order to dominate its cagemates, an explanation of the act as an effort to maintain a constant physiological state seems a little farfetched.

The Concept of Psychological Needs

One way of handling this difficulty is to postulate the existence of additional nonorganic drives or needs, usually called psychological needs. Among the psychological needs proposed by various writers are needs for activity *and* for relaxation, for security *and* for new experience, for self-assertion *and* for self-abasement, for imitativeness *and* for creative self-expression, for work *and* for leisure, for beauty *and* for practicability, for protection *and* for independence, for emotional security *and* for excitement, for superiority, for dominance, for status, for possession of children, for recognition, for achievement, for affection, for value, for ownership, for knowledge, for power, for prestige, and for "value-in-general."

It should be obvious that this conceptual scheme gets into difficulties since it leads to the postulation of contradictory goals. If we are free to postulate a new psychological need to explain any act otherwise inexplicable, the list will grow and grow. As someone has said, this method could lead to the postulation of a psychological need for pumpkin pie in October.

In spite of the way this theory of mixed physiological-psychological needs frays out into confusion and conflict, it is popular at the present time. For one thing, it provides a convenient formula for explaining anything that anyone has ever done. If none of the many conflicting drives can explain an act, a new drive can easily be added to the list. But it is impossible to predict by this method what an individual is going to do because it offers us no way of knowing which of the many conflicting hypothetical drives will be operating. As a result, applied psychologists, whose planning often requires a fairly accurate prediction of what an individual will do in a particular situation, do not find it helpful.

This puts the psychologist in the same awkward position as the other social scientists. Economists could go about their work with more confidence if the psychologists could give them a reliable psychology to work with; but the psychologists cannot solve their problem of prediction of individual human behavior by the physical-science methods most of them have been taught to prefer. Until the physiologists give them a better base to work on they cannot even begin to attack the problem.

In the meantime we are confronted with pressing problems of education, rehabilitation, and social reconstruction and planning for which a better understanding of human nature is essential. Without it we cannot be sure of our techniques or our goals. It is not safe to try to fit these problems into a theoretical framework which, no matter how bright its prospects for the future, is inadequate for that purpose now. Because they are expected to deal with human beings now and cannot wait for the physiological approaches to be perfected, many educational, clinical, and social psychologists are exploring the possibilities of other points of view.

The Group as a Determiner of Behavior

Two different and, to some extent, complementary approaches seem to be developing. The first uses the principle which Professor Emerson has rather happily called social homeostasis. Like physical organisms and other dynamic fields, the social group exists independently of any of its individual parts. It may exist long after all of its individual parts have been replaced; in fact it may continue to exist *because* some of its parts have been sacrificed or discarded. We can predict that so long as the society exists someone will be carrying out the functions required for its existence. As long as the society exists we can be confident that someone is playing these required roles. In an authoritarian society we can expect to find, for instance, leaders, followers, and the scapegoat minority or foreign enemies which are necessary to keep the followers in willing obedience to the leaders. If all of these roles, and many subsidiary ones, were not played the society would collapse.

Another characteristic that human societies and living organisms share with other dynamic fields is that their response to their external environment is selective. The type of response evoked by an environmental change depends upon the nature of the society or the organism; and changes which evoke a violent response from one society will elicit no response from another. A frequently cited example of this selectivity in the social field is Linton's study of the Tanala-Betsileo.[6] These two Madagascar tribes apparently shared the same culture until the Betsileo shifted from dry rice culture to wet rice culture. The wet rice culture has a number of economic advantages since it gives a higher yield, provides for better conservation of the soil, and can be carried out by single families. Since the system does not require frequent removal to new land it has the further advantage of enabling families engaged in wet rice culture to live in better and more permanent homes. Nevertheless, one of the Tanala clans which took up the new method soon abandoned it because it interfered with their religious ceremonies.

This same study furnishes other examples of the way in which societies function as dynamic fields. Because of the interdependent character of the organization in such a field, changes in one part of the field will affect, sometimes drastically, all other parts of the field. Once the Betsileo took up wet rice culture a profound change in their society followed. The fact that the land suitable for such cultivation was scattered and in small plots which could be cultivated more or less permanently made private ownership of the land desirable. Since the cultivation was by families rather than by clans (as it had been before), the ownership was by families. Class distinctions began to appear as a result of differences in family wealth. Slaves acquired economic value. Because the limiting factor in production was water, a strong central power to control irrigation

[6] A. Kardiner and R. Linton, *The Individual and His Society*, New York, Columbia University Press, 1939. Also in T. Newcomb and E. Hartley, *Readings in Social Psychology*, New York, Henry Holt and Company, 1947.

became essential. The result was that the Betsileo developed a "rigid caste system with a king at the head, nobles, commoners, and slaves." In consequence the individual Betsileo has a different style of behavior and different behavior goals from the individual Tanala.

The recent studies of social class in American communities abound with examples of the ways in which class membership helps determine the values, goals, and aspirations of individual Americans. In "Yankee City,"[7] in the early 'thirties, the typical upper-class member believed in heredity and manners as determinants of worth and status. He wanted money, not as an end in itself, but as a means of living "properly" in the family house, surrounded by symbols of the family position in the community, which it was his goal to maintain. The members of the middle class, on the other hand, believed in the power of money and education and wanted them both in order to gain higher status. The typical member of the 25 per cent of the population who constituted the lower-lower class cared little for education and looked on money as something to be spent for immediate satisfactions. The different social classes thus seem to obey different laws of economics. Kinsey[8] has similarly called attention to the difference in attitudes toward sex among the different social classes.

Man is fundamentally a social animal. As an isolated individual he does not amount to much and he seems to know it. In spite of the accusations often made that the group holds its members back from progress and self-fulfillment, the truth is that, whatever our role, we can achieve it only in cooperation with others. Lewin[9] demonstrated that people change their ways of living faster in groups than they can individually. They also seem to think more effectively when they do it together. In one experiment[10] Shaw

[7] W. L. Warner, The Social System of a Modern Community, New Haven, Yale University Press, 1941.

[8] A. C. Kinsey, Sexual Behavior in the Human Male, Philadelphia, W. B. Saunders Company, 1948.

[9] K. Lewin, "Group Decision and Social Change," in T. Newcomb and E. Hartley, Readings in Social Psychology, New York, Henry Holt and Company, 1947, pp. 314-315.

[10] M. E. Shaw, "A Comparison of Individuals and Small Groups in the Rational Solution of Complex Problems," Am. Jour. Psychol., XLIV, 1932, 491-504. Also in Newcomb and Hartley, ibid.

gave three reasoning problems to each of twenty-one individuals and to five groups of four people each. The individuals, working alone, arrived at correct solutions to only 8 per cent of the problems, the groups to 56 per cent. Group membership is important. Sobel,[11] in studying the psychiatric breakdown of army personnel in combat, found that after men had lost interest in defending their country, had forgotten to hate the enemy, were too tired to care about the immediate military objective and too frightened to pretend courage, they were still kept going by their loyalty to their immediate group. The effect of group membership on behavior in schools and factories has already been mentioned. As Murphy[12] puts it, ". . . so that we know his age, sex, subculture, and economic position . . . we can go a long way toward safely describing his personality." If we want to predict what a person will probably do in a given situation, the fastest way is to find what groups he feels part of and what his role is in the groups.

And yet the assumption that an individual behaves as he does because he is a member of a group which requires such behavior leaves a great many questions unanswered. Suppose that a man is a member of many different groups, as most people are nowadays. If the interests of these groups conflict, what will he do? The group-determinant hypothesis cannot tell us.

It is necessary to distinguish, at this point, between the rough hypothesis that the behavior of an individual will be that which is required by his social role and the more sophisticated principle of social homeostasis advanced by Professor Emerson. In a static society[13] like that of the social insects the difference can be ignored. The fact that a society has existed unchanged for a reasonable period of time indicates that it has developed the techniques necessary for its survival. As long as its environment remains unchanged such a society will continue to maintain itself, provided that its members

[11] R. Sobel, "Anxiety-Depression Reactions After Prolonged Combat Experience—the Old Sergeant Syndrome," *Bull. U. S. Army Medical Dept., Combat Psychiatry Supplement,* November, 1949, pp. 137-146.

[12] G. Murphy, *Personality,* New York, Harper & Brothers, 1947.

[13] A static society can survive only in a static environment. For reasons which will appear later it is unlikely that man will ever have such an environment. (He keeps changing it.)

continue to play their required roles.[14] But in human societies, even the most ancient of which are now being forced into constant change by the changes in their social and physical surroundings, the survival of the society is often possible only if the members break out of the traditional pattern and abandon their old roles for new ones.

This places us in an uncomfortable dilemma. If we follow the social-role hypothesis we are unable to explain social change or to predict its course or even its direction because social change requires a change in roles, which the theory does not explain. If we adopt the more subtle and inspiring concept of social homeostasis we cannot explain why some societies and groups fail to make the changes required for successful self-maintenance. Neither concept gives us much help in predicting the behavior of specific persons. Neither one explains why new groups are formed or what happens in situations which the social sanctions do not cover. They do not explain why some people disregard the sanctions of their native society to identify with and accept the sanctions of another.

Effective as they may be for other purposes, it does not seem that any of the psychological approaches we have described so far can give a clear picture of human purpose or human value. The physiological theories seem to imply that a society is good to the extent that it produces and distributes the goods necessary for the physical health of its members; but the fact that "psychological" needs have to be invoked to supplement the purely physiological needs indicates that people need something more than the physical necessities of life. It is hard to say just what this is, because the alleged psychological needs are so diverse and conflicting.

The social-determinant theories of behavior give a picture of value which is even more disconcerting because it seems to disregard completely the fate of the individual human being. The successful society, this approach implies, is the society which survives. Whether or not this society satisfies the need or helps fulfill the destiny of human beings in general or of specific persons in

[14] In insect societies the role is determined by the physical structure and the individual is physically incapable of changing its role. This is, except for some sex roles, not true of human beings.

particular is not pertinent to this point of view. It is reasonable to suppose that societies will have better chances for survival if their institutions and customs tend to keep their members alive, maintain their loyalty, and attract new adherents. In other words, the successful society must to some extent satisfy human need. But by itself the group approach, whose basic dynamism is the maintenance and extension of the group organization, gives us no inkling about what people need. The basic problem which must be solved before we can understand group dynamics thus turns out to be the problem of basic human values. What is the motivating purpose of human behavior?

THE INDIVIDUAL-FIELD APPROACH

At the present time a number of psychologists[15] appear to be more or less independently converging on a purely psychological theory of behavior which is more capable of dealing with the problems of human purpose and human values than the physiological and group approaches we have already discussed. These people do not form a school or group and do not share a formally organized body of theory, so that what follows is only my personal analysis of the general approach. The basic assumptions appear to be these:

1. The behavior of human beings, although it is often not appropriate to the immediate physical environment, is always appropriate to what is variously called the individual's psychological field, behavioral field, private world, assumptive world, perceptual field, or phenomenal field.

This is the crucial assumption of the approach. Instead of aban-

[15] I hesitate to name individuals because there are so many, but the following should be listed: in social psychology, G. W. Allport, Cantril, Coutu, Crutchfield, Klee, Krech, Lewin, Murphy, and Sherif; in clinical psychology, Combs, Lecky, Raimy, and Rogers; in education, Hopkins, Kelley, and Woodruff; and in the psychology of economic behavior, Hayes and Katona. The point of view owes much to the work of the Gestalt psychologists, particularly Kohler and Wertheimer; to the writings of L. K. Frank, A. Maslow, and R. H. Wheeler; and to the perceptual studies of Ames, Bruner, Murphy, Postman, and many others. See D. Snygg and A. W. Combs, *Individual Behavior*, New York, Harper & Brothers, 1949.

doning field dynamics because in the guise of organic homeostasis it is not adequate to explain all behavior, the individual-field psychologists keep the principle and move it to a conceptual causal field where it does work.

In terms of what we know about living organisms some such field is biologically necessary to animals with distance perception. Among those animals which remain small and live in the water or in a host organism, getting their food by drifting into contact with it or having it drift into contact with them, behavior is purely homeostatic. The only part of the physical environment which affects the animal or its behavior is that part which is in close contact with its surface. Such an animal lives in a behavioral field one molecule thick, and anything nutritive or noxious within that area is automatically dealt with. The individual has no choice of action and all animals of the species would respond in the same way.

An animal of this kind is unable to perceive food at a distance and move toward it, or to perceive danger at a distance and avoid it. It is completely at the mercy of its environment. If such a species is to survive one of two things has to happen. As one alternative its individual members might develop a high rate of reproduction and enough motility to scatter them so widely that a few, at least, would always be blundering into a favorable environment. Or, after developing motility, the individual organism might increase its chances for survival by developing distance perception[16] so that it could perceive food or danger at a distance and behave accordingly. But this presents a new problem. An animal able to perceive objects at a distance is now exposed to stimuli from a tremendous number of food and danger foci. An organism which responded simultaneously to all of the physical stimuli which bombard it from these sources would tear itself to pieces. In order to maintain its organization it must trim the confusing, stunning, incoherent field with which it is now in contact down to manageable size. It has to pick out that part of the physical field which is most important to the maintenance of its own organization at the moment and deal with

[16] This would necessitate a larger organism and therefore a slower rate of reproduction.

that, more or less ignoring the rest.[17] This "cut-down" field is the individual (or psychological) field.[18]

One important feature of the "cut-down" psychological field is that it has a time dimension. It includes a past and a future. For the organism whose behavioral world is limited to its immediate surface nothing exists except what is here and now; but the acquisition of distance perception automatically gives the field a time dimension. Food at a distance is not, for the organism, food now. If it is perceived at all as food it is food-in-the-future. As a result of this development great individual differences and apparent irrationalities in behavior begin to appear. The degree of choice required by the simplest type of distance perception results in wide differences between the individual fields of different individuals in the same physical situation.[19] And when an organism like man is able to symbolize and introduce into its psychological field objects and concepts not physically present, the range of possible behavior becomes tremendous. The behavior of individuals would be completely unpredictable if it were not for the next principle.

2.   The psychological field is an organized dynamic field. The immediate purpose of all of an individual's behavior, including his behavior as a perceiver, is the maintenance of organization in his individual field. If the field organization should disintegrate his

[17] When a man is being chased by a bull he is not likely to notice the mosquitoes.

[18] To realize in a small way how few of the stimuli physically present actually get into the individual's perceptual field, listen for the "s" sounds the next time someone speaks to you. They are so prevalent in English that many foreigners think of English as the "hissing language," but English-speaking people rarely hear them. They are too busy listening for the sense of what is being said.

[19] The irrationalities are only apparent. Behavior is judged irrational when it is not appropriate to the perceptual field of the observer. The sequence of plays chosen by a quarterback who is trying to coax the defense out of position to set up a breakaway play for a touchdown will appear foolish to a spectator who sees the situation in a shorter time perspective and thinks only in terms of maximum gain on the next down. And the spectator's choices would appear irrational to the quarterback.

physical organization could not be maintained.[20] If he loses faith in his perceptions organized behavior becomes impossible.[21]

The meaning and value of perceived objects and events are determined by the individual's field organization at the time. As examples we can take the different meaning and value to an individual of food before and after a heavy meal.[22] Our perceptions seem to follow dynamic-field principles in that events and objects are always interpreted in the way which will require the least change in the field. Suppose, for instance, that a large part of my perceptual field is organized around the belief that a certain man is an enemy. Then on an important occasion he treats me with kindness and generosity. The odds are that I will perceive his behavior as a subtle insult or a deliberate attempt to deceive. If he were unimportant to me, I would be able to change my perception of him as a result of his kind act; but since his supposed enmity plays an important role in my field organization, it will be easier to distort my perception of his act than to change the rest of my field to conform to the act. Many of the demonstrations devised by Ames and his associates at the Hanover Institute illustrate this principle.

3. The perceptual self is the part of the field which is per-

[20] The nausea of seasickness is a minor example of the breakdown of physical organization which occurs in a disorganized perceptual field. Workers at the Hanover Institute (See H. Cantril, *The "Why" of Man's Experience*, New York, The Macmillan Company, 1950; and E. C. Kelley, *Education for What Is Real*, New York, Harper & Brothers, 1948) report that subjects exposed to perceptual phenomena which they are unable to reconcile with one another frequently become nauseated.

[21] Cf. the difficulty of mirror drawing, as a mild example.

[22] The economic implications of this illustration are interesting. If the individual is satiated the food has no immediate value to him. In fact it may have a negative value if he has to dispose of it. However, if his field includes a perception of the future as one in which he will want to eat the food or in which he can exchange it for something else which he will want, it will be perceived as having value and he may save it. If he has a pressing immediate problem not relating to food, it is not likely that he will be aware of the food at all. If he has gone through experiences which have caused him to feel that food is always valuable, he may seek it out and eat it or hoard it even if it causes him physical discomfort to do so. Value depends upon the psychological field of the individual, and concepts of "true value" and "fair price" are psychologically unreal.

ceived as behaving. As a result it is the focal part of the field. The only aspects of the cosmos which seem important, indeed the only aspects which can enter the field at all, are those which are related to the self. If the principle of field organization is too abstract to be useful, we can paraphrase it by saying that the immediate purpose of all behavior is the maintenance of the behaver's perceptual field, particularly of his perceptual self.

This takes care of the problems of martyrdom and suicide, which are inexplicable by physiological principles and, in the case of suicide in our society where it is socially disapproved, by the concept of group role. It is not the physical self but the self-as-perceived, the perceptual self, which we are trying to preserve. A man who has come to think of himself as selfless and devoted to duty or to others will act so as to maintain that perception of himself, even at the expense of his life. There are strong connotations for character education here. A person who has been taught to perceive himself as an outsider will behave like an outsider, with no feeling of responsibility to the group. A person who has been taught to regard himself as a criminal has to maintain and enhance that concept of himself by believing that "only suckers work."

4. Because human beings are aware of the future, at least of its existence and uncertainties, it is not enough to maintain the perceptual self for the present moment. It has to be maintained in the future, built up and enhanced so that the individual feels secure for the future. And since the future is uncertain and unknown, no enhancement of the individual's experience of personal value,[23] no degree of self-actualization, is enough. Human beings are, by nature, insatiable. This should be an important point for the economists.

The ideal sought is a state in which the individual feels so much in harmony with the universe, so much a part of it, that he does not have to defend himself against any other part.[24]

[23] Terminology modified from H. Cantril, The "Why" of Man's Experience, New York, The Macmillan Company, 1950.

[24] It is significant that this state is said to have been achieved, at least in moments of ecstasy, by some of the saints. It probably involves the perception of the universe as one completely pervaded with infinite love and com-

Ways of Satisfying Need

Seen in this way, the many conflicting physiological and psychological "needs" which were discussed earlier turn out to be alternative ways of satisfying the individual's basic need for enhancement of his experience of personal worth and value. A more convenient classification of these alternative ways of satisfying need is given below. Since behavior is always determined by the individual field of the behaver, the method used by any individual in any situation will be one which is appropriate to his perceptions of himself and of the external situation at that particular time.[25]

MEANS OF MAINTAINING AND ENHANCING THE SELF

A. Change in body state leading to change in the perceptions of the self.
   1. Restoration of the body balance by eating, breathing, elimination, rest, etc.
   2. Blocking off organic sensations of fatigue, pain, or tensions indicative of personal inadequacies by the use of alcohol or drugs.
   3. Elicitation of an organic mobilization and increase in body strength by entering a dangerous or irritating situation; speeding, gambling,[26] etc.

---

passion for all living things. From this point of view the higher religions represent man's greatest insight in their recognition of the ultimate goal of human endeavor and their audacious attempt to move directly toward it.

[25] This concept is capable of bringing back the group role in a new form. It is now the individual's concept of what is required to maintain his picture of himself as a member of the group. If he does not perceive himself as a true member of the group his obligations, not being recognized, will have to be enforced, if at all, by police action. In a growing society the members seek and embrace their roles as means of self-enhancement. That is the reason the society is growing. This point of view supports Toynbee's hypothesis that a society whose members have to be held to their posts by coercion is disintegrating.

[26] Gambling also provides foundations for more convincing daydreams (D2).

B. Self-reassurance by demonstration of mastery, control, or superiority.
  1. Over people: Competition leading to victory over worthy opposition.[27] Other demonstrations of superiority by gossip, practical joking, scapegoating, making gifts, etc.
  2. Demonstration of control over material objects.
     a. Creative. Doodling to art.
     b. Destructive. Nailbiting to vandalism.[28]
  3. Accumulation of property, hoarding.
C. Reassurance and enhancement by association and identification with respected individuals and groups. Evidence of respect and love by respected persons. Feeling of identity with a great cause, of being part of a great movement.
D. By change in the nonself part of the field which places the self in a less threatened position.
  1. By change in the physical environment. Travel, moving, redecorating, etc.
  2. By daydreaming or fantasy, including that done by professionals. Radio, television, theater, fiction, etc.[29]

[27] Even if the individual is defeated he has enhancement through increase in body strength during the competition.

[28] Creative activities provide more permanent symbols of self-value than destructive activities, but they usually take longer and require more skill. Destructive acts therefore are more apt to be committed by an immature person or a person under great stress provided that they are not inconsistent with the perceptual self he is trying to enhance.

[29] Many activities help to satisfy the need for enhancement in several ways. The most satisfying sex experiences associate means A and C. Cigarette smoking, particularly for smokers who inhale, supplies a tissue irritant which causes a rise in blood pressure and an increase in heartbeat and amount of blood sugar (A2 and A3). The smoker also secures reassurance from manipulating an object and blowing smoke (B2). (Many smokers report that they get less pleasure from smoking in the dark.) He may also use smoking as a way of demonstrating membership in social groups (C) and gain a feeling of value by offering cigarettes and matches to people without them. It is small wonder that so many millions of dollars a year are spent for tobacco.

The Basis of Human Values

Looking at the problem of value from this point of view we can come to the following conclusions:

1. The basic goal of all individuals is for a feeling of increased worth, of greater value.

2. This goal is never completely reached. Given one success, one degree of self-enhancement, human beings will always aspire to more.

3. Satisfaction of the need for greater personal value can be and is sought in a number of alternative ways. Goods and experiences are of value to the individual only as they contribute to the feeling of personal worth.

We are now in a position to make some judgments about values. Since the individual can strive, with some success, for self-enhancement in a number of different ways, no single way is indispensable.[30]

THE SPECIAL STATUS OF ECONOMIC ACTIVITY

Although economic activity is only one of many ways by which the individual strives for an increased feeling of worth, value, and belonging, it is likely to demand a major portion of his time and attention. *Economic activity* takes a great deal of time because it is concerned with the control of "scarce" goods, that is, with materials and services that require conscious effort to get. Many of the scarce materials would be helpful to their possessor even if they were not scarce. Food and clothing, for instance, may be used to maintain or restore the body balance and increase the consumer's perception

[30] The only qualification is that if the individual fails to use the methods for seeking enhancement which also result in maintaining the body balance, he will die. As a usual thing he will use such methods because any marked physical disorganization results in such a change in the psychological field (See F. A. Beach, "Body Chemistry and Perception," in R. R. Blake and G. V. Ramsey, *Perception and Approach to Personality*, New York, Ronald Press, 1951) that the individual does act so as to restore the body balance. But this is not always the case.

of body strength. An automobile may be used to increase the driver's feeling of power and value, by helping him to earn his living, or by giving him a chance to exhibit skill and good judgment or daring. But objects or services do not have to be useful in such a direct fashion to be valuable. Scarcity alone can make an object valuable because the mere possession of a scarce object, provided it is sought by others, can be a constant and reassuring symbol of dignity, worth, and power. Air is necessary for self-maintenance but no one will derive the fullest possible satisfaction from air until it is bottled under expensive brand names and sold at such high prices that the consumers (and hoarders) are impressed by their own wealth, extravagance, and good taste. As things stand now we do a great deal of breathing but devote little attention to it. Since air is not scarce, breathing ordinarily presents no problems and therefore no opportunity for self-enhancement by overcoming obstacles.

At a social level in which the minimal physical necessities are so easily obtained that their possession arouses no pride, a great deal of time may be devoted to the economic struggle for such symbols of worth as modern kitchen equipment, antique (or ultramodern) furniture, mink coats, or a private office with its own water cooler, any of which would lose much of their value if they became more plentiful or if people quit competing for them. As long as such objects are scarce, it takes quite a bit of effort and ability or power to get them. As a result they have come to be, in the eyes of many, reassuring symbols of self-worth and status. Such people will sacrifice a great deal to get them. Superficially each individual has a large number of alternative symbolic goals available, but actually he can strive with hope and satisfaction only for the goals which are appropriate to his concept of himself and the situation. Failure to achieve the goals by which he has chosen to measure himself results in humiliation and anguish, which are not lessened by his power to achieve other ends which are not appropriate to his self-concept and are therefore not regarded as enhancing.[31]

[31] This gives additional importance to money or liquid assets whose possession appears to give assurance of ability to reach goals the individual has not yet thought of. The accumulation of money can thus become an important goal in itself.

The Psychological Function of Trade

This point of view, if it should come to be accepted as common sense, would lead to a better appreciation of the role played by the businessman in the production of values. It is sometimes assumed that value is an intrinsic property of the object and that anyone who buys an object for less than that value gets a bargain and anyone who pays more is a loser. This leads to the belief that neither the buyer nor the seller has produced anything. A business transaction, from this point of view, is a contest between two parties each of whom is trying to victimize the other by buying goods for less or selling them for more than their intrinsic worth. From this point of view business is attempted cheating and the model transaction is the purchase of Manhattan Island from the Indians.

From the individual-field point of view, however, both parties to a transaction may, and usually do, profit from it. Objects are valuable to people if they assist them in the satisfaction of their individual need for self-maintenance and enhancement. Since different people strive for satisfaction of this need in different ways, objects and experiences will have different values for different people, and both parties to an exchange which is free from coercion can be expected to profit by it. A model transaction, from this point of view, might be one between a starving man with a keg of water and a man suffering from thirst who has a surplus of food.

The Process of Choice

This approach also provides a conceptual framework for dealing with the process of choice. Lacking such a framework, economists have had to assume that anyone's choice of goals is perfectly free,

---

At the present time, however, the relative importance of this goal is probably declining due to inflation, high income taxes, and the divorce of ownership from control in the large corporations. In this type of organization the distinction between economic and political activities becomes very thin, as the struggle is not only for scarce objects but for scarce titles and positions, an increasing number of which require such special technical skills that their acquisition by outright purchase would be regarded as unethical.

limited only by the possibilities of the physical environment. In any actual situation the choice is much more narrowly limited since in order to be chosen an object or experience has to be perceived as a means by which the individual can approach closer to his goal. What will be chosen is thus determined by the nature and organization of the chooser's field at the instant of choice. People in the same physical situation will make different choices because they have different goals, or because they are in different stages of their progress toward their goals, or for a number of other reasons. A person under strong pressure, for instance, is likely to concentrate so strongly on his immediate goal that he will fail to perceive opportunities to by-pass it when they occur. When he feels threatened by intense and immediate loss of self-respect, the future aspects of his private field fade into the background and he acts "without foresight."

There is reason to believe that what people call "foresight" is related to the individual's concept of himself. The person who feels relatively secure in his feelings of personal worth does not need to concentrate so completely on the immediate problem and therefore has a better chance to see it in a broad perspective.

All of this seems to negate another assumption frequently made by economists, which is that the chooser is a completely rational and highly informed being capable of action in his own best interests.[32]

SELF-INTEREST AND ALTRUISM

The fact that man is potentially able to strive for satisfaction of need in many different ways gives us an answer to an important question, which may be stated in two different ways:

"Is man naturally good or evil?" or "Is man essentially altruistic or essentially selfish?"

Since we believe that a man's behavior may be either good or

[32] Advertisers know better and so do economists, but they have been forced into this position by a dearth of psychological knowledge. Since the psychologists have not furnished the kind of information about people that the economists have needed, the economists have had to go ahead and predict what a simplified hypothetical man would do.

evil, it seems to follow that a good society will help and encourage him to strive for enhancement in ways which further not only his own experience of personal value but the value experiences of others as well. The self-enhancement which accrues from an experience of being needed, from feeling part of a great movement, from contributing to something nobler and more important than our own lives, is just as natural and probably more lasting than the self-enhancement gained through successful aggression. In the long run it is better for the individual himself if he uses the socially desirable ways of seeking enhancement because such methods are not so apt to incite other people to thwart and resist him. There is no necessary conflict between the basic aspirations of the individual and the basic aspirations of others. There is no inevitable conflict between the individual and society.

Failure of Identification with Others

Let us consider, however, one way in which man may fall into antihuman behavior. The person who does not feel part of a social group will not behave as a member of the group. Even though a concept of himself as a just or honorable man may keep him from consciously self-seeking behavior at the expense of the people with whom he does not identify, his feelings and, as a result, his behavior toward them will be essentially selfish. Since the organization of our individual field is largely determined by our own need for a feeling of self-worth, it is easy for such a "good citizen" who does not feel one with his victims to commit great acts of aggression against people "for their own good" or in the name of justice, of patriotism, of economic law, or of preservation of the faith, and to do it in all sincerity and with a great feeling of rectitude. Law and ethics can help prevent injustice that we can recognize, but the best insurance against injustice is complete identification with the potential victim so that injury to the victim is injury to the self. The man who loves his neighbor as himself has not abandoned self-interest. He still seeks for self-maintenance and enhancement, but his self now includes his neighbor.

Identification with Others as the Basis of Ethics

It is on this base that human ethics seem to have developed best. It is true that on logical grounds it is to almost everyone's advantage to work together on the basis of "You scratch my back and I'll scratch yours." But attempts to explain existing systems of ethics or create new ones on the basis of enlightened self-interest seem to be psychologically unrealistic. For a society to survive it must receive from some of its members sacrifices, sometimes of their lives, for which it cannot compensate them in a material sense. A system of ethics based on *quid pro quo* could in no way command the degree of self-sacrifice required and secured in all societies. This self-sacrifice seems to be a manifestation of identification, love, and faith in something more important than our own lives.

There is a growing feeling among psychologists that self-acceptance is necessary before we can accept or love others. Rogers[33] has concluded on the basis of his clinical experience and research that a person who feels so threatened that he is preoccupied with the necessity for defending himself has little sympathy to give to others. Murphy[34] believes that to love others we have to love (accept) ourselves first.

The degree to which men can attain brotherhood with all men is still unknown. Professor Emerson,[35] looking at the problem against the background of millions of years of biological development, sees it as a goal which is almost assured. From a psychological point of view it does not seem impossible, given enough time. Man is certainly not averse to identifying himself with others. But he tends to identify most completely with comparatively small groups, probably because he can more clearly perceive his value to such a group.

The greatest obstacle in the way of universal brotherhood at the

[33] C. R. Rogers, *Client-Centered Therapy*, Boston, Houghton Mifflin Company, 1951. See also A. H. Maslow, "Self-Actualizing People: a Study in Psychological Health," in *Personality Symposia*, 39, No. 1, Values in Personality Research, W. Wolff, ed., New York, Grune and Stratton, 1950.

[34] G. Murphy, *Personality*, New York, Harper & Brothers, 1947.

[35] Chapter 10.

present time is not man's unregenerate selfishness and individualism. It is the fact that to give their lives meaning and dignity the people of the world have identified themselves with a great number of conflicting groups and causes for which many of them are prepared to sacrifice themselves *and others*.

Limitations of Individual Experience

It is not yet safe to assume that the process of identification with larger and larger groups can go on indefinitely. The individual field is at best only a limited version of reality, and as the group becomes larger and more complex it is more and more difficult for the individual to perceive his value and function in it and consequently to seek identification with it. Education can help; but no matter how highly educated we are, there are physiological and psychological limits to our ability to comprehend and identify with a complex society and many people in our society may already have approached those limits. There is something suspicious about the way one civilization after another gets to the point where there is a high degree of interdependence between people who are not personally acquainted and then goes into a decline.

Even if we should succeed in getting a better conception of our relation to others, the resulting feeling of brotherhood might be disappointingly mild. The "cut-down" nature of the perceptual field makes it impossible for us ever to achieve as warm a feeling of identification with all as we now have with some. The more people we identify with, the less time and interest we can give to each. It may follow that a man who loves all of mankind equally will not love any one person much.

This brings us to the second source of evil in human nature. It lies in our inability to recognize or accept the limited nature of our perceptual fields. As has been pointed out earlier, the individual's personal field is a limited and often distorted version of reality. Nevertheless, it is the only version he has and he has to trust it. This naïve assurance that our private experience is a valid representation of reality is dangerous. It breeds atrocities. Most of the great enormities of human history have been committed in the name of what the perpetrators believed to be noble causes. They would have been ashamed to commit such atrocities for purely selfish reasons.[36]

There is no reason to suppose that human beings will ever become omniscient, so this source of evil seems certain to remain with us permanently. However, there are reasons for believing that its effects may be alleviated. In a society of people better able to accept themselves and therefore better able to accept others, there would be a greater respect for and acceptance of the corrective insights of others and less disposition to seize on a worthy cause as an excuse for aggression against others.

COMPARISONS BETWEEN SOCIETIES

Since there are many ways in which people can secure some degree of self-actualization, it is reasonable to suppose that there can be many different "good" societies. However, if we judge a society by its contribution to the value experience of individual human beings, a society is good to the extent that it enables its members and neighbors to live with health, security, self-respect, and dignity. It is good to the extent that it enables its members and neighbors to feel adequate to live with reality and, in consequence, to perceive it without distortion. Such a society will institutionalize and encourage techniques of production and cooperation among its members. Each member will have "an opportunity to work, to feel personally successful, and to sacrifice for some cause which to him is important. Each person must have opportunity to feel that his life has meaning, importance, and purpose."[37] Such a society will be continually changing. "No successes and no recognition can be enough to give anyone the permanent feeling of adequacy and self-assurance that he needs. Further achievement and growth are always necessary. As a result no society which attempts to remain static can adequately satisfy the needs of its members. A 'good so-

[36] Compare the mannered observance of the "laws of war" in the admittedly selfish dynastic wars of the eighteenth century with the savagery and ferocity of the religious wars of the sixteenth and seventeenth centuries and the "wars for humanity" of the twentieth.

[37] D. Snygg and A. W. Combs, *Individual Behavior*, New York, Harper & Brothers, 1949, p. 200.

ciety' must provide its members with opportunities for self-enhancement by pioneering in new fields and at ever more difficult problems."[38]

THE NATURE OF SOCIAL CHANGE

From this point of view there is nothing inevitable about the direction of social change. The Marxist ideas of inevitable communism and the Greek idea of inevitable cycles, both of which seem to have been based on the short-time trends of a single civilization, are equally mistaken. No two societies develop in exactly the same direction because when a "hitch" develops in a society the possibilities for solving it are limited by the character of its individual members and the potentialities of its physical and social environment. These differ in all societies.

In human societies, particularly in civilizations, people are constantly pushing against the frontiers for better ways of satisfying their individual need. Sometimes (frequently in our own society) such a push[39] is so successful that it opens up a whole new field of possibilities and problems and creates a crisis because the society has no established practice for dealing with them. In such a situation, with social precedents vague or absent, each member of the

[38] Snygg and Combs, *op. cit.* To the writer the approach which has been described seems to argue against the planned society, particularly if the goal of that society is a static state of perfection. It seems to be a valid corollary of the individual-field approach that planning for other people is ineffective because each has his own individual organization of values and goals which are relatively unrecognized by others. In addition planning by a few for the many is sure to be less realistic than the active explorations of the many because it is based on fewer points of view about nature and about people. Planning by a few in authority is especially dangerous because by reason of their authority and responsibilities they are certain to have developed goals and aspirations not shared by the other members of the society. The result is, all too often, a solution which does not win cooperation and which has to be enforced, if at all, by force, thus splitting the society and destroying its unity.

[39] The temper tantrums of a baby and the discovery of nuclear energy both represent such pushes. One difference is that our society has already developed techniques for dealing with temper tantrums.

society has to make his own decision and in doing so he helps to change his society for the better or for the worse. This is a ticklish moment because there are opportunities for disaster if the attempted solutions are based on false analogies with problems which have already been solved or if they are otherwise based on false concepts of reality. In our own society an increasingly large proportion of our problems have to do with people both in our society and outside of it. In this situation erroneous concepts of human nature are particularly dangerous.

XIII

Secular Values and Religious Faith

by Theodore M. Greene
Professor of Philosophy and Master of Silliman College, Yale University

Two distinct but related problems are of crucial importance in this project and of grave concern to all thoughtful men and women in our society—the problem of evaluation and the problem of religious faith. The problem of evaluation concerns the nature of values and our knowledge of them. Are they objective, universal, and discoverable? If so, how can we assess man's conflicting apprehensions of them; if not, how can we escape demoralization? The problem of religious faith concerns the existence and nature of God and man's knowledge of Him. How assess the competing claims of atheism, agnosticism, and the bewildering variety of man's religious faiths? The presuppositions and criteria of responsible evaluation have been discussed by philosophers in our culture since the days of Socrates, and no agreement among contemporary philosophers is in sight. Equally controversial is the question whether religious faith is ever valid, and, if it is, under what conditions. This question too has been of perennial interest to philosophers since ancient times, and the cleavage today between skeptics and believers is as deep as ever.

It is appropriate that the philosophical perspective on these issues be included in this volume along with other perspectives. No contemporary philosopher, however, can presume to speak for his fellow philosophers. The dominant trend is still toward a "relativism" which denies that values have any objective reality and insists that they are merely human ideals arising out of, and en-

365

shrined in, social conventions and institutions. Contemporary "naturalism," "realism," "instrumentalism," and "positivism" all prescribe some such interpretation, and this general position has been greatly reinforced in recent years by psychological, anthropological, sociological, and historical inquiry. The following analysis of values and evaluation must therefore be taken as expressing the position of a minority, though perhaps a growing minority. It will have to be assessed by the reader for whatever plausibility and cogency it may seem to him to possess.

The same can be said for the ensuing account of religious faith. It is not intended to convince the religious skeptic but to indicate, however briefly, what seem to me to be the nature and presuppositions of a "liberal" interpretation of the Christian faith.

It seems appropriate to discuss the problem of values first, and in "secular" terms, since it concerns all of us, the religious skeptic no less than the believer. This order of presentation should not be taken to imply, however, that values, if they are in any meaningful sense objective, are unrelated to an equally real Deity, or that religious faith is irrelevant to a belief in objective values. I believe, however, that a case can be made for the objectivity of values without recourse to theology.

I need hardly add that both of the ensuing discussions are greatly oversimplified and grossly inadequate. The issues at stake are much too complex, and the current interpretations of them are much too various, for adequate treatment in brief compass. All that I can here attempt is to sketch, in cursory fashion, what seems to me to be the most reasonable approach to both issues.

I. THE STATUS OF VALUES AND THE CRITERIA OF RESPONSIBLE EVALUATION

The problem of values and evaluation is simultaneously an epistemological problem, i.e., concerned with the nature and criteria of knowledge, and an ontological problem, i.e., concerned with the nature of reality. A claim to knowledge of objective values is arbitrary and irresponsible if it fails to provide intelligible and applicable criteria of knowledge. Knowledge, in turn, must be a knowledge of something real with a character of its own and, at least to some degree, humanly knowable. We need not concern ourselves with hypothetical aspects of reality which are, in fact, humanly unknowable. But we should certainly concern ourselves with the objective reality, or unreality, of knowable values, since evaluation can be said to be valid or invalid in the sense of being true or false only if it is directed to values which are real and objective in some meaningful sense. It is precisely this reality which is today so widely denied or questioned; and such denial or doubt leads quite logically to the conclusion that evaluations are neither true nor false but merely "emotive" expressions of socially conditioned preferences which are ultimately irrational.

The issue before us, then, is perfectly clear-cut and unambiguous, however complicated may be its solution. Is our universe completely neutral to man's hopes and fears, welfare and misery? If so, does it not preclude the very possibility of valid or invalid evaluations, though still permitting mankind to assess its own cumulative well-being and frustration, generate its own ideals, and exert itself to realize them? In such a universe, values would certainly not be objective in the sense here defined.

The issue should not be confused by the fact that all human societies have been found by anthropologists to have more or less well-established value systems, and that these socially accepted values are sometimes referred to as "objective" when contrasted with the "subjectivity" of the private feelings and emotions of individual men and women. Societies do attach value to various objects, activities, and attitudes; and these evaluations are reflected in speech and overt behavior and can therefore be studied by social scientists. This merely demonstrates, however, the factuality of human evaluations, individual and corporate. It leaves quite untouched the question whether some of these evaluations are more valid, that is, more adequate to the nature of values in themselves, than other evaluations. Most sociologists and anthropologists would, I believe, be the first to insist on this distinction between socially "objective" and ontologically "objective" values, since it enables them to continue their studies of contrasting cultural patterns of social evaluation without committing themselves to the reality or unreality of what they would be inclined, with Professor Linton, to call "transcendental" values.

Let us, in attempting to analyze this problem, ignore for the moment all theological claims for Revelation and, indeed, the entire traditional religious perspective, and proceed in purely secular terms. And let us start with certain rather obvious generalizations.

1. The Self Experiencing the World

The all-embracing basic fact with which we seem to be confronted is that man is a complex and dynamic being in continual and vital relation to an environment which is also complex and dynamic. It is also clear that these three factors—the self and its total environment, and the multiple relations between them—are distinguishable but not independent of one another. The history of Western philosophy records many attempts to analyze and understand "man," "experience," and "reality" in isolation from one another, and all these attempts, however illuminating in various respects, must be judged to have failed. The only "reality" which we can analyze fruitfully is the actual "world" which man encounters and which he can in some measure come to know. The only "human nature" we can effectively explore is that which comes into being in this orderly world and which matures and evolves in lively interaction with it. "Experience" can be understood only in terms of this interaction of self and world; that is, as an emergent "field" or "process" whose nature is always determined by both poles—the nature of the world to which the self reacts and the nature of the self which finds its world and reacts to it.

The "complexities" of self, world, and emergent experience can be analyzed in several complementary ways. We can start with the self and analyze it in terms of inherited aptitudes and of socially conditioned patterns of behavior acquired after birth. Experience can be analyzed into its irreducible components and its distinctive types—e.g., perceptual, social, moral, aesthetic, and religious. Man's exploration of the world about him can be focused upon distinctive (though never isolated or unrelated) aspects of its complex nature—its inorganic structures and processes, its living species and the rhythms of their growth and evolution, mankind as organized into complex societies, etc.

Wherever we start, however, we are sooner or later impelled to relate our findings to the ultimate matrix of all inquiry, which is summarized in the formula "self experiencing its world." The world we explore leads us back to ourselves as part of this world and as the agents who explore it and exploit it. The self we study is a self with a biologically determined heredity, born into a society of other selves, and living in a world of nature which possesses an orderly and coercive character of its own. The human experience we seek to understand remains unintelligible save insofar as we examine it as the total response, active and passive, conscious and unconscious, of the self to its total effective environment.

Only in this context can such phenomena as truth and error, health and disease, progress and regress, be ultimately understood. Only in proportion as man, conceived of as a conscious being capable of knowledge, makes progress in correctly apprehending himself and his environment can he meaningfully be said to advance in knowledge and his judgments to exhibit more truth and less error. If there were no mind capable of knowing and no reality capable of being known by it, there would be no knowledge at all, no truth or error, no cognitive experience. Whatever skeptical arguments philosophers may devise regarding the reality of the self, the world, or the possibility of knowledge, the actuality of all three and therefore of degrees of truth and error *must*, in *some* sense, be presupposed, even by the skeptics themselves. The Sophist Gorgias inevitably lapsed into a threefold self-contradiction when he declared, "There is nothing, and even if there were something we could not know it, and even if we could know it we could not communicate it to others"; for in this very utterance he sought to *communicate* what he believed he *knew* about the *actual nature of things*.

Similarly, health and disease can ultimately be understood only in this same all-embracing context of the self successfully or unsuccessfully adapting itself to its total environment. This applies to health narrowly defined in purely physical terms. It applies also to mental health, that is, to man's successful adaptation to the social environment in which he finds himself. Health, physical and mental, and its concomitant satisfactions, are the rewards of such adaptation; physical ill-health and psychic disorder and the misery that attends both are the penalties of maladaptation.

The concepts of progress and regress also become meaningful only if an additional characteristic of living creatures, and particularly of man, is duly recognized. This is the factor of distinctive individual and generic potentialities. Each identifiable living species has a multitude of distinguishing evolutionary potentialities, and each member of each species possesses at birth a unique configuration of the characteristics of his species which determines his special individual capacities for growth. The fact that all life is "dynamic" means, among other things, that each species seems to possess within itself a drive or *élan* to perpetuate itself and to produce out of itself new species with new distinguishing characteristics. Similarly, each living individual is impelled not only to preserve its own life but also to realize, during its lifetime, its own innate potentialities. How successful this impulse to growth and "self-realization" is in any particular case depends, as far as we can tell, upon the innate capacity for growth of the individual and also, to a large extent, upon a favorable physical and social environment. An individual can thus be said to have achieved his own proper destiny in proportion as, during his lifetime, he has been able to realize or actualize his potentialities; and mankind, as a very distinctive species, can be said to progress in proportion as it realizes the cumulative human potentialities of the human race.

This brings us, by an apparently indirect route, back to our immediate problem of values and evaluation. The purpose of my preamble has been to try to set this problem in a realistic and intelligible perspective. The claim that values are objective should, I suggest, mean merely that man's evaluations do not differ *in kind* from his nonevaluative (i.e., factual) cognitions, best exemplified in the natural sciences. His evaluations constitute a distinctive type of response to various aspects of his total environment; they too have a referent to which they too can be more or less adequate. In short, man responds to his *total* environment in two complementary ways —factually and evaluatively. He is continually asking two different but related questions: What is it? and, What is its actual or potential value? Both questions are meaningful and answerable, since his environment possesses both a factual and a value character.

This assertion can perhaps be clarified with the help of some distinctions and the dismissal of some unnecessary confusions.

2. Embodied Values

The only values we actually encounter are *embodied* values; that is, values which seem to us to be embedded in, and therefore to characterize, concrete things, events, institutions, practices, attitudes, etc. We actually encounter and enjoy not Beauty in the abstract but beautiful objects; not Efficiency, but efficient machines, individuals, and operations; not Justice, but more or less just laws and practices; in short, not Value, but objects, persons, and acts that seem to us to possess value of one sort or another. We feel, and normally believe, that we ourselves really encounter these value characteristics in the persons, objects, processes, etc., which we judge to possess them in some degree. It requires a very sophisticated argument to make even plausible the suggestion that the picture I judge to be beautiful is in fact wholly neutral and aesthetically no different in value from any other picture or human artifact; that a law I judge to express some degree of justice is in fact *merely* a social convention; that my strong impulse to regard human beings as possessed of intrinsic value is nothing but a widespread fiction and that, in fact, men, women, and children are, in and of themselves, totally lacking in value. There can, I think, be no question that the universal verdict of philosophically unsophisticated men is that the "world" which we encounter exhibits value structures and possesses, to varying degrees, characteristics or qualities which we label "values" of various designatable types.

We are here at the very heart of our problem. The sophisticated skeptic would have us believe that nothing has a value in its own right and that we unconsciously project our human preferences into whatever we approve. He is therefore compelled to accuse mankind in general—not merely the untutored "common man," but all artists and critics, all political and social reformers, all moralists and prophets—of being victims of a universal illusion: the illusion, namely, of believing that some "things" are more beautiful, more just, etc., than others. In the process of indicting the entire human race he inevitably indicts himself, since a major presupposition of his entire argument is, of course, that truth is better than error and that his analysis of the value problem is therefore more valuable, because truer, than alternative analyses. Consistency would compel him to deny this presupposition, and such a denial would destroy the basis of his own argument. What is particularly striking about skepticism of this type, however, is the questionable implication that whereas man has evolved in continuous adaptation to his environment, and whereas his cognitive faculties, as well as his bodily skills, have developed in response to a reality capable of calling forth such response, his highly developed capacity to evaluate has to all intents and purposes developed *in vacuo*, that is, in an environment wholly innocent of the characteristics which would make evaluations true or false, valid or invalid.

It is universally admitted that unless an individual's hunger leads him to eat nourishing and nonpoisonous foods he will die; that man can live safely and with comfort in his physical environment only in proportion as he learns its laws and appropriately adapts himself to them; that animal and human societies will not survive or prosper save insofar as social behavior takes due account of the actual needs of its individual members. In all these areas evolution and growth, individual development and institutional cooperation, are explained *functionally* in terms of a more or less successful (i.e., realistic) adaptation to the environment in question. And such adaptation is universally regarded as involving, at the conscious level, progressive *understanding* of the characteristics which the environment in question *actually* possesses.

Yet man is supposed by the skeptics to have developed his evaluative capacities miraculously, without benefit of an objective order possessing value characteristics of its own, i.e., in a world obedient to physical laws but devoid of aesthetic, moral, or religious regularities and urgencies. Mankind, save for the sophisticated skeptic, is thus accused of wholesale schizophrenia. Man is believed to be capable of progressively rational response to his physical environment, but condemned to wholesale illusion in all his evaluations; to be more or less successfully realistic in his orientation to "fact," but systematically unrealistic and escapist in his preoccupation with values.

No self-respecting philosopher will care to appeal either to common sense or to universality of belief as a criterion of truth; nor will he wish, in general, to deplore sophistication. But this particular brand of sophistication, so widespread today in academic circles and seeping so rapidly into the common mind, should not, I believe, be allowed to triumph by default. The burden of proof surely rests with the skeptic. It is up to him to explain in evolutionary terms the rise of what he regards as this universal human illusion, to try to defend the skeptical thesis without self-contradiction, and to make its acceptance rationally compelling.

Some of those whom I have here labeled as skeptics will at this point wish to argue that man's social environment differs sharply from his physical environment; that, though the physical world of the physicists and astronomers may itself be innocent of all values, it has nevertheless produced out of itself living organisms and, finally, mankind; and that men have, in all societies, created their own values, established standards, and envisaged ideals. Hence, they may insist, human evaluations can be said to be more or less adequate according to the criterion of human satisfaction and welfare, even though the rest of reality, both organic and inorganic, is innocent of and indifferent to human values and evaluations. My answer, in brief, is that if we view mankind in the perspective of cosmic evolution, we seem to be confronted with two large alternatives. Either the "nature" out of which life and human life has evolved actually possessed, in potentiality, what has become actual in time, or else cosmic evolution must be regarded as a continuous process of creation of something out of nothing. The latter view seems to me to involve the unnecessary and most implausible acceptance of a continuous, utterly irrational miracle; the former view seems to assert the thesis here defended—namely, that the values which men create and discover do have a source and an anchorage in ultimate reality.

3. *Ideal Standards*

All evaluations have a second characteristic, which must now be noted. They always involve an explicit or implicit reference to an *ideal standard*. For the values which are actually encountered in their concrete embodiments are never judged to be "perfect." They are always judged to be more or less adequate exemplifications of values which somehow transcend all possible embodiments. By reference to those transcendent values the most nearly perfect of finite manifestations must be judged to be inadequate and imperfect. Thus, no one with a sense of, and passion for, justice will regard any act, law, or person as perfectly just, that is, as embodying complete and absolute justice. No informed critic will claim absolute beauty or absolute artistic excellence for any work of art; least of all will the creative genius who has produced it. No spiritually sensitive person will judge any human act or person to be perfectly holy. Here the parallelism to the scientific and philosophical search for truth is inescapable. No competent scientist or philosopher with an ounce of humility will presume to equate his truths—that is, his insights and discoveries—with the whole of truth or with truth in its unblemished completeness.

Here three widely current confusions must be mentioned and if possible dispelled, since they have so greatly contributed to obfuscation and because they have all been used to strengthen the case of the sophisticated skeptic.

A.   The first is the supposition, deriving in our Western tradition from Plato, that values, to possess real objectivity, must be reified, i.e., conceived of as things (*res*) or eternal "objects" in some timeless realm of their own. This interpretation can be seen today to reflect an unconscious materialism; that is, the uncritical assumption that, to be "really real," a value such as justice or truth must have a substantive character in the manner of material objects (even though not subject, as they are, to time and change). Such reification is no doubt very natural but it is quite unnecessary. We can today conceive of reality in other than substantive quasi-material terms.

B. It is also commonly supposed that a belief in absolute values necessarily involves the claim that at least some men can know them adequately, and that this knowledge of them is therefore as absolute as these values themselves are asserted to be. This claim has, through the centuries, received some support from philosophers and theologians in their more arrogant moments. It must be admitted that the voice of pretended omniscience has been too often heard, and all too often from men whose basic beliefs should have dictated humility and the recognition of human finitude as basic human virtues. Such arrogance is wholly inconsistent with the spirit of scientific inquiry, philosophical speculation, moral insight, responsible criticism of art, or prophetic religious utterance. The claim of any finite man or institution to absolute knowledge cannot possibly be regarded as a necessary corollary of a belief in absolute values. Any such pretension involves the fallacy of misplaced absoluteness; that is, the fallacy of attributing to finite comprehension, which is never absolute, the absoluteness of an "object" only partially apprehended.

It might be urged that the best way to minimize the danger of absolutizing our human conceptions of absolute values would be to stress basic attitudes rather than ultimate objectives—e.g., the attitude of a man who is trying to act justly, rather than the nature of absolute objective justice. This suggestion does indeed reflect the Socratic spirit of inquiry: his primary concern with the quest for knowledge, his rejection of all conventional dogmas, and his critical dissatisfaction with all human solutions of basic philosophical problems. It is also consistent with his passion for intellectual honesty and moral integrity, his respect for personality, etc. We must not forget, however, that these attitudes of Socrates were rooted in basic beliefs, e.g., in cosmic justice—"Be assured that no harm can befall a good man either in this life or the next!" In short, what we find in Socrates is (a) a passion for justice, intellectual honesty, etc., *plus* (b) an abiding faith in objective justice and intelligible order, *plus* (c) profound humility and caution regarding man's most adequate apprehensions of cosmic justice and cosmic structure, *plus* (d) the courage to take a firm stand on practical moral issues (*cf.* his refusal to break the laws of Athens by escaping from prison). In all these respects Socrates can serve as a model of full-bodied liberalism; he is a luminous exemplification of responsible attitude, fervent belief, intellectual caution, and practical courage —all in happy and healthy balance.

C.   A third and more serious difficulty can best be expressed in two straightforward questions: Can absolute values be known by mortal man even partially? If so, cite instances; if not, what sense is there in asserting their reality? My answer to these questions will probably not satisfy the convinced skeptic; but it is, I believe, the only answer that can be given and it is also, I would urge, meaningful and plausible. It is that absolute values are, by definition (man being what he is and they being what they are here conceived to be), unknowable in their absolute completeness. They are, nonetheless, *partially* apprehensible and apprehended; they also constitute necessary points of reference in any responsible normative inquiry.

Here again we are at the very heart of our problem, approached now from the side of human cognition and its implications. When a scientist admits, or indeed insists, that his present insights, though superior to those of his predecessors, are still imperfect and partial and therefore sure to be superseded by the insights of his successors, he is describing these insights of his as finite. Finite in relation to what? Partial by reference to what?

In the first instance, in relation to, and by reference to, more adequate insights which his successors will doubtless achieve if scientific inquiry continues in the future as it has in the past. But this is not the whole meaning of his insistence that his scientific insights are merely finite, for he will also wish to record his conviction that all his human successors, however much they may come to know, will still never be able to transcend their finitude and achieve scientific omniscience. This means that integral to all scientific inquiry is the recognition that *all* human knowledge is necessarily finite. But, again, finite by reference to what?

This question, I would urge, is not only a meaningful question but also one that demands an answer. And the only answer that can be given is, by reference to absolute truth. This truth can be defined quite easily as the quality characterizing that hypothetical set of propositions which, in conjunction, would do complete justice to the reality under investigation. Absolute truth, so defined, constitutes the inescapable presupposition of all assertions of cognitive finitude. Without it as a point of reference (however empty, for us, in content) the concept of finite truths has no ultimate meaning.

The same analysis is applicable to justice, beauty, and the other basic values whose reality our multiple evaluations presuppose. To equate any concept or any instance of human justice with absolute justice would reflect unpardonable arrogance and invite ruthless tyranny; witness the countless historical occasions on which the claim to infallible rightness has led to cruel suppression of heresy. To deny, on the other hand, that mankind is striving in various ways in his several societies to achieve greater justice than has been achieved in the past, or to assert that his most conscientious efforts to make his laws just are all the fruit of a pathetic illusion, on the ground that justice ultimately has no meaning and that no laws are actually more or less just than any alternative laws, is to lapse into a sophisticated cynicism which should, at the very least, be asked to justify itself. Is it not far more reasonable to say that men, since time immemorial, have been seeking for justice and have been encouraged to continue their costly efforts only by the belief that they were striving toward objective justice, though neither they nor their descendants would ever, as finite human beings, succeed in completely apprehending or actualizing it?

D.   One further objection can be dealt with briefly, though a full study of its implications would be a long and difficult task. The complaint is frequently voiced that such a theory of value presupposes an ultimately static universe and contradicts the possibility that reality may be, through and through, an evolving and creative process. Whatever the difficulties in trying to conceive of change without any base of permanence, or of progress without any fixed point of reference, the foregoing argument for objective values does not necessarily imply either of these contrasting metaphysical theories. All that is here asserted is that what man responds to in his multiple evaluations, insofar as they are realistically oriented, is an integral part of his ultimate environment and not merely a fiction of his individual or collective creative imagination. Objective values are as real as any other major aspect of his world, as discoverable by man, and, as far as human experience indicates, as orderly and coercive.

This, I submit, is what is (or should be) meant by the assertion that there are "spiritual laws" in the universe. We can here usefully define the spiritual in secular terms as referring to the value components, both finite and absolute, of man's effective environment and his evaluative responses to these components. The assertion that there are "spiritual laws" can then be taken to mean that man and his world are so made that man's normative aspirations do not arise in a normative vacuum and that their effects are never the result of sheer accident or chance; but rather that man, as a being who seeks to envisage, actualize, and enjoy values, is, in these distinctively human activities, as subject to objective regularities and coercions as he is in his purely physical traffic with the physical world around him.

More concretely, the results of love and of hatred, of integrity and lack of integrity, of justice and injustice, etc., are just as invariable as are the mechanical results of physical behavior or the physiological results of nutrition or malnutrition. Man never *really* "gets away" with anything at *any* level of conduct, even though he may seem to do so. All our acts are subject to objective laws and are followed by predictable consequences. All health and growth, both physical and spiritual, depend upon knowledge of, and conformity to, relevant objective laws and structures. In short, man's evaluations should be conceived of as his attempts, more or less wise and successful, to adapt himself to those aspects of his total orderly environment to which these evaluations are addressed.

4. *Criteria of Evaluation*

What, then, can be said regarding workable criteria for responsible evaluation? Philosophers who believe in such criteria will formulate them in terms of the more embracing criteria of knowledge to which they subscribe; once again I cannot give the correct philosophical answer but only the answer which seems to me to be most adequate and useful.

The workable criteria are the twin criteria of "coherence" and "correspondence." By "correspondence" I mean here full recognition of actual present (and future) value experiences, my own and those of others; by "coherence" I mean the scope and logical consistency of the conceptual interpretation of these experiences. So defined, these are the generic criteria of all human knowledge here adapted to the distinctive nature of value experiences and insights in a manner strictly parallel to the way in which these same generic criteria are adapted in scientific inquiry to the distinctive nature of man's sense perceptions and his scientific interpretations of them. What is here assumed is (a) that all human knowledge issues from the interpretation of evidence and is reliable in proportion as the evidence is reliable (i.e., accurately observed) and in proportion as the interpretation is conceptually consistent, both internally and with regard to other accepted interpretive concepts; and (b) that the real world which we encounter in experience presents itself to us in significantly different types of experience, whereas the mind which does the interpreting is one and the same mind subject to the same laws of logical consistency.

The value experiences here referred to, to which the fullest justice must be done, are not easy to describe. They always involve, first of all, a more or less intense emotional component. Extreme rationalists have tried to ignore or minimize this emotive factor, but have always thereby radically distorted the experience they sought to comprehend. Skeptics, past and present, have gone to the other extreme in attempting to reduce evaluation to its emotional component, and this attempt has necessarily resulted in robbing the act of evaluation of all cognitive significance. Responsible critics of the arts, moralists, jurists, etc. have more or less successfully hit the mean between these extremes. They have recognized the universal presence of emotion in all evaluation and the resultant danger of subjective bias, emotionalism, and sentimentality; but they have clung to the conviction that the emotional response of a trained and mature person to a value situation need not be a distorting factor and can be a source of genuine normative insights. Their confident but cautious reliance on emotion clearly indicates that emotions are believed by them to occupy in total evaluation a role analogous to that of sensations in total sense perception. We can usefully recall

Kant's famous dictum that "concepts without percepts [sensations] are empty, percepts without concepts, blind," and suggest a parallel formula regarding evaluation, *viz.*, "Evaluative concepts not rooted in emotional responses are empty; mere emotions are blind." In short, emotional response seems to be our characteristic response to value situations, and we seem to be completely dependent upon such response for any genuine insight into such situations.

But just as sense data, though equally essential to scientific knowledge, can be variously interpreted and misinterpreted, so can primitive emotional responses. In the area of sense perception we must recognize the possibility of hallucination, and of more or less serious illusion, as well as of reliable perceptions approximating to, though never reaching, the ideal of perfectly accurate or "veridical" perception. Similarly, in evaluation, we must recognize the possibility of really pathological emotional response (where the emotion is entirely unjustified by the objective situation) and of varying degrees of sentimentality, as well as of reliable evaluations approximating more or less closely to, but never wholly reaching, the ideal of perfectly accurate or "veridical" evaluation.

There is also in all evaluation a Gestalt component, that is, the more or less inclusive apprehension of a total configuration. We apprehend and evaluate various parts of a work of art in their relation to each other and to the work as a whole; we apprehend and judge moral acts and motives in the wider contexts of character and social environments; etc. Recognition of this factor is an important safeguard against the temptation to seek for isolated value elements in value situations or to attach undue weight to artificially isolable feelings of satisfaction or dissatisfaction, pleasure or pain. The beauty of a picture is not one among many sensory elements in it but a function of the picture as a whole; and our mature enjoyment of the picture is not independent of our sensory perception of its lines and colors or of our imaginative and conceptual comprehension of its subject matter and expressed content, but rather the affective aspect of our total response to the picture as a whole. Similarly, an informed moral judgment is synoptic, embracing the total relevant situation in which value is judged to be embodied more or less adequately.

5. *The Middle Road between Absolutism and Relativism*

This account of values and evaluation needs of course to be greatly refined and sharpened, and many awkward problems concerning the nature of values and our knowledge of these values call for further careful exploration. In our times, moreover, my entire approach and its basic presuppositions must be defended in detail against skeptical query and hostile attack. All I have been able to do is to try to indicate a position other than that of contemporary relativism (as defined on page 365) and to urge that *some* such position should be accepted as a framework for the type of responsible evaluation which all men of integrity and good will would wish to believe in and to express in their own thought and conduct.

That the problem we have been considering is of major importance is brought home to us when the question arises as to the possibility of appraising the merits and defects of various contrasting types of human societies and their respective value systems. The uncompromising relativist dismisses any such attempt as, *in principle,* futile and meaningless. Specific acts, he will argue, are in fact evaluated by the members of a given society in terms of *its* scale of values, and the scale of values of another culture can be appraised as a whole from the point of view of the society to which the evaluating agent belongs. The former appraisal is "objective" *within* the society in question, in contradistinction to the "private" desires or preferences of any member of that group. Appraisal of one culture according to the standards of another culture, in turn, must remain wholly irrational and arbitrary unless there are, in some sense, transcultural values and a transcultural criterion for evaluation. The systematic denial that such values exist would seem to carry with it inevitably the denial that any such criterion is discoverable or defensible.

The urgency of the problem can be underlined by citing a test case. All anthropologists are thoroughly committed to the validity, in principle, of the scientific method of inquiry. They are unanimously convinced that it is superior, as a method of arriving at a true understanding of contrasting societies and their institutions, to superstitious reliance on magic, sorcery, frenzied trance, etc. What is the thoroughgoing relativist to say about this deep-seated and empirically supported conviction? Historically, the scientific method as we know it has arisen in our own Western culture, and allegiance to it is as distinctively a characteristic of the "best" thinking in our society as is reliance on magic, etc., in various "primitive" cultures. Nor would our anthropologists believe and act as they do had they not been "socially conditioned" to this pattern of belief and behavior. Are we to conclude that this faith, which all educated nonscientists share with them, is *merely* a product of social conditioning, *merely* a characteristic of our culture, but *in principle* no more defensible than the belief in and practice of magic?

Indeed, we can go a step further and ask the extreme relativist on what rational or objective basis he would defend the thinking and the conclusions which constitute his own relativistic theory. Is this theory itself merely a cultural phenomenon which, in principle, is in no way superior to, or more valid or truer than, any rival theory? How can he defend or argue for his own theory if, according to its conclusions, objective truth is ultimately meaningless?

May I repeat that an authoritarian absolutism which asserts not only the objectivity of values but the infallibility of at least some human apprehensions of them is *not* the only alternative to such "nihilistic" or self-destructive relativism. We need not leap out of the relativistic frying pan into the fire of authoritarian dogmatism. We can, and should, struggle to maintain a middle course between these extremes by accepting the objectivity of values and "spiritual laws," by believing that man has made, and can continue to make, progress toward their more adequate apprehension, but also by never forgetting that all human evaluations have been, are, and must be finite and fallible.

It is indeed the case that all human evaluations are inevitably "conditioned" both psychologically and socially. To deny this is to assert sheer nonsense and to fly in the face of everything we know about man, cognition, evaluation, and human development. All beliefs are the beliefs of individual persons with a background of personal experience that is bound to influence them radically. And all human beings are born into, and grow to maturity in, a specific society and culture which of course profoundly affects their personal outlook on life and all their insights and beliefs.

But this is true of *all* men, wise and stupid, and *all* beliefs, informed and uninformed. The validity of beliefs is a totally independent question and can be dealt with only at a totally different level of inquiry. A relatively false and a relatively true belief are equally "conditioned," both psychologically and socially. It is always illuminating to explore these conditioning factors, particularly when the emergent belief is privately or culturally warped. But there is no excuse for committing the genetic fallacy of supposing that the value of anything, including a belief, is determined by its antecedents. Its value must be assessed, if it is to be assessed at all, on other grounds. I have attempted to indicate a fruitful nongenetic approach to this problem of responsible assessment or appraisal. If this approach seems unsatisfactory, I can only urge that a more satisfactory approach be sought for with the utmost urgency, for a nihilistic relativism is certainly both indefensible and disastrous in its effects.

II. Man's Religious Quest

Faith in a "living God" is not identical with, or reducible to, a "secular" belief in the values of truth, beauty, and justice. The crucial difference between them is that values are, in most forms of secular idealism, conceived of as passive, awaiting man's discovery, as "nature" awaits scientific inquiry; whereas nearly all the religions of mankind attribute to their deity or deities a dynamic character by virtue of which they enter into human life on their own initiative. Natural regularities and the "spiritual laws" of the secularist may be said to "manifest" themselves in their spatio-temporal embodiments, whereas the gods or God are believed, in one way or another, to "reveal" themselves to mankind. This revelation, moreover, is conceived of as a source of both light (or insight) and power (or strength), with the result that man is believed able to do "with God's help" what he could not do without this divine assistance. In short, religious faith asserts more regarding the universe than does a secular idealism and presumes to offer man greater resources than does a humanistic "philosophy of life."

This is certainly true of historical Christianity. Since the present study includes a Christian evaluation of our society, it is essential that at least some of the distinctive claims of Christianity be clearly formulated and that the problem of the validity of religious faith in general, and of the Christian faith in particular, be honestly faced. Professors Bennett and Niebuhr have restated certain basic Christian affirmations and have developed some of the main social implications of the Christian faith. I shall restrict myself to some of the presuppositions of this faith and to the general claim that enlightened religious beliefs are valid and can be tested for their validity.

1. *Diversities and Similarities*

If we approach the problem from the epistemological point of view, as seems inevitable in our predominantly skeptical society, the first presupposition calling for recognition is that religious beliefs are not "all of a piece," equally valid or equally invalid. There is as great a difference between primitive superstitious religious beliefs and mature enlightened religious beliefs as there is between the crude interpretations of nature advanced by Thales and other pre-Socratics and the highly disciplined scientific beliefs of leading scientists today. More specifically, it is agreed by all informed students of Christianity that the Christian religion has developed out of a primitive Hebraic cult, through centuries of prophetic criticism and purification, through the cataclysmic events recorded in the New Testament, and finally through nearly two thousand years of ecclesiastical and theological evolution since New Testament times. It is recognized also that contemporary Christian beliefs differ greatly, in their extremes, not only in content but in enlightenment—as greatly as contemporary quackery differs from modern medical theory and practice.

This recognition of crucially different degrees of religious enlightenment and maturity should be coupled with the recognition that all religious faiths and practices have a common element which justifies the application of the descriptive term "religious" to all of them. This common denominator has been defined in many different ways, and perhaps never better than by Professor Paul Tillich as man's "ultimate concern for the Ultimate." This formula has the merit of emphasizing (a) man's deep-seated conviction that there is something in the universe of ultimate concern to him, and (b) his conscious or unconscious search for it in all cultures and ages. It has the further merit of leaving room for the greatest variety of "concerned" searches for this Ultimate and a corresponding variety of interpretations of its essential nature. Finally, it makes possible the recognition that "religious" concern, search, and emergent belief need not, and should not, be identified exclusively with their traditional ecclesiastical manifestations. Such an identification sharply differentiates the "secular" from the "religious" and thus, by definition, denies that an ultimate concern outside of the framework of organized religion may be as genuinely religious as are traditionally orthodox expressions of such concern.

Professor Tillich's formulation of the essence of religion must, however, be supplemented in the important respect referred to in an earlier paragraph. Most, though not all, forms of religious belief assert the reality of a *dynamic* divine principle which does not passively await man's self-initiated discovery but actively intrudes itself into human life and the course of human history. This divine principle has of course been conceived of in enormously different ways—in many alternative animistic, polytheistic, pantheistic, deistic, and monotheistic patterns of belief. But common to all of them, however crude or refined, is the conviction that the deity or deities are, in some sense or other, dynamic forces or agents eliciting a type of human response notably different from man's appropriate responses to truth, beauty, justice, and equity. The crucial formula of religion is "human response to a Divine initiative."

The nature of this human response will of course depend upon how this divine dynamic power is conceived of. Man's characteristic effort may be to escape the unwelcome intrusion of an unfriendly deity or to bribe a potentially cooperative deity to be of help; or his response may express itself in a feeling of gratitude and obedience to a deity conceived of as righteous and forgiving love.

But as Rudolf Otto pointed out in his famous "The Idea of the Holy,"[1] deity is always apprehended, however superstitiously or maturely, as possessing a distinctive quality which Otto entitled the "numinous" or the "holy." Whatever is sincerely worshiped—whether it be familiar or unfamiliar spirits, or the gods of ancient Greece, or a Roman emperor, or nature, or the God of enlightened Christianity—the worshiper regards the "object" of his worship as holy and therefore worthy of his "reverence."

A further characteristic of all the historic religions is their tendency to evoke a total human response and to make demands upon the whole life of man. Religious faith, in any of its well-developed forms, involves man's emotions, imagination, and reason, his thought and his conduct; and it carries with it, at least by implication, resources and obligations relevant to all human activities. This is less true of some less developed religions and of religions that have retrogressed in the direction of formalistic sterility. One can distinguish between vital religious faiths, on the one hand, and more or less ossified and stereotyped religious beliefs, on the other, by the fact that the latter are of only peripheral concern to the believer and fail to provide him with an embracing and dynamic "way of life," whereas the former challenge his entire personality and qualify much, if not all, of his thought and behavior.

It follows from what has been said regarding divine initiative that all vital religion is felt by the believer to be in some sense revelatory. The deity who is worshiped is never believed to be wholly unknown and unknowable, and such knowledge as is available is always believed to be, at least in part, the result of a divine self-revelation. Once again, the accounts given by primitive religions and by the great world religions of both the manner and the content of such divine revelation differ greatly, but that such revelations have taken place and, as some religions assert, continue to take place is commonly acknowledged by the religious believer.

The religious consciousness is equally insistent, however, that man is never able fully to comprehend the divine mystery, however luminously it may reveal itself to him. Deity always remains, for

[1] Translation by John W. Harvey, New York, Oxford University Press, 1936.

the humble and sincere worshiper, both partly knowable and known and partly hidden and unfathomable. This partially explains the haunting fear which characterizes some religions and the sense of awe with which even the God of Christianity is apprehended and worshiped.

Equally emphasized is the importance of responding in an appropriate way to what is thus divinely revealed. The generic receptive attitude is, as has been said, the attitude of reverence, though such reverence can vary from cringing superstitious fear, at one extreme, to enlightened awe and joyful gratitude, at the other. But this reverence does not exhaust man's proper response to deity; he is also under obligation to express this awe in appropriate forms of worship and in appropriate behavior toward his fellow men. In some religions moral and social conduct have, it is true, become largely divorced from specifically religious beliefs and practices, but such divorce can fairly be regarded as a symptom of loss of religious vitality and therefore as the mark of religious retrogression. It is a safe generalization that all vital religions emphasize the importance of appropriate behavior both toward the deity and toward other human beings. Religion, in short, tends, in proportion to its vitality, to demand of man a total and affirmative response to what is believed to be the divine offer and the divine command.

All the religions known to us are simultaneously private and corporate. Religious beliefs are always conserved (with greater or less evolving modification) in a religious tradition; provision is always made for some forms of shared public ceremonial and worship; and this tradition and these forms of worship are safeguarded and implemented by some sort of religious institution or "church." Religion, in short, is universally a more or less highly organized social phenomenon. Even the solitary members of what Professor Tillich calls the "latent church" are bound together, however unconsciously, by a common attitude or ethos and a shared repudiation of all traditional forms of religious organization in their society. A completely solitary and idiosyncratic or individualistic religious faith would seem to be a contradiction in terms.

But every religion that possesses any real meaning and value for the worshiper is also, and essentially, a private relationship between the individual and the deity who confronts him. This "I-Thou" relationship reflects man's ultimate solitariness and the fact that he must finally make his own decisions and commitments and face in solitude the ultimate fact of death. Once again, religions differ greatly in emphasis. Some move far in the direction of public ceremonial and sacerdotal responsibility at the expense of private worship and the personal responsibility of the believer. Others minimize ritual and public worship and emphasize private devotion and dedication. No vital religion, however, is exclusively social on the one hand, or wholly private and individual on the other.

2. The Appraisal of Conflicting Religious Faiths

It follows from these generalizations that any *a priori* wholesale condemnation *or* approval of religion in all its enormously diverse forms is inadmissible. "Religion" has expressed itself in the greatest variety of ways—in superstitious beliefs as well as beliefs that honor human reason and are adjusted to man's growing knowledge of the world; in fanatical frenzy and in quiet devotion; in cruel persecution and in heroic self-sacrifice; in extreme reactionism and in militant social reform. Running through all its diverse manifestations is discernible the golden thread of man's search, now pathetic, now tragic, now noble and now debased, for that in the universe which is able to complement his finitude and redeem his sinfulness. This search, however perverse and distorted, must be respected whenever it is sincere. But we find also in all religions, the "highest" as well as the "lowest," evidence of man's deep-seated proclivity to idolatry, i.e., the worship of false gods unworthy of his reverence. This idolatry, which reappears stubbornly in the most highly developed religions and in the most enlightened worshipers, must be recognized and combatted for what it is—man's apparently ineradicable proclivity to absolutize the finite and to reverence such lesser gods or idols.

It therefore behooves us to judge religion in its diverse forms as discriminatingly and open-mindedly as possible. Such an approach dictates as sympathetic an understanding of world religions other than Christianity as possible; an honest critique, affirmative and negative, of Christianity itself in its major variants; and, finally, a careful philosophical analysis and assessment of the most enlightened religious claims to valid insights. I can of course attempt none of these difficult tasks at this time; I must limit myself to a brief mention of certain crucial problems with which such an embracing inquiry would have to deal and to the clarification, if possible, of a few highly controversial issues.

A. We must distinguish, first of all, the proper authority with which prophetic and redemptive religion judges the "church" and all its spokesmen, as well as the prevailing ethos and the institutions of its culture, society, and historical period, from the arbitrary and indefensible authoritarianism that reflects some form of pious idolatry. When Jesus was described as one "speaking with authority," the authority ascribed to him was very different from the legalistic authoritarianism of the Scribes and Pharisees. The authority which they claimed for their laws and judgments was the authority of a tradition and a synagogue which had become rigid and highly conventionalized and which the ecclesiastical powers sought to impose upon man from without. In contrast, the authority with which Jesus was felt to speak was the inwardly compelling and persuasive authority of one whose life, speech, and character proclaimed their own spiritual authenticity. The secular and human analogue would be the authority with which a great mathematician, scientist, or artist speaks to those who have the ears to hear and the minds to understand. Similarly, the authority which an informed believer finds in a long and tested religious tradition finds a secular analogy in the authority which we today ascribe to pure science or to medicine as traditions worthy of our high respect. Religion at its spiritual best speaks with tremendous authority, but religion become authoritarian thereby proclaims its spiritual bankruptcy.

B. Enlightened religious faith must be distinguished from blind credulity, on the one hand, and the pretense to logical certainty, on the other. No alleged "proof" of God's existence has ever demonstrated to the hilt, beyond all peradventure, that the God of religious worship exists. Yet no enlightened believer will tolerate the assertion that his faith is wholly blind and credulous. Informed religious faith bases itself upon a mass of "evidence" which can be labeled in omnibus fashion as "religious experience," and also upon as rigorous and honest reflection—theological, psychological, historical, and philosophical—as has been employed in any purely secular inquiry. The emergent belief of the religiously sensitive and reflective person is therefore held by him in both a "confessional" and an "apologetic" spirit. In company with his fellow believers he declares, "This we have seen, and heard, and encountered, and this we must therefore confess and proclaim"; and in company with all the reflective minds in his tradition he declares, "This seems to us to be the most reasonable and compelling interpretation of our individual and corporate experiences." These two approaches are of course interrelated and, ideally, fused into a single body of interpreted evidence, but believers of differing aptitudes and interests will naturally stress and develop different aspects of the total supporting "argument."

C. The claim that religious faith need not be wholly blind raises inevitably the problem of the criteria by which the critical and reflective mind may, and in fact does, appraise claims to valid religious insight. These criteria, like the criteria of nonreligiously oriented evaluations, are the generic criteria of all knowledge adapted to the distinctive type of experience referred to as "religious." No theology can survive if it divorces itself from such experiences; ultimately it is no more than the best available interpretation of them. Similarly, no religious experience, however intense or momentarily coercive, is self-authenticating. It is the cumulative pattern of infinitely various yet mutually reinforcing experiences, viewed in the light of a mutually reinforcing set of theological concepts (these experiences and these concepts evolving within a religious tradition and in a more or less cohesive religious community), which, in total impact upon the reflective and sincere believer, generate in him the faith he lives by. Nor are the insights of the prophets and the saints self-authenticating, however true and profound they may in fact be. We can assure ourselves of their truth and profundity only by checking them against other pronouncements, for which truth and profundity are also claimed; against our own relevant experiences, for whatever they may be worth; and against the whole corpus of relevant articulated knowledge available to us.

Here, as in science, searching individual insights are invaluable, but they must always be subjected to whatever *appropriately* "objective" tests can be devised; for only thus can their validity be assured and the invalidity of alternative claims to insight be demonstrated. Only thus can whatever is eccentric and warped in the manner in which they have been apprehended and expressed be recognized and, at least partially, pruned away. That all this evidence and all this theorizing can produce in man no more than a reasonable and well-considered faith is obvious. But it is equally obvious that such a "faith" should not be contrasted with "knowledge" but should rather be assessed for its measure of reasonableness and its degree of uncertainty and risk. Religious faith, in short, is a venture—for many, a blind and superstitious venture; for others, a venture not only based on private experience and reflection but powerfully supported by a mass of shared experience and cooperative reflection over many centuries.

D. At this point a major difficulty arises. How, it can be asked, is an authentic religious experience possible without prior commitment, and how can such commitment be reconciled with any religious claim to objectivity? This is a genuine problem which must be squarely faced, but it is not insoluble. The solution depends upon man's ability to move dialectically, back and forth, between an attitude of commitment and an attitude of critical scrutiny. This is of course by no means a phenomenon unique to religion; it happens continually in friendship and politics, in artistic creation and the critical response to art. A value situation can be fully understood only if it is "entered into," in the spirit of participation and commitment; yet it can be judged objectively only if it is viewed, as it were, from a distance, with impartial fairness and critical rigor. These sound like mutually incompatible attitudes and approaches, and there is indeed question as to whether they can in fact prevail in any given individual at the same instant. But there is no question that they can, with effort and self-discipline, be made to succeed one another in a slower or faster rhythm. We need not pretend that this dialectical swing and counterswing is easy, or that

anyone with deep conviction can achieve complete objectivity even
in his most critical moments. Nonetheless, the solution of the
problem must certainly be sought along this road of dialectical tension and swing.

3. *The Genius of Protestantism*

This is precisely the road which the Protestant attempts to travel.
He believes that the Christian Gospel can be truly comprehended
only from within, through active participation in the life of the
Christian community and acceptance of its rich spiritual heritage.
He accepts as definite and normative God's revelation of Himself
to the Hebrew prophets and, uniquely, in Jesus Christ. He therefore accepts as his standard the love which he finds perfectly exemplified in the life and death, the character and teachings, of the
historical Jesus whom he accepts as the Christ, the Son of God, the
Incarnation of the eternal Logos. The nature of this love will, he
believes, dictate not a repudiation but a radical transvaluation of
all secular values, as the Great Commandment was declared by
Jesus to have embraced and transcended the Ten Commandments
of Mount Sinai.

This does not mean, however, that God is believed to have revealed Himself exclusively through prophetic utterance and in
Jesus as the Christ; nor does it mean that the Christian theologian is
indifferent to values and spiritual laws as they manifest themselves
in nature, human nature, and the course of history. On the contrary, he finds in man's common or "secular" experience pointers
to and confirmations of the values which are given in Revelation.
For, since the God of Revelation is believed to be the creator and
sustainer of the world, it is expected that signs of His purpose can
be discerned by the spiritually sensitive observer in His (and our)
world in space and time. Similarly, the Christian belief that God
"created" the world and is the "source" of all objective values does
not mean that His "fiat" is arbitrary or "irrational," or that the "new
law" of love, as revealed in Christ, is inconsistent with "the old law
that was from the beginning" and that manifests itself in the structure of creation. This new law is conceived of rather as the "ful-

fillment," not the "destruction," of the old law. It is one and the same God, the source and ground of all order, meaning, and value in the universe, who has manifested Himself in all creation, in all times and to all peoples, but with special clarity to the prophets and saints and uniquely in Jesus as the Christ.

The Christian theologian welcomes, therefore, the spiritual insights of other religions as well as the wisdom of the "secular" philosopher and scientist, historian and artist. He believes, however, that, apart from the direct or the indirect influence of Christian faith, human understanding of objective values and of the spiritual laws to which they are subject is apt to be gravely distorted. Hence, the continuous renewal of a true vision of basic values does, he is convinced, depend upon Revelation.

The Christian believer is thus deeply commited to an "experimental" approach to all human problems—to theological and philosophical as well as economic and social problems. He values open-minded receptivity, both spiritual and factual; he believes that man's quest for insight is endless, that no authentic insight will ultimately be jeopardized by honest and searching criticism, and that responsible experimentation and search at every level of inquiry will always be productive of new insights. He is convinced that only thus can a mature and intellectually responsible faith be achieved.

III. The Factor of Language

One of the most crucial factors both in secular evaluation and in articulated religious faith is the factor of language. The semantic problem embraces all attempts to express and communicate what are felt to be normative insights, both secular and religious. Such insights, we have said, depend upon a total integrated response to a total value situation by all of a man's "faculties"—his imagination and his emotion no less than his intellect or reason. These insights (whether authentic or not) can therefore be expressed only in a language which can serve as an adequate vehicle for so complex a response to so complex a situation. My thesis, had I the space to develop it, would be that, as regards the verbal languages, it is "poetic" language, whether in verse or prose, and, as regards other means of communication, it is the languages of the so-called fine arts, notably music, architecture, painting, sculpture, and the dance, which, in their several ways, and, of course, only when expertly used, provide man with his most accurately expressive languages of evaluative expression and communication.

"Poetry" is the most important of these languages and it is in some ways the richest and most expressive. Witness the preponderant reliance on poetic, in contrast to abstract and purely conceptual, discourse in the Scriptures of all the great world religions. The reason for this can, I think, be explained. Evaluation addresses itself to value "situations," that is, to situations (including things, events, and persons, singly and in combination) in which universal values are believed to be encountered in concrete embodiment or in which it is felt that value could and should be so encountered. Our evaluative responses to such situations, in turn, are, I have urged, simultaneously emotive, imaginative, and conceptual. "Poetry" is the fitting vehicle for such response and for the expression and communication of such evaluation because poetry is, in essence, the concrete embodiment, in appropriate images, of "universals." Its genius is precisely its ability to express the universal in and through particular images. In the process, the significance for man of these universal values is "brought home" to us with an emotional intensity comparable to, and sometimes even greater than, the emotional intensity of firsthand confrontation of value situations.

Purely conceptual discourse, even when it concerns values, appeals only to the intellect and is intended to evoke no more than intellectual apprehension and consent. But to "realize" values involves far more than merely acknowledging them intellectually. It involves actually encountering them and feeling their quality and urgency as well as apprehending them in their multiple varieties, combinations, and settings. Hence the grave limitation (as well as the merit of conceptual lucidity) of purely conceptual language as expressive of the full meaning and significance of love and friendship, justice and cruelty, etc.

When we come to consider the distinctive semantic problems of religious expression and communication we are confronted with an even harder task. It is to find a language somewhat adequate to the nature of deity as apprehended by the believer. The difficulty is twofold: it derives in part from the unfathomable mystery of God, but, no less, from the inadequacy of all human language to express accurately even those aspects of the divine nature which the believer feels himself in some measure to apprehend.

It is this second difficulty which constitutes the central semantic problem of religious discourse. All human languages are necessarily anthropomorphic, scientific prose no less than religious poetry, though some uses of any type of language reflect a cruder anthropomorphism than others. These anthropomorphic languages which man has developed reflect his predominant preoccupation with things and persons. Hence, in trying to describe the God of Christianity the Christian theologian has really only two choices: to describe Him in impersonal terms, devised and adequate for natural objects and events; or in personal terms, devised and adequate for human beings. He normally chooses the latter alternative as less inadequate and inappropriate to the necessities and insights of religion. But, in proportion to his religious enlightenment, he makes heroic efforts himself to remember, and to remind his hearers, that all ascription of human attitudes and attributes to the Deity is merely analogical, containing a germ of truth and much inevitable anthropomorphic distortion. He insists that God is righteous, but that His righteousness differs from ours, not absolutely, yet in both degree and quality; that His love is not wholly beyond human apprehension, particularly as it manifested itself in the historical Jesus, but that it nevertheless transcends all that we can ask or think, etc.

The dangers and pitfalls involved in using language in this analogical manner, and the comparable risk of harmful ambiguity in the religious use of poetry and the other artistic vehicles of religious expression, cannot be denied. Yet these languages, so used, would seem to be the only halfway adequate languages at the disposal of the believer. Meanwhile, the Psalms, the Parables, the Thirteenth Chapter of I Corinthians, the finest theological writing of St. Paul and his theological successors, great religious music and architecture, painting and sculpture, religiously expressive and sacramental ritual—all testify to the notable clarity and power with which these languages can be used to bring home to us what the articulate religious believer wishes to express and to communicate to others.

The foregoing cursory analysis of values and evaluation and of religious belief is offered with due apology for its great inadequacy. I have tried, in what I have said about religion, to provide a brief prologue to the chapter by Professor Bennett and to Professor Niebuhr's Conclusion, so that the reader who comes to the volume without much sympathy for the Christian position which they accept as valid may perhaps be helped by an initial clarification of difficulties that, in our secular age, continually bedevil the honest inquirer. Enough genuine difficulties remain after all unnecessary obfuscations have been cleared away; the least we can do is to try to avoid controversy over false issues and to do our best at least to understand one another.

XIV

A Theological Conception of Goals for Economic Life

by JOHN C. BENNETT
Professor of Christian Theology and Ethics,
Union Theological Seminary

Christian theology is systematic thought concerning the nature of God and man and concerning man's salvation. It includes the development of doctrines about the implications of Christian faith and it provides the basis for the ethical standards by which the Christian ought to live. This chapter is an attempt to consider the goals of economic life from the point of view of Christian theology in its Protestant form.

There is no universally accepted formulation of the implications of Protestant theology for economic life. It is not possible in such a chapter as this to expound an orthodox body of thought which, if understood, would settle most of our questions. Protestant thinking that deals with economic life must draw out the implications of Biblical faith, but this must be done in an exploratory way in the face of new problems or at least new urgencies which were quite unknown to the Biblical writers and to the classical theologians who have created the patterns of thought dominant in most branches of the Church. Their deepest assumptions about God and man can be related to these new problems and urgencies, but that must be done by us.

In recent years there has been a continuous process of corporate Christian thinking about economic life marked especially by the work of great ecumenical conferences. In the report of the Oxford Conference on Life and Work in 1937 there is a statement that illustrates this contention that we must relate fundamental assumptions to new problems. The statement deals with the possibilities of production which now enable men to overcome "the kind of poverty which is crippling to human personality." The report makes the following claim concerning the significance of this fact of productivity:

This possibility marks off our time from the period of the New Testament and from other periods in which Christian thinking about economic life has been formulated. In the light of it the direction of Christian effort in relation to the economic order should henceforth be turned from charitable paternalism to the realization of more equal justice in the distribution of wealth.[1]

To relate Christian faith to a dynamic economy and to the decisions of men who know that they need not accept existing standards of living as divinely ordained is a task which recent generations of Christians have had to undertake in a fresh way. The dynamic economy made possible by modern technology and the new hopes of neglected and exploited peoples of the world are better indications of the divine purpose than static structures presided over by a small class that has used Christian doctrines to defend its privileged position.

The Purpose of the Economy

Economic institutions exist for the sake of the production and distribution of goods and the provision of services on which the existence and the welfare of the community depend. How economic goods are related to other goods can be left to other chapters to clarify in detail. The important point is that these institutions exist to meet human needs. How needs are related to wants of various kinds which go beyond needs also raises many difficult questions. The primary emphasis here must be placed upon needs and upon needs of the whole population. The fact that needs are relative to

[1] *The Oxford Conference Official Report*, Chicago, Willett, Clark & Company, 1937, p. 87. The Oxford Conference report is the most competent and most representative corporate statement of modern Christian social teaching in the non-Roman churches.

the cultural situation should not confuse us, for an estimate of such needs in any particular situation—for example, under urban conditions in the United States—provides essential data for Christian thinking concerning the economic institutions in that situation.

This essential purpose of economic activities and institutions underlies everything that will be said later about the relation between economics and Christian faith. There is implicit in this conception of the purpose of economic activities and institutions a test of those activities and institutions on which economists have put special emphasis: the test of effectiveness. No degree of justice in the organization of economic life can compensate for failure to be efficiently productive, for on this depends the capacity to provide adequately the food, the clothing, the shelter, and other goods which are required by the community. Those who represent Christian theology and ethics are tempted to underestimate the significance of this test of effectiveness in their concern to apply ethical tests, just as economists have often shown an opposite kind of one-sidedness and have declared the independence of economics from ethics.

Autonomy of the Economic Order and Its Limitations

The characteristic tendency in both thought and action since the sixteenth century has been the tendency to separate the sphere of economics from that of Christian theology and ethics. In part this has been a justifiable rebellion against the effort of the Church to impose laws in detail upon the economic order which would have prevented developments within it that have proved to be creative. The medieval Church attempted to regulate economic life in the light of principles that did not fit the new vitalities which began to develop during the later Middle Ages. The Catholic Church and the reformers failed to prevent the rise of modern capitalism, and elements in the doctrine of the reformers, especially Calvin, actually provided strong spiritual support for the development of the institutions and the ethos of capitalism.

There has been a long debate over the exact relationship of modern capitalism to various forms of Protestantism. One conclusion that can be drawn from the debate is that later Calvinism did create a religious spirit that was favorable to individual initiative, to habits of industry and thrift, to the development of moral sanctions for the endless accumulation of wealth, and even in some cases to the moral condemnation of the poor. The emancipation of economic life from control by the Church and even from Christian criticism was greatly aided by the complacent assumption of a pre-established harmony between efforts of individuals to seek their own advantage and the welfare of the community as a whole. It was assumed that injustices would be automatically eliminated if economic activities were given free rein.

So the economic order came to be regarded by many Christians as having its own laws which were autonomous in relation to any detailed guidance or criticism from the Church, and indeed the economic order as a whole was itself regarded as a demonstration of the working of divine providence. It was not autonomous in relation to God. This made no practical difference because there was no way of recognizing divine judgment upon the economy except in terms of the laws of the economic order. Christians and secularists would not, under such conditions of thought, differ in their estimate of economic activities. The sheer momentum of modern capitalistic institutions encouraged this tendency to keep them independent of Christian criticism, because the Church, even if it had felt the need to do so, would have had difficulty keeping ahead of these new developments. Also, the concern of the economist to preserve a manageable area for his scientific study underlined the autonomy of economic life. The theologian today, partly because of a fresh understanding of the doctrine of sin and partly because he is wise after many events, can recognize the extent to which Christian complacency concerning the essential justice of economic institutions was encouraged by the fact that the Christian interpreters themselves were largely drawn from or were dependent on social groups that had benefited most from the developing economy.

But complacency about the sufficiency of automatic self-correction in the economy is no longer possible except on the part of a sheltered few. Most observers, whether they are Christians, liberal secularists, or theoretical Marxists, would agree that the separation of economic life from ethical criticism did lead to vast exploitation and misery; that it did tend to dehumanize culture; that it did result in an intolerable inner conflict in the motives of men. Economic activities are now almost universally judged in terms of some values which cannot be derived from a study of economic processes themselves.

The Christian can put what has happened within the Church in terms of the following change of thought: It is not enough to say that economic processes in themselves reveal God's purpose for economic life; we must bring to economic life what we know of God's purpose for the whole of human life as it is known to us in Christ. The Christian must reject as a deadly heresy the idea of two absolutely different standards, one for the Kingdom of God or the Church or the personal relations of men, and another for the economic order. God as known in Christ is the Lord of all life.

The first claim that the Christian theologian must make with reference to the economic order is that it is not fully autonomous; that it stands under the judgment of God as known in Christ. But he must admit that there is a relative autonomy in the economic order. Failure to admit such relative autonomy is to invite the kind of reckless declaration of independence from all Christian standards which has had such evil consequences.

To say that the economic order has relative autonomy means, among other things, that there are aspects of it for which there is no distinctively Christian guidance. There is no Christian guidance concerning the given economic possibilities in a particular situation. All ethical demands, Christian or non-Christian, must be made in the light of the actual resources of a country in comparison with the size of its population. Also, there is no Christian guidance concerning the cause-and-effect relationships within economic processes. These are not to be separated from all ethical concerns, however, for it makes a great difference from the point of view of Christian ethics what the consequences of a particular economic policy will be. The choice of a policy in the light of what are expected to be its consequences is an ethical choice, but the prediction of the consequences depends upon a technical judgment. It is a matter of Christian concern to find policies that will prevent inflation, with its injustice to large segments of the population, or to prevent unemployment; but whether or not a particular policy will have either result, or whether the result of such a policy will have by-products that are so evil that the policy must be rejected, is a technical question.

It is important to guard against a common misuse of technical judgments. They often become smoke screens for judgments which are really based upon special economic interests. Any discussion of problems of taxation will include many technical judgments, but in public debate they are usually used to prove that the burden of taxation should fall on some group other than the one that is offering them as arguments. It is essential to be sensitive to the difference between the elements in such an argument which are technical and morally neutral from those which are controlled by economic interest or by moral purpose. On large questions of public policy there is usually a confusion of technical issues with other issues to which Christian moral judgments are highly relevant.

There are issues involved in most questions of policy which are primarily neither economic nor ethical though having economic and ethical relevance. As an example, take the problem of incentive. This is a psychological problem with important moral implications. It is not a problem for which the psychologist can give conclusive guidance. Economists have often assumed a psychology of incentives of an acquisitive kind as though it were axiomatic. Christian and secular idealists have sometimes assumed an opposite psychology of altruistic incentives as though it were a sure description of what could be expected to become the human situation if only various changes were made in the economic system. Both have been partly mistaken in the substance of their judgments and both have failed to realize that they were confusing psychological judgments with either economic or moral judgments. There are many questions on which no professional group can claim to have the last word, which are neither purely ethical nor purely technical, which call for a kind of wisdom about human life which is only too rare.

I. THE IMPLICATIONS OF SPECIFIC CHRISTIAN DOCTRINES FOR ECONOMIC LIFE

A. *The Doctrine of God*

There are obvious ways of relating Christian ethics to economic life. These will be discussed later. Here I shall deal with the implications of Christian doctrine for economic life. Ethics depends upon doctrine. It deals with what the Christian ought to do in the light of the nature of God and man, in the light of what God has done for man's salvation. A common way of distinguishing between theological doctrine and ethics is to say that the former is concerned with the understanding of what *is* ultimately real and the latter with what we *ought* to do.

I. THE TRANSCENDENCE OF GOD. It is important to put side by side two aspects of Christian teaching about God: the transcendence of God and the revelation of God in Christ. God transcends every human idea, every human system. "All the nations are as nothing before him" (Is. 40:17). "For as the heavens are higher than the earth, so are my ways higher than your ways and my thoughts than your thoughts" (Is. 55:9). At the center of Biblical teaching about God is the warning against idolatry, which is the natural human tendency to put a finite object in the place of God. This transcendence of God might be understood in such a way as to cause him to be irrelevant to all human problems, but Christians believe that God has demonstrated his love for man, his solidarity with man, and that he has done so supremely in the life and death and resurrection of Jesus Christ.

These two aspects of the Christian faith in God eliminate two common religious tendencies: the tendency to think of God as so remote that we can know nothing about his purpose and the tendency to find the clue to his purpose in some structure of nature or history. I have indicated the danger of the latter tendency in connection with the economic order when the so-called laws of economics as understood at a particular time are assumed to be a natural revelation of the divine will. These two aspects of Christian faith in God are the basis for judgment of every human ideal and achievement. In particular the Christian warning against idolatry is of great significance when men are tempted to put a social system —whether it be Soviet communism or any other system—in the place of God. The American form of idolatry which takes the form of the idealizing of our institutions is better disguised than the Communist because it is often expressed through the use of Christian symbols, but it causes great religious and moral confusion in American life. Fortunately our American culture is not authoritarian, and American idolatry is a common private tendency rather than an official creed.

The temptation to absolutize any culture, any scheme of values, or any economic institutions or objectives is ever with us, and the surest protection against it may be found in Christian faith. It is of special significance that this revelation of God has its center in the Cross, which is the sign of the rejection of Christ by the various agents of culture in the first century. Today we can say of Christ that, rejected by his own nation, he belongs to no natural human group, and he is the sponsor of no social system. The fact that he lived under humble conditions, born in a stable, the son of a carpenter, is a sign of God's indifference to human conceptions of rank. Jesus' own saying that "the first shall be last" does not have initially an economic reference but it is characteristic of Jesus' habit of overturning the world's usual way of arranging people.

2. THE CHRISTIAN DOCTRINE OF CREATION. Of more direct significance for economic life is the Christian doctrine of creation. It has two elements which need special emphasis. One is that the created world is essentially good. There is in the Christian view of the world no absolute dualism which denies the value of any aspect of creation. The doctrine of the fall is a symbol of the faith that sin is not characteristic of the essential nature of man. There is no ultimate contrast between body and spirit according to which the things of the body or of the material world are evil. In fact, the Christian teaching about sin locates the chief source of sin in the spirit of man, in his pride, his self-sufficiency, his idolatry. The economic life of man is not to be morally rejected on the ground that

it is so largely concerned about material goods. It is true that "man does not live by bread alone," but in the Lord's prayer there is a petition for daily bread. It is often suggested that the use of the elements of bread and wine in the Communion is a symbol of the importance of the material basis of life for Christian faith.

A second element in the doctrine of creation is that it forms the basis for Christian thinking about property. Any system of ownership must take account of many factors that will differ from situation to situation, but there are basic Christian convictions about property by which Christian thinking about systems of ownership should be guided. Most important of all is the conviction that God is the only absolute owner of property. Insofar as man has the right to use the resources of the earth he must regard this right as a trust. According to the report of the Oxford Conference (1937), from which I have already quoted, "It should be reaffirmed without qualification that all human property rights are relative and contingent only, in virtue of the dependence of man upon God as the giver of all wealth and as the creator of man's capacities to develop the resources of nature."[2]

The most obvious implication of this conception is that the resources of the earth were intended for the use of all persons and not for a privileged minority.[3] The tendency for individuals and small

[2] *Op. cit.,* p. 100.

[3] Dr. J. M. Clark raises this question in a memorandum: "In terms of this principle, does the American people rank as a privileged minority? What is its duty toward other peoples? Suppose your specialists report that the handing over of given resources to certain other peoples would mean handing them into the exploitive control of a smaller and more grasping minority, extending less benefit to the masses under them than American 'exploiters' would extend? Or if the abolishing of bars to immigration is an issue, suppose they report that the long-term result would be to people the more prosperous areas of the world not perhaps to the present density of India or China, but near enough to it to impoverish these areas without raising the level of prosperity in the areas now overcrowded or reducing their overpopulation? Suppose it was concluded that this would lower our standards of social morality—a poor country can't afford high standards of diffused welfare—and is not a feasible route on what one of the papers (Boulding, p. 78) has called 'the long climb' from equality of poverty to equality of plenty?"

groups to gain control of these resources on a large scale and for indefinite periods for their own exclusive use is always an affront to the Creator. Christians originally accepted private property as a concession to human sin. The Catholic tradition following Thomas Aquinas accepts the necessity for private property and gives good reasons for its constructive contribution, but St. Thomas limited the right to the use of property on the principle that sharing with those who are in need is a matter of justice.[4] Always in the background there was the idea that in a world not distorted by the fall communal ownership of property would be natural.

This radical doctrine never became embodied in institutions, but it remained in the background as an ultimate basis for criticism of institutions. Catholic and early Protestant conceptions of property always involved a limit in principle to accumulations of property and to the right of individuals to use for *themselves* property of which they are the owners. Later Protestantism lost sight of this idea of limits, but it continued to acknowledge the principle that God is the only absolute owner by insisting on the duty of stewardship. This came to be in practice a means of justifying complete ownership of the greater part of one's wealth if a portion of it was given to the Lord. The principle of stewardship should mean that all of one's possessions are to be used in the light of God's purpose.

Christian teaching about property lost its edge very early because it came to be generally assumed that any prevalent system of ownership existed by divine appointment and was to be explained as a necessary consequence of the fall of man. The deeper criticism of private property continued to be expressed by monasticism, but the ordinary lay Christian who owned property did not ask why he should be a beneficiary of the fall in this respect. As we shall see, Christian teaching about human nature does provide justification for private property within limits; but it should also provide an effective warning against the sinful tendency to justify almost endlessly institutions and policies which serve only selfish interests and per-

---

[4] "In this respect man ought to possess external things, not as his own, but as common, so that, to wit, he is ready to communicate them to others in their need." *Summa Theologia*, Part II, ii, 66.2.

mit some people to exploit others through the use of the power over their lives which often accompanies ownership of property.[5]

3. DIVINE PROVIDENCE—HUMAN FREEDOM AND AUTHORITY. Another aspect of Christian faith in God which has implications for economic life is faith in divine providence, which usually interacts with some recognition of human freedom. Most Christian theologians have affirmed God's ultimate control over history without denying the freedom of men to resist God's purposes. Even Calvin, whose system is the most thoroughgoing assertion of the divine sovereignty, conceded something to human responsibility, if inconsistently, when he emphasized the idea that man is the author of his own sin. God who causes "the wrath of men to praise him" overrules their very disobedience and uses it for his own purposes. There are many theologians who, while they believe that God will not be defeated by human sin, are careful to prevent the ultimate faith from canceling out the sinful and tragic character of much human history, and who see in the Cross the kind of overcoming of evil by God which is costly to God himself. In other words, God does not override human wills and gain his way by sheer omnipotence but suffers the consequences of man's resistance.

The implications of these ideas about God and man that are most relevant to economic life can be seen if one raises the question:

[5] The Oxford Conference report developed the outlines of a Christian doctrine of property under present conditions. After affirming the relative and contingent character of all human property rights, it emphasized the following points: that "the existing system of property rights and the existing distribution of property must be criticized in the light of the largely non-moral processes by which they have been developed"; that every argument for private property is an argument for its widest possible distribution; that the social consequences of the exercise of property rights should always be considered; that the contribution of the community in the production of all wealth is an essential factor; that distinctions should be made between various forms of property. On this last point the report says: "The property which consists in personal possessions for use, such as the home, has behind it a clearer moral justification than property in the means of production and in land which gives the owners power over other persons" (pp. 100-101). This does not mean that only property for personal use is really justified, but rather that the temptation to abuse all other forms of property rights needs to be emphasized.

Does Christian teaching about divine providence constitute a ground for the pious acceptance of the *status quo* as divinely ordained? There is no doubt that Christians have often interpreted their faith in these conservative terms. Paul's injunction about "subjection to the higher powers: for there is no power but of God; and the powers that be are ordained of God" (Romans XIII 13:1) has been the proof text for conservatives in every period. There has been a conflict throughout Christian history between conservative interpretations of divine providence and revolutionary imperatives which arise from the faith that God loves all men and seeks their welfare. Paul's words in Romans XIII need to be balanced by words even more familiar in the worship of the Churches: "He hath put down the mighty from their seats, and exalted them of low degree. He hath filled the hungry with good things; and the rich he hath sent empty away" (Luke 1:52-53).

Today there is a remarkable converging of Christian traditions in the rejection of socially conservative interpretations of divine providence. There is a releasing of the socially radical imperatives in Christian faith, and I shall try to indicate in this chapter that these have a validity for us that is more than that of a contemporary Christian ideological fashion.

I believe that there are two reasons for this shift of emphasis. The first is the fact that old structures which in other periods seemed to be static and to have a certain majesty because of their association with tradition have gone. The divine right of holders of power and privilege in the contemporary world has lost all plausibility. In mid-nineteenth-century England there was a popular saying: "God bless the squire and his relations and help us all to keep our stations." History has done too much to the squires and to the stations of the working classes in England to make such sentiments possible today. The changes that have come in our period have often led to greater evils, especially in the form of totalitarianism, than existed under the old social hierarchies; but they have also opened up new possibilities for the submerged classes and races which can no longer be denied even by conservatives who might prefer the old institutions for themselves.

A second factor that has helped to demolish conservative interpretations of divine providence consists of the new voice and the new power that have come to what I have called the submerged classes and races. In some cases they have raised up their own Christian interpreters. This is particularly true of that part of the world which so recently was regarded complacently by Western Christians as ordained to be ruled imperialistically by the West. The Churches of Asia have been able for some decades to talk back to the Churches of Europe and America and in doing so have effectively changed the outlook of Christians in the West. In the case of the working classes there has been great moral pressure on the Church, often as by an outside force, and this pressure has had a profound effect on the Christian conscience within the Church. The rise of the various forms of "Social Christianity," of which the "Social Gospel" was but the American Protestant form during a particular period (roughly from 1880 to 1930), has been the result of the interaction between the Christian conscience illumined by fresh response to Biblical faith and these pressures from the contemporary working-class movements. The pressure of Marxism on the mind of the Church has been important, both as an actual corrective to much Christian thinking and as a stimulus to find alternative Christian solutions for the problems of the groups to which it appealed. In the United States the leadership of both the Protestant and the Catholic branches of the Church has taken the labor movement with great seriousness. The Catholics have had more ambitious programs for influencing the labor movement than the Protestants because organized labor is so large a part of the Catholic constituency.

One consequence of this new opportunity to speak for themselves that large groups of people have acquired is that it has deflated Christian tendencies to defend special privilege or unchecked power over others on paternalistic grounds. Paternalism has a better appearance when those who are on the receiving end are unable to say frankly what they think of it. Paternalistic use of power may at times represent a step forward over exploitation that has previously existed, but it needs to be kept under close moral scrutiny because it so easily becomes a defense of a structure that may be essentially unjust and which may deny those who are its supposed beneficiaries the opportunity to develop their own capacities. During periods in which institutions seemed static, paternalistic expressions of Christian love were the best way of improving the condition of the poor and oppressed. But today Christian love as it seeks the welfare of all social groups cannot be content with philanthropy as a substitute for efforts to achieve more equal justice.

B. *The Christian Doctrine of Man*

There has been in recent years a marked revival of interest in the Christian doctrine of man, and the implications of this doctrine for economic life have been much discussed. There is no space here to outline the doctrine, but it is essential to emphasize two aspects of it. The first is the conviction that man is made in God's image, responsible to God, with unique dignity and possibilities derived from this relation to God. The second is that man universally and persistently tends to be sinful. This second conviction means that tendencies toward pride and self-centeredness are present on every level of human life. The religious root of these tendencies is man's failure to recognize his dependence upon God, and the social consequences of these tendencies are to be found in all varieties of injustice. The sinfulness of man's mind and spirit is shown most clearly in his tendency to defend imperialistic exploitation by means of theory and even by means of a distorted idealism. Pride and self-righteousness when they are identified with idealism and often with religious sanctions greatly aggravate antisocial consequences of economic self-interest because they cause a conflict between social and economic systems to become an ideological and religious conflict with great increase of bitterness and intransigence.

In this Christian conception of the universality and persistence of sin, there are at least four implications for economic life.

1. PRESSURES OF INDIVIDUAL AND GROUP SELF-INTEREST. There is, first, a warning against the ways in which judgments about economic issues are warped by self-interest or the narrow interest of a particular group. This does not mean that we must accept the idea of economic determinism, though those who are unaware

of the extent to which economic factors do determine the opinions and loyalties of men are especially vulnerable to their influence. Also, this does not mean that the individual is always controlled, even so far as his judgments are influenced by such economic factors, by conscious and deliberate selfishness. Many other elements confuse the situation. He may have a sense of solidarity with a group and he is assured that the interests of his group are on the side of the general interest. Usually there are economists, clergymen, and editorial writers who are ready to assure him that such is the case. Moreover, the social experience of any individual is limited, and it is extremely difficult for him to see the world from the point of view of any nation or social class other than his own. Conscious economic motives are more effective as the common denominator of motive in a nation or a social class than they are in the case of an individual. The idea of the person as an "economic man" is a monstrosity. He is more likely to be driven by the hunger for affection, the desire for social approval or status, than by conscious economic interest.

Within the Church it should be natural for people to become aware of their tendency to be influenced by the pressures of group interest. The peculiar illusions, the peculiar forms of self-righteousness, of each class should be made so apparent that they become a part of the confession of sin. Too often this does not happen, and instead religious symbols are used to support the illusions of a particular congregation. This is one point at which a deliberate effort of the Church to open itself to correction by its own Gospel is imperative.

2. USE OF POWER WITHOUT RESPONSIBILITY. Christian teaching warns against all irresponsible forms of power, whether they be political or economic. Economic power is often less obvious than political power and it tends to be more irresponsible than political power under the conditions of political democracy. One reason for thinking that the modern criticism of paternalism by Christians is more than a reflection of modern culture is that it takes account of the truth in old ideas about sin which were strongly held in other periods by Christians who did not apply them realistically to them-

selves in their social relations. Defenders of slavery, of privileged oligarchies, of the unchecked power of employers, though they often believed in this Christian teaching about sin, seemed blind to their own peculiar temptations as men of power. This is evidence of the truth of that teaching. Today labor unions are still resisted by many Christians who should know from their Christian faith that they need to have their own power checked by the power of a union. Labor leaders also should recognize that their power should rest on democratic foundations and should be subject to check by society as a whole. Abraham Lincoln, in this respect, was a sounder theologian than most of the more orthodox Christians of his time when he said: "No man is good enough to govern another without that other's consent."[6]

3. OVERSIMPLIFICATION OF PROBLEM OF INCENTIVE. Christian teaching about man should also warn us against easy solutions of the problem of incentive. The consistent Socialist has wrongly assumed that this problem would not exist in a socialized society in which all would be working for the common welfare. On the other hand, the capitalistic theorist has usually neglected the moral dangers in a society that puts its chief emphasis upon the motive of self-interest. He assumes too readily the innocence of self-interest because in a competitive society those who are seeking their own profit are supposed to be serving the common good. We have learned from bitter experience that the cultural support for unlimited acquisitiveness trains men in tendencies to which they are already inclined and causes them to develop institutions for the exploitation of the community in their own interests.

Christian teaching about human nature points toward economic institutions which make use of self-interest to get efficient work done. The best of us need prodding by the necessity of earning a living, for it is easy to let down and, even if we work, to neglect tasks that are uncongenial. Here there is one basis for accepting private property as good for man, though any argument for private property as a source of incentive is an argument for its wide distribution. On the other hand, it is also important to avoid placing

[6] Speech at Peoria.

such great temptations before man's selfish desires that they warp character in ways that are antisocial. If wealth is honored as the chief mark of success, great encouragement may be given to economic activities that are in themselves useful but which may be so carried on that personal character or the moral climate of society will be deeply corrupted.[7]

4. THE YEARNING FOR PANACEAS. The Christian view of human nature also constitutes a warning against panaceas and utopias. Both the doctrine of sin and the recognition of man's finiteness are involved here. We must avoid fatalistic or pessimistic doctrines that set definite limits to possible advance. Christian teaching should encourage us to seek solutions of our problems. But it is important to realize now that there are no over-all and no absolute solutions. Each solution will create new and often unexpected problems. Also, in the search for solutions there is the tendency to overemphasize one essential value at any given time—the value of freedom in some situations and the value of order or security in other situations. Moreover, gains that are made do not remain secure. There is always the danger of their being corrupted. The more effective and more concentrated forms of power which go with many of our solutions create the possibility of more oppressive forms of tyranny than existed in earlier periods. Loyalty to the public interest and personal integrity are always necessary foundations for sound economic and political institutions, but these qualities are precarious. They do not grow easily and a community or a culture can lose them.

One of the chief points of conflict between Christianity and communism is the Communist assumption that communism has the key to absolute solutions of economic and social problems. The most fateful miscalculation of Communists is their conviction that,

[7] Much needs to be done to follow up the studies of incentive that indicate that motives of a noneconomic sort such as group solidarity or social approval are more important for industrial efficiency than economic motives. Cf. Elton Mayo, *The Social Problem of an Industrial Civilization*, Cambridge, Harvard University Press, 1945. There is a difference between incentives for efficiency and incentives for investment in new enterprises which needs study from the Christian point of view.

if only they push hard enough, and by whatever means are necessary, to establish their power and to destroy the capitalistic elements in society, they will achieve both justice and freedom. The idea that the totalitarian state created to accomplish this purpose will disappear seems to them to guarantee the freedom. This conviction that, no matter how ruthless and oppressive and treacherous their dealing with persons may be, the good society will assuredly come as a result of success in their revolution makes it easy to justify any enormity that seems expedient on the way. How far the men in the Kremlin or the present Communist party bosses in various countries really believe in the new freedom that is expected, according to the theory, to follow the withering away of the state may be open to question. But there is no doubt that multitudes of their followers are attracted to communism by this promise and that they are helped to endure the tyranny because they are confident that it is a temporary expedient.

The Christian should be able to detect three illusions in this one aspect of the Communist faith: (1) the illusion that any society will be as securely just and free as the one which they promise; (2) the illusion that this good society can be brought about by change in external institutions, because it is assumed that the capitalistic form of property is the root of all evil; (3) the illusion that the dread results of terror and tyranny can be wiped out if only the terror and the tyranny are successful in destroying the opposition.

THE INDIVIDUAL AND THE COMMUNITY

So far in the discussion of the doctrine of man I have emphasized the implications of the Christian teaching about the universality and persistence of sin. There is another aspect of Christian teaching about man that may be even more important as we face the present conflict between social systems. It is the Christian conception of the person in relation to the community. Christian support cannot be claimed for either a consistent individualism or a consistent collectivism. The person is a member of several communities. This membership is an essential part of his nature. He develops self-consciousness in social relations and his purposes and loyalties are for the most part social. But no community owns him fully, for he is responsible to God who transcends all communities. Personal freedom has its deepest source in this responsibility of the person to God. And yet God is also God of the communities to which the person belongs. He wills their welfare. Responsibility to God includes responsibility for the welfare of the various communities of which the individual person is a member. Such responsibility often involves the attempt to adjust the conflicting interest of various communities.

I have stated as briefly as possible a view of the person which is implied in Christian faith. This view is incompatible with an atomistic individualism as an account of the nature of the person, and with any form of economic individualism which gives the pursuit of economic gain for the self primary place in the moral life. Responsibility to God and the sharing of God's concern for the welfare of the community should have that place. This view is equally incompatible with any collectivism which rides roughshod over the consciences or the welfare of the members of society, which regards any persons as no more than expendable instruments, or as mere obstacles to be relegated to some human scrap heap. Insofar as the conscience of a society is influenced by the Christian view of the person, it will preserve a strong sense of responsibility for the welfare of even its most objectionable members. The Church should go beyond secular society or the state in this redemptive concern.

C. Christian Salvation

Christian teaching about salvation concerns the goal of human life and the means by which God seeks to draw men to that goal. The goal understood in its ultimate context is eschatological in the sense that it transcends the life of persons and communities within history. All our experiences of salvation in the course of our lives in this world are regarded by Christians as intimations of a fulfillment by which God will establish his Kingdom. The otherworldly dimension of Christian faith has grown dim in the modern liberal Church and there has been a concentration upon the fulfillment of God's purpose in history through the progress of mankind. The most widely accepted criticism of the liberal theology of recent decades, especially as expressed in the Social Gospel, is that it is built on expectations concerning the human future in history which are as remote from the conditions of human existence as they are from the faith of the New Testament. This does not mean that progress is impossible, but that endlessly cumulative progress is unlikely. There are many reasons for recognizing that most social gains are precarious; that they create new and perplexing problems; that they may be undone by such catastrophes as atomic war or the spread of totalitarianism. The Christian faith that the meaning of the life of any one of us does not depend entirely upon what it contributes to historical progress fits the spiritual need of our generation.

It is possible to move, from this recognition of the mistakes in recent expectations, in two quite different directions. Many Christians, especially on the European continent, have developed an emphasis on eschatology that threatens the significance of the development of communities and institutions in history. On the other hand, the view that prevails in most of the Churches and which, with different emphasis, is expressed by both Catholic and Protestant theologians is that God's final Kingdom is a fulfillment of human history and not a negation of it. As I should express it, though God's Kingdom transcends every social achievement, we do serve God in each endeavor to raise the level of human life, in every new embodiment of justice and mercy and fellowship in our communities.

Salvation as we know it in Christian experience includes at least two elements. The first is the awareness of being forgiven or accepted by God (Justification). The second is growth in a life of obedience and love (Sanctification). These do not represent two separate processes that can be chronologically distinguished. Gratitude for forgiveness is primary because it is the ultimate source of Christian motive, and the Christian's awareness of being forgiven is the deepest corrective for self-righteousness. Moreover, awareness of being forgiven is the ultimate Christian basis for the "self-acceptance" which is essential for spiritual health. Growth in obedience and love cannot be left to itself without effort, without attention to the improvement of moral understanding, without personal discipline; but the faith of one who has already been forgiven is the true source of this growth. This faith itself depends upon response to what God has done to reveal himself and to draw men to himself in Christ, and this response comes normally through the mediation of Christ to men by the Church.

So abbreviated a discussion of Christian salvation may seem arrogant to the person who does not accept Christian presuppositions. There are approaches to this experience of salvation apart from Christ, and Christians themselves often seem far removed from it. It is difficult for Christians to make claims for Christian faith without seeming to make claims for themselves in depreciation of others. This is the last thing that should be intended. The story of the Pharisee and the Publican is a perfect statement of what should be the Christian approach to all problems of comparison. It would not be intellectually honest for the Christian to obscure his conviction that, whatever be the saving work of God apart from any conscious relation to Christ, we do have in the Gospel the context in which all experiences of salvation can best be understood. The hunger for an equivalent of what Christians mean by forgiveness or justification is abundantly evident in the understanding by clinical psychology of the need for acceptance by whatever is regarded by a person as having most authority in his world.

What does this discussion of salvation have to do with economic life? I shall emphasize two points of connection between them.

1.   ECONOMIC CONDITIONS AS OBSTACLES TO SPIRITUAL GROWTH. There is an economic basis for the kind of welfare which at least removes obstacles to salvation. This is an extremely difficult point because it is certainly true that some of those who have known the saving influence of God most deeply have been great sufferers, and they have possessed few of the things that most of us regard as necessary for welfare. What has the Cross to do with economic welfare? It is also true that a high standard of living can be a great obstacle to salvation. It can create a sense of self-sufficiency and, seemingly, take the place of God. I think that there is a close analogy between the relationship of welfare and personal salva-

tion and what Arnold Toynbee suggests about the relationship of a favorable environment and the health of a civilization. Toynbee says that society needs the stimulus that comes from hard conditions, problems that call for determined effort; but that conditions can be so hard that they inhibit and crush rather than stimulate. When life is too easy and soft we find obstacles to salvation. Poverty and hunger, on the other hand, can be so great that they are only destructive. Their destructiveness can be seen most clearly in their effect upon children.

⌈These conditions which are favorable to salvation cannot be measured quantitatively on a universal scale. There are many considerations which depend upon particular cultural situations. For example, (1) housing conditions in a modern city may have disastrous effects on family morale, and family morale will affect the emotional growth of children in ways which are important for Christian salvation. (2) The sense of injustice which grows out of the contrasts between wealth and poverty may be the source of soul-destroying bitterness and a great obstacle to fellowship. (3) Archbishop Temple has emphasized the spiritual consequences of unemployment. He says: "The worst evil of such unemployment, whether due to cyclical or to more permanent conditions, is its creating in the unemployed a sense that they have fallen out of the common life." He adds that this feeling that they are not wanted is "the thing that has power to corrupt the soul of any man not far advanced in saintliness."[8] (4) Persons are corrupted by the moral climate created by great emphasis on personal financial gain, by false standards of success, by almost unconsciously dishonest advertising and salesmanship, by the commercial stimulation of materialism and vulgarity in popular tastes. This subtle type of corruption instead of providing clear moral issues, the facing of which produces character, undermines character before people are aware of what is happening.⌋

There are more indirect consequences of economic policies and decisions which are today perhaps more fateful than ever. The clearest example is the influence of economic policies on political institutions. If ways are not found to prevent large-scale unemploy-

[8] *Christianity and Social Order*, New York, Penguin Books, p. 12.

ment in industrialized countries or to solve the problem of agricultural poverty elsewhere, totalitarianism in its Communist form or in some other form is sure to spread. The spiritual effect of totalitarian tyranny upon the people is another subject. Here it is enough to call attention to the effect of economic conditions in bringing on such a tyranny. No matter how evil conditions become there will be some saints or heroes who will seem to be the greater because of what they have had to overcome, but children and the majority of persons are likely to be spiritual victims.

2. SPIRITUAL HEALTH AND ECONOMIC EFFECTIVENESS. A second point of connection between economic life and Christian salvation is that Christians who are saved in any sense, who are at some point in the process of growth in obedience and love, will serve their neighbors through producing goods to meet their needs and through seeking economic policies and institutions which will favor the kind of welfare I have described as a condition for salvation. In other words there are economic conditions for salvation and economic fruits of salvation. What is involved in the Christian economic activity that should be a fruit of salvation will be discussed in the next section on Christian Ethics and Economic Life.

There is one problem which requires much exploration that I shall mention here. Should the Christian limit himself in what he does for the neighbor to that which he regards as essential to the neighbor's salvation according to the distinctively Christian conception of salvation? I am sure that the answer is No, but I doubt that the basis for that answer has received adequate attention. The doctrinal source of the answer would be related to the Christian doctrine of creation as contrasted with the doctrine of salvation or redemption. God has created the world to be used. Man is justified in making use of the resources of the earth for purposes that are not directly related to salvation. The whole modern development of science and technology and most pursuits of aesthetic values are justified by the Christian judgment concerning the essential goodness of God's creation. All human invention and all human artistic achievements are elaborations of that creation.

The human consequences of technology are both good and bad. What it has done to make possible wider community and more devastating conflict is ever before our minds. It has created the so-called mass man, but it has liberated countless men from drudgery, hunger, disease, and ignorance. The Christian is not intended to go about with a narrowly moral or religious yardstick to measure what is good for his neighbors. He will be guided by the claims of many forms of human good which have their proper place and which become dangerous only when they lose that place and become, in isolation, the chief objects of devotion.

There are undoubtedly many dilemmas here. There is an endless accumulation of material things which are good in themselves but which crowd out more meaningful interests. It is difficult to define the nature of Christian vocation as it is related to the production of each new gadget. It would be curious advice, however, to suggest that those who make use of most of the older gadgets, including the typewriter on which this is being written, should sanction no newer ones. There is no chance that the present tendency toward technological complexity will be reversed unless an atomic war destroys most of the resources on which it is based. This tendency means that what first may seem to be gadgets become necessities. If deprived of them now, large populations would starve or their health would be endangered. So a critical attitude toward our preoccupation with these "things" should not cause Christians who take for granted their own use of such necessities to discourage production of them for others. There may be some spots in the world where a kind of technological innocence can be preserved, but the great underdeveloped areas of Asia have such vast populations that only far-reaching development in technology can save people from the kind of poverty that crushes the soul.

Christian salvation cannot guarantee economic institutions which are adequately productive or just, but the Christian has reason to expect that new impulses that have their source in the spirit of God and are expressed in lives of integrity and self-giving will be effective in the economic order. All communities are made up of mixed populations, and only a minority in most communities is open to a direct appeal to the Christian conscience. But we can think of God as working always through social necessities that are on the side of justice as well as through the consciences of men.

The most fortunate societies will be those in which the redemptive impulses that come from God's spirit, and the pressures that come from various forms of social necessity or from political movements which represent a certain rough justice, are kept in close relation to each other. When that is the case, those who represent these redemptive influences will do things that have social relevance; and others who represent the various social forces without which large-scale changes in society are impossible will become sensitive to a wide range of social values. The best way, perhaps the only way, of keeping these factors in close relation to each other is to emphasize the responsibility of Christians, while representing these redemptive influences, to take their place in the world as citizens and as participants in economic life.

II. CHRISTIAN ETHICS AND ECONOMIC LIFE

The distinctive element in Christian ethics is the primacy of love, the self-giving love that is known fully to Christian faith in the Cross of Christ. The distance between love, so understood, and the concrete problems of economic life may seem so great as to make Christian ethics irrelevant to those problems. This would be so on most occasions if we were to think only of Christian love in its ultimate form in situations that call only for complete self-sacrifice. Such love means a radical caring for the welfare and dignity of the neighbor, and the neighbor is every man who is within reach, who is affected by what we do or leave undone. This caring involves service to the community of which the neighbor is a part and to the institutions on which his welfare depends. It involves the serving of many values which contribute to the welfare of the neighbor. The content of Christian ethics cannot be deduced from love alone; but love is the ultimate source of motive and the ultimate corrective for the attitudes and choices of the Christian.

Christian love must be related to concrete economic choices by way of values which are not distinctively Christian. I refer to such values as order, justice, freedom, and efficiency.[9] Justice may be thought of as the overarching social value that governs the relationship of other values, but here I am limiting it to the narrower idea of distributive justice.

These values are interdependent in the long run. No society can achieve one of them in a stable form without also embodying the others in some measure. But there is no universal principle by which these values must be related. Certainly there is no Christian law governing them which enables us to judge exactly how much emphasis at a given time ought to be placed on each of them. Why are these values Christian values at all? The answer is that Christians, from the motive of love, must seek whatever values are essential for the welfare of persons. There are also values in personal life, such as integrity, which economic institutions may in practice encourage or hinder and by which, therefore, they must be judged.

1. *Justice in Distribution—among Persons*

Justice in distribution must always be under the criticism of the principle of equality. The effort to achieve absolute equality of income, however, would involve a degree of regimentation that would destroy many forms of personal freedom. It would also deprive economic institutions of the incentives which are essential for efficiency. Even if a society were made up entirely of committed Christians, they should recognize that they are not immune to the temptation to slackness, to the temptation to neglect work which is uncongenial. In any existing society the pressure of necessity and the pull of some economic advantage are, within limits, desirable if the economic system is to be adequately productive. But these considerations do not remove the claims of equality. Contrary to the habits of most societies, the burden of proof should be on every form of inequality. The defense of particular forms of inequality

[9] The economists in this symposium illumine the question: At what price in connection with one value do you achieve other values? They are most sensitive about losses in freedom and efficiency. See chapters by Clark and Knight especially.

by their beneficiaries is an almost universal expression of the sin of man that Christian teaching emphasizes.

One form of equality which has greatest strategic importance is equality of opportunity for all children. This means that they should have, as far as it is technically possible and as far as it is consistent with the stability of the family, equal access to the means of health and to the education suitable to their capacities. There are many inevitable inequalities. No planning can make doctors and teachers of equal effectiveness available to all children, regardless of economic factors. But inequalities which are the result of family income alone are the kind to be emphasized in this context. This is a case where, even if it is at the risk of undermining incentive, the tendencies toward inequality need continuous correction.

The relation between Christian love and the economic motives of the Christian is a perennial problem with which Christians have struggled from the beginning. If some degree of inequality is good for the productivity of economic institutions, where may the line be drawn? Should the Christian accept anything for himself beyond what most of his neighbors receive? Unless a relatively privileged Christian suspects that everything that he says on this subject has in it an element of rationalization of his own privilege, he is probably deceiving himself.

Many things are said in this connection which have truth in them. There are family responsibilities; it is unfair to force upon one's family standards which some of the members may not fully understand or accept. There are professional responsibilities which call for income to meet expenditures that may not be required of everyone. There are the difficulties in knowing how best to divest oneself of privilege in a way that will really benefit others whose need is greatest. We become involved in a particular way of life with its standard of living and it is often difficult to see where to reduce that standard without doing positive harm to someone.

The suspicious factor in these arguments is that they can be stretched so indefinitely. It is a rare thing to find a person who cannot use them to defend his income no matter how large it is! Christian distrust of all wealth is never far away from any honest reflection on these problems. Jesus did not lay down a law on this matter, but his words about the "needle's eye," about Dives, and about the rich fool are there to haunt us.

2. *Justice in Distribution—among Nations*

When we move from this discussion of the problem of unequal wealth in personal terms to the consideration of unequal wealth as between nations, the issues become more complicated. As the world's richest nation, the United States faces great moral dilemmas. We will not share our wealth as much as is possible because of the pull of national self-interest, but even if we were to decide to go far in sharing wealth we should find that there are limits to doing it in ways that are really helpful. This nation seems fated to have a continuously rising standard of living. This is a moral embarrassment in relation to other nations, but it is a moral problem in itself if it means that the American people will have too many possessions for their own spiritual good. Any slowing up of our economy would mean unemployment with its fateful consequences for our free institutions. We are tied to a dynamic economy. We cannot reject it morally because a great increase in production is needed to meet the needs of a part of our own population and those of most of the population of the world. We have an enormous responsibility to find ways of sharing our wealth constructively with less privileged nations; but, whatever we do in this respect, the wealth will increase here at home. We are tempted and we shall continue to be tempted in our fatness to make a god out of prosperity.

Both in personal life and in the life of the nation there is a real tension between Christianity and the general trend of our economic life. There will be Christians who, feeling the burden of this tension, will try to find some way of living a much simpler life, of reducing their standard of life deliberately to a point nearer to the standard of living of the least privileged groups. Monasticism at its best has been influenced by this same concern to renounce the acquisitiveness and materialism of the world, and Protestants have often sought a personal or community discipline inspired by this same protest. This type of sectarian withdrawal from the main stream of contemporary society can make a positive contribution to the ethical sensitivity of those who remain in that main stream; but this contribution will be dependent in large measure on the degree to which those who choose such a discipline are free from self-righteous illusions. They should realize that they depend in innumerable ways upon the larger society with its more callous economic behavior. They should also realize that if their protest became popular it would have disastrous effects upon an economy, the effectiveness of which is essential for the welfare of most of the human race. They must also realize that not many people with family responsibilities can make such a choice.

Most Christians, of course, will have to find their vocations in the economy. They can believe that, in spite of all the moral problems it creates, it does represent good possibilities of life to countless millions who in other periods have been little more than beasts of burden. The visitor to some Asian countries today is impressed by the misery of the lot of the ordinary man, for which no claims to a higher spirituality in the culture compensate. There is a materialism of poverty as well as a materialism of wealth.

When we ask what in detail a Christian should do, the Protestant answer must be in terms of the idea of vocation and the idea of stewardship—two threadbare words which need to be reclaimed. There are no rules that can be laid down as to what occupations are good and what are to be rejected, or as to how much anyone should receive. The Reformation swept away for Protestants the contrast between sacred and secular callings and established the principle that a Christian can serve God significantly in any constructive occupation. But criticism of particular occupations does need to be emphasized together with the improvement of possibilities of service in them. As for income, it would be a great gain at present if Christians quite generally became sensitive to the moral issues involved, and if this sensitivity caused them to keep raising the question as to how much they ought to spend on themselves. One mark of Christian sensitivity would be an open-minded attitude toward proposals advanced in the interests of the community as a whole which may bring some economic loss or sacrifice to oneself.

3. Christianity and Economic Systems

Contemporary discussion of economic issues is related to the choice of economic systems. The arguments about capitalism and communism and socialism are always with us. Christians have lived with many economic systems, and it cannot be too much emphasized today that there is no one Christian system. This does not mean that systems are unimportant, but it does mean that Christian thinking should avoid doctrinaire stereotypes and slogans. There has been a remarkable consensus in contemporary Protestant thought on this matter. The Amsterdam Assembly of the World Council of Churches (1948)[10] criticized both communism and capitalism on several specific grounds. It also called attention to ideological illusions which are characteristic of both: in the case of communism, the illusion that "freedom will come automatically after the completion of the revolution"; and in the case of capitalism, the illusion that "justice will follow as a by-product of free enterprise." This type of thinking limits the alternatives between which Christians should choose. It helps us to find a way forward if we can rule out paths which have been very tempting to many Christians. If we criticize both one-sided individualism and one-sided collectivism, there remains in between a broad area for constructive experiment.

The most controversial problem is the problem of the relation of the state to economic activities. Here again the Amsterdam Assembly pointed the way in general terms by emphasizing both the need of accepting the responsibility of government for the "coherent and purposeful ordering of society" and the need of a large measure of pluralism in society. The Amsterdam report said that "centers of initiative in economic life must be so encouraged as to avoid placing too great a burden upon centralized judgment and decision."[11] This is vague if one is looking for a definite policy, but in relation to present controversies it is the kind of guidance that is most needed.

[10] Official Report, op. cit., Section on The Church and the Disorder of Society.

[11] See especially chapter by MacIver in present volume.

To assume that the more the state acts the better things will be is as wrong as it is to assume that the state is the only threat to personal freedom.

There is no Christian economic system, but there are immediate goals for economic life that do have a claim upon Christians. Whatever name we may give to the economic institutions of our society, we must ask of them whether or not they serve these goals. I shall mention two such goals as illustrations. One is the preservation of a large measure of economic stability and the avoidance of socially destructive periods of unemployment or inflation. The other is the prevention of any private centers of economic power from becoming stronger than the government as the political organ of the community. The choice of means for reaching such goals involves the technical problems often mentioned in this chapter, problems for which there is no specifically Christian guidance. There is a responsibility resting on every Christian to discover the best available means. The Christian expert and the Christian citizen, rather than theologians or the Church acting in its corporate capacity, must bear the chief burden of that responsibility.

4. The Church and Its Function in Relation to Economic Life

The Church is the community of all who have faith in God as revealed through Christ. It is not intended to be a community of righteous men but of men who confess their sins. It is not a community made up of people who agree on political or economic questions. It is a community made up of all classes. That is actually the case today in America; the difficulty is that the divisions between denominations and even more between local churches tend to follow lines of race and class. But the point that needs emphasis is that the Church in its constituency transcends political and social divisions, and in its purpose it transcends all particular social purposes. It exists for the worship of God and to mediate to men the saving grace of God. It becomes involved in economic issues because its members are deeply affected for good or ill by economic conditions and because they are called upon to make decisions which affect the welfare of others.

The influence of the Church upon the economy should be effective on several levels.

1. It should help to improve the moral and spiritual climate in which economic institutions function. The moral assumptions that are taken for granted in a culture are more important than all particular efforts to improve institutions. If there is little integrity or compassion in the hearts of people, no institutional reforms are likely to gain their ends.

2. The Church as the community of worshiping people from all social groups can help in the overcoming of the most stubborn economic conflicts. There has been no more tragic failure of the Church anywhere than its failure in some countries to keep within its fellowship the large body of industrial workers. Class conflict has been most destructive when it has been the conflict between Christian upper and middle classes and "proletarian" workers who have made a religion out of Marxism. Differences of opinion within the Church on many economic issues are a sign of health.

3. The Church in its teaching can give guidance concerning the ends of economic life and concerning the temptations against which Christians must continually guard themselves. This chapter as a whole points to the kind of corporate guidance that the Church should be able to give to its members.

4. The most concrete activity of the Church in the economic order will be the daily decisions of its members as citizens and in their various occupations. The Church should inspire its members to organize for definite political action on economic issues of moral significance and to seek to find concrete solutions of economic problems in connection with their work in the world. It should encourage them as they make experiments which in their concreteness go far beyond the kind of guidance which the Church itself can give. It should not dictate to its members as they try to find more concrete solutions, but it does have a responsibility to help its members come together to discuss the problems raised by their political activities or their daily work.

The Church as an institution has a responsibility to set its own house in order. It cannot persuade others when its economic behavior is flagrantly inconsistent with its own teachings. When its divisions are in part expressions of pride and snobbery, its exhortations directed to the world are little heard. When its policies as employer are thoughtless and even callous, it can do little to improve industrial relations in the secular order. It should listen to its own teaching and be brought to repentance by its own gospel. The Church, however, should not become ingrowing and concentrate on perfecting itself before it does what it can to influence the economic life of the community. Its members need Christian guidance now for their decisions as citizens and as participants in the economic order.

Conclusion

XV

The Christian Faith and the Economic Life of Liberal Society

by REINHOLD NIEBUHR
*Dean of the Faculty and the William E. Dodge, Jr.
Professor of Applied Christianity,
Union Theological Seminary*

I

The "liberal" society which gradually emerged out of the disintegration of the medieval culture and the feudal-agrarian economy is generally characterized by democratic political institutions and by an organization of economic life which dispenses, as far as possible, with the political, and even the moral, control of economic activities.

It was the great achievement of classical economic liberalism to gain recognition of the doctrine that the vast system of mutual services which constitute the life of economic society could best be maintained by relying on the "self-interest" of men rather than their "benevolence" or on moral suasion, and by freeing economic activities from irrelevant and frequently undue restrictive political controls. It released the "initiative" of men to exploit every possible opportunity for gain and thus to increase the resources of the whole of society, at first through the exploitation of commercial opportunities and subsequently through the endless development of technical and industrial power. This new freedom was, in fact, so necessary for the growth of modern commercial-industrial society that it is difficult to determine whether modern commerce and industry developed because they were freed from traditional controls, or because their vitalities and complexities simply broke down moral and political controls which were no longer

433

able to contain the vast flood of new energies or to preserve significant restraints amidst mounting complexities.

The doctrine of classical economic liberalism accompanied its emancipation of economic life with a theory calculated to set the mind and conscience of society at rest about the possible moral and political consequences of this new freedom. The theory was that justice would be the inevitable consequence of a free play of all competitive vitalities. The "free market" would automatically check disbalances of power and privilege. If it offered exorbitant profits provisionally, these would be dispelled in the end by attracting a larger number of competitors to rich pasture lands. In the same manner, meager returns, whether in wages or in profits, would be ultimately redressed by reducing the labor force and capital of the enterprise in a given field.

This assurance of the beneficent effect of a "hidden hand" which controlled the actions of men beyond their conscious contriving, of a "pre-established harmony of nature" which transmuted all competitive strivings into an ultimate harmony, was obviously a more dubious doctrine than the basic assurance that men must be engaged primarily through their self-interest to participate in the vast web of mutual services which has always characterized man's economic life and which increasing specialization of labor has made ever more intricate.

The perpetual debate among economists from the days of Adam Smith to our own may be said to center on the problem of how the indubitable benefits of freedom and initiative which flowed from the truth of the basic doctrine may be preserved, while the errors in the ancillary doctrine are corrected. The chapters by outstanding economists and social scientists in this volume revolve around this theme. It is equally significant that, while none espouse the doctrines of classical liberalism in their purity, there is nevertheless considerable difference in emphasis: on the contrasting perils of the loss of initiative if the economic process is subjected to too rigid controls, on the one hand, and the possibility of injustice if disproportions of economic power are not corrected by political power, on the other. (Professor Boulding's chapter may be usefully compared with Professor MacIver's on this issue.)

In this debate it became more and more apparent that many cherished values of civilization are not protected by the operations of a "free market" (which are accurately defined in Professor Clark's chapter) and that there are conflicts in society which are not composed within the limits of a self-regulating competition. The errors and miscalculations which gave liberal society an undue confidence in the possibilities of an automatic harmony of economic and social interests may be finally reduced to two primary ones. (1) The liberal theory was strangely blind to the factor of power in man's social life and more particularly to the possibility that great disproportions of power would result in injustice. This error was the more fateful because it was introduced into Western social thought at the precise moment when a technical society began to develop. This society would quickly transmute the static inequalities of a feudal society into dynamic ones. (2) The liberal theory was informed by an economic rationalism which tended to equate every form of self-interest with economic interest. It believed men both capable of acting, and inclined to act, upon the basis of economic interest and so obscured the motives of political and religious passion and interest, of ethnic and other loyalties, which impinged upon the economic sphere and were the very stuff of the sphere of politics.

There was consequently little in the liberal theory by which the great centralizations of power in modern economic society could be dealt with morally or politically. Modern society was actually subjected to more violent economic and other conflicts than more traditional and organic communities, thus offering ironic refutation of the liberal concept of social harmony and a self-regulating competitive struggle. The violence of the social conflict was accentuated by the fact that those classes of modern society (particularly in Europe) which suffered most from the periodic dislocations of a supposedly self-regulating economy, and from the poverty which follows inevitably upon powerlessness in competition, became informed by a social creed (Marxism) which contained even more miscalculations than the liberal creed which it challenged. In place of the concept of a natural social harmony it advanced the idea of an inevitable class conflict between propertied and propertyless classes. For the picture of a society in which prudence and competition seemed to have made power an irrelevance, it substituted the idea of a power conflict in which the powerful would become ever more so and the weak ever more exploited until, in a remarkable historical denouement, the powerless would become powerful by the force of their social resentments, the strength of their greater numbers, and the grace of a remarkable historical dialectic operating inexorably to redress the disbalances of history.

In place of the liberal fear of political power and obtuseness toward the realities of economic power, Marxism substituted a theory which assumed that all economic power would be destroyed through the abolition of the right of possession. Since the theory failed to take account of managerial power in the economic realm, the vaunted "socialization of property" actually permitted a concentration of both economic and political power in the hands of a single oligarchy. This oligarchy was allowed to assert its power without any significant restraints, for Marxism in its pure form had found the source of self-interest purely in the institution of property. Its oligarchs, being without property, were therefore supposed to be governed by interests identical with those of the "proletariat" in whose name they governed.

The miscalculations of pure Marxism have resulted in so odious a system of tyranny that the classes in Western society who benefit most from an unregulated economy are persuaded that the validity of their creed can be most simply established by pointing to the grievous errors in the Marxist dogma. But the whole social history of the Western world refutes this simple belief. For the healthiest democracies of the Western world have preserved or regained their social and economic health by using political power to redress the most obvious disbalances in economic society, to protect social values to which the market is indifferent, and to prevent or to mitigate the periodic crises to which a free economy seems subject. They have been prompted to these measures by political parties, primarily composed of workers, who were informed by modified and more democratic versions of the Marxist creed. And even when, as in America, the workers were not directly influenced by Marxist thought, they learned not only to set the organized economic power of the trade union against the organized power of finance and industry but also to organize politically. Through their political power they sought to enforce their demand that the community establish minimal social securities and that it intervene in the economic process whenever it seemed possible and desirable to do so in the interest of welfare.

The debate about the limits and possibilities of a free economy has, in short, not been an academic one. It constitutes the very stuff of political life and controversy in the Western world in the twentieth century. The debate has been inconclusive, and must continue to be so. It is inconclusive because only the most grievous extremes of the two warring creeds have been refuted by experience, while the wisest communities have mixed the two creeds in varying proportions. It is clear that absolute economic freedom fails to establish sufficient justice to make it morally viable. It is also clear that consistent socialization or even regulation of property unduly maximizes political power, replaces self-regulating tendencies in the market with bureaucratic decisions, and tends to destroy the initiative which helped to create modern technical efficiency.

Assuming that Western society will preserve sufficient economic and social health to ward off the virulent version of Marxism, which still takes root wherever there is great poverty or distress, it is probable that the healthier nations will, in varying ways, experiment with various combinations of "freedom" and "planning," but will also seek to avoid the perils of inordinate power, whether political or economic. Both justice and freedom may be secured if the mistake is not made of believing that the one flows inevitably from the other. The question, how much liberty should be risked to establish justice, or justice sacrificed to preserve liberty, will be illumined by able social scientists, as it has been done in this volume. They will arrive at various compromise solutions according to principles admirably stated in Professor Knight's chapter and illustrated in practically every other chapter.

But the question will also continue to be the subject of party conflict. In this conflict, one may expect that those classes in society which suffer most from dislocations in the economic process and benefit least from disproportions of power in economic society will espouse the cause of "control" and "planning." Those classes, on the other hand, which have most to gain from risk-taking and most to give through imaginative initiative will naturally be more zealous to preserve freedom in the economic process and most convinced that the whole structure of democratic freedom rests upon this one freedom. These ideological distortions are inevitable, as James Madison foresaw, and one may be grateful that in a healthy democracy it is not possible for either side to transmute the truth it holds into error by blindness to the truth cherished by the opposing side. For both sides in this ideological struggle obviously have hold of a truth which must be supplemented by the truth which the other side cherishes.

The ideological struggle is apparent internationally as well as nationally. The so-called "free" world, which is united in rejecting totalitarian collectivism, does not have absolutely common convictions on the relation of freedom to justice. A nation as wealthy as our own is more inclined than the poorer nations of Europe to prefer freedom to justice and to believe that justice can be achieved with only a minimal control of economic life. So obviously are our thoughts on these issues conditioned by the economic circumstances of our various nations that this particular symposium will be found to have accents which Europeans will find characteristically American, despite the learning and circumspection of the several authors.

II

The question is how the Christian faith enters this debate or makes significant contributions to its solution. Most thoughtful readers will observe that several authors, social scientists of great repute, have considered the ethical problems of our economic life without explicit recourse to uniquely Christian standards of judgment. Yet they are practically unanimous in finding no source for ethical standards in pure economic analyses and in recognizing that ethical norms are nevertheless either implicitly or explicitly involved in the judgments which economists and other social scientists make about our common life. All of these ethical judgments might, however, be reduced to varying interpretations of the concept of "justice." No doubt the Christian heritage of our civilization colors our ideas of justice, even when the civilization has become highly secularized. But no civilization can exist without some notion of justice, for it is not possible to form a real community if its several members do not have the desire to "give each man his due."

Does the Christian faith add anything significant to the concept of justice? The most immediate answer to this question is that it subordinates justice to an even higher standard, that of love. According to Christ, "all the law and the prophets" are summarized in the twofold love commandment, which enjoins both the love of God and the love of the neighbor. However, if it is assumed that the Christian contribution to economic and political life is simply contained in the purity of its ethical ideal of love (an assumption which some modern versions of the Christian faith have sought to inculcate), the relation of Christianity to man's economic and political life would seem to become even more problematic. For the question would then arise whether this ideal has any relevance to the organization of economic or political society. The most ideal social possibility for man may well be so perfect an accord of life with life that each member of a community is ready to sacrifice his interests for the sake of others. But, as David Hume observed, politics (and for that matter economics too) must assume the selfishness of men.

It is certainly significant, as Professor Snygg suggests in his chapter, that the highest religious visions of the good life always culminate in the concept of this perfect accord. The ideal of love is not superimposed upon human history by scriptural, or any other, authority. Human existence, when profoundly analyzed, yields the law of love as the final law of human freedom. Man's unique freedom, in which he rises indeterminately above his determinate existence, requires that his life be fulfilled not within himself but in others. It also requires that this realization of himself in others should not be pursued merely from his own standpoint. That is, he cannot regard others simply as tools and instruments of his self-realization.

Yet that is precisely what he is inclined to do. Any religious faith which merely discovers the law of love but does not also make men aware of the other law, that of self-love, is a sentimental perversion of Christianity. It is a perversion which lacks true inwardness of religious experience. For in such experience men become aware, as St. Paul testified, not only of the final law of life but of another law "which wars against the law that is in my mind."

It is from the standpoint of both of these laws, from the recognition of the validity of the one and the reality of the other, that Christianity must make its contribution to the organization of man's common life, whether in economic or in political terms. From the standpoint of the law of love every scheme and structure of justice will be recognized to be tentative and provisional. Not merely the positive law of particular communities but also the notions of justice, from the standpoint of which positive law is criticized, are touched by interest and passion. They always contain an ideological element, for they tend to justify a given equilibrium of power in a given historical situation.

It was an achievement of Catholic moral theory that it recognized the necessity of standards of justice for the institutional life of mankind below the level of love. But it was a weakness in the theory that love became a "counsel of perfection" and lost its dialectical relation to the law of justice. Justice, meanwhile, was conceived in terms of classic rationalism. It was assumed that human history, like nature, had an inflexible structure to which human actions must conform. The standards of human conduct and of human association, ostensibly derived from an inflexible "natural law," were, however, conditioned by the peculiar power relations of the feudal-agrarian culture. Such standards could not be applied adequately to the new economic vitalities and interests developed by the rising middle-class civilization.

The consequence of this situation was the open rebellion of middle-class life against traditional standards of justice. They had become instruments of injustice precisely because they covered particular historical social forms with the aura of the absolute. In the relation of religion to culture it is important to distinguish sharply between the absolute and the relative. If the authority of religion is used primarily to give absolute validity to relative values, the consequence is a fanaticism which Professor Knight (Chapter 7) deprecates as a characteristic fruit of religion. It is characteristic from the standpoint of modern culture to ascribe fanaticism to religion, and not without cause. It is, however, significant that modern culture, which hoped to destroy religious fanaticism by the power of reason, did not anticipate the even more grievous fanaticisms of modern political religions which would express themselves in the name of reason and of science. Modern culture did not, in short, measure the depth of this problem, or rightly gauge the persistence with which men will use standards of justice as instruments of their interest and use religion to obscure, and thus to aggravate, the ideological taint in their reasoning about justice.

A modern Protestant analogue to Catholic conceptions of "natural law" is the tendency of certain types of Protestant pietistic individualism to endow "natural law," as eighteenth-century rationalism conceived it, with religious sanction. Thus the characteristic prejudices of middle-class life, its tendency toward extravagant individualism, its lack of a sense of community or justice, its devotion to the principles of laissez faire, are falsely raised to religious absolutes; and confusion is worse confounded. Recently there has been a strong recrudescence of this type of thought in Protestant circles; and it has been so heavily financed by interested political and economic groups that its ideological corruption is even more evident than was the religious support of traditional "natural law" concepts at the rise of modern commercial society.

Standards of justice may be said to be (1) expressions of the law of love, insofar as the love of the neighbor requires a calculation of competitive claims when there is more than one neighbor and (2) a practical compromise between the law of love and the law of self-love. They are a compromise in the sense that norms of justice seek to arrive at an equitable adjustment of conflicting claims, assuming the selfish inclination of men to take advantage of each other. A Christian contribution to standards of justice in economic and political life must therefore not be found primarily in a precise formulation of the standard. It must be found rather in strengthening both the inclination to seek the neighbor's good and the contrite awareness that we are not inclined to do this. The inclination to seek the neighbor's good must be accompanied by an awareness that every norm of justice is but a very relative approximation of this goal. The awareness that even good men are not consistently inclined to do this will lay bare the ideological taint, the corruption of self-interest, in every historic standard.

Thus a genuine Christian contribution to the ideological conflict in democratic society must serve to mitigate, rather than aggravate, the severity of the conflict; for it will prevent men from heedlessly seeking their own interests in the name of justice and from recklessly denominating value preferences, other than their own, as evil. If Christian piety or any other kind of piety does not yield these fruits of humility and charity, it must be consistently rejected as the "salt that has lost its savor."

III

This interpretation of the contribution of Christian faith to a sane and viable organization of modern economic life would seem, however, to be in conflict with what we have already defined as the creative idea of classical economic theory: the idea of the necessity and legitimacy of making use of self-interest for the purpose of achieving a more flexible system of mutual services than the rigid moral and political controls of traditional culture made possible. It seems to be in conflict because the Christian analysis of human motives arrives at a critical estimate of the force of the same self-interest which economic life must harness. This supposed conflict has, in fact, persuaded some economists to regard Christianity as a vast system of wishful thinking, which practical men had better disregard. For Christianity seems to suggest that men not only should, but also could, love their neighbors as themselves if they tried hard enough. But practical men must assume the persistence of self-interest in human affairs. This confusion has been heightened by some modern highly moralistic versions of the Christian faith. In those the solution of our economic problems has been sought by suggesting that we need only to substitute the "service" for the "profit" motive to cure the ills of our society. This solution not only ignores the persistence and the power of self-interest in human affairs, but it also obscures the fact that most men seek whatever they seek not simply for themselves but in the service of some community, more particularly the family. (See Professor Knight's chapter on this issue.) The problem of the human community is not so much that of egoism as that of alteregoism. It is the problem of finding an equitable distribution of the values of life, not between individuals but between various groups, most particularly between families.

If, then, the power of self-interest, whether egoistic or alteregoistic, cannot be simply transmuted or suppressed and must therefore be used, what becomes of the Christian definition of this power as "sin"? The correct answer to that question involves a more rigorous distinction between the presuppositions of the Christian faith and those of modern culture than has thus far been made. For the self-interest which was rightly harnessed in modern economic theory and practice was wrongly defined by it as the harmless survival impulse which man shares with all creatures. From the eighteenth century to the present moment it has been a tendency in modern culture, particularly in its naturalistic versions, to interpret human actions and motives in terms as analogous to nature as possible. When modern thought speaks of "laws of nature" which govern history and furnish the norms of human action, it means the concept to be taken literally. These modern "laws of nature" are not laws of reason intuitively known. They are even more dubious concepts. They are supposedly objective forms, analytically discerned. That is why historical evolution could be regarded as merely an extension of natural evolution. The numerous analogies between human history and natural history (as described, for instance, in Professor Emerson's chapter), made inevitable by man's affinities with other creatures, are usually emphasized unduly and the uniqueness of man's freedom is not fully appreciated.

The consequence of this error is that the whole drama of human history is falsely interpreted. On the one hand it is regarded as subject to laws of natural development as if the freedom of the human agent, who is both a creator and a creature of the historical process, did not introduce incalculable elements into the human drama. On the other hand this excessive determinism always finally gives way to an excessive voluntarism. At some point in the evolutionary process man is supposed to come into complete control of his own destiny. The reason this is regarded as possible is that the "mind" which is supposed to control the historical process is assumed to be akin to the disinterested mind of the natural scientist, even as the historical stuff which is to be mastered is assumed to be akin to the unconscious impulses of nature. Actually the stuff of history is much more recalcitrant to control than the stuff of nature. The simple will-to-live of nature has been transmuted by human free-dom into the will-to-power, on the one hand, and into the desire-to-live-truly, that is, to fulfill the essential norms of human exist-ence, on the other.

Furthermore, the "mind" which is supposed to bring historical destiny under control is a mind much more organically and deeply involved in the process to be controlled than the mind of the nat-ural scientist is involved in the nature which he observes. There is, therefore, no simple "man" who can or cannot come into control of historical destiny. There are various men and groups of men who have contradictory notions of what man's destiny is. At the present moment, while the liberal world dreams of bringing history under human control, its practical statesmen and its common people are preoccupied with a desperate struggle against a horrible tyranny which is trying to do exactly what some dreamers in the liberal world had hoped to do: that is, bring all of history under the control of an elite of scientists, in this case of "Marxist-Leninist" scientists.

The pretensions of complete disinterestedness by this elite are of course bogus. But so are, in a greater or lesser degree, those of any elite which pretends to speak for "man." Nor are the corrup-tions of their reason the inertia of "unintelligent and unconscious processes." The corruptions are due to a curious compound of the will-to-live-truly and the will-to-power. They are in short uniquely human corruptions due, not to the inertia of natural impulse, oper-ating against the more inclusive purposes of mind, but to the pre-tensions of man as creature that he is not creature but a creator without qualification. If Communist pretensions have become par-ticularly noxious (as compared with the more innocent dreams of the liberal world), that is due not so much to any particular defect in the Marxist scheme of managing history (though there are many obvious errors in it), but to the fact that the theory actually provides for the investment of a specific group of elite with actual power. The fury which they exhibit in its use may be regarded as the inevitable consequence of the exercise of too absolute power, on the one hand, and as the consequence of the frustration when pretended omnipotence and omniscience meet recalcitrant forces in history, not obedient to their mind or will.

Human desires and ambitions, as Professor Snygg rightly observes (Chapter 12), are without natural limit. The Christian's faith can make no greater contribution to the organization of man's common life than its interpretation of the root of this inordinacy. For according to the Christian faith man is on the one hand a free spirit, "made in the image of God," who rises indeterminately in his consciousness over nature, history, and self. He cannot, therefore, be contained or explain the meaning of his life within the limits of any system of nature. But he is on the other hand a creature, driven by natural impulses and limited by conditions of time and place. These limitations reach into the very pinnacles of spirit, even as the freedom of spirit reaches down into every natural impulse and transmutes it into something less determinate than the impulses of other creatures. (One need only to consider how the sex impulse, possessing a purely biological function in nature, is related to almost every creative and destructive force in the total human personality.) Thus from a genuinely Christian standpoint man can never be understood merely from the standpoint of his involvement in nature, on the one hand; nor can he, on the other, be regarded as a potentially discarnate spirit in whom historical development is progressively actualizing this potential. On the contrary, the evils to which human history is subject arise precisely from those forms of inordinacy which are rooted in man's vain effort to deny his creatureliness.

If we now return to the problem of the organization of economic life and to the necessity of harnessing self-interest, it will become apparent not only why it must be harnessed and not merely suppressed but also why the self-interest has a different dimension than was assumed in the theories of classical economics and in the whole of modern naturalistic thought. Self-interest must be harnessed for two reasons. It is too powerful and persistent to be simply suppressed or transmuted. Even if individual life could rise to pure disinterestedness so that no human mind would give the self, in which it is incarnate, an undue advantage, yet it would not be possible for collective man to rise to such a height. The institution of the family would alone prevent a simple substitution of "motives of service" for "motives of profit," as we have seen. For the self as "breadwinner" will seek to serve his family by seeking gain for his toil.

But self-interest must be allowed a certain free play for the additional reason that there is no one in society good or wise enough finally to determine how the individual's capacities had best be used for the common good, or his labor rewarded, or the possibilities of useful toil, to which he may be prompted by his own initiative, be anticipated.

Yet the self-interest which is thus engaged is not some harmless survival impulse as found in nature. It is not simply satisfied, as physiocratic theory assumed, when human toil yields returns adequate for man's primary needs. For human desires and needs rise indeterminately above the biological level. Self-interest expresses itself above all in what Bertrand Russell has defined as the "desire for power and glory." The two are so intermingled that we need not, for present purposes at least, distinguish them. Thomas Hobbes was able to describe this dimension of self-interest, which was obscured in the thought of his contemporaries, primarily in terms of desire for prestige. He spoke of the "constant competition for honor and prestige" among men. Yet his description yields a sense of the will-to-power lacking in the thought which lies at the foundation of liberal economics.

Because it did not recognize the unlimited nature of all human desires in general and of the desire for power and glory in particular, classical liberalism naturally underrated both the reality of the contest for power in man's social and economic life and the injustices which would result from great inequalities of power. In common with liberal thought, Marx obscured both the lust for power in the motives of men and the factor of power in social life. Self-interest is interpreted by Marxism, as by liberalism, primarily in terms of the economic motive, that is, as the desire for gain. The original state of man's innocency was, according to Engels, disturbed by "greed and covetousness." But since these inordinate desires were attributed to the corruption of the institution of property, it was possible for Marx to envisage an ideal state of society on the other side of the abolition of property. In this post-revolutionary society human needs and desires would be as limited and would achieve as simple a harmony as the liberal culture imagined possible on this side of a revolution.

Thus the foundation was laid for the tragic conflict in modern social history between two great political credos. In this conflict both creeds, in their purer form, generated monstrous contrasting evils from an essentially identical mistake. In the case of pure liberalism it was believed possible to abandon the whole economic life of man to a "natural system of liberty" because the forces in competition in the economic sphere were regarded as essentially determinate and of potentially equal strength. They were neither. Just as human freedom accentuates inequalities found in nature, so also a technical society accentuates the inequalities of more traditional societies. Marxism, on the other hand, allows the power impulses of an uncontrolled oligarchy to express themselves behind a façade of innocency, erected by the dogma that the possession of property is the only source of inordinate desire. In the one case the perils to justice arising from economic power, particularly from inequality of power, are not recognized. In the other case, the perils from the combination of economic and political power in the hands of a single oligarchy are obscured.

Thus the errors of both those who abjure every effort to control human enterprise and those who would bring it completely under a plan rest upon false estimates of the desires and ambitions of men which furnish the stuff of human history. The self-interest of men must be used, rather than merely controlled, not only because it is too variable and unpredictable to be simply controlled but also because the corruption of self-interest among the oligarchs, who would control it, is actuated by ambitions and power lusts, more dangerous than is dreamed of in either philosophy. On the other hand, the self-interest of men, when uncontrolled, does not simply create a nice harmony of competitive striving. That is why the healthier modern societies constantly experiment with social strategies in which neither creed is followed slavishly.

In arriving at this wisdom of "common sense," modern nations are revealing in the field of economics and politics insights into the character of human nature and history which belong to the Christian view of man and which both pure liberal and radical political theories have tended to obscure. This view of man recognizes that (in Pascal's phrase) the dignity and the misery of man are inextricably united. This is to say that both the creative and the destructive possibilities of man's actions in history are derived from the same uniquely human freedom. The misery (that is, man's capacity for evil) develops when he extends his power and wisdom beyond the limits of man as creature. The dignity of man implies his capacity to manage his own destiny and to create communities and social harmonies in which moral and political wisdom outwit the short-range desires and ends of man as creature. The evil in man implies the constant possibility of the corruption of this creative capacity. Therefore he is not to be trusted with too much power and his wisdom as manager of historical destiny is not to be relied on too unqualifiedly.

The Christian faith in its various historic forms has of course become involved in various errors which illustrate these corruptions. Sometimes it has championed concepts of justice or freedom which were ideologies of the strong. Sometimes it has exceeded secular culture in moralistic illusions based upon the idea of the dignity and goodness of man but lacking in understanding of man's capacity for evil. Sometimes it has fled from these errors into a quasi-Christian Marxism. In this view collectivistic economics is espoused in the name of brotherhood, but the perils of power in the collectivist organization of society are not seen.

A genuine Christian faith must always be ready to recognize the periodic involvement of its own historic forms in the various errors against which its true genius forces it to contend. It may be significant, however, that the healthiest national communities of our epoch are those in which the treasures of the Christian faith have never been completely dissipated and in which therefore the fratricidal conflict of modern technical society has been mitigated. For the cherished values of toleration, without which a democratic society would become impossible, are the fruit of a charitable understanding that all human wisdom is limited, that self-interest taints all human virtues, and that there is a similarity between our own evil and those against which we contend.

IV

A viable democratic society cannot, of course, exist merely by tolerant understanding of the inevitability and the universality of the taint of self-interest in all the various positions taken by competing groups in the community. If each group were merely intent upon its own interests and if it used general concepts of justice merely as screens for these interests, the society would disintegrate into warring camps. Such cultures as the Confucian, for instance, have been unable to establish stable community on a wider level than that of the family because there was no moral impulse to affirm interests above those of the family. A healthy community requires that every family and every economic and social group should have, in addition to concern for its own welfare, some genuine devotion to the "general welfare." One must leave the concept of "general welfare" somewhat vague because it must include not only the welfare of the national community but that of the nascent world community.

The progressive development of ever wider communities in the history of mankind is accounted for by the fact that every individual has the ability to achieve some detachment from the communities to which he is bound by nature (the family) and by nature and history (ethnic and other communities), and that this ability is subject to historic growth. The wider the communities, whether national or international, the less they can count on organic, sub-rational, and submoral forces of cohesion and the more they must depend upon man's conscious sense of responsibility for the welfare of others than those who are peculiarly his own. In other words the law of love is the final law of human freedom; and the words of Christ, "If ye love them that love ye, what thanks have ye?" accurately state the indeterminate character of the love commandment, expressing the obligation of the individual to ever wider communities than those to which he is immediately bound.

While, as we have already observed, the love commandment is

always partly contradicted in actual life by the immense force of self-love, particularly the self-love of groups and collectives, it remains nevertheless the law of life. Any theory of community, whether religious or secular, which presents the commandment to love the neighbor as the self as a simple moral possibility inevitably obscures the realities with which the political and economic order must deal. On the other hand, the "realistic" tradition in Western social thought has consistently committed the error of underestimating man's residual capacity for justice, which is to say, his genuine concern for his neighbor. This inclination to be concerned with life, beyond the immediate community in which the self lives, is strengthened by genuine religious piety. For in such piety the freedom of the self over its immediate necessities and ambitions is heightened and the self's profound and ultimate relation to all other selves is illumined.

When this religious impulse is deficient or lost, life sinks, not so much to an individualistic, but to a narrower and narrower level of alteregoism, that is, to a containment of life within some narrow community of family or clan. Then the immediate and limited communities of mankind exhaust the concern of the self for others, leaving the larger communities, whether national or international, in the anarchy of warring particular interests or a purely coerced unity. A creative relation of the Christian faith to the problems of society therefore requires that both the law of love be affirmed and the fact of the persistence of self-love be fully recognized. The Christian faith is most creative when this is done not formally by the mere preaching of precept but by the force of a genuine piety which emancipates the self from its narrower loyalties and at the same time makes it conscious of their persistence and force.

A Christian faith, informed by Biblical norms, cannot issue either in an optimism which obscures the power of particular loyalties offering their resistance to the wider loyalties, or in the type of realism which denies man's capacity for the wider loyalties or even the binding force of such loyalties. For a truly Christian interpretation of the radical character of human freedom must illumine both the creative and the destructive possibilities of that freedom. A truly religious analysis of human experience must lead to a consciousness of both of these possibilities, not merely as social facts to be observed, but as intimate facts which the self may experience and know in his own life.

If such a relation between the Christian faith and the economic and political life of mankind is established, there will be little inclination to invest the whole capital of religious sanctity in particular norms of justice or specific technical structures of economic and political life. They will not be despised, because it will be recognized that the complexity of competing claims in the community requires that norms of justice be constantly defined and redefined, and that the power of particular interests in a community requires that balances and equilibria of power be constantly constructed and reconstructed. They must be reconstructed because new vitalities constantly enter into the field of concern, and old balances become unjust under new conditions.

But the whole capital of religious sanctity must not be invested in these norms. For these systems and structures of justice are not eternal norms to which life must perennially conform but rather *ad hoc* efforts to strike a balance between the final moral possibilities of life and the immediate and given realities. If certain moral, social, and economic traditions have become firmly established, they will not be lightly cast aside. The more it is recognized that there is not one single rational and just method of organizing the life of the community, the more will an established historic method be given due reverence, the more so if there is no illusion that some other method will overcome every past evil or be immune to opposite evils. A proper understanding of the historical and contingent nature of these various structures of justice will discourage both the revolutionary ardor which is always informed by some illusions and the conservatism which pretends that established norms are absolute.

V

The relation of the Christian faith to economic, as to political, life is not exhausted in its real or potential influence upon the moral and social norms of a community, nor in the insights which disclose the heights and depths of human conduct. All religion is an expression of the meaning of human existence. The Christian religion is unique in expressing the meaning of human existence in terms which partly involve and partly transcend man's historic existence.

The significance of man's life upon earth is affirmed, and all historic duties and tasks are taken seriously. But the Christian faith also insists that the final pinnacle of meaning transcends all possibilities of history. It is recognized that physical survival may be bought at too high a price. Thus Christ declares: "Fear not them which kill the body but are not able to kill the soul; but rather fear him which is able to destroy both soul and body in hell" (Matt. 10:28). This implies that the self in its integrity of spirit is not identical with the self as a physical organism, and it is recognized that there are situations in which men must choose to die rather than to buy their survival at the price of this integrity. In the same spirit Christ asks: "What shall it profit a man if he shall gain the whole world and lose his own soul" (Mark 8:36)? The question suggests that the physical advantages of life can be bought at too high a price. The warnings in the Scripture against covetousness are frequent and explicit; and they are justified by the observation that "a man's life consisteth not in the abundance of the things which he possesseth" (Luke 12:15). In Christ's parable of the rich fool, the effort to protect the future against all contingencies by heaping up wealth is rebuked by a reminder of the brevity of the life of all men. "Thou fool, this night thy soul shall be required of thee" (Luke 12:20).

The final question about the relation of the Christian faith to the economic life of liberal society is concerned with the legitimacy of these warnings and their relevance to a society in which economic efficiency tends to become the final norm by which all things are judged. While our contributors in this volume have generally accepted Professor Lionel Robbins's definition of economics as the study of the relationship between human ends and scarce means (thus eliminating the problem of ultimate ends from the scope of economics), Professor Heimann (Chapter 4) rightly calls attention to the fact that the general effect of modern economic rationalism has been to exalt the economic means of gain or of efficient production into final ends of human existence. According to Professor Heimann the effect of this tendency has been that "society has relinquished its control of economic activity and has in turn been made into an appendix to that which is now constituted as economic life."

One might question whether this indictment is as true now as it was at the beginning of the Industrial Revolution, and whether there has not been a consistent tendency in the healthier modern communities to subordinate economic activity to the wider purposes of the community. The quickness with which a liberal society responds to external peril and harnesses its productive power to the purposes of military defense is a proof of the continued sovereignty of the community over its economic life. Yet such an example hardly meets Professor Heimann's indictment. For what a community may define as its supreme *ad hoc* end in a moment of crisis need not seriously affect what the culture of that community defines as the very end of human existence.

The problem is whether what Professor Heimann defines as modern "economic rationalism" has not placed so much emphasis upon the tangible ends of life, in contrast to the more intangible values of life, that we have in effect created a culture in which all the Biblical warnings are disregarded. This is a particularly serious problem for the United States because we are being criticized by both friends and foes in Asia and Europe for having become obsessed with the tools and gadgets of life. When we speak rather idolatrously of the "American way of life," our friends and critics profess not to be certain whether we are recommending certain standards of political freedom or are extolling our living standards. The latter have reached heights of opulence beyond the dreams of avarice for most of the inhabitants of the world.

Sometimes we seem to believe that these living standards are the fruit and the proof of our virtue; at other times we suggest that they are the necessary presuppositions for a virtuous democratic national life. In the one case we follow our Puritan tradition, which did not seek after prosperity in the first instance but was nevertheless certain that since "Godliness was profitable unto all things," prosperity was a mark of divine favor and a reward of virtue. In the other case we draw upon the Jeffersonian tradition in our national heritage. The Jeffersonians believed that the superior virtues of American democracy would be guaranteed primarily by the ampler economic opportunities of our virgin continent. These would avert for America the severity of the social struggle and the subordination of man to man in the overcrowded life of Europe. The Jeffersonian interpretation has one merit of recognizing that democracy is viable only in a society in which the economic margins are sufficient to prevent a desperate struggle for the economic resources of the community.

Whatever the merit of either interpretation, it is now apparent that there is no such simple coordination between economic welfare and the moral, spiritual, and cultural life of the community as we had supposed. The criticisms which European and Asian nations make of our cultural and spiritual life may not always be just. Frequently they are prompted by envy of our good fortune, and seem to rest upon the presupposition that virtue and good fortune are completely incompatible. An impoverished world is, indeed, involved in curious inconsistencies in its relation to a wealthy and powerful preponderant nation. For on the one hand the poorer nations insist that they require our help in establishing greater economic efficiency and productivity as a basis for a healthy democratic life. On the other hand they seem to believe that our wealth is proof of our vulgarity and possibly even of our unjust exploitation of others.[1]

The widespread criticisms of American prosperity and of American culture are usually not based upon distinctively Christian presuppositions. They therefore prove the more convincingly that the issue involved is not the mere rejection of an illegitimate Christian "otherworldliness" in favor of a more unequivocal affirmation of the meaning of man's historic existence. The issue is the relation be-

---

[1] A significant example of the latter indictment is the propaganda pamphlet of the followers of Aneurin Bevan in the British Labour Party. The pamphlet, entitled *One Way Only*, is based upon a simple Marxist assumption that the superior American productivity is an indication of the exploitive character of American capitalism.

tween man's immediate and ultimate ends. The question to be resolved is whether the satisfaction of immediate ends will inevitably
contribute to the achievement of the more ultimate ends.

In considering this question we must note that man's economic
activities are devoted in the first instance to the satisfaction of his
primary needs of food, shelter, and security. Ultimately, of course,
men bring economic effort into the support of every end, spiritual,
cultural, and communal. (This fact gives justification to Professor
Lionel Robbins's definition of economics.) It cannot be denied,
however, that economic activity is always devoted in the first instance to these primary needs and that modern economic "rationalism" gives these needs a preference because they are, as Professor
Heimann insists, more "tangible." The proof is furnished by the
fact that a nation which indubitably has the highest living standards cannot boast of the highest achievements in the moral and
spiritual quality of its culture.

Naturally any community will devote economic productivity to
other than primary needs as soon as these primary needs are tolerably met. Therefore economic efficiency and increased productivity
will support all higher cultural activity. Human culture depends
in fact upon the ability of an economy to establish margins of welfare beyond the satisfaction of primary needs.

There are, however, two reasons why the relation of economic
efficiency to culture is subject to a law of diminishing returns. The
first is that human needs and desires are, as previously observed,
essentially indeterminate. There is therefore no natural limit for
their satisfaction. The place of the automobile in the American
economy is an effective symbol of this fact. The mobility which it
provides is not exactly a "primary" need. But neither is it basically
a cultural one. Yet the satisfaction of this need for mobility takes
precedence over many needs, some of them cultural and others
actually more primary. It is a question, for instance, whether the
possession of a home has not been subordinated in the American
economy to the possession of an automobile. Even if there had not
been such an influence as "economic rationalism," which emphasized the more tangible values, human nature, under whatever culture, would have been inclined to exploit economic margins for

immediate satisfactions in preference to more ultimate ones. There is therefore no "natural" system of preferences which will guarantee that economic means will not become ends in themselves and that tangible and immediate satisfactions will not usurp the devotion of men to the exclusion of more ultimate ones. One possible wrong preference involves that the "dignity of man" as a producer is violated for the sake of achieving a high degree of productivity in favor of man as consumer. Furthermore, highly efficient economies may become involved in vulgarities to which more traditional cultures are immune. For in the more traditional cultures the imagination has not been prompted to seek and to desire the unlimited on every level of human satisfactions.

The second reason for the law of diminishing returns in the relation of efficiency to culture is the fact that technical efficiency is more effective in providing the basis for cultural and spiritual values than in contributing to its heights. The invention of writing, and subsequently of printing, were fateful chapters in the cultural history of mankind. Culture depends upon communication. And these arts of communication were creative instruments for all social, as well as for more purely spiritual, achievements of mankind. But the subsequent inventions which made "mass" communication possible and which culminated in the achievement of radio and television have had the general effect of vulgarizing culture. Some of this effect will be eliminated when the instruments are brought more effectively under the control of artistic and cultural purposes. But the degrading which is due to the necessity of reaching a total audience rather than selective groups with special interests will undoubtedly remain.

These diminishing returns in the realm of culture are symbolic of the general relation between quantitative and qualitative aspects of life. The quantitative increase of the comforts and securities of life, and of the technical efficiencies which furnish the foundation for every type of human achievement, does not lead to an indeterminate increase of the highest possibilities of life, measured culturally or spiritually. No degree of economic security can finally obviate the basic insecurity of human existence, finally symbolized in the fact of death. If preoccupation with these securities creates a culture in which human beings are incapable of coming to terms with life's basic insecurity through a serenity of faith, the culture stands under Christ's condemnation of the rich fool.

No technical efficiencies can guarantee the perfection of the poet's art, and no system of card indexing can assure that the historian will have an imaginative grasp of the drama of history which he seeks to portray. While a democratic society requires both a high degree of literacy among its citizens and enough economic margins to prevent the social struggle from becoming desperate, nevertheless the problems of social justice cannot be solved indeterminately by creating so much abundance that the question of justice is less desperately argued because the goods of life need not be divided too equitably.

There are certain problems of human togetherness which we assume to have solved in America because our expanding economy has postponed them. The original expansion of the economy through an advancing frontier and the subsequent expansion through ever new achievements of technical efficiency have created the illusion of life's unlimited possibilities. Actually human existence is definitely limited, despite its apparently unlimited possibilities. The serenity of man and the sanity of his life with others finally depend upon a wisdom which knows how to come to terms with these limits. This wisdom of humility and charity must be derived from a faith which measures the ends of life in a larger context than that which the immediate desires of man supply.

For this reason the Christian faith has a very special function and challenge in a culture in which a high degree of technical efficiency has been attained. If it becomes too defensive about its alleged "otherworldliness," if it fails to call attention to the limits of the "abundance of things a man possesseth" in achieving the serenity and charity without which life becomes intolerable, if it does not define the dimensions of life which create the possibility of contradiction between the desire to survive and the desire to live in integrity of spirit, if, in short, it capitulates uncritically to the cult of technical efficiency and the culture of abundance, it must lose its uniqueness as religious faith. Perhaps this is the issue on which the Christian faith must come most directly to grips with the prevailing mood of a technical culture. Such a culture is in mortal danger of "gaining the whole world" but "losing its own soul." Certainly its idolatrous devotion to technical efficiency has accentuated a peril which Jesus perceived, even in a culture in which the tendency to seek after treasures which "moths corrupt and thieves break through and steal" had not been accentuated by the modern preoccupation with material comfort and physical security.

It would, of course, be foolish to deny the moral and spiritual significance of the "conquest" of nature in our civilization or to yearn after the poverty-stricken conditions of nontechnical societies. Man has been given a rightful dominion over the forces of nature; and the whole history of human civilization is a history of his gradual extension of that dominion. But it is also true that this dominion cannot annul nature's final triumph over man; for even the most powerful and comfortable man must finally submit to the common fate of death. The only possible triumph over death for man is a triumph of faith, which is to say a conception of the meaning of life from the standpoint of which death is not the annulment of all meaning. In the Bible the effort of man to establish the meaning of his existence upon the basis of his own power and intelligence is consistently interpreted as the root of all evil. The rich fool who builds his barns for future security has not reckoned with the fact that he may die any moment. Those who build great houses are accused by the Psalmist, with subtle psychological insight, of having the "secret thought that they will continue forever."

The nonchalance of faith's triumph over life and death is succinctly expressed in the Pauline word: "For whether we live, we live unto the Lord: and whether we die, we die unto the Lord; whether we live therefore or die, we are the Lord's" (Romans 14:8). In many ways the most basic distinction between secularism and a genuine Christian faith is at this precise point. From the standpoint of the Christian faith no achievements of culture and civilization can finally give man security. On the contrary most of the evils of life arise from the fact that man seeks frantically to establish absolute security by his power, wisdom, or virtue.

The preoccupation of a technical civilization with the external securities of life is due partly to a natural tendency of every culture to extol its unique achievements. Modern man has been remarkably successful in technics and is naturally prone to overestimate the significance of his success in this enterprise for the total problem of human existence. But there is also a deeper religious issue in this idolatry. The frantic pursuit of the immediate goals of life is partly occasioned by an uneasy awareness that this pursuit has not resulted in its promised happiness and by a consequent final and desperate effort to reach the illusive goal of happiness by a more consistent application of principles of efficiency.

If there is such motivation in the current preoccupations of a technical society, particularly in America, they may well be regarded as abortive, but also dangerous, efforts of the spirit of "secularism" in unconscious and therefore purer form to bring human destiny under the control of human power.

This problem is the most serious challenge to the Christian faith. It is the more serious because it cannot be solved by a simple denial of the significance of man's conquest of nature. It can be solved only by recognizing the moral and spiritual resources in the technical achievements on the one hand and by recognizing their limits on the other. The final limits remain the same for the most advanced as well as for the most primitive society.

Index of Subjects

Index of Names